Drug Use
and
Abuse
A Guide to Research Findings

Drug Use
and
Abuse
A Guide to Research Findings

Volume 2: Adolescents _____

Gregory A. Austin
Michael L. Prendergast

Foreword by Dan J. Lettieri

ABC-Clio Information Services
Santa Barbara, California
Denver, Colorado
Oxford, England

Library of Congress Cataloging in Publication Data

Austin, Gregory A.
  Drug use and abuse.

  Includes indexes.
  Contents: v. 1. Adults — v. 2. Adolescents.
  1. Drug abuse—Abstracts. 2. Psychotropic drugs—
Abstracts. 3. Drug abuse—Periodicals—Indexes.
4. Psychotropic drugs—Periodicals—Indexes.
I. Prendergast, Michael L., 1946—   . II. Title.
[DNLM: 1. Substance abuse—In adolescence—Abstracts.
2. Substance abuse—In adulthood—Abstracts. 3. Substance
dependence—In adolescence—Abstracts. 4. Substance
dependence—In adulthood—Abstracts.   ZWM 270 A935d]

RC564.A95   1984   616.86'3   84-3015

ISBN 0-87436-412-4 (v.1)
ISBN 0-87436-413-2 (v.2)
ISBN 0-87436-414-0 (set)

10 9 8 7 6 5 4 3 2 1

ABC-Clio Information Services
2040 Alameda Padre Serra, Box 4397
Santa Barbara, California 93103

Clio Press Ltd.
55 St. Thomas Street
Oxford, OX1 1JG, England

Manufactured in the United States of America

CONTENTS

LIST OF ABSTRACTS

VII. Drug Use among High School Students and Adolescents

VIII. Drug Use among College Students and Young Adults

IX. Drug Use among Ethnic Minority Youth

X. Studies on Marijuana and Hallucinogens

FOREWORD

It is rare to feel both pleased and honored to write a foreword. I shall not hesitate to express my enthusiasm for *Drug Use and Abuse*, an exciting, original, and innovative two-volume set. At the turn of the century, the social psychologist William McDougal compared the cyclical reemergence of concepts to "old wine in new bottles." As anyone who has ever written a scientific literature review will attest, the two fatiguing impediments in compiling such a review are (a) locating the material and (b) sorting and assembling the distinct findings into digestible portions. *Drug Use and Abuse* greatly diminishes those impediments and may prove to be new wine in new bottles.

Unencumbered by the conventional methods used in presenting other collections of research abstracts, Drs. Austin and Prendergast have prepared a comprehensive guide to the findings of federally funded research on drug use and abuse. More importantly, they have created a refreshingly unique approach to the research literature that clearly represents a new landmark in information dissemination.

The creative component of this work lies in its treatment of the findings of each study represented. The lengthy abstracts of each study include purpose, methodology, findings, and conclusions. Research findings (called "kernels") within each study are separately numbered, and the nine indexes refer the user to specific findings as well as to the corresponding abstract. The value of this approach is evident in the fact, for example, that a user interested in marijuana is able to locate information on that drug in reports primarily dealing with other drugs as well as from studies on marijuana itself.

These volumes should ease the burden on busy researchers by helping them locate quickly research findings on the use and abuse of a particular drug and by presenting such findings in a succinct form. For anyone concerned with the pressing problem of drug abuse, I heartily recommend these digestible volumes and volumes of digests.

Bon appetit!

Dan J. Lettieri, Ph.D.
National Institute on Alcohol Abuse
    and Alcoholism
Division of Extramural Research
Rockville, Maryland

ACKNOWLEDGMENTS

The completion of this project required the help and cooperation of many people. We were particularly fortunate to have had the advice and encouragement of Dr. Dan Lettieri at the National Institute on Drug Abuse, whose suggestions and guidance were invaluable. Special acknowledgment is due to the Principal Investigators who reviewed the abstracts of their research. The accuracy and completeness of the volume have been much improved by their cooperation. Any mistakes remain the responsibility of the editors. We also wish to acknowledge the support provided by the staff of NIDA's Research Division, Psychosocial Branch, in helping us identify research projects.

The abstracts were written by Marcelline Burns, Nancy Fitzgerald, Boris Odynocki, and Karen Shannon. Bill Burger wrote the various programs that made these computer-produced volumes possible. The abstracts were input and corrected by Annette Lightell and Barbara Garrison. Additional tasks in preparing the volumes were carried out by Beverly Barnett, Bohdan Futala, Sandy Greig, Steve Harmon, and Dieanna Harper. The project was partially funded by NIDA research grant R01DA02836.

INTRODUCTION

Drug Use and Abuse consists of two separate, self-contained volumes that summarize and index in detail the findings of 238 studies on the psychosocial aspects of drug use and abuse, most of which were produced under federally-funded research grants. The studies were carried out between 1970 and 1980, although some of the documents are dated as late as 1982. The two volumes are divided on the basis of user characteristics: Volume 1 consists of studies of adult populations; Volume 2, studies of adolescent and college-age populations. Organizing the studies in this way also resulted in the two volumes being divided on the basis of drugs studies: although both volumes contain studies that are concerned with multiple or general drug use, Volume 1 is mainly devoted to opiates; Volume 2, to marijuana and hallucinogens. Each volume consists of two major parts: (1) lengthy abstracts listing the research findings themselves; and (2) a series of indexes that make it possible to locate specific findings of interest. The numbering of the abstracts is sequential: those in Volume 1 run from 1 to 125; those in Volume 2, from 126 to 238. Within each volume, the abstracts are grouped into topics and within topic alphabetically by author. The topic divisions for Volume 1 are Characteristics of Opiate Use and Adult Users, Treatment of Drug Dependence, Relationship between Drugs and Crime, Drug Use among Women, Drug Use among Ethnic Minority Adults, and Miscellaneous Studies of Adult Drug Use. The topic divisions for Volume 2 are Drug Use among Adolescents, Drug Use among College Students and Young Adults, Drug Use among Ethnic Minority Youth, and Studies on Marijuana and Hallucinogens.

These volumes differ from other collections of abstracts on drug abuse in three respects. First, the purpose, methodology, findings, and conclusions of each study are abstracted at length, with particular attention focused on the findings. This is not an annotated bibliography to all drug research literature; rather, it is a detailed guide to the findings of major federally funded psychosocial drug research. Second, each discrete finding is separately numbered and indexed. The indexes refer the user not simply to abstracts but to particular findings of interest. This makes it possible, for example, to identify information regarding marijuana in a study on heroin use that might otherwise be overlooked. Third, we have summarized the results of unpublished as well as published research reports. Our abstracts may therefore be the only accessible source for the findings of difficult to acquire unpublished papers.

Selection Criteria

The first criterion for inclusion in this volume was that the research had been funded at least part by a federal grant since 1970. This was done for two main reasons. First, most large-scale drug research in the United States is federally funded because of the time and expense involved, the controversial nature of the research, and the need for guarantees of confidentiality to sample populations. Second, it provided a convenient selection criterion for identifying a manageable sample of studies that represented the range questions, methodologies, and results in psychosocial drug abuse research generally. Every effort was made to identify the psychosocial drug research grants funded by the National Institute on Drug Abuse or its predecessors between 1970 and

1980, and the Principal Investigators for the grants were contacted to assure that we had acquired all the important publications dealing with their research findings.

Not all publications from a given grant have been abstracted. The original pool of documents numbered 500. From these we eliminated documents that did not qualify as "drug abuse research," as defined below, or that were duplicative in reporting results. In the context of these volumes, "drug abuse research" means the empirical study of the psychological, sociological, epidemiological, treatment, and prevention aspects of drug abuse. Documents reporting on historical, theoretical, clinical, or methodological research were excluded from abstracting. Even if a document did fall within the definition of "drug abuse research," it was not abstracted if it was a literature survey, book review, comment on a paper, dissertation or thesis, programmatic recommendation, program description, or popular article. The types of literature that have been selected for abstracting are journal articles, papers in edited books, conference papers, final reports, prepublication papers, government publications, and other formal scientific presentations of research; most abstracts are of journal articles.

Description and Organization of Abstracts

The *List of Abstracts* that appears after the Contents provides the Abstract Number and the author(s) and title of each document abstracted. The page number on which each abstract begins is also given. The abstracts are arranged under the various topics for each volume. Although most of the abstracts were easily assigned to one of the volumes and to one of the topics within that volume, a small number did not readily fit into any of the topics or they could have been placed under two or more topics. The decision of where to put them was necessarily arbitrary.

What primarily sets the abstracts that appear here apart from those in other volumes of abstracts is the Findings section, which consists of a list of "kernels," that is, discrete, self-contained statements of specific research findings reported in the document being summarized. The kernel format provides quick access to specific research findings on a wide variety of subjects. Each kernel is indexed for sample characteristics (age, ethnicity, sex, etc.), research design information (methodology, instruments) and topics (drugs studied, social factors in drug use, psychological disorders associated with drug use, treatment programs, etc.). The subject indexes at the end of each volume specify which kernel(s) of an abstract deal with a particular subject. Thus, after consulting the appropriate index, the reader can turn directly to the indicated kernels in order to find the information of interest, rather than having to read the entire abstract for the information.

In writing the abstracts, we found that some types of research fit more easily into the kernel format than others. The format is well suited to experimental research and small-scale surveys, in which findings are relatively discrete. Ethnographic research, however, often describes a complex and interrelated set of behaviors, attitudes, and values, and the findings of such research were more difficult to divide into self-contained kernels. A somewhat different problem arose with large-scale survey research, which usually results in a large report consisting of hundreds of findings. To summarize all or even most of the findings would defeat the purpose of the abstract. For ethnographic and large-scale survey research, only the more important or more general findings were summarized.

The abstracts consist of six sections: citation, summary table, purpose, operational definitions, findings, and conclusion, each of which is described below.

> *Citation.* Presents the bibliographical information on the article being abstracted in six fields, each field being identified by a two-letter abbreviation: Abstract Number (AN), author(s) (AU), title of the document (TI), source of the document (journal, book, conference

paper, etc.) (SO), institutional affiliation of the first author (IN), and number of references in the document (RF).

Summary Table. Consists of a chart with ten fields that specify various characteristics of the sample and the research design. The fields are as follows:

> DRUG
> TYPE
> NUMBER
> SEX
> AGE
> ETHNICITY
> LOCATION
> METHODOLOGY
> INSTRUMENTS
> CONDUCTED

The information for the table was taken from the document being abstracted. When an item of information was not found in one document but could be determined from another by the same author, that item was included in the summary table of the first document, but placed in square brackets, thus: ETHNICITY: [white; black]. When the information for a field could not be determined, "not specified" was used. For Sex and Ethnicity, the number or percentage of subjects in each group was provided where such information was available. For the Drug and Ethnicity fields, if more than four terms were applicable, the terms "multidrug" and multiethnic," respectively, were used.

Purpose. Describes the background or rationale for the study, the sample and the research procedures, and other information that might help in understanding the results of the study.

Operational Definitions. Provides explanation for terms used in the findings section that may not be self-evident or that are defined by the author of the document in a certain way for purposes of organizing or analyzing the data. For instance, abstract 050 refers to treatment programs A, B, and C; these three programs are briefly identified in the operational definitions section of the abstract. This section does not appear in all abstracts.

Findings. Lists specific research findings from the document being abstracted in the form of statements known as "kernels." Each kernel is preceded by a number (1, 2, 3, etc.), which in combination with the Abstract Number provides a unique reference for each kernel in the volumes. The page number(s) of the document from which the finding was taken follows each kernel.

Conclusion. Summarizes the main results of the study and any conclusions or recommendations discussed in the document.

These informational abstracts are not intended to replace the original documents, but they do provide an orderly and detailed presentation of the procedures, findings, and conclusions of a study. The kernels summarize results that were reported in the text of the document; information found in tables was not abstracted, except in a small number of cases where such information had to be included in order to make a statement in the text meaningful. The abstracts do not include evaluative or critical comments. No attempt was made to standardize the terminology used by different authors. After the abstracts were written, they were sent to the Principal Investigators, who were requested to review them for accuracy and completeness. The abstracts were then revised in accordance with the corrections or suggestions made by the Principal Investigators.

Indexes

The index at the end of Volume 1 covers the abstracts appearing in that volume; the index in Volume 2 covers both volumes. The Author Index consists of an alphabetical listing of authors; each author name is followed by the Abstract Number and document title. All names that appear as authors in the abstracts are included in the Author Index.

There are nine subject indexes: Topic, Drug, Sample Type, Sex, Age, Ethnicity, Location, Methodology, and Instrument. The format of the first six subject indexes is as follows: under an index term, each reference consists of the Abstract Number, the title of the document, and the numbers of the kernels that match the index term. The format of the Location, Methodology, and Instrument indexes is the same, except that it does not include references to kernels since a given term in these indexes (e.g., New York; longitudinal survey; Taylor Manifest Anxiety Scale) applies to the study as a whole rather than to particular findings. The title of the document is included in the index entries to aid in the selection of abstracts of interest. The indexes point to both explicit and implicit information in the indicated kernels. For example, a particular kernel may not say anything about the age of the sample, but the kernel has been indexed for this variable. Similarly, a kernel will not state that the finding was gathered in a correlational study, but it will be so indexed in the Methodology Index. The implicit information in a kernel may be easily discovered by looking at the Summary Table of the abstract.

The terms in each index are arranged alphabetically, with two exceptions. The terms in the Age Index are listed chronologically. The terms in the Drug and Topic Indexes are arranged by category rather than strictly alphabetically. For example, in the Drug Index, "methaqualone" will not be found after "methadone," but under the category DEPRESSANTS after "barbiturates." In the Topic Index, "religious factors" is found under the category SOCIAL FACTORS, while "religious program" is found under the category TREATMENT PROGRAMS. At the beginning of each subject index, the index terms are listed in the order in which they appear.

The basis of the subject index terms and their arrangement was the list of descriptors used by the National Institute on Drug Abuse, Division of Research, in its data base of NIDA-funded research projects. The abstracts found in these volumes were written and indexed to be compatible with the NIDA data base. For indexing the abstracts, new categories were created (location, methodology, instrument), and new terms were added to the Topic Index.

VII. DRUG USE AMONG HIGH SCHOOL STUDENTS AND ADOLESCENTS

AN: 126
AU: Andrew, K.H.; Kandel, D.B.
TI: Attitude and behavior: A specification of the contingent consistency
     hypothesis
SO: American Sociological Review, 44:298-310, 1979
IN: Columbia University, New York, New York
RF: 26

SUMMARY TABLE

DRUG: marijuana
TYPE: high school students
NUMBER: 5,258
SEX: male and female
AGE: high school
ETHNICITY: white; black; Puerto Rican
LOCATION: New York State
METHODOLOGY: longitudinal panel survey
INSTRUMENT(S):   questionnaire
CONDUCTED: 1971-1972

PURPOSE

This study sought to test the contingent consistency hypothesis that social
pressures reinforce the effect of attitude on behavior. The attitudes and
behaviors studied pertain to marijuana use; the contingent effects tested were
those of parents and peers. The analysis was based on a two-wave panel survey
using a random sample of students attending public high schools in New York State
during the school year 1971-1972. Questionnaires were distributed to students in
18 schools in fall of 1971 and in spring of 1972.

FINDINGS

1. The relationship between marijuana-related attitudes and marijuana use was
fairly high. But when a measure of group norms was included along with attitude
in an equation predicting frequency of marijuana use, much of the apparent effect
of attitude turned out to be spurious. Peer influence had a stronger additive
effect than attitudes (p. 307).

2. Cross-sectional analyses revealed interaction effects between attitudes and
situations: in the earliest stage immediately preceding onset of marijuana use,
all the effects of the situational variables were additive (p. 308).

3. Interactions between attitudes and situation appeared among those adolescents
who shifted from being nonusers to becoming frequent users (p. 308).

4. Attitudes towards marijuana had only a moderate impact on marijuana use when
less extreme change or no change was occurring (p. 308).

5. Being a member of a peer group where marijuana use was highly prevalent
facilitated rapid and heavy involvement in marijuana use (pp. 303-304).

6. The greater influence of peers than of parents on adolescent marijuana use may be the result of the greater reliance of adolescents on peers than on parents in matters related to adolescent life style and also of the greater visibility of certain adolescent behaviors to peers than to parents (p. 308).

CONCLUSION

This study tested the contingent consistency hypothesis that social pressures reinforce the effect of attitude on behavior. It was found (after a cross-sectional and two-wave longitudinal analysis) that peer-related norms had the greatest interactive impact, while parental norms exerted very little impact. The study could not demonstrate whether contingent effects on attitudes among individuals undergoing rapid behavioral change derive regularly from social influences. Future research should focus upon redefining a population in terms of its particular developmental stage of participation in a behavioral sequence so as to specify those conditions when contingent consistency is most likely to remain in effect.

AN: 127
AU: Berberian, R.M.; Thompson, W.D.; Kasl, S.V.; Gould, L.C.; Kleber, H.D.
TI: The relationship between drug education programs in the greater New Haven
     schools and changes in drug use and drug-related beliefs and perceptions
SO: Health Education Monographs, 4:327-376, 1976
IN: Yale University School of Medicine, New Haven, Connecticut
RF: 19

SUMMARY TABLE

DRUG: multidrug
TYPE: junior and senior high school students
NUMBER: 13,606
SEX: male; female
AGE: junior and senior high school
ETHNICITY: black (11%); white (87%)
LOCATION: Greater New Haven, Connecticut
METHODOLOGY: longitudinal, comparative survey
INSTRUMENT(S):   questionnaire; interview
CONDUCTED: 1970-1973

PURPOSE

Many researchers would agree that drug education has failed. Yet few studies
support such beliefs. Most studies that attempt to evaluate drug education have
examined the educational process or some intermediate outcome. The purpose of
this research was to evaluate the effects of drug education with an application of
a broad epidemiological approach. Data on adolescent drug use in the Greater New
Haven area between 1970 and 1973 were analyzed in relation to information on drug
education programs in 33 schools from which the sample was selected. Drug use
rates and measures of beliefs and perceptions before and after exposure to drug
education programs were compared to the rates and measures of control students
(matched for grade in school) who did not have any drug education.

OPERATIONAL DEFINITIONS

Assembly: during either Year One or Year Two, a minimum 90% of students attended
at least one assembly or film dealing with drugs.

Regular course work: course work in drug education taught in regular classes.

Special course: a course dealing primarily with drugs or related topics taught
during Year One or Two.

Staff training: some of the school staff received special training in drug
education or drug counseling.

FINDINGS

1. Drug education, in general, did not have a strong, consistent influence on
drug rates or on drug attitudes and beliefs (p. 366).

2. For the 8th-, 9th-, and 10th-grade cohorts, there were smaller increases in drug use for schools that implemented drug education programs than for schools that did not (p. 366).

3. For the 7th-grade cohort, there were slightly greater increases in drug use for those schools that implemented drug education than for those that did not (p. 366).

4. Of five types of drug education--"assemblies," "regular course work," "special course work," "staff training," and a combination of staff training with two or more others--not one was consistently associated with changes in drug use (p. 366).

5. Drug education was generally associated with relatively small increases in the proportion of students knowing where to obtain cannabis (p. 367).

6. For drugs other than cannabis, drug education was positively related to increased knowledge of where illegal drugs could be obtained in the 7th-grade cohort; the relationship was negative for the 8th-, 9th-, and 10th-grade cohorts (p. 367).

7. Changes in beliefs regarding the harmfulness of cannabis were not related to drug education (p. 367).

8. Changes in perception of the harmfulness of noncannabis drugs were significantly related to drug education (p. 367).

9. Drug education did not change the students' perception of the legal risks of drug use (p. 367).

10. The students anticipated lenient treatment for drug use in a school whose staff was trained in drug problems. Students receiving drug education in regular course work or assemblies did not anticipate lenient treatment (p. 367).

11. Students who received drug education in regular course work viewed cannabis and noncannabis drugs as harmful and endorsed school restrictions on their use (p. 368).

12. Students who received drug education in their regular course work had lower rates of alcohol and cannabis use than did students who had other types of drug education (p. 368).

13. In the 7th-grade cohort, a strict school policy against drugs was related to a small net reduction in drug use. At the high school level, a strict drug policy was associated with some increase in alcohol use (p. 368).

14. Schools with regular courses and assemblies in drug education exhibited somewhat lower drug use rates, whereas schools with special courses had higher drug use rates (p. 368).

15. In general, students who received drug education in assemblies or regular courses, compared with those who had other types of drug education, had higher perceptions regarding the harmfulness of drugs, lower anticipation of going to jail for drug use, and higher anticipation of strict reaction from school authorities to the discovery of drug use (p. 369).

CONCLUSION

If the goal of drug education is defined as prevention of drug use, then the evidence collected during this study indicates that drug education has indeed failed. No significant changes were observed during the implementation of drug education. However, some useful observations were made. One of them was that younger cohorts revealed certain undesirable effects of drug education on drug use (higher rates of increase among youths in schools with some drug education). Another observation was that older cohorts modestly benefitted from drug education. The conclusion may be drawn that drug education should be started at higher grades, not lower.

AN: 128
AU: Blum, R.H.; Garfield, E.F.; Johnstone, J.L.; Magistad, J.G.
TI: Drug education: Further results and recommendations
SO: Journal of Drug Issues, 8:379-426, 1978
IN: Program in Drugs, Crime and Community Studies, Stanford University, Stanford,
      California
RF: 16

SUMMARY TABLE

DRUG: multidrug
TYPE: sixth-grade and seventh-grade students
NUMBER: 1,413 (763 actually completed all tests)
SEX: male and female
AGE: 10-13 years
ETHNICITY: primarily white
LOCATION: two suburban California communities
METHODOLOGY: comparative, longitudinal survey
INSTRUMENT(S): questionnaire
CONDUCTED: 1976-1977

PURPOSE

In an earlier study comparing modes of drug education and their effects on
students in primary and middle-level California schools, drug education was seen
to have an impact on two measures: stability (the extent to which a youngster's
use remains the same rather than expanding either in frequency or use or kinds of
use) and spread (the extent to which new classes of drugs are used). Both
didactic instruction (information only) and process education (discussion groups
employing values clarification and decision-making and emphasizing personal,
interactive, and affective components) were compared with a control group which
received minimal information. Drug education, particularly the didactic
experience, was found to have greater impact in reducing spread, but the control
group showed more stability. The present study was designed to confirm and extend
the earlier study; sixth-grade students, who had shown the greatest sensitivity
to drug education, were followed for two years. Sixth-grade students (N=1,413)
from five schools in two suburban California communities were exposed for two
years to five modes of drug education and tested at four different points in time
(at the start and end of sixth and seventh grades). Only 763 children completed
all four tests, due to problems of scheduling, transfers, etc. The five modes of
drug education studied were a control group (four hours of drug education per
year), a didactic group (information only for nine hours), a discussion group
(eleven hours of discussion and four hours of information), a combined information
and discussion group (nine hours of discussion and six of information), and a
parent-designed curriculum group. The latter had to be abandoned because of lack
of participation on the part of parents. Results from the four tests and the four
remaining modes of drug education were analyzed statistically to determine the
impact of drug education. Other variables such as sex, teacher effect, and
student reactions were also considered.

FINDINGS

1. A trend toward ever earlier nonmedical drug use among children was confirmed; sixth graders in this sample used more drugs more regularly than sixth graders studied four years earlier (p. 420).

2. Classification of children's drug use was scalable, using the following hierarchical scale (from most frequent to least frequent): 1) abstainer, 2) low frequency of use of beer, wine, spirits, and tobacco; 3) high frequency of use of beer, wine, spirits, and tobacco; 4) low marijuana use; 5) high marijuana use; 6) low amphetamine, barbiturate, and hallucinogen use; 7) high amphetamine, barbiturate, and hallucinogen use; 8) low heroin/cocaine use; 9) high heroin/cocaine use. Prior drug use was 95% predictable based on known present use (p. 420).

3. Teachers who were interested in providing drug education were more liberal politically and in their own drug views than those less interested (p. 420).

4. For youngsters who began the sixth grade with a previous history of low use of alcohol and tobacco, the information only method of drug education produced greater stability (no change in use level over time) and restrained extreme expansion (new drug use did not embrace a wide range of other drugs nor as great a frequency of use) (p. 420).

5. For youngsters who began sixth grade with a previous history of frequent use of alcohol and tobacco, the four modes of drug education achieved the following results: 78% of the control group (minimal education), 56% of the information only group, 48% of the discussion only group, and 38% of the combined discussion-information group remained stable in their drug use. The percentages of students who went on to extreme progressions of drug use were 22% for the combined discussion-information group, 35% for the discussion only group, 45% for the information only group, and 67% of the control group. Thus, although the least drug education resulted in the most stability, it also increased the risk of extreme drug expansion (pp. 420-442).

6. The most powerful predictors of drug use were levels of drug use at the beginning of sixth grade and history of inhalant use. Being female predicted lower drug use scores (p. 421).

7. The only drug education mode significantly associated with average scores on levels of drug use over two years was the combined information-discussion method. Teachers contributed significantly to the average scores depending on their role as regular faculty or as part of the study's research staff; there were likewise individual teacher differences and interactions between teachers and educational modality (p. 421).

8. When the drug use of all sixth grade students was analyzed without consideration of starting level of drug use, the least drug education contributed most to stability in drug use patterns, while discussion methods contributed more to expanded use. The drug education modes of combined information-discussion and discussion only both contributed to reduced use over time (p. 421).

9. About 75% of the sixth-grade students in this study reported complete satisfaction with their drug education, regardless of the type of program. About half of the students considered the intent of the program to be moral, that is, making them stop drug use. Fifty-eight percent reported that the drug education

they received influenced their decisions about drug use (p. 422).

CONCLUSION

Drug education has an impact on sixth and seventh grader's nonmedical psychoactive drug use. This impact can be stabilizing, stimulating, restraining, or reducing. The effect varies with the type of drug education presented and with outcome criteria. The least drug education is most often associated with stability (drug use remaining the same). However, if the outcome desired is reduction from current use levels, a combined discussion-information educational mode is preferable. A second choice modality is the information only method, which appears both to maintain stability and to retard spread for youngsters with low levels of initial drug experience. Drug education programs appear to work best when an information-giving component is included; process modes, without a factual basis, risk not only destabilizing use and not restraining spread, but even of facilitating spread as a function of individual teacher effects. Drug education should be given just prior to and during expected transitional upsurge periods of drug use, and not after habits of use are well established.

AN: 129
AU: Brook, J.S.; Gordon, A.S.; Brook, D.W.
TI: Perceived paternal relationships, adolescent personality, and female
     marijuana use
SO: Journal of Psychology, 105:277-285, 1980
IN: Department of Psychiatry, Mt. Sinai School of Medicine, New York, New York
RF: 21

SUMMARY TABLE

DRUG:	marijuana
TYPE:	adolescent females
NUMBER:	36
SEX:	female
AGE:	adolescence
ETHNICITY:	white
LOCATION:	New York, New York
METHODOLOGY:	correlational survey
INSTRUMENT(S):	interview
CONDUCTED:	not specified

PURPOSE

The study evaluated three models (independent, mediational, interdependent) of the relationship between paternal characteristics, the adolescent daughter's personality attributes, and her marijuana use. Thirty-six white adolescent females were interviewed. Questionnaire items were used to develop scales reflecting the paternal domain and scales reflecting the adolescent personality domain.

FINDINGS

1. Within the paternal domain, the adolescent girl's marijuana use was negatively related to paternal warmth and child-centeredness and to the girl's identification with her father (p. 280).

2. In the personality domain, marijuana use by adolescent females was negatively related to conventionality, intolerance of deviance, responsibility, and autonomy, and positively related to flexibility and interpersonal aggression (p. 281).

3. Results of the study support an independent model; the paternal domain was significantly associated with the daughter's marijuana use, with control on personality; and the daughter's personality domain was significantly related to marijuana use, with control on the paternal domain (p. 281).

4. Seventy percent of the variance in the adolescent female's marijuana use could be explained by the combined influence of paternal and adolescent personality domains (p. 282).

CONCLUSION

Paternal factors and adolescent personality attributes were found to be
independently related to the daughter's use of marijuana. Personality factors may
lead to marijuana use despite a positive father-daughter relationship, or the girl
with a non-drug-prone personality may become a user given a conducive
father-daughter relationship. Nonuse is directly correlated with a close and
affectionate relationship with the father. The female users are unconventional,
less responsible, more tolerant of deviance, more likely to engage in aggression,
receptive to change, and more dependent. Although there is a unidirectional
influence of the father on the daughter, there are also interactive processes, and
a girl's drug behavior may modify the paternal domain.

AN: 130
AU: Brook, J.S.; Lukoff, I.F.; Whiteman, M.
TI: Correlates of adolescent marijuana use as related to age, sex, and ethnicity
SO: Yale Journal of Biology and Medicine, 50:383-390, 1977
IN: School of Social Work, Columbia University, New York, New York
RF: 23

SUMMARY TABLE

DRUG: marijuana
TYPE: adolescents
NUMBER: 403
SEX: male (202); female (201)
AGE: 13 to 17 years
ETHNICITY: white (124); black (141); West Indian black (138)
LOCATION: Brooklyn, New York
METHODOLOGY: comparative, correlational survey
INSTRUMENT(S):   interview; questionnaire
CONDUCTED: not specified

PURPOSE

Although many studies have been conducted concerning the demographic, personality, and environmental factors related to adolescent drug use, few have focused on the interactive processes among these variables. In a study involving adolescents (N=403) from three different ethnic backgrounds in New York, three interactive processes were investigated: (1) the relationship between adolescent marijuana use and a number of personality-attitudinal dimensions; (2) the relationship between perceived environmental factors and adolescent marijuana use; and (3) the relationship of these correlates to marijuana use as a function of sex, age, and ethnicity.

FINDINGS

1. Nineteen percent of the adolescents interviewed reported having used marijuana at least once; neither sex nor ethnicity was related to marijuana use (p. 386).

2. The 16-to-17-year olds reported more marijuana use (29%) than did the 13-to-15-year old subjects (11%) (p. 386).

3. Adolescent marijuana users had significantly lower scores on social desirability scales and significantly higher internal locus of control and tolerance of deviance scores than did nonmarijuana users (p. 386).

4. Among the marijuana users, blacks and West Indians were found to be more assertive than whites (p. 386).

5. West Indian nonmarijuana users expected more satisfaction of needs from their family than users. But users in general tended to expect their affection, recognition, and dependency needs to be fulfilled by friends (p. 387).

6. Adolescent marijuana users reported being closer to their friends than to their parents, while nonusers were closer to their parents (p. 387).

7. Adolescent marijuana users reported more involvement in deviance and more friends and family members who used marijuana than did nonusers (p. 387).

8. Nonusers of marijuana reported higher school grades, more time spent on homework, and less frequent cutting of class than did marijuana users (p. 388).

CONCLUSION

Results of the study indicated a relationship between personality and perceived environmental factors and adolescent marijuana use. Two processes were seen as related to adolescent drug use: social nonconformity at the personality, institutional, and social levels, and the modeling effects of family and peers. In general, these patterns persisted across different ethnic, sex, and age groups.

AN: 131
AU: Brook, J.S.; Lukoff, I.F.; Whiteman, M.
TI: Peer, family, and personality domains as related to adolescents' drug
     behavior
SO: Psychological Reports, 41:1095-1102, 1977
IN: School of Social Work, Columbia University, New York, New York
RF: 28

SUMMARY TABLE

DRUG: marijuana; multidrug
TYPE: adolescents
NUMBER: 403
SEX: male (202); female (201)
AGE: 13 to 17 years
ETHNICITY: white (124); black (141); West Indian black (138)
LOCATION: Brooklyn, New York
METHODOLOGY: correlational survey
INSTRUMENT(S):   interview
CONDUCTED: not specified

PURPOSE

An attempt was made to learn more about the interrelations among family, peer, and
personality domains and their relationship to adolescent drug use. Three models
which have been used to explain this behavior were investigated: the
interdependent, mediational, and independent models. Adolescents (N=403) from
three different ethnic groups were interviewed at home, and answered questions
concerning their personality, peer and family relationships, and drug use.

FINDINGS

1. Nineteen percent of the adolescents interviewed reported having used marijuana
with or without other illicit drugs. However, the majority of drug users
indicated having used only marijuana (p. 1098).

2. The 16-to-17-year olds reported more marijuana use (30%) than did the
13-to-15-year old subjects (10%) (p. 1099).

3. Scores on personality scales indicated that adolescent drug use was related to
less conformity, high internal locus of control, and a greater tolerance of
deviance (p. 1099).

4. Drug users were more susceptible to peer than to parental influence, and they
expected satisfaction of their dependency, affection, and recognition needs from
their peers (p. 1099).

5. Adolescent drug use was positively related to deviant behavior by relatives
and to drug use by parents and family members (p. 1099).

6. Each of the three domains studied (personality, peer, family) was
significantly and independently related to adolescent drug use (p. 1100).

CONCLUSION

Results confirmed the independent model of adolescent drug use. Family, peer, and personality factors each influenced the patterns of drug use regardless of the prominence of the other two domains. Future attempts at intervention should take all domains into consideration if they are to be maximally effective in curbing adolescent drug abuse.

AN: 132
AU: Brook, J.S.; Lukoff, I.F.; Whiteman, M.
TI: Family socialization and adolescent personality and their association with
     adolescent use of marijuana
SO: Journal of Genetic Psychology, 133:261-271, 1978
IN: School of Social Work, Columbia University, New York, New York
RF: 21

SUMMARY TABLE

DRUG: marijuana
TYPE: adolescents and their mothers
NUMBER: 284
SEX: male (144); female (140)
AGE: 13-17 years
ETHNICITY: American black (93); white (97); British West Indian black (94)
LOCATION: Brooklyn, New York
METHODOLOGY: correlational survey
INSTRUMENT(S):   interview
CONDUCTED: not specified

PURPOSE

Adolescents and their mothers were interviewed in a study designed to examine the
impact of family socialization practices and adolescent personality/attitudinal
characteristics on marijuana use by the adolescents. Multiple regression analysis
of the interview data permitted the examination of the relationship of
theoretically relevant variable sets. Five scales for the parents and three
scales for the offspring were developed based on correlations of interview items.
Adolescents were classified in terms of marijuana use: no marijuana, only
marijuana, marijuana plus other illicit drugs. The respondents were drawn from a
low social class, urban population.

FINDINGS

1. Maternal assertion, educational expectations, educational aspirations, number
of rules enforced, and parent-child engagement in present-day activities were
negatively correlated with marijuana use by the adolescent children (p. 265).

2. Adolescent marijuana use was positively correlated with rebellion against
parental rules, tolerance of deviance, and internal locus of control (p. 265).

3. The combined influence of parental socialization and adolescent
personality/attitude variables accounted for 21% of the variance in marijuana use,
but each area also exerted an independent effect as demonstrated by the lack of
interaction between significant variables (p. 265).

4. Parental socialization and adolescent personality and attitude appear to be
independently related to adolescent use of marijuana (p. 268).

CONCLUSION

Parental socialization factors and adolescent personality/attitudinal attributes were found to have independent effects on marjuana use by the adolescent, with each comprising a set of conditions sufficient for marijuana use. Parent socialization had a direct effect, rather than acting "through" the adolescent's personality or attitudes. Similarly, the adolescent personality had a direct relation to marijuana use.

AN: 133
AU: Brook, J.S.; Lukoff, I.F.; Whiteman, M.
TI: Initiation into adolescent marijuana use
SO: Journal of Genetic Psychology, 137:133-142, 1980
IN: School of Social Work, Columbia University, New York, New York
RF: 23

SUMMARY TABLE

DRUG: marijuana
TYPE: adolescents and their mothers
NUMBER: 183
SEX: male (90); female (93)
AGE: 13-17 years
ETHNICITY: American black (57); white (62); British West Indian black (64)
LOCATION: Brooklyn, New York
METHODOLOGY: longitudinal, correlational survey
INSTRUMENT(S):   interview
CONDUCTED: 1974; 1977

PURPOSE

A sample of adolescents and their mothers was interviewed in 1974 and again in 1977 in a longitudinal study of marijuana use. The relationship of three domains (personality/attitudes, peer relationships, and family socialization practices) to the initiation of marijuana use was studied. Data were obtained by in-person interview with both the adolescent and the mother, using items and scales theoretically related to adolescent marijuana use.

OPERATIONAL DEFINITIONS

Initiates: adolescents who began use of marijuana between 1974 and 1975 and who used it at least twice in that period.

FINDINGS

1. Thirty-two percent of the adolescents began to use marijuana during the time between the first and second interview (p. 136).

2. Thirty-seven percent of the initiates reported use a few times a year, 29% reported use once a month to several times a month, and 34% reported use once a week or more often (p. 136).

3. The personality/attitude variables which characterized marijuana users in comparison to nonusers were tolerance of deviance, lower educational aspirations and expectations, and less conventional attitudes (p. 137).

4. In terms of family variables, mothers of initiates in comparison to mothers of nonusers were less assertive, were less likely to be involved with their children in activities of shared responsibility, had lower educational expectations for their children, and had lower expectations that their own needs for dependency, affection, and recognition would be met within the family (p. 138).

5. Initiates were more likely than nonusers to be peer oriented rather than parent oriented (p. 133).

6. Family and personality domains made significant and independent contributions to adolescent initiation to marijuana use (p. 139).

7. With personality, family, and demographic variables controlled, the peer domain was not significantly related to adolescent initiation to marijuana use (p. 139).

8. In a significant interaction, adolescents with a nonconventional mother and with marijuana-using friends were most likely to initiate marijuana use (p. 140).

9. In a significant interaction within the family domain, mothers who had low expectations for their children and who had an internal orientation were most likely to have children who initiated marijuana use (p. 140).

10. Adolescents whose mothers had high expectations and whose relatives were not involved in deviance were least likely to initiate marijuana use (p. 140).

CONCLUSION

The adolescents' personality and family relationships (but not peer relationships) were found to be significantly related to marijuana use. Each was independently related to marijuana use and by itself might comprise a set of sufficient conditions for subsequent use. Among the adolescent personality and attitude variables which were found to be relevant were a tolerance of deviance, unconventional attitudes, and low expectations for educational recognition or achievement. In terms of family influence, the marijuana initiates' mothers had low expectations, were not involved with their adolescent children, and were themselves nonconventional and passive. It appears that peer determinants correlate with marijuana use because both are heavily influenced by the other two factors of personality attributes and family relationships. In support of peer influence, adolescents who have unconventional mothers and who also are part of the marijuana subculture are more likely to initiate marijuana use. Both internal factors (personality) and external conditions (family) exert significant influence on adolescent marijuana use.

AN: 134
AU: Brook, J.S.; Whiteman, M.; Brook, D.W.; Gordon, A.S.
TI: Paternal determinants of male adolescent marijuana use
SO: Developmental Psychology, 17:841-847, 1981
IN: Department of Psychiatry, Mt. Sinai School of Medicine, New York, New York
RF: 27

SUMMARY TABLE

DRUG: marijuana
TYPE: male college students and their fathers
NUMBER: 246
SEX: male
AGE: 18 years (mean)
ETHNICITY: white
LOCATION: New Jersey
METHODOLOGY: correlational survey
INSTRUMENT(S):   questionnaire
CONDUCTED: not specified

PURPOSE

White male college students at a large state college in New Jersey and their fathers were administered questionnaires which assessed various personality and socialization factors as well as marijuana use. Only males whose fathers had not been absent from the home at any time during their life for more than two years were eligible to participate in the study. Analyses were based on scales grouped under three domains: Father Personality Attributes, Father Socialization Techniques, and Adolescent Personality Attributes. Three models were suggested to describe interactions of these domains: interdependent (in which case all three would act together to influence marijuana use), mediational (in which case one would be prepotent, remaining statistically significant despite control on the remaining domains), and independent (in which case each domain would be associated with marijuana use despite control on the others). These models were tested using hierarchical multiple regression analysis with marijuana use versus nonuse as the dependent variable. Finally, the adolescents were placed in three groups according to their average use of marijuana, and a three-group multiple discriminant function analysis was performed to determine those factors which distinguished nonusers, experimental users, and regular users.

FINDINGS

1. Fathers of marijuana-using adolescent sons were more likely than fathers of nonusers to be unconventional and to score higher on measures of psychopathology; their personality characteristics included tolerance of deviance and of marijuana use, impulsivity, masculinity, depression, poor object relations, and difficulty in interpersonal relations (p. 843).

2. Fathers of adolescent sons who did not use marijuana were more likely than fathers of marijuana users to have established a close, affectionate relationship with their sons and to serve as role models for their sons; paternal socialization techniques that were related to a son's use of marijuana included lack of child-centeredness, lack of affection, and lack of father-son

communication and involvement, while the son's identification with his father was inversely related to marijuana use (p. 843).

3. Adolescent marijuana users were more unconventional and interested in stimulus seeking than nonusers; marijuana use was positively related to lower school achievement, tolerance of deviance, less responsibility, and more rebelliousness and sensation seeking (p. 844).

4. When the domains of Paternal Personality Attributes, Paternal Socialization Techniques, and Adolescent Personality Attributes were analyzed in regards to marijuana use among male college students, it was found that adolescent personality attributes remained significantly correlated with marijuana use despite control on the other domains, or, in other words, mediated between paternal factors and marijuana use (p. 844).

5. Paternal affection and psychological adjustment (as judged by good object relations and nonimpulsivity), which were otherwise associated with less marijuana use for adolescent sons, were associated with greater marijuana use when mitigated by rebelliousness in the adolescent son (p. 844).

6. A father's intolerance of deviance, when found together with a sense of responsibility in his adolescent son, led to the least marijuana use among college males (pp. 844-845).

7. For a group of male college students and their fathers, those adolescents who did not use marijuana were most conventional and least interested in stimulus seeking, and had fathers who were the most conventional, well-adjusted, and affectionate, while the regular marijuana users were the most unconventional, least well-adjusted, and coldest. Experimental users and their fathers displayed attributes between those of the regular users and nonusers (p. 845).

CONCLUSION

A mediational model most accurately depicts the way in which a father may influence his son's use of marijuana. The data are consistent with a causal patterning in which the father's personality and his child-rearing practices have an effect on his son's personality, which in turn affects the son's marijuana use. The son's personality is the mediating factor. Fathers who were most unconventional, least well-adjusted, and coldest were most likely to have sons who used marijuana regularly. Adolescents who were regular marijuana users were more likely than nonusers to be unconventional and sensation seeking. The adolescents' personality is important not only by itself but as a synergistic or mitigating effect on paternal traits. Sons who are conventional and have conventional fathers are less likely to use marijuana, while the positive effects of a father's well-adjusted personality and warm relationship with his son may be weakened if the son is highly rebellious. This mediational model implies that fathers who are well-integrated and traditional in orientation establish sound psychological relationships with their sons, which facilitates the development of certain personality attributes in their sons that insulate them from marijuana use. Furthermore, sons who identify with their fathers tend to develop personalities which insulate them from drug use. The factors associated with marijuana use were the same factors which distinguished between regular, experimental, and nonusers. Although these findings describe a general proneness to marijuana use, risk factors such as peer use of marijuana, availability of marijuana, and peer relationships may also affect marijuana use. These findings suggest that

intervention strategies should be aimed at changing an adolescent's general
orientation towards unconventionality and sensation seeking; attention should
also be given to enhancing those paternal factors which hinder the development of
those adolescent characteristics.

AN: 135
AU: Brook, J.S.; Whiteman, M.; Brook, D.W.; Gordon, A.S.
TI: Fathers and sons: Their relationship and personality characteristics
      associated with the son's smoking behavior
SO: Journal of Genetic Psychology, 142:271-281, 1983
IN: Department of Psychiatry, Mt. Sinai School of Medicine, New York, New York
RF: 23

SUMMARY TABLE

DRUG: tobacco
TYPE: male college students and their fathers
NUMBER: 246
SEX: male
AGE: 18 years (mean)
ETHNICITY: white
LOCATION: New Jersey
METHODOLOGY: correlational survey
INSTRUMENT(S):   questionnaire
CONDUCTED: not specified

PURPOSE

White male college students at a large state college in New Jersey and their
fathers were administered questionnaires which assessed various personality and
socialization factors as well as tobacco use. Only males whose fathers had not
been absent from the home at any time during their life for more than two years
were eligible to participate in the study. Analyses were based on scales grouped
under the three domains of Father Personality Attributes, Father Socialization
Techniques, and Adolescent Personality Attributes. Three models were suggested to
describe interactions of these domains: interdependent (in which case all three
would act together to influence tobacco use), mediational (in which case one would
be prepotent, as demonstrated by its remaining statistically significant despite
control on the remaining domains), and independent (in which case each domain
would be associated with tobacco use despite control on the others). These models
were tested by using hierarchical multiple regression analysis with tobacco use
versus nonuse as the dependent variable.

FINDINGS

1. Fathers of adolescent sons who smoked cigarettes were more "traditionally"
masculine in orientation, more impulsive, less well-adjusted, and more tolerant of
tobacco and marijuana use than fathers of nonsmokers (p. 274).

2. Fathers of adolescent sons who smoked cigarettes were less affectionate and
supportive, spent less time with their sons, did not center attention on their
sons, used harsh techniques of discipline, and had lower expectations for their
sons than fathers of nonsmokers. In addition, there was less communication
between fathers and sons who smoked, and adolescents who smoked were less likely
to identify with their fathers (p. 275).

3. Male college students who smoked cigarettes when compared to nonsmokers were more rebellious, more impulsive, less responsible, and more tolerant of deviance (p. 276).

4. When the three domains of Father Personality Attributes, Father Socialization Techniques, and Adolescent Personality Attributes were analyzed in regards to tobacco use among male college students, it was found that each of these domains was associated with tobacco use despite control on the remaining domains, suggesting that an independent model best describes the interaction between these factors and tobacco use (p. 276).

5. Fathers who were well-adjusted and viewed as role models by their sons (factors associated with less tobacco smoking among adolescents) were more likely to have sons who smoked if their sons were rebellious and sensation-seeking (p. 277).

6. Adolescents who were rebellious or obsessive (factors associated with tobacco smoking among adolescents) were even more likely to smoke if their fathers were permissive or nonsupportive (p. 277).

7. Highly impulsive fathers who did not communicate with their sons were more likely to have sons who smoked cigarettes than those who were impulsive but did communicate with their sons (p. 277).

CONCLUSION

An independent model best describes the way in which the three domains of Paternal Personality Atttributes, Paternal Socialization Techniques, and Adolescent Personality Attributes affect tobacco use among adolescents, with each domain seeming to have an independent relationship with and constituting a set of sufficient conditions for adolescent tobacco use. Thus, adverse paternal personality attributes are operative even in the context of effective paternal socialization techniques and positive adolescent personality attributes; ineffective paternal socialization techniques are associated with tobacco use despite benign paternal and adolescent personality attributes; and adverse adolescent personality attributes are associated with tobacco use despite optimal paternal conditions. The findings regarding fathers of smokers suggest certain conclusions: (1) the nature of the affectional bond between father and son is important, with a positive bond making smoking less likely; (2) fathers of nonsmokers have higher expectations for their sons and stress development of independent behavior which leads to a sense of control over the environment; (3) harsh, critical, and punitive fathers are more likely to have sons who smoke, perhaps because smoking is used as a way of coping with feelings of inadequacy; (4) adolescent males who identify with their fathers are less likely to smoke, while smokers might be seen as identifying with the masculine image portrayed in cigarette ads as compensation for the lack of an adequate role model; and (5) the father who spends a great deal of time with his son is less likely to have a son who smokes. Certain interactions between father and son also relate to adolescent smoking. The effectiveness of a well-integrated or emulated father may be mitigated by his son's sensation-seeking or nonconventional attributes. Also, a father's lack of control and support increases the possibility that a maladjusted or rebellious adolescent will smoke.

AN: 136
AU: Brook, J.S.; Whiteman, M.; Gordon, A.S.
TI: Maternal and personality determinants of adolescent smoking behavior
SO: Journal of Genetic Psychology, 139:185-193, 1981
IN: School of Social Work, Columbia University, New York, New York
RF: 22

SUMMARY TABLE

DRUG: tobacco (cigarettes)
TYPE: adolescent tobacco users and their mothers
NUMBER: 39
SEX: male
AGE: 16-20 years
ETHNICITY: white
LOCATION: Brooklyn, New York
METHODOLOGY: correlational survey
INSTRUMENT(S):   interview
CONDUCTED: not specified

PURPOSE

Thirty-nine males, ages 16-20, and their mothers were interviewed separately in a study of the maternal determinants and personality attributes of adolescent tobacco users. Both the mothers and the sons were asked about attitudes and the mother's child-rearing practices. In addition, the sons were asked about their own personality characteristics. Three different patterns of interconnection were explored: (1) certain personality predispositions and maternal factors might have to exist simultaneously to stimulate smoking behavior; (2) one set of factors might mediate the relationship of the other; (3) personality and maternal factors might each have an independent relation to smoking behavior. Scales were developed separately for mothers and adolescents based on interview responses that measured the various maternal and adolescent factors.

FINDINGS

1. Correlational analysis of personality attributes showed that adolescents whose thought and behaviors met conventional societal standards were less likely to smoke (p. 189).

2. Personal autonomy among adolescents was negatively correlated with smoking, suggesting that nonsmokers do not lack independence (p. 189).

3. The more traditional the mother's ideology and behavior and the higher her expectations for her son, the less her son smoked (p. 189).

4. Maternal factors of affectional interaction, satisfaction of the child's needs for recognition and dependence, and encouragement of his independent status related negatively to smoking behavior (p. 189).

5. Adolescent males who identified with their mothers were less likely to smoke, but if the boy identified with a mother who herself smoked, then he was likely also to smoke (p. 190).

6. Adolescent personality attributes and maternal characteristics had an interdependent relationship to adolescent tobacco use; maternal factors must be associated with the adolescent personality attributes to make their effects felt and vice versa (p. 190).

CONCLUSION

Both maternal factors and adolescent personality attributes must co-exist in order for adolescent tobacco use to occur. Smokers, in comparison to nonsmokers, are less in control of their impulses, less responsible and autonomous, more rebellious, and more aggressive. Given these personality predispositions, tobacco use occurs given certain maternal orientations or practices, or as a modeling of maternal behavior. Maternal intolerance of deviance and high expectations for the son are negatively related to tobacco use. Positive affective exchanges were found to be more frequent between mothers and nonsmokers. In sum, both maternal conditions and the adolescent's personality play a role in smoking behavior.

AN: 137
AU: Brook, J.S.; Whiteman, M.; Gordon, A.S.
TI: The role of the father in his son's marijuana use
SO: Journal of Genetic Psychology, 138:81-86, 1981
IN: School of Social Work, Columbia University, New York, New York
RF: 8

SUMMARY TABLE

DRUG: marijuana
TYPE: adolescent males
NUMBER: 71
SEX: male
AGE: 16-20 years
ETHNICITY: American black (17); white (30); British West Indian black (24)
LOCATION: Brooklyn, New York
METHODOLOGY: correlational survey
INSTRUMENT(S):   interview
CONDUCTED: not specified

PURPOSE

Adolescent boys were interviewed in order to assess their perceptions of
paternal/maternal warmth, child-centeredness, control through guilt, autonomy, and
identification. The study examined paternal characteristics in relation to the
adolescents' marijuana use, both as a sole determining dimension and in
interaction with other aspects of the family. The analysis controlled for
maternal influence on the father-son relationship. The 71 male adolescents were
also questioned about their use of marijuana.

FINDINGS

1. Maternal variables were not found to be significantly related to the sons' use
of marijuana (p. 83).

2. Findings suggest that nonusers of marijuana were more likely to have warm
mothers and fathers who do not use control through guilt (p. 84).

3. Marijuana users reported that their mothers were not child-centered and that
their fathers did not grant them sufficient autonomy (p. 84).

4. In comparison with marijuana users, nonusers were more likely to describe
their fathers as centering attention on them and showing warmth (p. 83).

CONCLUSION

The degree of paternal affection was found to be related to the son's use of
marijuana. Boys whose fathers are not warm and child-centered are more likely to
use marijuana. The absence of both maternal affection and paternal tolerance in

control and authority relates to more marijuana use. These findings are subject to differing interpretations. Although the findings can be interpreted as indicating that paternal characteristics are the antecedents of adolescent marijuana use, it is also possible that the adolescent's use of the drug leads to changes in paternal affection and control.

AN: 138
AU: Elinson, J.; Josephson, E.; Zanes, A.; Haberman, P.
TI: A Study of Teenage Drug Behavior
SO: Final Report, NIDA Grant R01DA00043, 1977
IN: Division of Sociomedical Sciences, School of Public Health, Columbia
     University, New York, New York
RF: 69

SUMMARY TABLE

DRUG: multidrug
TYPE: junior and senior high school students
NUMBER: approximately 33,000
SEX: male and female
AGE: high school
ETHNICITY: white; black; Puerto-Rican; Chicano
LOCATION: United States (cross-sectional)
METHODOLOGY: longitudinal survey
INSTRUMENT(S): questionnaire
CONDUCTED: 1970-1975

PURPOSE

In order to contribute to the data on nationwide trends in youthful drug use,
33,083 junior and senior high school students in 22 selected schools across the
nation completed questionnaires on drug use in 1971. Two years later, in 1973,
students at the same schools were again asked to complete questionnaires; 31,993
did so. Of this number, 8,136 had also responded to the first questionnaire;
students in this group constituted a panel, and the information they provided was
used to measure and analyze changes in drug behavior and factors related to those
changes. Other studies were also undertaken to supplement the information
provided by the trend and panel studies: (1) Drug use questionnaires were
administered to 500 chronic absentees from two of the participating high schools,
both of which had extremely high rates of absenteeism. (2) A study conducted in
1971 compared data on drug use from questionnaires completed by students in eight
junior high schools, three on the West Coast and five on the East Coast. (3) The
results of the fourth in a series of national household sample surveys of
adolescents ages 12 to 17 conducted in 1971, 1972, 1973, and 1974-1975 were
reported. (4) A study conducted in early 1974 compared drug use information
provided by 3,788 adolescents ages 11 to 16 attending a comprehensive school in a
new town in Southern England with data obtained from the original United States
trend study. (5) Another cross-cultural study was carried out in 1974, comparing
data obtained from 3,904 Puerto Rican high school students in New York City with
data obtained from Puerto Rican high school students in Puerto Rico. The report
contains many more findings than are summarized below.

OPERATIONAL DEFINITIONS

Recent use: use of a drug during the two months previous to the survey.

FINDINGS

1. More than two-thirds of junior and senior high school boys reported drinking alcohol apart from a family setting in 1971 and 1973, with the proportions of girls being almost 10% lower in each year. There was an increase between 1971 and 1973 in reported use of alcohol and in frequency of use. The proportions of drinkers rose dramatically by grade in both years, with almost twice as many twelfth graders reporting alcohol use as seventh graders in both years (p. 3.22).

2. In 1971, two-fifths of junior and senior high school boys and a slightly larger percentage of girls reported smoking cigarettes. In 1973, the proportion of girls who had ever smoked increased to one half whereas the proportion for boys showed a smaller increase. The proportion of smokers gradually increased from the seventh to the ninth grade in both years, reaching a plateau of between slightly more than two-fifths but less than one-half from the ninth to the twelfth grade (p. 3.22).

3. After alcohol and cigarettes, marijuana was the drug preferred by junior and senior high school students in 1971 and 1973. In 1971, two-fifths of the boys and one-third of the girls reported ever using marijuana; by 1973 the percentages were one-half of the boys and more than two-fifths of the girls. Frequency of use also increased. Between two-thirds and three-quarters of boys and girls reporting any use of marijuana indicated use in the previous two months in both years. The largest percentage of marijuana users among tenth-grade students in 1973 reported use 60 times or more, while in the earlier grades students usually reported use once or twice or 3-19 times ever. The percentage of students who had not tried marijuana but would like to do so decreased between 1971 and 1973; for both years, more girls were in this category than boys and percentages increased by grade level (pp. 3.22-3.25).

4. After alcohol, cigarettes, and marijuana, barbiturates were the most frequently used drug by junior and senior high school students. About one-seventh of both boys and girls reported ever using barbiturates in 1971, increasing in 1973 to slightly less than one-fifth for both. About one-half of those reporting any use indicated recent use (in the last two months). Both total and recent use increased by grade level, with the sharpest increase occurring between the eighth and ninth grades and a stabilization occurring for twelfth graders in both years (pp. 3.25-3.26).

5. Slightly less than one-seventh of both male and female junior and senior high school students reported any use of amphetamines in 1971, rising to about one-sixth in 1973. The percentages reporting recent use also increased. The proportion of total and recent users increased with grade level in both years, although there was some leveling in total use by the twelfth grade and recent use reached a plateau after the tenth grade (p. 3.26).

6. About one in every nine junior and senior high school boys reported ever using LSD in 1973; this was slightly higher than the percentage reporting such use in 1971. Girls were less likely to use LSD in both years. Other psychedelics were used slightly more often (2% more often than LSD) by both boys and girls in both years. Reported recent use of LSD and other psychedelics in both years increased up to tenth grade and tended to stabilize thereafter (pp. 3.26-3.27).

7. More than one in ten junior and senior high school boys and less than one in ten girls reported any glue use in 1971 and 1973, with a slight increase in use between the two years. Reported recent use of glue showed a definite inverse

correlation with grade, with seventh and eighth graders more likely to use glue than twelfth graders (p. 3.27).

8. There was more cocaine use reported by junior and senior high school students in 1973 than in 1971, more use among boys than girls, and in each successive grade. Percentages of users were small, ranging from 4% of girls in 1971 to 12% of boys in 1973 (pp. 3.27-3.28).

9. Heroin was the drug with the least reported use (both ever and recent) by junior and senior high school students. Although there was a slight increase in total use (from 3.7% to 4.9%) and recent use (from 1.4% to 2.2%) by boys between 1971 and 1973, use by girls showed no change. Most heroin use appeared to be experimental and was almost equally likely to take place at any grade level (p. 3.28).

10. In 1971, half (50%) of those in a panel of junior and senior high schol students reported having drunk alcohol and over a third (35%) reported having smoked cigarettes. Two years later, in 1973, the percentages had increased to 76% for alcohol and 42% for cigarettes. Between 1971 and 1973, the use of marijuana increased approximately 25%-30%, while the use of other drugs increased 9%-10% for barbiturates, 7%-11% for amphetamines, 4%-6% for LSD, 5%-8% for other psychedelics, and 1%-2% for heroin. An increase in glue sniffing experience was reported by seventh and eighth graders, more than by ninth and tenth graders. The largest changes in experience with alcohol and cigarettes took place in the lower grades, and changes in experience with marijuana steadily increased at about the same rate for each grade level (pp. 4.4-4.5).

11. There were no differences between male and female students in a panel of junior and senior high school students with respect to increased experience with drugs, except that girls showed a larger increase in cigarette smoking than boys (p. 4.5).

12. Three times as many of the same junior and senior high school students had used marijuana recently in 1973 as in 1971. Twice as many had used barbiturates and amphetamines recently as two years earlier. Cocaine, LSD, and other psychedelics all showed net increases. Only heroin and glue showed no net change in recent use (p. 4.6).

13. In 1971, two out of three students from a panel of junior and senior high school students who had ever tried marijuana were using it currently, as compared to one out of four of those who had ever tried glue. About half or more of those who had tried barbiturates, amphetamines, and psychedelics other than LSD used these drugs currently. By 1973, the ratio of active users to ever marijuana users had changed, with three out of four users reporting current use, while active heroin users dropped to one out of three and active glue users dropped to one out of five (p. 4.7).

14. Between 1971 and 1973, the ratio of recent users to ever users of cocaine increased for each grade level in a panel of junior and senior high school students, but ratios declined for barbiturates, LSD and other psychedelics, and glue in each grade (pp. 4.7-4.8).

15. Students from a panel of junior and senior high school students who were nonusers of marijuana in 1971 wre more likely to initiate use of marijuana by 1973 if they talked with friends about drugs, had a history of absenteeism from school, participated in school protests, had positive attitudes towards marijuana use,

were often or sometimes offered drugs, and reported themselves as unhappy.
Race-ethnicity, religious identification, socio-economic status, self-appraisals
of health and nervousness, parents' use of sleeping pills or tranquilizers,
students' concern about the approval of parents or peers, and general attitudes
about drug use had little bearing on initiation of marijuana use (pp. 4.10-4.23).

16. Using multivariate analysis on selected antecedent variables, it was found
that friends' use of marijuana was the the most predictive variable of subsequent
initiation to marijuana use for a panel of junior and senior high school students
interviewed in 1971 and 1973. The next most important variables, in order of
importance, were participation in school protests, grade-point average, church
attendance, and school absenteeism. However, only 64% of those who had all five
drug-related attributes began using marijuana, and 17% of the students who had no
such traits did initiate marijuana use, suggesting that other factors also
influenced initiation of use (pp. 4.70, 4.74).

17. Senior high school students who were frequently absent from school were
considerably more likely than other students to use alcohol and cigarettes, as
well as marijuana and other illicit drugs (p. 5.20).

18. West Coast junior high school students consistently reported more drug use
than their East Coast counterparts, especially the use of illicit drugs (except
heroin, which had been tried by 2% of both groups). Marijuana was the illicit
drug of choice on both coasts, with glue and tranquilizers following
(pp. 6.4-6.8).

19. More than three-fourths of junior high school students who used illicit drugs
had also smoked cigarettes and nine-tenths had also used alcohol. Thirty-six
percent had only used marijuana or hashish, and almost 75% of those who had used
other drugs also used marijuana (p. 6.9).

20. Junior high school students who used illicit drugs were more likely than
those who did not to be older, to have lower educational expectations, to have
lower grade-point averages, to be absent from school more often, to engage in
school protests, and to be more independent of their parents (p. 6.18).

21. Junior high school students on the West Coast were more accepting of the use
of illicit drugs than those on the East Coast; the West Coast students were also
more likely to report that illicit drugs were easy to obtain and that their
friends used such drugs (pp. 6.13-6.17).

22. The proportion of adolescents ages 12-17 who reported using marijuana at
least once remained relatively constant during three nation-wide surveys conducted
in 1971, 1972, and 1973 (ranging from 15% to 17%), but increased markedly (to 22%)
in 1974-1975. The proportion of experimenters (less than 9 uses) remained
relatively unchanged between 1971 and 1975, but the proportion of occasional users
(10-59 times ever) and frequent users (60 or more times ever) increased 6% in each
category. The proportion of nonusers who wanted to try marijuana dropped from 12%
in 1971 to 5% in 1974-1975. Older adolescents and those living in the West and
Northeast reported the most ever use and recent use of marijuana. Rates of use
for other drugs remained relatively stable during the same time period. Reported
cigarette, alcohol, and other drug use was highly correlated with marijuana use in
1974-1975, as were favorable attitudes towards legalization and use of marijuana
by friends. Adolescent marijuana users were less likely than nonusers to expect
to continue education after high school and to think they should obey laws they
did not like (pp. 7.2-7.7).

23. Marijuana was the illicit drug most often used by English adolescents, with 6% reporting ever use, which compared to more than half of American high school students reporting ever use. Percentages of English adolescents reporting use of any other illicit drug were lower than 6%, although the proportions who used alcohol and cigarettes were comparable (though slightly lower) than percentages for American adolescents. English adolescents who used marijuana differed markedly from nonusers: they tended to be older, from broken homes, male, less motivated educationally, more dissatisfied with school, more often absent from school, less close to their parents, much more likely to use alcohol and tobacco, much more positive in their attitudes towards drug use, and much more likely to have used other illicit drugs than nonusers (pp. 8.2-8.6).

24. Puerto Rican high school students in New York City reported higher use of legal and illegal drugs than Puerto Rican high school students in Puerto Rico. Alcohol was the legal drug of choice of both groups, with 63% of the New York sample reporting use compared to 46% of the Islanders; cigarette use was also more prevalent in the migrant group (52%) than in the Islander group (33%). Marijuana was the preferred illicit drug for both groups, but only 11% of the Islanders reported any use compred to 45% of the migrant group. Barbiturates were the second illegal drug of choice for both groups, with 4% of the Islanders and 12% of the migrant group reporting such use. The migrant group was more tolerant of deviance and drugs and also reported higher use of illegal and legal drugs by peers, parents, and self (pp. 9.13-9.14).

CONCLUSION

Marijuana was the illicit drug of choice for American high school students, and both ever use and frequency of use increased between 1971 and 1973. For a panel of high school students first questioned in 1971 and again in 1973 about marijuana use, 53% remained abstainers and 29% initiated use; initiation of use was related to social milieu, role performance, and specific attitudes toward drug use. For those who were marijuana users in 1971, 10% increased use, 4% remained the same, 2% decreased use, and 2% stopped use. A special study of chronic absentees from two high schools revealed that absentees reported considerably more use of drugs than students at the same schools. In 16 other high schools, frequently absent students reported more use of almost all drugs than students who attended more regularly, regardless of the characteristics of the student body or the location of the school. In a special study of eight junior high schools conducted in 1973 on the West and East Coasts, West Coast students reported more use of illicit drugs and both users and nonusers reported more favorable attitudes toward drugs than their East Coast peers. In four consecutive national household surveys, the proportion of adolescents ages 12 to 17 who reported having used marijuana increased from 15% in 1971 and 1972, to 17% in 1973, and to 22% in 1974-1975. Marijuana use was correlated directly with reported use of cigarettes, alcohol, and other drugs. A comparative study of secondary school students conducted in a small English city in 1974 revealed far less use of illicit drugs than in any of the United States communities studied; only 6% of the English adolescents reported any use of marijuana. Perhaps for this reason, those who reported such experiences turned out to be far more deviant by various attitudinal and behavioral measures than their counterparts in the United States. In a comparative study of Puerto Rican high school students conducted in 1974 in New York City and in Puerto Rico, those in New York reported considerably more drug use. Marijuana was the illicit drug of choice for both groups; however, while 45% of the Puerto Rican students in New York City reported ever having used marijuana, the corresponding figure for students in Puerto Rico was only 11%.

AN: 139
AU: Gould, L.C.; Berberian, R.M.; Kasl, S.V.; Thompson, W.D.; Kleber, H.D.
TI: Sequential patterns of multiple-drug use among high school students
SO: Archives of General Psychiatry, 34:216-222, 1977
IN: Institution for Social and Policy Studies, Yale University, New Haven,
      Connecticut
RF: 15

SUMMARY TABLE

DRUG: multidrug
TYPE: high school students
NUMBER: 1,094
SEX: male and female
AGE: 16.3 years (average)
ETHNICITY: white (87%); black (12%); Puerto Rican (1%)
LOCATION: New Haven, Connecticut
METHODOLOGY: cross-sectional survey
INSTRUMENT(S): questionnaire
CONDUCTED: 1972-1973

PURPOSE

Studies concerning patterns of multiple drug use have indicated a sequential
pattern in the progression from marijuana to heroin, although the patterns have
not been clear. This study investigated whether drug users progress from
marijuana to heroin via specific intermediate drugs, whether there is one path
taken or many towards heavy drug use, and whether drug users abandon the original
drugs once they have moved to another. To help answer these questions, students
(N=1,094) from 20 high schools in New Haven and surrounding towns completed
questionnaires and participated in informal discussion sessions concerning their
drug use history. To control for potential nonresponse bias, nonrespondants were
compared with respondents on available sociodemographic and school participation
dimensions.

FINDINGS

1. A moderate (though significant) relationship existed between grade in school
and use of cigarettes, barbiturates, amphetamines, cocaine, and heroin (p. 217).

2. Students reported a considerable amount of drug use: alcohol, 75%;
marijuana, 52%; cigarettes, 39%; hashish, 34%; barbiturates, 18%;
amphetamines, 18%; LSD, 12%; mescaline, 10%; glue, 9%; cocaine, 6%; and
heroin, 2% (p. 218).

3. Multiple drug use was prevalent; 58% of the students reported use of more
than one drug and 44% had used three drugs or more. Forty-three percent of the
students reported that they were still multiple drug users at the time of the
survey (p. 218).

4. With the exception of glue and cigarettes, the use of drugs was a highly
interrelated set of behavior patterns (p. 218).

5. The use of alcohol was almost as strongly associated with the use of "harder" drugs as was the use of marijuana, with the exception of the relation between alcohol and heroin use (p. 218).

6. A progressive pattern of "ever" drug use existed in the population studied, although as students progressed from one drug to another, they did not tend to give up the drugs they started with (p. 219).

7. Those students who reported current use of the least frequently used drugs reported using the more frequently used drugs as well (p. 219).

8. Although analysis indicated a progressive pattern in frequency of drug use among high school students, it did not demonstrate that individuals necessarily began using drugs in the same order (p. 219).

9. The temporal sequence of drug use was as follows: first, regular cigarette smoking, followed by alcohol, marijuana, hashish, barbiturates, amphetamines, LSD, mescaline, heroin, and cocaine. This sequence, however, was not correlated to frequency of use for a particular drug (p. 221).

10. Use of a particular drug was positively associated with the use of other drugs, although these associations were not strong in the cases of glue and cigarettes. This suggests that cigarettes and glue probably play little role in an orderly progression of drug use (p. 222).

11. According to the list of temporal progression of drugs used, students who progressd beyond hashish were about equally likely to go next to barbiturates, amphetamines, LSD, or mescaline. Most students, however, did not progress beyond these four drugs unless they had used all four of them (p. 222).

CONCLUSION

A progressive pattern of multiple drug use was found, although students did not give up use of the original drugs (i.e., cigarettes, alcohol, and marijuana) when they progressed to heavier drugs. The steps begin with (in temporal order) alcohol, marijuana, and hashish; then barbiturates, amphetamines, LSD, or mescaline are about equally likely to be used, but in no particular sequence; finally heroin and cocaine. No consistent pattern was found for glue and cigarettes. Results indicated that the use of both alcohol and marijuana was strongly associated with the use of other drugs. Although a pattern of a stepping-stone progression in drug use was supported in general, it appears that the underlying processes involved in this progression of polydrug use are more complex than were originally anticipated.

AN: 140
AU: Graeven, D.B.; Folmer, W.
TI: Experimental heroin users: An epidemiologic and psychosocial approach
SO: American Journal of Drug and Alcohol Abuse, 4:365-375, 1977
IN: Department of Sociology, California State University, Hayward
RF: 12

SUMMARY TABLE

DRUG: heroin
TYPE: heroin users
NUMBER: 120 (44 experimenters; 76 addicts)
SEX: male and female
AGE: 19 to 29 years (retrospective: high school)
ETHNICITY: primarily white
LOCATION: San Francisco-Oakland, California
METHODOLOGY: retrospective, descriptive survey
INSTRUMENT(S):   interview
CONDUCTED: 1975

PURPOSE

This study addressed two issues regarding adolescent heroin use: (1) the role of experimental heroin use in the diffusion of a heroin epidemic and (2) the psychosocial factors that differentiate between those experimenters who use heroin only a couple of times and those who have more frequent patterns of use. The conceptual framework of the study was that adolescent drug use is the result of a breakdown in the mechanisms for social control (particularly the family and the school) and of a corresponding increase in the influence of deviant peers. Interviews with students who were experimental heroin users and heroin addicts were conducted in 1975 at two high schools in the San Francisco-Oakland area that had experienced heroin epidemics between 1965 and 1974. In addition to information on drug use patterns, the interview elicited measures of family life, high school and peer involvement, involvement with the criminal justice system, and personality. In 1975, interviews were conducted with subjects who had been experimental heroin users or heroin addicts at two high schools in the San Francisco-Oakland area that had experienced heroin epidemics between 1965 and 1974.

OPERATIONAL DEFINITIONS

Levels of heroin use: low (once or twice), moderate (3-30 times), high (over 30 times).

Epidemic: an epidemic of heroin use at two high schools in the San Francisco-Oakland area from 1965 to 1974.

FINDINGS

1. Frequency of heroin use among experimental users was: 29% more than 30 times, 33% between 3 and 30 times, and 38% once or twice (p. 368).

2. During the period of the heroin epidemic, those students who became addicted were more likely to have used heroin in the early years of the epidemic, whereas experimenters were more likely to have used heroin in the later years (p. 368).

3. Of all the people identified as heroin users, 51% became addicts, most of them having used heroin early in the epidemic (p. 368).

4. As the epidemic progressed, the method of using heroin the first time shifted from injection to snorting. As snorting became more popular, experimental use increased and the rate of addiction decreased (p. 368).

5. As the epidemic progressed, heroin addicts became isolated from other drug users, thus reducing the amount of reinforcement on heroin experimenters to increase their use (p. 368).

6. Addicts were more likely to introduce others to heroin than were experimenters: addicts introduced an average of 6 new users to heroin; experimenters, an average of 2.9 (p. 369).

7. Compared with low experimental heroin users, moderate and high users used amphetamines, LSD, and barbiturates more frequently and were more likely to be involved in polydrug use both during and after their high school years (p. 369).

8. For the three levels of experimental heroin users, the length of use for alcohol, marijuana, and LSD was similar (p. 369).

9. High experimental users of heroin used amphetamines, barbiturates, and heroin for a longer time than low experimental users (p. 369).

10. About 40% of experimenters with moderate or high levels of heroin use had used heroin in the year of the interview (1975) (p. 369).

11. In 1975, high experimental users of heroin reported a higher rate of heroin use than current use of other drugs, suggesting that heroin is the drug of choice for the high experimental user (p. 369).

12. In 1975, moderate experimental heroin users reported high rates of use for amphetamines and barbiturates as well as for heroin, suggesting that moderate experimental heroin users tend to be polydrug users (p. 369).

13. Eighty-three percent of the high and 79% of the moderate experimental heroin users had used the drug once or twice a month over a period of three years or more (p. 369).

14. For the three levels of experimental heroin users, the percentages of intravenous injection at first use were similar. Heroin was more likely to be the first drug used intravenously for low (46%) and moderate (44%) experimental heroin users, whereas this was true for few (9%) of the high users. High experimental heroin users were more likely to have taken a variety of drugs intravenously, compared with low and moderate users (pp. 369-370).

15. Compared with moderate and high experimental users, low users seldom paid for heroin for their first use, seldom introduced anyone else to the drug, and had lower satisfaction with their heroin experiences (pp. 370-371).

16. All three levels of experimental heroin users had similar rates of frequent exposure to drugs, except for heroin. Compared with moderate and high experimental heroin users, low users were exposed to various drugs more often than they used them. These results suggest that exposure to drugs is not an adequate explanation for the amount of heroin and other drug use by experimental users (p. 371).

17. Compared with moderate and high experimental heroin users, low users had less trouble in high school, were less likely to have been on probation since high school, and were less likely to be unemployed (p. 372).

18. With regard to family life, the percentages of intact families were similar for the three levels of experimental heroin users; high users said that in their families there were fewer rules, less intimacy with their parents, and less closeness, compared with low users (p. 372).

19. Compared with low experimental heroin users, high users exhibited lower self-esteem and a less positive view of the future while in high school (p. 372).

20. Compared with low and moderate experimental heroin users, high users were less involved in academic subjects and were more likely to feel marginally involved in school (p. 372).

CONCLUSION

The results lend support to previous findings that there exists a pattern of experimental use that is continued over a period of several years. High school students who used heroin early in the epidemic were more likely to become addicts, while those who used heroin later more often became experimental users. The increase of experimental use in the later years of the epidemic may be explained by the increasing popularity of snorting rather than intravenous injection and by the increasing isolation of heroin addicts from other drug users. With regard to psychosocial factors, experimental users who used heroin frequently had weaker ties with school and family, more involvement with the criminal justice system, and less positive views about themselves and the future. Such personality factors are similar to those considered to be important in causing other adolescent deviant behavior.

AN: 141
AU: Graeven, D.B.; Graeven, K.A.
TI: Treated and untreated addicts: Factors associated with participation in
     treatment and cessation of heroin use
SO: Paper presented at the National Drug Abuse Conference, 1977. 23 pp.
IN: Department of Sociology, California State University, Hayward
RF: 9

SUMMARY TABLE

DRUG: heroin
TYPE: heroin users
NUMBER: 76
SEX: male and female
AGE: 19 to 29 years
ETHNICITY: primarily white
LOCATION: San Francisco-Oakland, California
METHODOLOGY: retrospective, comparative survey
INSTRUMENT(S):   interview
CONDUCTED: 1975

PURPOSE

This paper examines three aspects of treatment in heroin addicts: (1) differences
between treated and untreated addicts with regard to family life, high school and
peer involvement, and personality; (2) the use of heroin and other drugs by
treated and untreated addicts; and (3) differences between those who stopped and
those who continued using heroin with regard to treatment experience, background
factors, and drug use. Interviews were conducted with heroin addicts who had been
addicts at two high schools in the San Francisco-Oakland area that experienced
heroin epidemics between 1965 and 1974.

OPERATIONAL DEFINITIONS

Four levels of treatment: no treatment; one or two treatment contacts; three to
six treatment contacts; seven or more treatment contacts.

FINDINGS

1. Eighty-one percent of the addicts interviewed had been in a treatment program;
the types of treatment used were: detoxification programs, 76%; residential
programs, 60%; outpatient treatment, 35%; methadone maintenance, 20%; private
physician, 16%; penal institutions, 16%; religious programs, 12%; others, 10%
(p. 6).

2. Treatment experience was not related to parents' occupation or education
(p. 7).

3. Untreated addicts were slightly younger than treated addicts: median age 22
years vs. 24, 23, and 25 years for other three levels of treatment, respectively
(p. 7).

4. Treatment experience was not related to marital status (p. 7).

5. Compared with treated addicts, untreated addicts were less often in trouble during high school (suspension, trouble with police, run-away from home); less likely to have spent time in jail since high school; more often employed; and more likely to have had some college education (p. 7).

6. The level of treatment was not related to academic involvement or peer association (p. 7).

7. Untreated addicts reported somewhat higher trust in friends while in high school, whereas treated addicts more often reported low openness with friends (p. 7).

8. None of the treatment levels could be differentiated by attitudes toward the future (p. 7).

9. Addicts who had been in treatment exhibited lower self-esteem than those not in treatment (p. 8).

10. With regard to family life, untreated addicts, as compared with treated addicts, more often described their families as close, had more family rules, and were under more pressure from their parents (p. 8).

11. Untreated addicts and addicts with one or two treatment contacts generally began heroin use later than addicts with more treatment experience (p. 9).

12. Compared with treated addicts, untreated addicts took less time to kick heroin during the worst time, were less likely to have a habit of more than $100 during their run, were less likely to have used heroin for four years or more, and were less likely to have introduced others to heroin (p. 9).

13. Untreated addicts had a smaller heroin habit than treated addicts; the size of the habit was directly related to the level of treatment experience (p. 9).

14. With regard to the use of other drugs, untreated addicts were less likely to have been dependent on amphetamines than treated addicts, and were more likely to have used LSD, amphetamines, and barbiturates during the year preceeding the interview (p. 9).

15. By 1975, the percentage of untreated addicts who were not using heroin (52%) was nearly the same as that of those having one or two treatment contacts, while addicts with more treatment contacts were more likely to have used heroin in 1975. Also, untreated addicts were less likely to have used heroin three or more times a week during 1975 than treated addicts (p. 10).

16. Among untreated addicts, those not using heroin as of 1975 did not differ from those still using heroin with regard to trouble in high school, academic involvement in high school, or educational achievement; nonusers had less contact with the criminal justice system, were less often married, more often employed, had higher levels of peer association, and less often belonged to a deviant group (p. 11).

17. Among treated addicts, nonusers of heroin in 1975 were less likely to have belonged to a deviant group in high school, had more trust in high school friends, and were less likely to be open than continuing users (p. 11).

18. Among untreated addicts, those not using heroin as of 1975 reported more family activities, more perceived closeness in the family, and more pressure from parents, whereas continuing users reported more family rules and more family fights (p. 12).

19. Among treated addicts, those not using heroin as of 1975, when compared with continuing users, were less likely to have intact families, reported fewer family activities, were less likely to describe their family as close, indicated less openness with parents, and had more family rules, although the differences between the two groups were small (p. 12).

20. Personality characteristics prior to beginning heroin use did not differentiate as much between those who stopped or continued using heroin as they did between those who entered treatment and those who did not (p. 13).

21. Among untreated addicts, those not using heroin in 1975 had larger habits in high school than those still using heroin; both groups had similar percentages of current LSD and amphetamine use, but a much higher percentage of current heroin users reported barbiturate use (p. 13).

22. Among treated addicts, current users of heroin had larger habits during their longest run than nonusers as of 1975; users also had a somewhat higher proportion of using other drugs (p. 13).

23. Untreated heroin addicts had a better family background, more positive self-esteem, less involvement with the criminal justice system, and smaller heroin habits than treated addicts (pp. 13-14).

24. Untreated heroin addicts were more likely to cease heroin use than addicts with frequent treatment experience (p. 14).

25. Untreated heroin addicts who had stopped using heroin had less involvement with the criminal justice system and a more supportive family than untreated addicts still using heroin (p. 14).

26. Treated heroin addicts who had stopped using heroin had slightly poorer family backgrounds than those still using heroin (p. 14).

CONCLUSION

In this study, untreated addicts had more positive experiences with their families and more positive feelings about themselves than treated addicts; thus, it is important that generalizations about the personality characteristics of addicts be based on data from both treated and untreated addicts. Since untreated addicts were likely to have high levels of heroin use and were more likely to cease heroin use, it is evident that some heroin users can regulate their habit such that treatment is not necessary. Thus, it may not be the best policy to try to identify untreated heroin users who have not chosen to enter treatment and who have a supportive family life, because the likelihood of their stopping heroin use is higher than those who go through treatment.

AN: 142
AU: Graeven, D.B.; Jones, A.
TI: Addicts and experimenters: Dynamics of involvement in an adolescent heroin
     epidemic
SO: Paper presented at the National Drug Abuse Conference, 1977. 13 pp.
IN: Department of Sociology, California State University, Hayward
RF: 11

SUMMARY TABLE

DRUG: heroin
TYPE: heroin users
NUMBER: 156 (plus 47 controls)
SEX: male and female
AGE: 19 to 29 years (retrospective: high school)
ETHNICITY: white (85%); Mexican-American (11%)
LOCATION: San Francisco-Oakland, California
METHODOLOGY: retrospective, comparative survey
INSTRUMENT(S):   interview
CONDUCTED: 1975

PURPOSE

In recent research, areas with a high incidence of heroin addiction have been
labelled macroepidemics and then studied as such (epidemic model). The purpose of
this study was to apply the epidemic model to an outbreak of an adolescent heroin
addiction in a suburban community of the San Francisco-Oakland metropolitan area
between 1965 and 1974 and to determine the history of the epidemic. Another goal
was to describe and analyze the patterns of involvement for those who only
experimented with the drug and for those who became addicted to it. The addict,
experimenter, and exposed population were identified, and a random sample of
persons who had no exposure to heroin was selected for comparison. The study
sample was selected from the yearbooks of two high schools in the area. The time
period of the study was divided into three phases: early phase (1965-1967),
middle phase (1968-1970), and late phase (1971-1974).

OPERATIONAL DEFINITIONS

Epidemic: an epidemic of heroin use at two high schools in the San
Francisco-Oakland area from 1965 to 1974.

Epidemic phases: early phase (1965-1967), middle phase (1968-1970), late phase
(1971-1974).

Experimenter: someone who had used heroin at least once but who never became
dependent on it.

Exposed person: someone who was physically present when heroin was being used,
but never used it.

FINDINGS

1. Among addicts, there was a rapid increase in the incidence of heroin use in the early phase of the epidemic, which was followed by a decline (p. 4).

2. Among experimenters, there was a more stable distribution of heroin use over the first six years (1965-1970) of the epidemic than among addicts (p. 4).

3. A more stable distribution of heroin use among experimenters (between 1965 and 1970) was followed by a peak in 1971 (p. 4).

4. In the last year of the epidemic (1974), 29% of the addicts had not used drugs. Eight percent of the addicts reported a modal use of heroin less than one or two times a month. Sixteen percent had a modal use of one or two times a week. Forty-seven percent of addicts reported a modal use of drugs three or more times a week (p. 5).

5. Sixty percent of the experimenters reported no use of heroin in the last year of the epidemic (1974). Thirty-three percent of the experimenters reported use of the drug less than twice a month. Seven percent of the experimenters reported a modal use of drugs once or twice a week (p. 5).

6. Ten years after the onset of the epidemic, about one-third of the addicts reported no use of heroin (p. 5).

7. At the end of the epidemic (1974), about half of the heroin users reported a frequency of heroin use sufficient to produce dependence (p. 5).

8. The heroin epidemic in the two high schools paralleled increased polydrug use among high school students (p. 5).

9. In the first phase of the heroin epidemic, addicts had the highest use of all drugs (alcohol, marijuana, LSD, speed, and barbiturates) compared with the experimenter, exposed, and comparison groups (p. 5).

10. In the second phase of the epidemic, addicts had the highest use of marijuana and barbiturates, with experimenters having a somewhat higher use of alcohol, LSD, and speed (p. 5).

11. The addicts were more likely to get involved in high polydrug use than the experimenter, exposed, or control groups (p. 5).

12. Once addicts got involved with heroin, they cut back on their use of other drugs (p. 5).

13. Ninety-three percent of the early phase addicts first used heroin while high school students. Eighty percent of the mid-phase addicts and 44% of the late phase addicts first used heroin while still in high school (p. 6).

14. Fifty-five percent of the experimenters first used heroin in the early phase of the epidemic; 66% first used heroin in the mid-phase of the epidemic; 24% did so in the last phase (p. 6).

15. Seventy-eight percent of the addicts and 83% of the experimenters were most likely to obtain heroin for first use from a previous user (p. 6).

16. Eighty-one percent of the experimenters obtained their first heroin free, while only 54% of the addicts first obtained their heroin free (p. 6).

17. The median length of time from initial use to addiction was twelve to eighteen months in the first phase of the epidemic, and four to six months in the middle and late phases (p. 8).

18. Addicts "turned on" an average of six new heroin users, and experimenters about three (2.9), with both groups introducing heroin to more people in the early phase of the epidemic than in the middle or late phases (p. 8).

19. Both addicts and experimenters were more likely to inject heroin as the first method of use in the early and mid phases of the epidemic. Injection as a first method of heroin use decreased markedly by the late phase of the epidemic, with a corresponding increase in snorting as a first method of heroin use (p. 7).

CONCLUSION

It was found that the patterns of involvement in heroin use were different for the heroin addicts and for the heroin experimenters. Addicts were more likely to demonstrate high levels of polydrug use before trying heroin; they paid more frequently than experimenters for their initial heroin use and more frequently enjoyed the heroin experience the first time; also, they more frequently attracted others to heroin. The highest rates of addiction occurred in the early phase of the epidemic, but the highest rate of heroin experimentation occurred in the late phase. Heroin use is highly contagious in the early stages of an epidemic. One implication of the findings is the importance of developing an intervention program as early as possible in a heroin epidemic.

AN: 143
AU: Graeven, D.B.; Schaef, R.D.
TI: Personality development and adolescent heroin use
SO: Social Work Research and Abstracts, 13:24-29, 1977
IN: Department of Sociology, California State University, Hayward
RF: 35

SUMMARY TABLE

DRUG: heroin
TYPE: heroin users
NUMBER: 203
SEX: male (147); female (56)
AGE: 19 to 29 years (retrospective: high school)
ETHNICITY: white (85%); Mexican-American (11%)
LOCATION: San Francisco-Oakland, California
METHODOLOGY: retrospective, correlational/comparative survey
INSTRUMENT(S):   interview
CONDUCTED: 1975

PURPOSE

Drug abuse among adolescents may be the result of young people trying to come to terms with normal adolescent problems of growing up rather than of a pathological personality. To examine this possibility, subjects who had attended two high schools that experienced a significant increase in heroin use between 1965 and 1974 were asked how they felt about themselves in high school. The interview was designed to obtain measures of sexual identity, future orientation, self-esteem, and self-concept. Subjects were divided into four levels of heroin involvement: addiction, experimentation, exposure (but nonuse), and nonuse (controls). In addition, the study compared males and females to determine if any differences existed between the sexes on the four personality variables and to assess the implications of those differences (if any) for treatment.

OPERATIONAL DEFINITIONS

Levels of heroin involvement: addiction, experimentation, exposure (but nonuse), and nonuse (controls).

FINDINGS

1. Males and females who had been involved in heroin use reported greater use of other drugs than did controls (p. 27).

2. Compared with controls, males involved in heroin use were more likely to say they were somewhat or very outgoing with females and less likely to say they were shy (p. 27).

3. The measurement of sexual identity (degree of shyness or ease with the opposite sex) did not discriminate between the levels of heroin involvement for females (p. 27).

4. Both male and female addicts said they had more sexual experiences than their friends (p. 27).

5. For males and females, there were significant correlations between the level of involvement with heroin and the frequent and regular use of other drugs during sexual activity (p. 17).

6. Although there was no significant correlation between a scale of males' attitudes toward the future during high school and their involvement with heroin, on one item within the scale, males who used heroin did not think that the future looked as bright as males not involved with heroin (p. 24).

7. For females, there was a significant correlation between a negative view of the future and use of heroin (p. 27).

8. The total score on a self-esteem scale was not significantly related to the level of heroin involvement for males, but for certain items the relation was significant: males involved with heroin more frequently said that they wished they had more self-respect and often reported that they felt no good at all. Males who had used heroin more often said that they felt they did things as well as others (p. 27).

9. Low self-esteem was significantly related to use of heroin among females. Compared with nonusers, female heroin users said they felt useless at times, and felt not satisfied with themselves (p. 27).

10. On a self-concept scale, males who used heroin, especially addicts, reported a more positive description of themselves by peers than nonusers. Male heroin users gave descriptions of themselves that were significantly lower in self-esteem than those of nonusers. Descriptions by parents of the male subjects while in high school (as reported by the subject) had no significant relation to heroin involvement (p. 27).

11. Compared with female nonusers of heroin, females who used heroin had significantly lower ratings on three self-concept measures: peer description of subject, parental description of subject, and subject's self-description. For the second and third measures, none of the female addicts or experimenters were rated as having a high self-concept (p. 28).

12. How the subjects felt about themselves while in high school was significantly related to heroin use by females, but not by males (p. 28).

13. At the time of the interview, the subjects' feelings about themselves were significantly related to heroin use by males, but not by females (p. 28).

14. Of males who had stopped using heroin, 81% said they felt good about themselves at the time of the interview, whereas only 45% of the males still using heroin so responded (p. 28).

15. Of females who had stopped using heroin, 100% said they felt good about themselves at the time of the interview, whereas only 7% of the females still using heroin so responded (p. 28).

16. For both males and females, the use of heroin was clearly related to the subjects' feelings about themselves, with continued use related to more negative feelings (p. 28).

CONCLUSION

The relationship between personality factors and heroin use is clearly different
for males and females. Adolescent females who became involved in heroin use had a
negative orientation toward the future, a low self-esteem, and a negative
self-concept. For males, although certain aspects of self-esteem and self-concept
appear to be related to adolescent heroin use, in general there was no significant
relationship between personality variables and heroin use. With regard to sexual
identity, both males and females who were involved in heroin use said they had
more sexual experience than their friends. It appears that for some adolescents
heroin use is a way of coping with anxiety about sexual identity. Such a finding
suggests that one strategy for drug abuse prevention is to provide adolescents the
opportunity to discuss problems of sexual identity and sexuality. For females,
the results point to a drug abuse prevention program which would develop positive
self-concept, self-esteem, and future orientation. Since personality variables do
not appear to be related to heroin use in males, prevention strategies directed
toward them may have to use techniques of peer group socialization.

AN: 144
AU: Graeven, D.B.; Schaef, R.D.
TI: Family life and levels of involvement in an adolescent heroin epidemic
SO: International Journal of the Addictions, 13:747-771, 1978
IN: Department of Sociology, California State University, Hayward
RF: 39

SUMMARY TABLE

DRUG: heroin
TYPE: heroin users
NUMBER: 156 (plus 47 controls)
SEX: male (72%); female (28%)
AGE: 19 to 28 years (retrospective: high school)
ETHNICITY: white (85%); Mexican-American (11%)
LOCATION: San Francisco-Oakland, California
METHODOLOGY: retrospective, correlational survey
INSTRUMENT(S):   interview
CONDUCTED: 1975

PURPOSE

To examine the relation of family life to different levels of heroin involvement, four levels of heroin involvement were identified and various measures of family cohesiveness were determined through interviews with the subjects. The levels of heroin involvement were addiction, experimentation, exposure (but no use), and no use (control). These levels of involvement were correlated with the following measures of family cohesiveness: emotional cohesion, behavioral integration, supportive integration, conflict interaction, external control, and adolescent evaluation of parents. The data were collected as part of research on an adolescent heroin epidemic which occurred between 1965 and 1974 in a lower middle- to middle-class suburb of the San Francisco-Oakland metropolitan area.

OPERATIONAL DEFINITIONS

Levels of heroin involvement: addiction, experimentation, exposure (but nonuse), and nonuse (control).

FINDINGS

1. Males involved in heroin use had less communicative intimacy with both parents and came from families with a high amount of conflict between parents and between parents and children. They gave lower evaluations of both parents, and more often came from broken homes (p. 761).

2. No relation was found between male heroin involvement and closeness to parents, family activities, or number of rules (p. 761).

3. Female involvement in heroin use was significantly related to less feeling of closeness to both parents, less intimacy with the father, a lower evaluation of the father, less participation in family activities, more rules, and a higher amount of conflict between parents and children (pp. 761-762).

4. There was no correlation between female heroin involvement and intimacy with the mother, evaluation of the mother, parent conflict, or family intactness (p. 762).

5. For females, a poor relationship with the father remained the most important factor contributing to their heroin involvement. But their relationship with the mother was also a contributing factor. For males, heroin use was explained more by a poor relationship with the mother and the greater amount of conflict at home (pp. 762-763).

6. In a primarily white, suburban population, the quality of the adolescent relationship with the parent of the opposite sex was determinative in heroin involvement or noninvolvement (p. 763).

7. Subjects who were more involved with heroin used larger amounts of other drugs such as alcohol, marijuana, psychedelics, amphetamines, and barbiturates than those with lower heroin involvement (p. 763).

8. Both males and females with higher involvement in heroin use were more frequently in trouble in high school than those with lower involvement (p. 763).

9. A lack of intimacy with both parents, a lower adolescent evaluation of both parents, and a higher amount of parent conflict and parent-child conflict were related to greater use by male heroin users of psychedelics, amphetamines, and barbiturates (p. 766).

10. For heroin-using females, increased use of psychedelics, amphetamines, and barbiturates was related to less intimacy with the father and less participation in family activities. Closeness with the father was related to psychedelic and barbiturate use and to trouble in high school (p. 766).

11. The more alcohol a female used, the more intimate she was with her mother (p. 766).

CONCLUSION

Male heroin users had a low degree of supportive interaction with both parents, lower evaluations of the parents, a high amount of conflict between family members, and a greater incidence of broken homes. Although good family relations tended to insulate against heroin use, it did not deter those who used heroin from becoming addicted. For females, good family relations insulated them against addiction, but it did not deter them from experimental use of heroin or from involvement in situations where heroin was used. An increase in the emotional cohesion of the family, supportive interaction, and behavioral integration, and at the same time a decrease in the amount of conflict and greater reliance on internal rather than external controls, could prevent heroin and drug abuse.

AN: 145
AU: Huba, G.J.; Alkin, M.S.; Bentler, P.M.
TI: Is coca paste currently a drug of abuse among high school students?
SO: Journal of Drug Education, 11:205-212, 1981
IN: Department of Psychology, University of California, Los Angeles
RF: 4

SUMMARY TABLE

DRUG: coca paste
TYPE: high school students
NUMBER: 688
SEX: male (228); female (460)
AGE: 17-18 years
ETHNICITY: white (442); black (109); Mexican-American (105); Asian-American
                 (32)
LOCATION: Los Angeles, California
METHODOLOGY: descriptive, correlational survey
INSTRUMENT(S):   questionnaire
CONDUCTED: 1980

PURPOSE

It has recently been contended that coca paste, an inexpensive unrefined form of
coca, will become a new substance of abuse among adolescents and young adults. In
order to determine whether or not there were substantial rates of coca paste use
among high school students in Southern California, which has generally been a
gateway for illicit drug trafficking, questionnaires on drug use containing
specific items on coca paste were administered to 688 eleventh and twelfth graders
in a Los Angeles high school during March and April of 1980. Use rates for coca
paste were correlated with use of other drugs, knowledge about coca paste, peer
use, and perceived availability of the drug.

FINDINGS

1. Although the sample of Los Angeles high school students reported at least
moderate use of illicit drugs such as marijuana (51.3% of the males and 47.8% of
the females), liquor (57.8% and 54.1%, respectively), PCP (5.7% and 6.7%), and
cocaine (20.2% and 19.1%), only a very small percentage (1.8% of the males and
1.1% of the females) reported use of coca paste (p. 208).

2. For the sample of Los Angeles high school students, there were relatively low
levels of reported coca paste use and knowledge; 98.2% of the boys and 98.9% of
the girls had never used it, only 13.2% of the boys and 7.6% of the girls had ever
heard of coca paste, and only nine students reported occasional use during the
previous six months. Six individuals reported bad experiences on coca paste
(p. 209).

3. The majority of the Los Angeles high school students questioned (96.1% of the
males and 96.6% of the females) did not have friends who used coca paste and most
felt that it would be difficult to get access to the drug or did not know how to
do so. Only 5.2% of the boys and 2.8% of the girls felt it would be easy or very
easy to obtain coca paste (p. 209).

4. High school students in Los Angeles who used other drugs frequently and marijuana in some quantity were more likely than other students to report that they knew about coca paste and that they either used it or had friends who did (pp. 210-211).

CONCLUSION

There was an extremely low number of adolescents in Los Angeles during March and April of 1980 who had any knowledge of coca paste; the percentage of users was very small, and most adolescents reported that their friends did not use coca paste and that they did not have access to a source of the drug. Those who had used coca paste, who knew friends that had, or who knew how to obtain it were more likely than nonusers to use other illicit drugs frequently, and marijuana in some quantity, but these correlations may simply be due to the tendency of individuals who are heavily involved in the drug culture to claim knowledge of another drug. The findings indicate that use of coca paste was not an integral part of the youth drug culture in Los Angeles in the spring of 1980.

AN: 146
AU: Huba, G.J.; Wingard, J.A.; Bentler, P.M.
TI: Adolescent drug use and intentions to use drugs in the future: A concurrent
      analysis
SO: Journal of Drug Education, 9:145-150, 1979
IN: Department of Psychology, University of California, Los Angeles
RF: 7

SUMMARY TABLE

DRUG: multidrug
TYPE: junior high school students
NUMBER: 1,634
SEX: male (35.6%); female (64.4%)
AGE: [13.4 years (average)]
ETHNICITY: white (56.4%); Spanish (14.8%); black (23.6%); Asian (5.2%)
LOCATION: Los Angeles, California
METHODOLOGY: cross-sectional, correlational survey
INSTRUMENT(S):   questionnaire
CONDUCTED: not specified

PURPOSE

Although previous investigations have studied the causal and psychosocial factors
of adolescent drug use, few have studied the cognitive intentions, as opposed to
behaviors, held by youth concerning psychoactive drug use. An attempt to examine
the relationship between drug use and intended future drug use was made using
junior high school students (N=1,634) from metropolitan Los Angeles. The students
completed questionnaires asking about the number of times they had used particular
drugs and about their intentions to use these drugs in the future. The drugs
assessed in the study were cigarettes, beer, wine, liquor, cocaine, tranquilizers,
drug store medications used to get "high," heroin and opiates, marijuana, hashish,
inhalants, hallucinogens, and amphetamines.

FINDINGS

1. Owing to the young age of the students questioned, most of their drug use was
found to be basically experimental (p. 147).

2. A significant relationship was found between the junior high school students'
drug use and their intended future use (p. 148).

3. The junior high school students' intentions to use a particular drug in the
future were more accurately predicted by knowing their previous experience with
all drugs than by knowing previous experience with that specific drug (p. 149).

CONCLUSION

The results of the study indicated that the intentions to use a particular drug
were better predicted by all current drug-taking behaviors than by only the level
of use for that specific drug. In addition, the intention to use drugs in the
future was associated with current drug taking behavior in the junior high school

students studied. These findings indicate that additional factors besides current drug use are involved in determining whether the students will take a drug or not, and these factors must be considered in any future work concerning adolescent drug use.

AN: 147
AU: Huba, G.J.; Wingard, J.A.; Bentler, P.M.
TI: Beginning adolescent drug use and peer and adult interaction patterns
SO: Journal of Consulting and Clinical Psychology, 47:265-276, 1979
IN: Department of Psychology, University of California, Los Angeles
RF: 36

SUMMARY TABLE

DRUG: multidrug
TYPE: junior high school students
NUMBER: 1,634
SEX: male (35.6%); female (64.4%)
AGE: 13.4 years (average)
ETHNICITY: white (56.4%); Spanish (14.8%); black (23.5%); Asian (5.2%)
LOCATION: Los Angeles, California
METHODOLOGY: cross-sectional, correlational survey
INSTRUMENT(S):   questionnaire
CONDUCTED: not specified

PURPOSE

In an attempt to gain information about the social interaction patterns of drug
users, three questions were investigated. The first question concerned whether
there is a significant link between drug use and reported interaction patterns in
young adolescents. The second question was whether there exists a general
subculture of drug users. The final question was whether the subcultures of drug
users have the same interpersonal norms. To answer these questions, students
(N=1,634) from eleven schools in greater metropolitan Los Angeles were selected to
complete questionnaires concerning their drug use and their interactions with
peers, parents, and significant adults.

FINDINGS

1. Adolescent drug use was strongly related to interaction patterns with other
adolescents and significant adults (p. 273).

2. Adolescent hard drug users tended to know many adults who took pills to get
high and had many friends who used hard liquor or pills (p. 272).

3. The adolescent cigarette smoker tended to know many adults who had recently
smoked marijuana, drove frequently in cars with friends, and associated with
adolescents who cut classes and smoked cigarettes at school (p. 272).

4. A specialized pattern of peer and adult interaction associated with drug use
in general among adolescents was not found, although there were drug-specific
interactional patterns formed by adolescent drug users (p. 274).

5. The existence of a single, general drug culture that adolescents enter and
remain in as they increase their experimentation was refuted (p. 274).

6. Indicators of social deviance were not substantially related to any of the drug-use or social-interaction dimensions (p. 274).

7. Beginning adolescent drug users did not generally belong to groups with highly atypical social interaction and adjustment patterns (p. 274).

CONCLUSION

The results indicate that the present approach of dealing with adolescent drug use as a deviant behavior pattern may be insufficient. Although deviance may be related in some ways to drug use, the present data indicate that friendship circles or specific interaction sets also play a significant role in adolescent drug use; these roles are not indicative of general unconventionality or maladaptive behavior. Although it is possible that subsequent associations with people involved with drugs may lead to a general change in attitudes, friendships, or lifestyle, this change had not yet occurred by the ninth grade in the group of normal, healthy adolescents that was studied.

AN: 148
AU: Huba, G.J.; Wingard, J.A.; Bentler, P.M.
TI: Longitudinal analysis of the role of peer support, adult models, and peer
       subcultures in beginning adolescent substance use: An application of setwise
       canonical correlation methods
SO: Multivariate Behavioral Research, 15:259-280, 1980
IN: Department of Psychology, University of California, Los Angeles
RF: 35

SUMMARY TABLE

DRUG: multidrug
TYPE: junior high school students
NUMBER: 1,177
SEX: male and female
AGE: junior high school
ETHNICITY: white; black; Oriental; Spanish
LOCATION: Los Angeles, California
METHODOLOGY: longitudinal, correlational survey
INSTRUMENT(S):   questionnaire
CONDUCTED: not specified

PURPOSE

Adolescent drug use has been assumed to be one facet of a more general lifestyle
characterized by unconventionality and deviance. In a previous exploratory
investigation (see AN 147), the authors showed that while perceived supply and
support of drug use by peers are important concomitants of beginning substance
use, the perceived general characteristics of the peer environment are less
important. The present study was designed to determine whether or not knowledge
of perceived supply and support sources (the "support system") produces an
increment in prediction beyond that obtained from information about prior
drug-taking, and to determine whether or not the general aspects of the peer
culture can be used to predict subsequent drug-taking. Questionnaires were
administered to 1,634 7th, 8th, and 9th grade students in the Los Angeles area,
and follow-up questionnaires were completed by 1,177 of these adolescents a year
later. Each participant answered questions about drug use patterns and about his
or her interactions with parents, peers, and significant adults. Indications of
perceived adult use, perceived use among friends, and perceived supply from
friends were considered to be measures of the support system, while items
pertaining to more general characteristics of friends and interactions with them
(such as taking part in student government, getting together with friends outside
of school, cheating on an important exam, and cutting class) were considered to be
indicators of the peer culture. Canonical correlation analysis was chosen as the
primary statistical method for analyzing the data.

FINDINGS

1. Measures of peer culture produced little unique variance in ability to predict
drug use patterns for adolescents from one year to the next. However, second year
drug use was highly correlated to drug use in the previous year and to the support
system for substance use (pp. 271, 275).

2. Adolescents using various licit and illicit drugs interacted regularly with adults and peers who used the same substances and who served as sources of supply (p. 275).

3. Alcohol use and marijuana use were stable over a one year span for adolescents, while the use of "hard drugs" was only partially predictable from previous experimentation with these substances (pp. 275-276).

4. There was no evidence among a group of adolescents of a general drug use subculture which would predict drug use patterns, but rather different support systems existed for alcohol and marijuana use (p. 276).

CONCLUSION

Although both prior drug-taking behavior and a support system for drug use (including use and supply by friends and adult models for use) provide a significant increment in the multivariate prediction of adolescent drug use, there is no evidence that belonging to a counter-normative peer culture, specifically indications of mild levels of "deviance" or nonconformity in a school-oriented culture, enables prediction of drug use. Maladaptive or "deviant" characteristics in friends in a school environment (such as cheating on tests, not doing homework, etc.) do not add to prediction of drug use, nor do adaptive characteristics (such as belonging to clubs, involvement in student government, etc.) protect the individual from drug use. Rebelliousness may predispose an individual to belong to a counter-normative subculture, but only some of these subcultures represent support systems for drug use.

AN: 149
AU: Huba, G.J.; Wingard, J.A.; Bentler, P.M.
TI: Intentions to use drugs among adolescents: A longitudinal analysis
SO: International Journal of the Addictions, 16:331–339, 1981
IN: Department of Psychology, University of California, Los Angeles
RF: 9

SUMMARY TABLE

DRUG: multidrug
TYPE: junior high school students
NUMBER: 1,177
SEX: male and female
AGE: junior high school
ETHNICITY: white; black; Hispanic; Oriental
LOCATION: Los Angeles, California
METHODOLOGY: longitudinal, correlational survey
INSTRUMENT(S):   questionnaire
CONDUCTED: not specified

PURPOSE

Previous studies of high school and college youth have found that an expression of
intention to use drugs in the future is strongly correlated to later drug use. In
order to test the hypothesis that information about intended drug use among early
adolescents will add to information about current drug use in the prediction of
future drug taking, questionnaires about drug use and intended drug use were
administered to 1,634 junior high school students in Los Angeles. The following
year, follow-up questionnaires asking about drug use in the past six months were
completed by 1,177 adolescents, who made up the final sample.

FINDINGS

1. Second year drug use was significantly related to first year drug use for the
sample of adolescents. In addition, there was a statistically significant
correlation between first year intended drug use and second year drug use
(p. 335).

2. While information about first year drug use enabled strong predictions of
second year drug use for a group of California adolescents, intentions to use
drugs did not account for more than about 1% of the variance in a specific form of
subsequent drug use not accounted for by initial drug use (p. 335).

3. Adolescents who used primarily marijuana along with continued alcohol use and
who reported some tendency to experiment with other drugs in the second year of
the study had strong positive loadings for use of marijuana, hashish, and
cigarettes the previous year, as well as some use of liquor, tranquilizers,
heroin, inhalants, and stimulants, and intentions of using marijuana as well as
cigarettes, cocaine, tranquilizers, heroin, hallucinogens, and amphetamines.
Adolescents who used primarily alcohol in the second year of the study had
indicated use of beer, wine, liquor, and cigarettes the previous year as well as
intentions to use beer, wine, liquor, cigarettes, and marijuana (p. 337).

4.   Second year use of marijuana was related to first year use of alcohol, and
second year use of alcohol was related to first year use of marijuana for a group
of young adolescents. However, neither of the two cross-over correlations was
very large, indicating a low rate of predictable change in use patterns (p. 338).

CONCLUSION

Intentions by early adolescents to use drugs provide information not contained in
existing drug use patterns when predicting drug use one year later, but the
relationships, while statistically significant, are weak. Given that cognition
provides only a small increment in predicting future drug-taking, the initiation
of drug use or a change in drug use among adolescents seems to be controlled by
more immediate factors than mental calculation of risks and benefits. Since
intentions to use drugs have low predictive value for future drug taking, drug
education programs should probably try to dissuade individuals from relying unduly
on peers for values and attitudes rather than to coldly and logically present the
risks of drug-taking.

AN: 150
AU: Johnston, L.D.; Bachman, J.G.; O'Malley, P.M.
TI: Drugs and the Class of '78: Behaviors, Attitudes, and Recent National Trends
SO: Washington, D.C.: Government Printing Office, 1979. 335 pp.
IN: Institute for Social Research, University of Michigan, Ann Arbor, Michigan
RF: 28

SUMMARY TABLE

DRUG: multidrug
TYPE: high school seniors
NUMBER: 17,800
SEX: male and female
AGE: approximately 18 years
ETHNICITY: not specified
LOCATION: United States (cross-sectional)
METHODOLOGY: cross-sectional survey
INSTRUMENT(S):   questionnaire
CONDUCTED: 1978

PURPOSE

Monitoring the Future, an ongoing, longitudinal cohort study conducted by the Institute for Social Research at the University of Michigan, has been gathering data on drug use among high school seniors since 1975 in order to develop an accurate picture of the current drug situation and current trends among young people. This study presents data derived from questionnaires given to a nationwide sample of high school seniors in 1978, and these data are compared to data derived from previous years.

FINDINGS

1. Nearly two-thirds of high school seniors (64.1%) reported illicit drug use at some time in their lives, although many (27.6% of the total sample or 43% of all illicit users) had used only marijuana. Over one-third of the seniors (36.5%) reported use of an illicit drug other than marijuana at some time (p. 4).

2. Nearly all high school seniors reported use of alcohol (93%) and three-fourths (75%) used cigarettes. Marijuana was the most widely used illicit drug (59%), followed by stimulants (23%), tranquilizers (17%), sedatives (16%), hallucinogens (14%), cocaine (13%), inhalants (12%), opiates other than heroin (10%), and heroin (1.6%). These drugs remain in about the same order when ranked for prevalence in the most recent month and most recent year, with the exception of inhalant use, which was used in the senior year by only a small proportion of those who had ever used inhalants (p. 4).

3. High school seniors reported the greatest daily use of cigarettes (28%, with 18.8% reporting they smoked half-a-pack or more per day), followed by marijuana (10.7%) and alcohol (5.7%). Less than 1% reported daily use of any other illicit drug: amphetamines, 0.5%; sedatives, 0.2%; tranquilizers, 0.1%; opiates other than heroin, 0.1%; hallucinogens, 0.1%; cocaine, 0.1%; inhalants, 0.1%; and heroin, less than 0.05% (p. 5).

4. In general, among high school seniors, higher proportions of males than
females were involved in drug use, especially heavy drug use. Males reported
higher rates for overall marijuana use and daily marijuana use (14.2% compared to
7.1% for females); males were two to three times as likely to use inhalants,
cocaine, and heroin as females and slightly more likely to use hallucinogens,
opiates other than heroin, and sedatives; and males accounted for a
disproportionate number of the heavy users of these drugs. Females were as likely
as males to use stimulants and slightly more likely to be frequent users;
although females used tranquilizers more than males, frequent use occurred about
equally for both sexes. Both males and females reported similar percentages of
the use of some illicit drug other than marijuana during the past year (pp. 5-6).

5. Among high school seniors, alcohol was used primarily by males, with 8.3%
reporting daily use compared to 3.2% of females. Equal percentages of males and
females (18.9% and 18.0%, respectively) reported smoking half-a-pack or more of
cigarettes a day, although regular male smokers seemed to consume a somewhat
higher quantity of cigarettes (p. 6).

6. The use of marijuana at least once among high school seniors increased from
47% in 1975 to 59% in 1978, with annual marijuana prevalence increasing from 40%
to 50%. There was practically no increase in the use of illicit drugs other than
marijuana; about 36% reported use of other drugs in each of the four years at
least once, and between 25% and 27% reported use in the year previous to the
survey. Because of the increase in marijuana use, the overall proportion of high
school seniors involved in illicit drug use increased from 55% in 1975 to 64% in
1978, with annual prevalence figures rising from 45% to 54% (pp. 8-9).

7. Except for the use of stimulants, which remained essentially unchanged, the
percentages of high school seniors reporting the use of illicit drugs other than
marijuana changed between 1975 and 1978. The annual prevalence of hallucinogen
use declined from 11% in 1975 to 9% in 1977, but increased slightly to 9.6% in
1978; percentages for frequent hallucinogen use showed the same pattern (1.0% in
1975, 0.7% in 1976, and 0.5% in 1977, with 0.6% reporting frequent use in 1978).
Cocaine use accelerated rapidly, with annual prevalence going from 5.6% in 1975 to
9.0% in 1978. Use of opiates other than heroin increased from 5.7% in 1975 to
6.4% in 1977, but annual prevalence in 1978 was down to 6.0%. Use of sedatives
declined from 11.7% reporting annual prevalence in 1975, to 9.9% in 1978, and
tranquilizer use also declined by 1978. Lifetime prevalence of heroin use dropped
very gradually from 2.2% in 1975 to 1.6% in 1978, but annual prevalence remained
constant for 1977 and 1978. Inhalant use showed a slight rise from 3.0% in 1976
(the first year data were collected) to 4.1% in 1978 (pp. 9-10).

8. The percentages of high school seniors reporting alcohol use increased from
85% in 1975 to 88% in 1978, but there was virtually no change in lifetime
prevalence of cigarette use, although in 1978 there was a drop (for the first
time) in monthly prevalence (p. 10).

9. There was virtually no change in the prevalence of daily use of illicit drugs
among high school seniors between 1975 and 1978, except for daily tranquilizer
use, which increased from 0.1% in 1975 to 0.3% in 1977, but decreased again to
0.1% in 1978, and daily marijuana use, which increased from 6.0% in 1975 to 10.7%
in 1978. Daily use of alcohol, which was 5.7% in 1975, was exactly the same in
1978 (p. 10).

10. There were few sex differences among high school seniors in overall drug use trends between 1975 and 1978, except that the percentage of males smoking half-a-pack a day or more of cigarettes remained constant (about 20%), while the rate of cigarette smoking for females increased from 16% to 19% (pp. 10-11).

11. Among high school seniors, most initial contact with illicit drugs occurred during the last three years of high school; each illicit drug, except marijuana, was used by fewer than 8% before entering tenth grade. Prior to tenth grade, 28% had used marijuana, 56% had used alcohol, and 20% had begun smoking cigarettes daily. Alcohol and marijuana use began during 10th, 11th, or 12th grade for 37% and 31%, respectively, and daily cigarette smoking began during those years for 12%. For each illicit drug class, less than half of the users began use prior to tenth grade; among those who used cocaine by senior year, only one in six had done so prior to tenth grade, but among marijuana users, just under half had begun before tenth grade, while for all other illicit drugs (except inhalants) the corresponding proportion was roughly one-third. Nearly two-thirds of inhalant users had used inhalants prior to tenth grade (p. 12).

12. When questioned about "great risk" of harm for the regular user of various drugs, high school seniors felt that heroin was most harmful (87%), followed by LSD (81%), amphetamines, barbiturates, and cocaine (all about 68%), and regular use of cigarettes (59%), while only 35% believed that regular use of marijuana involved great risk. Compared with the perceptions about the risks of regular use, many fewer seniors felt that an experimental or occasional user of any drug ran a "great risk" of harm (p. 14).

13. Very few high school seniors felt that having one or two alcoholic drinks daily involved great risk (20%), but 35% thought there was risk involved in having five or more drinks once or twice each weekend, and 63% felt that there was great risk in consuming four or five drinks daily (p. 14).

14. Between 1975 and 1978, the percentage of high school seniors associating drug use with personal risk declined, but this was most clearly evident in relation to experimental and occasional use. The greatest decline in perceived risk involved marijuana and cocaine, while the perceived risk of smoking cigarettes increased from 51% in 1975 to 59% in 1978 (pp. 14-15).

15. A majority of high school seniors expressed disapproval of regular use of illicit drugs, ranging from 68% disapproving regular marijuana use to 92% disapproving regular cocaine use and 98% disapproving regular heroin use. Smoking a pack (or more) of cigarettes daily was disapproved by 67%, and drinking of two or three drinks daily was disapproved by 68%. For all drugs, the rate of disapproval was highest for regular use and lower for experimental or occasional use; while 68% disapproved of regular use of marijuana, only 44% disapproved of occasional use and 33% disapproved of experimental use (p. 15).

16. Between 1975 and 1978, in spite of a decline in the perceived harmfulness of most drugs among high school seniors, the percentages of students who expressed disapproval of drug use remained nearly the same, although there seemed to be more tolerance of marijuana use and experimental alcohol use (p. 15).

17. A majority of high school seniors believed that public use of illicit drugs (other than marijuana) should be prohibited by law; 60% favored prohibition of marijuana use in public, 50% favored prohibition of getting drunk in public, and 42% favored prohibition of cigarette smoking in public. Substantially fewer students believed use in private should be illegal (pp. 15-16).

18. Between 1975 and 1978, the views of high school seniors on public use of drugs remained virtually the same, while the percentage favoring prohibition of private use of illicit drugs declined somewhat; the percentage favoring public prohibition also declined slightly between 1975 and 1977, although this latter trend reversed (but not significantly) between 1977 and 1978 (p. 16).

19. A third of the high school seniors favored the legalization of marijuana, 30% believed marijuana use should be treated similar to a parking violation, and 22% believed use should be a crime. Two-thirds agreed that sale of marijuana should be legal if use were made legal. Should marijuana use become legal, most high school seniors said their use (or nonuse) of the drug would be little affected (p. 16).

20. A large majority of high school seniors stated that their parents would disapprove or strongly disapprove of their use of any drug. Over 95% felt that their parents would disapprove of regular marijuana use, experimental LSD or amphetamine use, or having four or five drinks a day. Although marijuana use was seen as receiving the least parental disapproval, 83% felt that their parents would disapprove of even experimental use. Parents were also expected to disapprove strongly (89% to 91%) of occasional marijuana use, taking one or two drinks nearly every day, and pack-a-day cigarette smoking (p. 17).

21. The great majority of high school seniors reported that their friends would not condone the use of illicit drugs other than marijuana, and nearly two-thirds had close friends who they felt disapproved of regular marijuana use or daily drinking (p. 17).

22. Perceived parental and peer norms regarding drug use reported by high school seniors did not change between 1975 and 1978 except in regards to marijuana use, for which perceived disapproval of use at each level (experimental, occasional, regular) dropped, and in regards to cigarette smoking, for which the perceived level of disapproval of regular smoking increased from 55% in 1975 to 60% in 1977 (p. 18).

23. Reports by high school seniors of exposure to friends using drugs and of other people using drugs were consistent, and reports on exposure to any drug use and exposure to friend's use paralleled figures on the senior's own use, with the highest levels of exposure involving alcohol and marijuana. Thirty percent of all seniors said that most or all of their friends got drunk at least once a week and 39% reported often being around people using marijuana (pp. 18-19).

24. High school seniors in 1978 were more likely than seniors in 1976 to report exposure to marijuana use and cocaine use, while there was some decrease in exposure to barbiturate use and LSD use; exposure to the use of other drugs remained fairly constant (p. 19).

CONCLUSION

A majority of high school seniors in 1978 reported illicit drug use at some time in their lives, although many (43% of all illicit drug users) used only marijuana. The two major licit drugs, alcohol and tobacco, were used most frequently, followed (in decreasing order) by marijuana, stimulants, tranquilizers, sedatives, hallucinogens, cocaine, inhalants, opiates other than heroin, and heroin. Daily use of any drug was highest for cigarettes, followed by marijuana and alcohol, but less than 1% used any other drug daily. Males were more likely than females to use drugs, and to use them more frequently. When data from seniors in 1978 were compared with data from seniors in 1975, 1976, and 1977, the greatest changes occurred in the use of and attitudes toward marijuana; marijuana use and exposure to marijuana use increased, while attitudes of disapproval and harmfulness declined. There was a similar though smaller trend for cocaine use, which was the only other illicit drug that increased in use. Disapproval of regular cigarette use increased slightly, and there was a slight decline in monthly prevalence of cigarette use. Attitudes toward alcohol use were mixed, with more seniors disapproving of minor, daily use of alcohol than of weekend binge drinking, thereby reflecting the actual use pattern of alcohol, which was towards weekend binges.

AN: 151
AU: Johnston, L.D.; Bachman, J.G.; O'Malley, P.M.
TI: Highlights from Student Drug Use in America 1975-1980
SO: Rockville, MD: National Institute on Drug Abuse, 1980. 113 pp.
IN: Institute for Social Research, University of Michigan, Ann Arbor, Michigan
RF: 0

SUMMARY TABLE

DRUG: multidrug
TYPE: high school seniors
NUMBER: approximately 17,000
SEX: male and female
AGE: high school
ETHNICITY: not specified
LOCATION: United States (cross-sectional)
METHODOLOGY: cross-sectional survey
INSTRUMENT(S):   questionnaire
CONDUCTED: 1975-1980

PURPOSE

The Monitoring the Future project has been collecting data on drug use and related attitudes from high school seniors during the spring of each year, beginning with the Class of 1975, in order to develop an accurate picture of current prevalence of drug use and trends in use among this population. Each year approximately 17,000 male and female high school seniors in representative high schools across the United States have completed the questionnaires. Only major findings on prevalence in 1980 and trends from 1975 through 1980 are reported.

OPERATIONAL DEFINITIONS

Daily use: for all drugs, except cigarettes, use of the drug on 20 or more occasions in the preceding 30 days.

FINDINGS

1. Drug use was widespread among high school seniors in 1980, with nearly two-thirds (65%) reporting use of any illicit drug, and nearly two out of every five (39%) reporting use of an illicit drug other than marijuana (p. 9).

2. Marijuana was the most widely used illicit drug among high school seniors, with 60% reporting some use in their lifetime, 49% reporting some use in the past year, 34% reporting some use in the past month, and 9% reporting daily use in the past month (pp. 11, 31).

3. After marijuana, stimulants were the illicit drug most often used by high school seniors (with a 26% lifetime prevalence), followed by inhalants (18%), cocaine (16%), hallucinogens (16%), sedatives (15%), tranquilizers (15%), opiates other than heroin (10%), and heroin (1%) (pp. 14-16).

4. The drug classes with the highest rates of discontinuation of use by high
school seniors were heroin (55% of previous users had not used in the past twelve
months), inhalants (56%), PCP (54%), amyl and butyl nitrites (49%), and
tranquilizers (43%) (p. 16).

5. High school seniors reported more use of the licit drugs, alcohol and
cigarettes than of any illicit drug. Nearly all students (93%) had tried alcohol
and 72% had used it in the past month; 71% reported trying cigarettes at some
time and 31% smoked at least some in the past month (p. 16).

6. Marijuana use among high school seniors apparently peaked in 1978 and 1979
after a long and dramatic rise. Annual and 30-day prevalence rates for marijuana
use changed very little between 1978 and 1979, and in 1980 both rates dropped for
the first time. Lifetime prevalence remained unchanged (p. 27).

7. Daily marijuana use among high school seniors increased almost two-fold
between 1975 (6.0%) and 1978 (10.7%). In 1979, 10.3% of high school seniors
reported daily marijuana use and daily use dropped in 1980 to 9.1% (p. 27).

8. Between 1975 and 1979, cocaine use increased rapidly among high school
seniors, rising from 5.6% in 1975 to 12% in 1979--a two-fold increase in two
years. However, in 1980, this rise abruptly stopped, with lifetime and annual
prevalence rising by only 0.3% to 15.7% and 12.3%, respectively; 30-day
prevalence actually dropped by 0.5% to 5.2%. The proportion of high school
seniors who reported daily cocaine use (0.2%) was the same in 1979 and 1980
(pp. 28-32).

9. Inhalant use among high school seniors rose steadily from 3.0% annual
prevalence in 1976 to 5.4% in 1979, but in 1980 annual prevalence decreased to
4.6%, largely due to a drop in the use of the amyl and butyl nitrites (pp. 29,
34).

10. Stimulant use among high school seniors, which remained relatively unchanged
between 1975 and 1978, increased in 1979 and continued to rise in 1980; annual
prevalence of use was 16.3% in 1977 and 20.8% in 1980, while daily use also rose
from 0.4% in 1976 to 0.7% in 1980 (p. 34).

11. Sedative use among high school seniors declined slowly between 1975 and 1979,
from 18.2% to 14.6%, but then increased very slightly to 14.9% in 1980 (p. 34).

12. Use of tranquilizers among high school seniors declined after 1977, with
lifetime prevalence dropping about 1% a year, from 18% in 1977 to 15% in 1980
(p. 34).

13. The prevalence of heroin use among high school seniors dropped steadily
between 1975 and 1979; lifetime prevalence decreased from 2.2% in 1975 to 1.1% in
1979 and 1980, and annual prevalence also dropped by half, from 1.0% in 1975 to
0.5% in 1979 and 1980, despite greater availability of heroin and a rise in 1979
and 1980 of perceived availability of heroin among students (p. 34).

14. The use of opiates other than heroin among high school students remained
stable at or near 6% every year from 1975 to 1980 (p. 35).

15. Hallucinogen use among high school seniors declined slowly from 11.2% annual
prevalence in 1975 to 9.6% in 1978, but the decline halted in 1979 and annual
prevalence was 9.3% in 1980. The use of LSD exhibited a pattern similar to the

drug class as a whole (decline in use from 1975 to 1977 or 1978, then stabilization), but the use of hallucinogens other than LSD continued to decline in 1979 and 1980, with annual prevalence dropping from 7.3% in 1978 to 6.2% in 1980, largely due to a decline in PCP use. PCP use decreased considerably between 1979 and 1980, dropping from 7.0% to 4.4% (pp. 29, 35).

16. There was a very gradual but steady increase in the prevalence of alcohol use among high school seniors between 1975 and 1978, with annual prevalence rising from 84.8% in 1975 to 87.7% in 1978 and remaining virtually constant afterwards at 88.1% in 1979 and 87.9% in 1980. The rate of daily alcohol use remained steady at about 6% from 1975 through 1980. However, binge drinking increased over that same interval, with the proportion of high school seniors reporting five or more drinks in a row during the prior two weeks rising from 37% in 1975 to 41% in 1979 and 1980 (pp. 29, 35-36).

17. Cigarette use among high school seniors apparently peaked in lifetime, 30-day, and daily prevalence in 1976 and 1977; 30-day prevalence rates dropped from 38% in 1977 to 31% in 1980, and daily cigarette use dropped over that same interval from 29% to 21%, while daily use of half-pack-a-day or more fell from 19.4% to 14.3%. The decline accelerated between 1979 and 1980 with daily use dropping by 4.1% (p. 36).

18. There was a steady decline in the perceived harmfulness of marijuana use among high school seniors from 1975 to 1979, but there was an increase in perceived harmfulness, particularly of regular use, in both 1979 and 1980, with the proportions of students feeling there is great risk in regular use increasing from 35% in 1978 to 50% in 1980 (p. 80).

19. There was a substantial and steady increase in the perceived harmfulness of cigarette smoking among high school seniors between 1975 and 1980, with the proportions who felt that pack-a-day smoking involved great risk increasing from 51% in 1975 to 64% in 1980 (p. 80).

20. The percentage of high school seniors who thought there was great risk in experimental use of cocaine dropped from 43% in 1975 to 31% in 1980, during a period of rapidly increasing use. Although the proportion seeing great risk in regular cocaine use dropped somewhat from 1975 to 1977, it remained fairly stable at around 69% from 1977 through 1980 (pp. 79-80).

21. In 1980 most high school seniors (71%) disapproved of smoking a pack (or more) of cigarettes per day; 69% disapproved of having one or two drinks daily, but only 56% disapproved of having five or more drinks once or twice a weekend, apparently because weekend binge drinking was more common among high school seniors than daily drinking (p. 81).

22. Between 1975 and 1977 there was a substantial decrease in disapproval of marijuana use at any level of frequency among high school seniors, but between 1977 and 1980 there was a reversal of that trend, with disapproval of experimental use rising by nearly 6% to 39% in 1980, disapproval of occasional use rising by over 5% to 50%, and disapproval of regular use rising by 9% to 75%, with the most rapid rise occurring between 1979 and 1980 (pp. 81-83).

23. Disapproval of the experimental use of barbiturates among high school seniors increased from 78% in 1975 to 84% in 1979 and 1980; disapproval of regular cigarette smoking also increased from 66% in 1976 to 71% in 1980. Both of these changes coincided with reductions in actual use (p. 83).

24. Between 1976 and 1979, the majority of American high school seniors believed that marijuana use should be legalized or decriminalized, but between 1979 and 1980 there was a sharp drop in the proportion favoring outright legalization (from 32% in 1979 to 26% in 1980), although the proportion favoring decriminalization remained stable at about 30% (pp. 86-87).

25. For each level of marijuana use (experimental, occasional, and regular), there was a drop in perceived disapproval by parents and friends of high school seniors from 1975 through 1977. However, this trend reversed between 1977 and 1980, especially for peer disapproval, and particularly in relation to regular marijuana use, with perceived peer disapproval of regular use rising from 64.5% in 1977 to 72.0% in 1980 (pp. 91, 93-97).

26. Except for marijuana use, there was little or no change between 1975 and 1980 in perceived parental disapproval of illicit drug use reported by high school seniors, with the great majority (91% to 99% depending upon the drug) believing that their parents would disapprove of even experimental use (pp. 90, 97).

27. The proportion of high school seniors saying that their friends would disapprove of them smoking a pack a day or more of cigarettes rose from 55% in 1975 to 74% in 1980, coinciding with an increase in expressed personal disapproval of regular smoking between 1977 and 1980, and a decline in cigarette smoking during the same period (p. 97).

28. There was a consistent discrepancy between the personal attitudes of high school seniors and perceived peer disapproval of alcohol use between 1975 and 1980, but the discrepancy narrowed substantially for the first time in 1980. The proportions of high school seniors reporting that their friends would disapprove of moderate (1 to 2 drinks) daily drinking rose from 63.2% in 1979 to 70.5% in 1980; for heavy (4-5 drinks) daily drinking, the proportions rose from 79.2% in 1979 to 87.9% in 1980. There was less perceived disapproval for weekend binge drinking, with only 46.6% of high school seniors feeling their friends would disapprove of such behavior in 1979, but this percentage also rose in 1980 to 50.6% (pp. 91, 97-98).

CONCLUSION

The 1980 survey of high school seniors revealed a number of significant changes in drug use patterns and attitudes. Regular cigarette smoking dropped sharply for both males and females, apparently because of a long-term increase in young people's health concerns about smoking as well as a sharp decrease in perceived peer acceptance of smoking. Daily marijuana use also dropped in 1980, following a period of dramatic increase; there were also decreases in annual marijuana use and monthly marijuana use, apparently for reasons similar to those for the decline in cigarette smoking. PCP use dropped markedly in 1980. Inhalant use also dropped slightly, in large part because of a decline in the use of amyl and butyl nitrite. Although cocaine use rose rapidly in the late 1970s, it remained stable between 1979 and 1980. Heroin use also remained constant in 1980, with only 1% of high school seniors reporting any use in their lifetimes. The overall proportion of students who used some illicit drug other than marijuana continued to rise in 1980, mostly due to an increase in stimulant use, which was the illicit drug most prevalent after marijuana. Methaqualone use also increased in 1980. Overall, drug use among high school students remained widespread, with nearly two-thirds of the high school seniors reporting use of an illicit drug, and nearly two out of every five reporting use of an illicit drug other than marijuana.

AN: 152
AU: Johnston, L.D.;   O'Malley, P.M.;   Bachman, J.G.
TI: Marijuana Decriminalization: The Impact on Youth, 1975-1980
SO: Final Report, NIDA Grant R01DA01769, May 1981. 85 pp.
IN: Institute for Social Research, University of Michigan, Ann Arbor, Michigan
RF: 20

SUMMARY TABLE

DRUG: marijuana
TYPE: high school seniors and follow-up panels
NUMBER: approximately 17,000 seniors per year
SEX: male and female
AGE: high school seniors; young adults
ETHNICITY: not specified
LOCATION: United States (cross-sectional)
METHODOLOGY: cohort sequential survey; follow-up panel survey
INSTRUMENT(S): questionnaire
CONDUCTED: 1975-1980

PURPOSE

This research project was undertaken primarily to determine if decriminalization
has had an effect on marijuana use by high school seniors and young adults and
secondarily to determine if certain variables such as attitudes and beliefs about
the drug, peer norms regarding use, and perceived availability were affected by
decriminalization. The Monitoring the Future study, a cohort-sequential study in
which questionnaires are administered to seniors each spring in representative
high schools across the United States, has been ongoing since 1975. In addition,
subsamples of participants from each year's senior class were mailed follow-up
surveys every year; two such panels were chosen each year to provide longitudinal
data about continuing use of drugs for seniors who reported heavy use of marijuana
or use of another illicit drug, and for all others. Four states (California,
Minnesota, Maine, and Ohio), which were labeled "early change states,"
decriminalized marijuana possession in late 1975 and early 1976, between the first
and second nationwide data collections, providing information about the effects of
decriminalization for a four-to-five year post-change period. In July of 1977,
three states (New York, North Carolina, and Mississippi), designated "late change
states," also decriminalized marijuana possession, providing an opportunity to
determine if there were any anticipatory effects since data were available both
before and after decriminalization. Comparisons were made between the early
change states, the late change states, and control states (all others) on lifetime
prevalence of marijuana use and frequency and recency of use from 1975 through
1980. Changes in use patterns were also analyzed for panels of seniors from the
classes graduating in 1975 and 1976. Finally, the impact of decriminalization on
intervening variables such as perceived availability of marijuana, attitudes and
beliefs about marijuana, and peer norms regarding use was analyzed using data from
the national samples for 1975-1980. Beginning in 1976, the high school seniors
were also asked what they thought was the prevailing law in their state regarding
marijuana possession and these findings were reported.

OPERATIONAL DEFINITIONS

Early change states: the four states--Ohio, California, Maine, and Minnesota--in which marijuana possession was decriminalized between November 1975 and April 1976.

Late change states: the three states--Mississippi, North Carolina, and New York--in which marijuana possession was decriminalized in July 1977.

Control states: all other states.

FINDINGS

1. When the data from the early change states were compared with the control states, there was no evidence of any positive effect of decriminalization on either lifetime prevalence rates, or frequency or recency of marijuana use. If anything, there was a small net loss in lifetime prevalence, and an even smaller net loss in frequency, relative to the control states, from 1976 to 1980 (p. 12).

2. There was no evidence of an anticipated increase in marijuana use in 1975 or 1976 prior to the passage of decriminalization laws in the late change states; rather, three of five observed changes were in the direction of a net loss relative to the control states (p. 13).

3. During the period from 1977 to 1980, after the passage of decriminalization laws in the late change states, levels of marijuana use remained comparable to those in the control states, with a slight net drop in the three prevalence measures (lifetime, annual, monthly use) and a very slight net increase in the overall frequency of use index (p. 14).

4. There was no increase in the proportions of the 1975 or 1976 panels of high school seniors who tried marijuana in the four to five years following decriminalization in the early change states. The rates of annual, monthly, and daily use were very similar to those for seniors from the control states for the first two to three years following decriminalization and, though the patterns were less clear for longer time intervals, there was very little or no systematic change on these measures (p. 19).

5. There was no anticipated increase in marijuana use among the panels of high school seniors graduating in 1975 and 1976 in the one-to-two years following graduation and before passage of decriminalization laws in 1977 in the late change states (p. 20).

6. When the proportion of total change in marijuana use occurring for the 1975 and 1976 panels of high school seniors during the period after graduation was compared for the early change, late change, and control states, the overall impression was one of random variation; in other words, there was no evidence of any positive or negative effect of decriminalization (p. 21).

7. Since the nationwide study of high school seniors began in 1975, nearly all seniors said marijuana was "fairly easy" or "very easy" to obtain, and decriminalization of marijuana possession in certain states had no discernible impact on perceived availability of marijuana (p. 22).

8. There was no evidence that decriminalization of marijuana in certain states
led high school seniors in those states to think marijuana was safer than high
school seniors in control states; in fact, there was a nationwide drop in
perception of marijuana as harmful between 1975 and 1977 and a rise between 1978
and 1980, and this pattern was consistent for seniors from both decriminalized and
nondecriminalized states (p. 24).

9. Individual levels of disapproval towards marijuana use as reported by high
school seniors nationwide dropped somewhat between 1975 and 1980 for the control
states; the early change states showed a comparable drop. For the late change
states, there was actually a cumulative increase in disapproval (p. 24).

10. Sizable numbers of high school seniors nationwide did not know the law
regarding marijuana possession in their state or had an incorrect perception of
the law for the years 1975-1980. In the states which decriminalized marijuana,
10-20% of the seniors still believed that possession could be penalized with a
jail sentence, while in control states, 30-40% incorrectly believed that a jail
sentence was not an option (p. 25).

CONCLUSION

There was little or no difference in marijuana use in terms of lifetime prevalence
and frequency and recency of use between states which decriminalized marijuana
possession between 1975 and 1980 and those that did not. There was no evidence
that marijuana use increased or that previous nonusers initiated use in the four
to five years following decriminalization in California, Minnesota, Ohio, and
Maine. Also, there was no evidence that young people began to use marijuana or
used it more frequently prior to decriminalization in Mississippi, New York, and
North Carolina; nor was there evidence of subsequent greater use in these states.
In fact, patterns of marijuana use remained fairly consistent nationwide. No
evidence was found that three variables which might have been affected by
decriminalization--perceived availability of marijuana, beliefs about the
harmfulness of marijuana, and attitudes of disapproval towards marijuana use--were
so affected between 1975 and 1980. Overall, the preponderance of the evidence
examined points to the conclusion that decriminaliztion has had virtually no
effect either on marijuana use or on related attitudes and beliefs about marijuana
use among American high school students and young adults.

AN: 153
AU: Johnston, L.D.; O'Malley, P.M.; Eveland, L.K.
TI: Drugs and delinquency: A search for causal connections
SO: In: Kandel, D.B., ed. Longitudinal Research on Drug Use: Empirical
     Findings and Methodological Issues. Washington, D.C.: Hemisphere Publishing
     Corp., 1978. pp. 137-156.
IN: Institute for Social Research, University of Michigan, Ann Arbor, Michigan
RF: 16

SUMMARY TABLE

DRUG: multidrug
TYPE: high school sophomores (initially)
NUMBER: 1,260
SEX: male
AGE: 15-23 years
ETHNICITY: white (93%)
LOCATION: United States
METHODOLOGY: longitudinal, correlational survey
INSTRUMENT(S):   interview; questionnaire
CONDUCTED: 1966-1974

PURPOSE

Data collected from a longitudinal study of a national sample of young men were
analyzed in an attempt to address the following questions: How strong is the
relationship between illicit drug use and other illegal activities? Is illicit
drug use associated with specific kinds of crime? Does illicit drug use lead to
an increase or decrease in subsequent delinquency? Does delinquency predict later
drug use? Information gathered from an initial personal interview and
questionnaire, plus four follow-up questionnaires, was examined for correlations
and changes over time in terms of drug use and delinquency measures (a theft and
vandalism index and an interpersonal aggression index). The drug users in this
sample were nonaddicted users of illicit drugs in high school.

FINDINGS

1. Illicit drug use was related positively and strongly to other types of illegal
behavior (p. 154).

2. The greater the degree of an individual's involvement with drugs, the higher
was his expected level of delinquency (p. 154).

3. Crimes against property had a higher correlation with illicit drug use than
did crimes against people (p. 154).

4. Of the specific property crimes investigated, those that were most strongly
related to illicit drug use were minor theft (under $50), shoplifting, and
trespassing (p. 154).

5. Heroin use was less related to minor theft (under $50) than was the use of
other illicit drugs, but it was more related to major theft (over $50) and to the
theft of car parts (p. 154).

6. Young men who used only marijuana scored lower than the other drug-using groups on two indexes of delinquency: theft and vandalism, and interpersonal aggression. Their level of interpersonal aggression was similar to that observed for abstainers (p. 155).

7. Most of the delinquency differences between the nondrug user and eventual drug-user groups existed before drug use ever began (p. 155).

CONCLUSION

Although illicit drug use is related positively to other forms of delinquent behavior, there is no evidence that the nonaddictive use of illicit drugs causes users to become more delinquent. Rather, the reverse causation seems more likely, that is, delinquency leads to drug use. Since both delinquency and drug use are deviant behaviors, they are likely to be adopted by individuals who are deviance prone.

AN: 154
AU: Kandel, D.B.
TI: Inter- and intragenerational influences on adolescent marijuana use
SO: Journal of Social Issues, 30:107-135, 1974
IN: New York State Department of Mental Hygiene, and School of Public Health,
     Columbia University, New York, New York
RF: 45

SUMMARY TABLE

DRUG: marijuana
TYPE: high school students and their parents
NUMBER: 8,206
SEX: male and female
AGE: high school
ETHNICITY: [black; white]
LOCATION: New York State
METHODOLOGY: cross-sectional, correlational survey
INSTRUMENT(S): questionnaire
CONDUCTED: 1971

PURPOSE

Answers to the following questions were sought: To what extent are youth
influenced in their drug use by their parents? To what extent are they influenced
by their peers? What is the concomitant and relative influence of parents and
peers? Under what patterns of generational relationships do these interpersonal
influences vary in importance? Analysis was based on data obtained from
adolescents, their parents, and their best school friends. The adolescent sample
of 8,206 was a multiphasic random sample representative of public secondary school
students in New York State, drawn from 18 schools within the state. Best school
friends were obtained from a subsample of five schools. In these five schools,
the entire student body completed questionnaires, and it was possible to obtain a
relational sample of matched student-friend dyads. Shortly after the school
survey, questionnaires were mailed to one parent of each student; 61% of the
parents contacted returned the questionnaires, and it was possible to match 49% of
all students with their parents through the use of self-generated identification
numbers.

OPERATIONAL DEFINITIONS

Psychoactive drugs: tranquilizers, barbiturates, stimulants, diet pills.

FINDINGS

1. Adolescent marijuana use was more strongly correlated with perceived maternal
than paternal use of psychoactive drugs (p. 116).

2. Adolescent marijuana use was directly related to the perceived degree of
parental drug involvement, but the association between adolescent marijuana use
and self-reported parental use of psychoactive drugs was much lower (pp. 116-118).

3. In matched parent-adolescent dyads, the relationship between adolescent marijuana use and parental self-reported drug use was small and appeared only in relation to mothers. Such relationships were stronger between girls and their mothers than between sons and their mothers (p. 117).

4. Self-reported parental alcohol use was correlated with adolescent marijuana use and was more important than self-reported parental use of tobacco or psychotherapeutic drugs (p. 119).

5. The lowest rates of adolescent marijuana use were observed in families in which parents neither smoked nor drank (p. 120).

6. Involvement in the adolescent subculture and involvement with other drug-using adolescents were the most important correlates of adolescent marijuana use (p. 120).

7. A strong relation existed between the adolescents' own marijuana use and their perception of their friends' use of marijuana (p. 120).

8. Adolescents' marijuana use was directly related to their best friend's self-reported use of marijuana (p. 120).

9. While both parents and best friends had an independent effect on adolescent marijuana use, the effect of peers was larger by far than the effect of parents (p. 122).

10. Drug use was directly related to the frequency of contacts with peers and to an orientation to peers away from parents (p. 123).

CONCLUSION

Estimates of parental influence on adolescent use of illegal drugs based on the child's perception of parental behavior exaggerated the importance of parents. Parental self-reports of certain types of drug behaviors, such as use of psychoactive drugs by mothers and use of alcohol by mothers or fathers, had some relationship to adolescent marijuana use; however, this effect was small. The influence of peers on adolescent drug use was greater by far. Certain parental drug-use patterns weakened, while others strengthened, peer influence. These findings validate a "cultural deviance" model of behavior and in particular the theory of differential association developed by Sutherland, which holds that although family conditions may set the stage for delinquent behavior, the child will not engage in such behavior unless models for delinquency are present in the peer culture around him.

AN: 155
AU: Kandel, D.B.
TI: Interpersonal influences on adolescent illegal drug use
SO: In: Josephson, E., and Carroll, E., eds. Drug Use: Epidemiological and
     Sociological Approaches. Washington, D.C.: Hemisphere Publishing
     Corporation, 1974. pp. 207-240.
IN: New York State Department of Mental Hygiene, and School of Public Health,
     Columbia University, New York, New York
RF: 55

SUMMARY TABLE

DRUG: multidrug
TYPE: high school students and their parents
NUMBER: 8,206
SEX: male and female
AGE: high school
ETHNICITY: [black; white]
LOCATION: New York State
METHODOLOGY: cross-sectional, correlational survey
INSTRUMENT(S): questionnaire
CONDUCTED: 1971

PURPOSE

To understand the role of intergenerational and intragenerational interpersonal
factors in the use of drugs, the following questions were explored: (1) To what
extent are youth influenced in their drug use by their parents? (2) To what
extent are they influenced by their peers? (3) What is the concomitant and
relative influence of parents and peers? (4) Under what patterns of generational
relationships do these interpersonal influences vary in importance? A two-wave
panel survey was carried out in 1971-1972 on a multiphasic representative random
sample of adolescents in high schools of New York State. Structured
self-administered questionnaires were given in a classroom situation to a random
sample of homerooms in 13 schools and to the entire student body in 5 schools.
The findings reported were based on the first wave of data collection.

FINDINGS

1. Adolescents who reported that their parents used tranquilizers, barbiturates,
or diet pills were more likely to be marijuana users than adolescents who did not
report such parental use. The association was stronger with perceived maternal
than paternal use (p. 217).

2. Adolescents' use of LSD, other psychedelics, methedrine, ups, downs, and
tranquilizers, opiates other than heroin, and inhalants increased in direct
proportion to the number of psychoactive drugs used by mothers but not by fathers
(p. 220).

3. Adolescent children of mothers who reported using all three types of
psychoactive drugs--tranquilizers, barbiturates, and stimulants--were at least
twice as likely to be users of an illegal drug other than marijuana than children
of mothers who used no psychoactive drugs (p. 220).

4. Parental influence on the child's drug use behavior exerted itself both through the use of psychotherapeutic drugs and through the use of alcohol and tobacco (p. 222).

5. Self-reported parental marijuana use and alcohol use was related to the use by their children of all illegal drugs, the strongest association being with marijuana (pp. 222-223).

6. Involvement with other drug-using adolescents was the most important correlate of adolescent drug use; it had a strong influence even without psychotropic drug or alcohol use by parents (pp. 225, 227).

7. Adolescents were more likely to be drug users if their brothers and sisters used marijuana than if their siblings did not use marijuana (p. 225).

8. Adolescent illegal drug use was highly correlated with both the perceived use of drugs by friends and the actual self-reported drug use patterns of best school friends, with self-reports of friend's use being the strongest association (pp. 225-227).

9. The overall association between marijuana use in friendship pairs was higher for girls than for boys (p. 226).

10. The effect of peers on adolescent drug use was larger by far than the effect of parents (p. 227).

11. Parental drug use behavior had an especially strong impact on adolescent drug use when illegal drug use was present in the child's peer group (p. 227).

12. Except for demographic characteristics (sex, age, etc.), the association between two friends' use of marijuana was stronger than for other attributes (school activities, peer activities, use of other drugs, political attitudes) (p. 230).

13. For adolescents who used drugs, their source of information about drugs was more likely to be friends or siblings, whereas nonusers more often got their information from school, television, or parents (pp. 231-232).

CONCLUSION

Parental influence on adolescent use of illegal drugs, based on the child's perception of parental use of psychoactive drugs, was greatly exaggerated. This influence appeared much smaller when based on the parents' self-reports than on the adolescents' perceptions. The effect of peers on the adolescents' drug use was much higher than the effect of parents. Given a situation in which peers used drugs, parental behavior modulated peer influence. Certain parental drug-use patterns weakened, others strengthened peer influence. These findings validate a "cultural deviance" model of behavior.

AN: 156
AU: Kandel, D.B.
TI: Reaching the hard-to-reach: Illicit drug use among high school absentees
SO: Addictive Diseases: An International Journal, 1:465-480, 1975
IN: New York State Department of Mental Hygiene, and School of Public Health,
      Columbia University, New York, New York
RF: 16

SUMMARY TABLE

DRUG: multidrug
TYPE: high school students
NUMBER: 105
SEX: male and female
AGE: high school
ETHNICITY: black; white
LOCATION: New York City
METHODOLOGY: comparative survey
INSTRUMENT(S):   interview; questionnaire
CONDUCTED: 1971; 1972

PURPOSE

The study was carried out to seek answers to the following questions: (1) Were
there differences in patterns of drug use between students present on the day of a
drug-use survey and those absent? (2) How representative were the sampled
absentees of the total absentee population? (3) What factors accounted for any
differences in the drug-use patterns of the absentees and the students present on
the day of the survey? Data were gathered through household interviews with
absentees and group administration of questionnaires to a self-selected sample of
absentees. Since it became apparent that those absentees interviewed in their
homes underreported drug use, the results in the report were based on the 44
absentees given the questionnaire as a group.

FINDINGS

1. The rates of drug use, particularly of illicit drugs, among absentees were
considerably higher than the rates of use among the regular students from the same
schools (p. 469).

2. Absentees more frequently than regular students shared the indicators of poor
school performance (frequent absence, low grades, and less time spent on homework)
that are usually associated with high rates of drug use (p. 470).

3. Considering the use of all illegal drugs, 58% of the absentees were drug
users, compared with 42% of the regular students; furthermore, absentees were
more likely to be multiple drug users (p. 471).

4. School surveys that ignore absentee students have underestimated the true
extent of drug use among the students enrolled in the school (p. 471).

5. Differences in drug use between absentees and regular students were strongest for girls and white adolescents, while the differences for boys and especially for blacks were much less marked. Absentee boys differed from regular students only in greater use of marijuana, while there was no difference between absentee blacks and regular students except for the use of marijuana and opiates other than cocaine, heroin, and methadone (p. 475).

6. Among whites, the rates of drug use for absentees were consistently much higher than for regular students (p. 475).

CONCLUSION

Absentees had higher rates of illegal drug use than their classmates who attended school more regularly. The same factors which were related to school absenteeism, such as poor performance and cutting of classes, were also related to higher rates of drug use among regular students and thus may partly explain the higher rates of use among the absentees. Absentees differed from regularly attending students in their greater involvement in deviant activities, including drug use. Thus, surveys based on responses from students in regular attendance will underestimate rates of drug use in direct proportion to the extent of absenteeism in the school.

AN: 157
AU: Kandel, D.B.
TI: On variations in adolescent subcultures
SO: Youth and Society, 9:373-384, 1978
IN: New York State Psychiatric Institute, and School of Public Health, Columbia
     University, New York, New York
RF: 17

SUMMARY TABLE

DRUG: multidrug
TYPE: high school students
NUMBER: 8,206
SEX: male and female
AGE: high school
ETHNICITY: [black; white]
LOCATION: New York State
METHODOLOGY: cross-sectional, correlational survey
INSTRUMENT(S): questionnaire
CONDUCTED: 1971-1972

PURPOSE

The position of youth in contemporary society is determined by adolescent
subcultures on the one hand, and by increased separation between parents and their
children on the other. In certain areas of their life, especially those relevant
to future life goals, adolescents turn to their parents, while in other areas they
prefer their peers. This paper elaborates the two propositions further. The
analysis was based on information gathered from a random sample of adolescents
(N=8,206) drawn from 18 public secondary schools in New York State during a
longitudinal study. The self-administered questionnaire completed by the students
included questions about drug use and about socio-demographic variables, quality
of family relationships, friends' drug use, and various aspects of lifestyles.

FINDINGS

1. Adolescents in marijuana-using groups were extensive users of other illicit
drugs (p. 378).

2. The lowest levels of drug use occurred among adolescents who had low peer
involvement and whose friends did not use drugs (p. 379).

3. The reported level of drug use in the peer group was a much more important
correlate of an adolescent's own use than was the degree of involvement with peers
(p. 379).

4. Adolescents who had marijuana-using friends and, in most cases, who used
marijuana themselves were alienated from their parents, whether or not they were
intensely involved with peers (p. 380).

5. Adolescents who were highly involved with friends who did not use marijuana
were much closer to their parents than those who were highly involved in
marijuana-using groups (p. 380).

6. Adolescents who were highly involved in marijuana-using groups spent less time on homework, were more likely to be absent from school, and were less likely to get good grades than adolescents in groups not using marijuana (p. 380).

7. Students in marijuana-using groups were much more likely to be involved in nonconforming activities than students in non-drug-using groups (p. 381).

CONCLUSION

Adolescents with non-marijuana-using friends expressed attitudes and behaviors revealing close relationships to parents and conformity to adult expectations. By contrast, adolescents with drug-using friends were estranged from their parents regardless of their degree of involvement with peers. The decisive factor shaping adolescents' feelings toward adults was not peer involvement as such, but involvement in a marijuana-using peer group. The findings are consistent with the seemingly contrary interpretations that drug use causes estrangement from parents, and that estrangement from parents facilitates involvement in drug use. Probably both mechanisms are involved in mutually reinforcing processes of influence.

AN: 158
AU: Kandel, D.B.; Adler, I.; Sudit, M.
TI: The epidemiology of adolescent drug use in France and Israel
SO: American Journal of Public Health, 17:256-264, 1981
IN: Department of Psychiatry and School of Public Health, Columbia University,
     New York, New York
RF: 43

SUMMARY TABLE

DRUG: multidrug
TYPE: French and Israeli adolescents
NUMBER: French sample: 499; Israeli sample: 609
SEX: French: male (53%), female (47%); Israeli: male (49%), female
                 (51%)
AGE: 14-18 years old
ETHNICITY: French; Israeli
LOCATION: Parisian metropolitan area; four major urban centers in Israel
METHODOLOGY: comparative, correlational survey
INSTRUMENT(S):   interview
CONDUCTED: 1977; 1979

PURPOSE

In order to obtain epidemiological data on substance use by adolescents in France
and Israel, two household surveys of urban youths 14-18 years of age were carried
out. The French sample included 499 French adolescents representative of youths
in the Parisian metropolitan area who were interviewed in spring 1977. The
Israeli sample included 609 Israeli adolescents residing in four major urban
centers in Israel (Jerusalem, Tel Aviv, Haifa, and Beer Sheba) who were
interviewed in spring 1979. Since both samples were urban, they were not selected
to be representative of the countries as a whole. Three dimensions of drug use
were examined: (1) ever use, (2) current use (in the month prior to the
interview), and (3) lifetime frequency of use. The data on use were then
correlated with demographic variables such as age, sex, father's education, and
religiosity (as determined by attending a religious school in Israel and frequency
of attendance at religious services in France). The patterns discovered were then
compared for both samples as well as for a sample of American adoelscents surveyed
in 1978 in New York State.

FINDINGS

1. For all drugs, the rates of ever use reported by adolescents in France
exceeded those reported by Israeli adolescents; these differences were relatively
small in the use of beer and wine, larger with respect to hard liquor and
cigarettes, and highest in the use of illicit drugs except tranquilizers. With
one exception (cigarettes), the higher the reported rate of use, the smaller the
difference between the rates reported in each country (p. 258).

2. The relative prevalence of current use (last 30 days) of various substances by
adolescents was very similar in both France and Israel; beer and wine were
reported to have been used by more adolescents than hard liquor, and the reported
rate of use of all legal drugs exceeded that of all illegal drugs. The only

difference pertained to cigarettes, which in France were used more frequently than all alcoholic beverages except cider, while in Israel the rate of cigarette use was lower than that of all alcoholic beverages (p. 258).

3. The lifetime prevalence of the use of illegal drugs by Israeli adolescents was very small, and it was nil for three drugs: psychedelics, amphetamines, and heroin (p. 258).

4. In France, the use of marijuana by adolescents was almost four times as great as the use of the next illicit drug (barbiturates and tranquilizers) (p. 258).

5. In both France and Israel, the use of any illicit drug was less prevalent among adolescents than the use of any licit substance, with the differences being greater in Israel than in France (p. 258).

6. For all drugs, in both France and Israel, the proportion of adolescents reporting current use (last 30 days) was much smaller than the proportion reporting ever use, but for all drugs on which comparisons were possible, the reported rates of current use were at least twice as high in France as in Israel (p. 258).

7. In France, about one-fourth of the adolescents who had ever used alcoholic beverages used them only once or twice, while between one-sixth and one-fourth used them 60 times or more. By contrast, in Israel there was a much lower percentage of heavy involvement with alcoholic substances (p. 259).

8. In Israel, 63% of the adolescents who had ever smoked cigarettes were no longer smoking, compared to 24% in France; 3% vs 12% were currently smoking a pack or more daily, and 12% vs 35% were currently smoking less than a pack a day (p. 259).

9. French adolescents used marijuana more experimentally than they used legal drugs, with less than 1% reporting use of marijuana 40 times or more; the use of other illicit drugs was even more rare. Among Israeli adolescents, the use of marijuana and/or hashish was less experimental than the use of wine and hard liquor (p. 259).

10. For various alcoholic beverages, cigarettes, and marijuana, French adolescents experimented with these drugs more extensively than Israeli adolescents and were more likely to remain users (pp. 259-260).

11. In both France and Israel, single drug rates of use increased monotonically with age, but the rate by which the use of any illicit drug increased with age was much larger in France than in Israel (p. 260).

12. In both Israel and France, males were more likely than females to report higher rates of lifetime experience with all drugs except barbiturates and tranquilizers. For tranquilizer use in France and barbiturate use in Israel, no differences in use by sex were apparent, and more Israeli females than males reported use of tranquilizers. Sex differences in drug use were greater in Israel than in France and were inversely related to the overall prevalence of use of each drug (pp. 260-261).

13. No consistent relationship was found between drug use and father's education (an index for socio-economic status) among adolescents in France and Israel (p. 261).

14. French adolescents who were religious reported lower percentages of the use of all drugs than nonreligious adolescents. In Israel, religiosity decreased the use of cigarettes, hashish/marijuana, and other illicit drugs, but there was little difference between religious and nonreligious adolescents in the use of wine, and more religious adolescents reported use of hard liquor than nonreligious youths. However, religious Israeli adolescents consumed fewer alcoholic beverages on any one occasion than nonreligious youths (pp. 261-262).

15. When data on drug use by French and Israeli adolescents were compared to data from an American sample of New York State high school students, it was found that French youths had rates of licit drug use at least equal to those of American youth. Illicit drug use was much higher among American adolescents than any French or Israeli; for example, 64% of American youths had tried marijuana in 1978 as compared to 23% of the French in 1977 and 3% of the Israeli in 1979 (p. 262).

CONCLUSION

The patterns of drug use among adolescents in France and Israel display differences as well as similarities. The overall order in lifetime and current prevalences of the use of legal and illegal drugs is identical for both countries, with legal drugs used by more youth than illegal drugs, and with marijuana used more frequently than any other illicit drug. However, while all four legal drugs have been tried in similar proportions in France, Israeli adolescents are less likely to have smoked cigarettes or drunk hard liquor than to have drunk beer or wine. French youths uniformly report higher lifetime and current use of all drugs, as well as more extensive drug involvement than Israeli youths. When compared with information on drug use by American adolescents in 1978, French adolescents report as high (or higher) rates of licit drug use, but much lower rates of the use of illicit substances. In each culture, the uses of legal and illegal drugs are highly correlated, with marijuana users more likely than nonusers to use legal drugs, with the correlation increasing with greater extent of marijuana use. Certain uniformities across countries appear in the relationship of drug use to socio-demographic variables: drug use increases through adolescent years, there are more male than female adolescents using each drug (except tranquilizers and sedatives), and there are no consistent associations between drug use and socio-economic status--all of which indicate that drug use shares certain features not affected by cultural specifics. The overall prevalence of drug use in a culture appears to be associated with two social processes: 1) a greater and more persistent involvement with drugs, as reflected in the proportion of adolescents who remain current users among those who have ever experimented with a drug and in the frequency of lifetime users of each drug, and 2) increased overall prevalence appears to be associated with a spread of the phenomena throughout all groups in society. These findings indicate that both for legal and illegal drugs persistence and degrees of involvement may be directly related to the overall prevalence of consumption levels in the society.

AN: 159
AU: Kandel, D.B.; Faust, R.
TI: Sequences and stages in patterns of adolescent drug use
SO: Archives of General Psychiatry, 32:923-932, 1975
IN: New York State Psychiatric Institute, and School of Public Health, Columbia
     University, New York, New York
RF: 30

SUMMARY TABLE

DRUG: multidrug
TYPE: high school students
NUMBER: Time 1: 8,206; Time 2: 7,250; Time 3: 1,635
SEX: male and female
AGE: high school
ETHNICITY: [black; white]
LOCATION: New York State
METHODOLOGY: longitudinal panel survey
INSTRUMENT(S): questionnaire
CONDUCTED: 1971-1972

PURPOSE

A major dispute revolves around the notion that use of certain substances leads to
the use of more serious drugs: for instance, use of marijuana is said to lead to
the use of heroin. Although supported by evidence, such associations do not
establish causal connections; most inferences about sequences of use of various
drugs have been based on cross-sectional data or on retrospective reports.
Nothing has been published on sequences of drug use based on prospective
longitudinal studies of respondents matched to themselves. This study attempted
to fill the gap. The findings on sequences of drug use over a period of several
months were described and analyzed. The study was based on a representative
random sample of high school students from 18 schools in New York State.

OPERATIONAL DEFINITIONS

Ranked drugs: drugs used by subjects were ranked on a Guttman scale as follows:
0, used none; 1, any legal drug (beer or wine, cigarettes, hard liquor); 2,
cannabis (marijuana or hashish); 3, pills (methamphetamine, other amphetamines,
barbiturates, tranquilizers); 4, psychedelics (LSD or other psychedelics); 5,
cocaine; and 6, heroin.

Time 1: fall 1971.

Time 2: spring 1972.

Time 3: winter 1972-1973 (data were collected at this timepoint only for a
subsample of seniors who graduated in 1972).

FINDINGS

1. Between the fall and spring of the academic year, most high school students (64%) retained exactly the same pattern of drug use (p. 925).

2. The higher the level of initial drug use, the smaller was the proportion of adolescents who maintained the same pattern of use during the subsequent period, with the exception of legal drug users who were more stable in their drug-use patterns than any other group, including nonusers (p. 925).

3. The majority of cannabis only users (55%) maintained the same cumulative pattern of drug use between fall of 1971 and spring of 1972, but only one third of users of pills, psychedelics, and cocaine and only 19% of heroin users used the same combination of drugs in spring of 1972 (p. 925).

4. Progression to higher-ranked drugs became less common and regression more common for high school students who reported high initial levels of use at Time 1. The use of a lower-ranked drug after the fall increased from 10% among Time 1 legal drug users to 58% among Time 1 heroin users, while the use of a higher-ranked drug ranged from 37% among Time 1 nonusers to 6% among cocaine users (p. 925).

5. Twenty-three percent of students continuing to use heroin discontinued the use of one or more lower-ranking drugs (p. 925).

6. For students who used drugs, the progression of use followed the sequence from nonuse to legal drugs to cannabis to pills to psychedelics to cocaine to heroin. For those who stopped using drugs, the same sequence occurred but in reverse (p. 927).

7. Legal drug use was a necessary step between nonuse and illegal drug use among high school students. Direct progression from nonuse to illicit use was virtually nonexistent (p. 927).

8. For those adolescents who were already using legal drugs, marijuana was a crucial introductory step towards illicit drugs (p. 927).

9. In the first stage of progression from nonuse of drugs to use, most nonusers who began using a drug started with beer or wine. In the second stage, most adolescents moved to using hard liquor and tobacco; smaller proportions of adolescents began using marijuana. In the final stage, adolescents used other illicit drugs (pp. 928-929).

10. For each type of drug, progression to a higher-ranked drug was positively related, and regression was negatively related, to the frequency of initial use (p. 930).

11. The number of legal drugs used and the frequency of use were associated with more progression to illegal drugs and with progression further along the scale. For adolescents who were heavy users of both hard liquor and cigarettes in the fall of 1971, 40% began using illegal drugs by spring 1972 and half progressed to the use of illicit drugs other than marijuana (p. 930).

12. The recency and frequency of drug use were associated with lower regression and stability of drug use and with higher progression. Among current cannabis users in fall 1971, 55% of those using marijuana several times a week or more

progressed to the use of other illicit drugs compared to 27% of those using
marijuana only once a month (p. 930).

CONCLUSION

Four major stages of involvement in drug use were identified: (1) beer or wine;
(2) hard liquor or tobacco; (3) cannabis; (4) other illicit drugs. These
findings increase our understanding of the process of involvement in drugs.
Although the results show a clear-cut sequence in the use of various drugs, they
do not prove that the use of a particular drug invariably leads to the use of
other drugs. Many adolescents stop at a certain stage of drug use without
progressing any further.

AN: 160
AU: Kandel, D.B.; Kessler, R.C.; Margulies, R.Z.
TI: Antecedents of adolescent initiation to stages of drug use: A development
     analysis
SO: In: Kandel, D.B., ed. Longitudinal Research on Drug Use: Empirical
     Findings and Methodological Issues. Washington, D.C.: Hemisphere Publishing
     Corporation, 1978. pp. 73-99.
IN: New York State Psychiatric Institute, and School of Public Health, Columbia
     University, New York, New York
RF: 70

SUMMARY TABLE

DRUG: multidrug
TYPE: high school students and parents
NUMBER: 8,206
SEX: male and female
AGE: high school
ETHNICITY: [black; white]
LOCATION: New York State
METHODOLOGY: longitudinal panel survey
INSTRUMENT(S): questionnaire
CONDUCTED: 1971-1972

PURPOSE

The onset of drug use by adolescents provides a unique opportunity to study the
processes of socialization, a study which requires both longitudinal analysis as
well as information about the various sources of influence upon an individual. In
order to study the impact of interpersonal relations between parents and
adolescents and between adolescents and their friends on initiation of drug use,
data were collected from a two-wave panel sample of 8,206 adolescents,
representative of public secondary students in New York State, who completed
questionnaires in fall 1971 (Time 1) and spring 1972 (Time 2). The use of
self-generated identification numbers permitted the matching of adolescents with
their parents and best school friends at Time 1 and with themselves at Time 2. It
must be noted that students who could not be measured at any point in time were
consistently different from those who matched, especially in drug usage, resulting
in an underrepresentation of drug users in the matched samples. For purposes of
analysis, cohorts of adolescents who had ever used the same drug or combination of
drugs at Time 1 were created, and subsequent initiation or continued abstention
within each cohort was correlated with variables relating to parental influences,
peer influences, and adolescent interpersonal interactions.

FINDINGS

1. Parents influenced adolescent initiation to hard liquor by providing role
models (p. 86).

2. Best friends' attitudes about the harmfulness of using hard liquor restrained
adolescents from starting to drink hard liquor (p. 86).

3. The degree of adolescent involvement in peer activities, such as frequency of getting together with friends, dating, attending parties, hanging around with a group of friends, or driving around, was an important factor in initiation to the use of hard liquor (p. 86).

4. The influence of the behaviors of parents and of peers on adolescent use of hard liquor was approximately equal in importance (p. 86).

5. Prior behaviors, including the extent of use of other drugs such as beer, wine, and tobacco and participation in forms of minor delinquent activity, were more important in predicting hard liquor use than either parental or peer influences (p. 86).

6. Parental attitudes and the closeness of their relationship with their children had some influence on initiation of marijuana use by adolescents. Adolescents who reported that their parents positively discouraged use of marijuana were less likely to begin using it than those who reported permissive parental attitudes (p. 87).

7. Perception by the adolescent and his/her best friend of marijuana use in their peer group was a relatively strong predictor of initiation of marijuana use, as was perception of peer approval of drug use. Perception of friends' behavior was more important than friends' self-reported use, suggesting that the overall extent of use in the peer group is a more important influence than use by a single friend. The general extent of exposure to peer influences and the availability of marijuana within the peer group were also important predictors of initiation of marijuana use. Each of these types of peer influence was more highly correlated with the initation of marijuana use than any parental influence (p. 87).

8. Certain adolescent behaviors (such as minor delinquent activities, cutting classes, low grades in school, political behavior, and liberal political orientation) and favorable attitudes toward the use of marijuana were the most important predictors of the initiation of marijuana use (p. 88).

9. Parental influences (especially the quality of the adolescent-parent relationship) on the initiation of illicit drug use other than marijuana were strong; lack of closeness was a particularly strong predictor, followed by the extent of control exercised by the parent, with greater control being associated with a tendency to start using other illicit drugs (pp. 88-89).

10. Parents who used hard liquor and psychoactive drugs (tranquilizers, stimulants, or barbiturates) were more likely to have children who began the use of illicit drugs other than marijuana. The father's impact was important insofar as he used hard liquor, the mother's impact insofar as she used psychoactive drugs (p. 89).

11. Best friend's use of all types of drugs was an important predictor of an adolescent's initiation into the use of illicit drugs other than marijuana (p. 89).

12. The more frequently an adolescent used marijuana, the greater was the probability that he or she used other illicit drugs (p. 89).

13. The most important predictors of adolescent initiation to the use of drugs other than marijuana were poor relations with parents, lack of intimacy with best school friend, extensive use of marijuana, use of other drugs by best school

friend, and feelings of depression (p. 90).

CONCLUSION

Drug use appears to proceed through specific stages, each one influenced by different predictors. For hard liquor, the most important predictor is involvement in minor types of deviant behavior. For marijuana, the most important predictors are peer influences and the adolescent's beliefs and values. For other illicit drugs, parental influence, particularly the quality of the parent-child relationship, is most significant. The finding that parental and peer influences on initiation into marijuana use were completely independent of each other throws doubt on the view expressed by previous researchers that the stronger the rejection of adult standards, the stronger the acceptance of peer standards, and vice versa. Both sources of influence can exert themselves independently of one another, for different kinds of behaviors.

AN: 161
AU: Kandel, D.B.; Single, E.W.; Kessler, R.C.
TI: The epidemiology of drug use among New York State high school students:
      Distribution, trends, and change in rates of use
SO: American Journal of Public Health, 66:43-53, 1976
IN: New York State Psychiatric Institute, and School of Public Health, Columbia
      University, New York, New York
RF: 42

SUMMARY TABLE

DRUG: multidrug
TYPE: high school students
NUMBER: 8,206
SEX: male and female
AGE: high school
ETHNICITY: black; white; American Indian; Oriental
LOCATION: New York State
METHODOLOGY: longitudinal panel survey
INSTRUMENT(S):   questionnaire
CONDUCTED: 1971-1972

PURPOSE

This longitudinal study of drug use among public high school students attempted to
link the responses and behaviors of the same respondents over an interval of five
to six months. A two-wave panel survey was carried out on a random sample of high
school students in New York State in the fall of 1971 and then in the spring of
1972. Data were collected through structured, self-administered questionnaires
given in classrooms. The response rate was 81% for Time 1 (fall) and 76% for Time
2 (spring).

OPERATIONAL DEFINITIONS

Ever use: use of a drug at least once.

Current use: any drug use during the 30 days preceding the surveys.

Regular use: use of a drug six or more times in that same 30-day period.

FINDINGS

1. More than one third (34.7%) of high school students used one or more illegal
drugs (p. 45).

2. The illegal drugs most frequently used by high school students were marijuana
(29.5%) and hashish (27.1%); amphetamines and barbiturates were also used by
14.1% and 12.3%, respectively. Use of LSD and other psychedelics was 8.6%;
cocaine, 3.9%; and heroin, 2.8% (p. 45).

3. A much greater proportion of adolescents had used alcohol or tobacco than any illegal drug (p. 45).

4. Use of hard liquor among high school students was highest in suburban areas of New York State and lowest in New York City (p. 45).

5. Overall rates of illicit drug use were highest among suburban high school students in New York State and somewhat lower in New York City schools (41% and 38%, respectively). They were lowest (28%) in upstate areas (p. 45).

6. The rates of illicit drug use consistently increased from the freshman to the senior year of high school (p. 45).

7. Boys were more likely to use hard liquor than girls, whereas differences between boys and girls for illicit drug use were smaller (p. 45).

8. White high school students were slightly more likely than blacks to have tried marijuana, and were more likely to have used psychedelics, pills, or inhalants; blacks were more likely to have tried heroin (p. 45).

9. American Indian high school students reported the highest rates of use for every drug except heroin (p. 45).

10. Oriental high school students reported by far the lowest rates of illicit drug use (p. 45).

11. For all drugs studied, experimental use (one or two times) by high school students was the most common pattern of use (p. 45).

12. The proportion of all high school students reporting very extensive drug use ranged from 6% for hard liquor and 7% for marijuana to 1% for illicit drugs other than marijuana (p. 45).

13. For each drug studied, the percentage of current users among the ever users was at least 28%, and as high as 65% for marijuana and 60% for hard liquor (pp. 46-47).

14. The proportion of current users (among ever users) increased with increasing age for hard liquor, tobacco, and cannabis (p. 47).

15. Those students who regularly used any drug, except tobacco and beer or wine, made up a very small percentage of the total sample (p. 47).

16. More than twice as many students had "ever used" hard liquor as had used marijuana (65% and 29%, respectively); but among users of these two drugs, the percentage of regular marijuana users (29%) was double that of hard liquor users (14%) (p. 48).

17. The proportions of regular drug users among current users increased slightly for most substances in the five-month period under study (p. 49).

18. Except for hard liquor, the proportion of high school adolescents who used no drugs between fall 1971 and spring 1972 was much larger than the proportions who remained users or who started to use. But three times as many students began to use a particular drug as those who stopped using that drug (p. 49).

19. Most illicit drug use by high school students was intermittent (p. 49).

20. Certain drugs were typically used by high school students in experimental fashion, whereas hard liquor and cannabis had more stable patterns of use over time (p. 49).

21. The percentage of students who began using marijuana between the fall and the spring was 6.9%; for hard liquor, it was 11.9% (p. 49).

CONCLUSION

Use of legal and illegal drugs was widespread among public high school students in New York State. The vast majority of students drank beer or wine (82%), smoked cigarettes (72%), or used hard liquor (65%). Thirty-five percent used more than one illegal drug. The most frequently used illicit drugs were marijuana and hashish. Although many adolescents had at some time tried a few illicit drugs, use of these drugs tended to be experimental or occasional. These findings suggest that public policy concerned with drug problems is misdirected, since it is concentrated on battling only illicit drug use. Taking into account that the use of legal substances is strongly related to the use of illegal drugs, public policy ought to be directed against the use of legal substances as well.

AN: 162
AU: Kandel, D.B.; Treiman, D.; Faust, R.; Single, E.W.
TI: Adolescent involvement in legal and illegal drug use: A multiple
     classification analysis
SO: Social Forces, 55:438-558, 1976
IN: New York State Psychiatric Institute, and School of Public Health, Columbia
     University, New York, New York
RF: 36

SUMMARY TABLE

DRUG: marijuana; multidrug
TYPE: high school students and their parents
NUMBER: 1,112
SEX: male and female
AGE: high school
ETHNICITY: [black; white]
LOCATION: New York State
METHODOLOGY: cross-sectional, correlational survey
INSTRUMENT(S):   questionnaire
CONDUCTED: 1971-1972

PURPOSE

To analyze the contributions of various background, personal, and interpersonal
factors to adolescent involvement in drug use, legal and illict, precise estimates
of correlations between factors were obtained through multiple classification
analyses carried out on a sample of matched adolescent, parent, and best
school-friend triads. To differentiate levels of drug involvement, three aspects
of illict drug behavior in adolescents were considered: (1) probability of using
marijuana; (2) frequency of marijuana use; and (3) among marijuana users,
probability of other illicit drug use. The analysis was based on data gathered
from a subsample of adolescent, parent, and best school-friend triads during the
course of a study of a random sample of 8,206 adolescents representative of public
secondary school students in New York State who were surveyed in fall 1971 and
spring 1972. Results reported here are from the fall survey.

FINDINGS

1. Sex, grade in school, or family income had little effect on marijuana use
among high school students when other variables were controlled (p. 442).

2. The most important factor in adolescent marijuana use was the best friend's
frequency of marijuana use (p. 445).

3. Psychoactive drug use by parents showed little relationship to adolescent
marijuana use. However, parental self-reported use of hard liquor was the fourth
most influential factor affecting adolescent marijuana use when all variables were
controlled (pp. 445-446).

4. Political attitudes and the level of participation in peer activities were the
second most influential factors in adolescent marijuana use after friend's
frequency of use. Drug use was highest among the most radical students and those

highly involved with their peers (p. 446).

5. Marijuana use among high school students was clearly the result of attitudinal and interpersonal processes (p. 446).

6. Compared with friends who did not use marijuana, marijuana-using friendship pairs were more likely to be politically radical, to do poorly in school, to be alienated from their parents, and to attend church rarely, suggesting that adolescent marijuana users form a subculture (p. 447).

7. Nearly half (48%) of the marijuana users among high school students had tried other illicit drugs as well (p. 448).

8. The most important factor related to multiple drug use by adolescent marijuana users was whether friends were multiple drug users; the next three factors in order of importance were closeness to parents, school performance, and depression (p. 449).

9. Progression from marijuana to more serious illicit drugs among high school students was more an expression of personal dissatisfaction and maladjustment than of participation in an adolescent subculture (p. 450).

10. When adolescents' use of the licit drugs, alcohol, and tobacco were included in the analysis of correlations between illicit drug use and other characteristics, use of illicit drugs by friends was still the most important variable influencing illicit drug use, but the adolescents' own use of hard liquor and cigarettes were the second and third most important variables affecting use of marijuana and illicit drugs and were the third and fourth most important variables affecting frequency of marijuana use (p. 451).

11. The overall level of involvement in peer activities (or sociability) was the most important factor influencing adolescents' alcohol use, followed by friend's use of alcohol (p. 453).

CONCLUSION

The data in this study supported the notion of stages in drug use involvement: alcohol and tobacco preceded marijuana, marijuana in turn preceded other illicit drugs. Three phases of drug involvement could be discerned: (1) use of legal substances, (2) use of marijuana, and (3) use of other illicit drugs besides marijuana. In the first stage, adolescents who enjoyed very high levels of activity and sociability with their peers began using socially acceptable substances--alcohol and tobacco. In the course of social activities, the adolescents came to know marijuana-using peers, and through them got involved in marijuana use. Those who were alienated from their parents, were depressed, or had negative feelings toward the establishment, church, school, or family then began using more serious illicit drugs.

AN: 163
AU: McBride, D.C.
TI: Parental and peer influence upon adolescent drug use
SO: Unpublished paper, 1978. 16 pp.
IN: Department of Psychiatry, University of Miami, Miami, Florida
RF: 0

SUMMARY TABLE

DRUG: multidrug
TYPE: high school students
NUMBER: 2,052
SEX: male and female
AGE: high school
ETHNICITY: white; Hispanic
LOCATION: eastern United States
METHODOLOGY: retrospective, correlational survey
INSTRUMENT(S):   questionnaire
CONDUCTED: not specified

PURPOSE

In the study of the etiology of deviant behavior, there exist two separate and
often exclusive theoretical orientations. The first, involving parental affect
and the attachment of the individual to his parents, sees the home and the family
environment as the primary and direct cause of delinquent behavior. The closer
and healthier the attachment to the parents, the less deviant behavior should
occur. The other position argues that delinquent behavior is related to the
degree of association with peers and that a learning of law-violating behaviors
must take place. An attempt was made to work within the framework of these two
traditions and explain the differences in the total drug use index by using the
relative and combined influence of parents and peers on individual drug using
behavior. Retrospective measuring techniques were used on a group of high school
students who completed questionnaires concerning their current drug use and their
relationships with parents and peers at age 12.

FINDINGS

1. A moderate inverse relationship between perceived attachment to parents at age
12 and current drug use was found. Of those students who were attached to their
parents, two thirds did not use illicit drugs at all, and only one third of those
not attached to their parents reported never having used illicit drugs (p. 10).

2. The larger the proportion of friends who were drug users at age 12, the more
likely it was for the individual to use drugs (p. 11).

3. Both parents and peers were found to affect the drug using behavior of
individuals regardless of the other (p. 14).

CONCLUSION

Both parents and peers were found to have a direct independent effect on adolescent drug use that remained for each when the other was statistically controlled. The implication is that in future research an integrative rather than an exclusionary approach might result in more powerful theoretical models.

AN: 164
AU: Margulies, R.Z.; Kessler, R.C.; Kandel, D.B.
TI: A longitudinal study of onset of drinking among high school students
SO: Journal of Studies on Alcohol, 38:897-912, 1977
IN: School of Public Health, Columbia University, New York, New York
RF: 26

SUMMARY TABLE

DRUG: distilled spirits
TYPE: high school students
NUMBER: 1,936
SEX: male and female
AGE: high school
ETHNICITY: black; white
LOCATION: New York State
METHODOLOGY: longitudinal panel survey
INSTRUMENT(S):   questionnaire
CONDUCTED: 1971-1972

PURPOSE

Analysis of initiation into the use of distilled spirits is crucial in
understanding the overall process of adolescent involvement in drugs. This study
investigated the factors which predict initiation into the use of distilled
spirits in a sample of high school students followed over the course of a school
year (1971-1972). Students were administered structured questionnaires in the
fall and spring of the academic year at an interval of five to six months. The
analysis was based on a sample of adolescents (N=1,936) who had never used
distilled spirits at Time 1 and relational subsamples of dyads of adolescents
matched to parents and best school-friends. Three areas of interest were
investigated: (1) parental influences, (2) peer influences, and (3) adolescent
intrapersonal characteristics.

FINDINGS

1. Neither the closeness of the adolescents' relationship with their families nor
their perception of parental control had a significant influence on the onset of
drinking (p. 904).

2. The example set by parents in the use of distilled spirits was more important
in the onset of drinking among their children than their attitudes towards
drinking (p. 904).

3. There was a correlation among adolescents between starting to drink and
perception of the number of friends who drink. This correlation was larger than
the correlation with the best friend's self-report of his/her drinking of
distilled spirits (p. 904).

4. Adolescents engaging in various social activities with their peers, such as
dating and attending parties, were more likely to start drinking than those who
did not (p. 904).

5. Participation in political activities and number of classes cut were important predictors of the onset of drinking (p. 905).

6. Prior involvement in minor delinquent activities provided one of the best predictors of the onset of drinking (p. 904).

7. Prior use of legal drugs was an important predictor of the onset of drinking for adolescents. Cigarette smokers were almost as likely as beer and wine users to progress to the use of distilled spirits during the five- to six-month interval studied (p. 904).

8. Friends became consistently more influential in starting drinking as adolescents progressed through high school (p. 907).

9. In spite of the greater pressures exerted by peers, parental influence on children's drinking did not decrease from he freshman to senior year of high school, indicating that parental and peer influences can operate simultaneously (p. 907).

10. Adolescents who continued to abstain from drinking in their last year of high school did so because of their belief in the harmful effects of alcohol (p. 907).

11. Initiation into drinking early in high school was associated with nonconforming behaviors (liberal political ideology and lack of religiosity); by contrast, when drinking was begun in the junior or senior years, it represented a conforming behavior for conservative students (p. 907).

12. Among adolescent girls, the examples set by parents and peers were significant predictors of their use of distilled spirits, whereas neither factor was important among boys (p. 908).

13. Believing that the casual use of distilled spirits is not harmful, participating in politics, and involvement in minor delinquent activities were significantly related to the onset of drinking for boys only, suggesting that girls who begin drinking distilled spirits are conforming to interpersonal role models, whereas boys do so as part of a complex of mildly deviant activities (p. 909).

14. Prior legal drug use predicted the use of distilled spirits for both boys and girls, although the use of wine and beer was a better predictor for boys than for girls (pp. 908-909).

CONCLUSION

Factors that determined the onset of drinking were social (situational) and psychological. Parental example and the influence of peers, particularly in the final years of high school, were the most important determinants of drinking. These influences and the closeness of parental ties were of greater relevance for girls. The following factors were important predictors of the onset of drinking among high school students: approval of drinking by parents and friends, having many drinking friends, deviant tendencies, and use of other legal drugs.

AN: 165
AU: Morrison, A.J.;   Kline, F.G.;   Miller, P.V.
TI: Aspects of adolescent information acquisition about drugs and alcohol topics
SO: In: Ostman, R.E., ed. Communication Research and Drug Education
      (International Yearbooks of Drug Addiction and Society, Vol. 3).   Beverly
      Hills, CA: Sage Publications, 1976. pp. 132-154.
IN: University of Michigan, Ann Arbor, Michigan
RF: 15

SUMMARY TABLE

DRUG: multidrug; alcohol
TYPE: adolescents
NUMBER: 300 subjects; 300 controls
SEX: male and female
AGE: adolescent
ETHNICITY: not specified
LOCATION: midwest
METHODOLOGY: experimental research
INSTRUMENT(S):   interview
CONDUCTED: not specified

PURPOSE

The authors examined the question: In what contexts and for what reasons do
audience members turn to the mass media for information they need about some
topic? Potential bases of information needs about two related topics, alcohol use
and abuse and drug use and abuse, were delineated. Cross-sectional and field
experimental survey research data were examined to determine how these information
needs relate to the perception of messages in most media and to the individual's
knowledge about these two topics. Relationships between audience needs and
evaluations of the importance of both topics and their information-scaling
activity regarding each topic were also analyzed. At Time 1, a random sample of
adolescents in two cities (one the experimental group, the other the control
group) were interviewed; then, a month-long drug or alcohol radio campaign was
broadcast in the experimental city. After the campaign, members in the original
subsample and in a second subsample were interviewed at Time 2.

OPERATIONAL DEFINITIONS

Time 1: the time of the interview before the drug or alcohol radio campaign.

Time 2: the time of the interview after the radio campaign.

FINDINGS

1. For the whole sample, more messages about drugs than about alcohol were
discriminated in the period before the initial interviews (p. 139).

2. The types of substances reported as used by adolescents did not predict either
discriminating messages or having knowledge of information sources about alcohol
or drugs (p. 140).

3. Knowledge congruency was significant when the father-adolescent dyad was considered for drug message discrimination and when the peer-adolescent dyad was considered for alcohol message discrimination (p. 140).

4. Those adolescents who talked with parents or peers perceived more messages about the drug and alcohol topics in mass media than did nontalkers (p. 141).

5. Adolescents who talked with peers about alcohol and drug topics knew more information sources than did nontalkers (p. 141).

6. Perceiving and recalling media messages about drugs and alcohol were related to knowledge of drug and alcohol information sources (p. 142).

7. Substance use, in general, did not effect the relationship between message discrimination and knowledge of information sources. For both alcohol and drugs, significant positive correlations held across all categories (polysubstance, marijuana/alcohol, alcohol, abstinence), except for marijuana/alcohol use (p. 142).

8. The radio campaign failed to stimulate message perception about either alcohol or drug topics (p. 144).

9. Those adolescents who heard the radio messages about alcohol nearly always knew more alcohol information sources than did those who heard no messages (p 146).

10. Talking with peers, father, and mother was related to perceiving the alcohol topic as important either at Time 2 only or at Time 1 and Time 2. Not talking with any partner was related to perceiving alcohol as important neither time or at Time 1 only (p. 147).

11. Only a small percentage (10%-15%) of the adolescents at either Time 1 or Time 2 indicated that they had sought information about either alcohol or drugs in the month before the interviews (p. 149).

12. Significantly larger proportions of drug information seekers were abstainers than users (p. 149).

13. Adolescents who talked with their fathers and mothers about alcohol use tended to seek information about alcohol at Time 1 or Time 2 (but not both) (p. 150).

14. Adolescents who talked to their partners (mother, father, peers) about drugs were much more likely to be information seekers at Time 1, Time 2, or both times than were nontalkers (p. 150).

CONCLUSION

The study focused on the relationships among three need states (perceived knowledge congruency, talking, and substance use) and four criterion variables (message discrimination, knowledge of information sources, topic importance, and topic information seeking). A clear set of relationships was established between talking and all four criterion variables, and almost no relationships between perceived knowledge congruency and these variables. With regard to the design and evaluation of drug and alcohol information programs, we must not think of the individual audience member as an isolated, passive recipient of this information. Instead, the needs of the audience members must be considered, especially since those needs may be derived from talking with parents or peers.

AN: 166
AU: O'Malley, P.M.; Bachman, J.G.; Johnston, L.D.
TI: Drug use and military plans of high school seniors
SO: Youth and Society, 10:65-77, 1978
IN: Institute for Social Research, University of Michigan, Ann Arbor, Michigan
RF: 9

SUMMARY TABLE

```
DRUG:           multidrug
TYPE:           high school seniors
NUMBER:         30,000
SEX:            males (48%);  females (52%)
AGE:            high school
ETHNICITY:      not specified
LOCATION:       United States (cross-sectional)
METHODOLOGY:    cross-sectional survey
INSTRUMENT(S):  questionnaire
CONDUCTED:      1976;  1977
```


PURPOSE

Drug use has been shown to be higher among men in military service than among those of similar age in civilian life. If such is the case, the question arises whether this higher rate is a result of military service itself (a socialization effect) or a result of the fact that individuals who enter the military tend to be heavier drug users already (a selection effect). In an effort to check for this selection effect, data gathered from surveys given to a nationwide cross-section of high school seniors in 1976 and 1977 were analyzed for correlations between plans to enter military service and present drug use.

FINDINGS

1. High school seniors (male and female) who expected to enter the armed forces tended to use cigarettes, alcohol, and marijuana slightly more than did seniors who did not expect military service; for illict drugs other than marijuana, use by seniors who did not expect to enter military service was somewhat more than use by seniors who did expect to enter the military (pp. 68-70).

2. High school seniors expecting to enter military service were no more likely than average to have used marijuana during their last year of high school (p. 73).

3. There were no significant relationships between the likelihood of military service and heavy alcohol use. Males reported heavier drinking than did females, and noncollege-bound high school seniors reported heavier drinking than did the college-bound (p. 72).

4. High school seniors who expected to enter military service were less likely to be illicit drug users than were other seniors; those male seniors who definitely expected to enter military service and did not expect to attend college were significantly less likely to use illicit drugs (p. 73).

5. For females who planned to attend college, those who expected to spend time in military service had a significantly higher rate of cigarette use than did those who had no such expectation. The difference for males was not significant (p. 72).

6. For students who did not plan to attend college, there was no significant relationship between the likelihood of military service and smoking (p. 72).

7. For males who were not college-bound, those who definitely expected to enter military service were significantly less likely to be recent heavy marijuana users (p. 73).

8. For males who were not college-bound, those who were definite about the likelihood of entering military service had significantly lower rates of illicit drug use (other than marijuana) (p. 73).

CONCLUSION

High school seniors who planned to enter military service did not differ in their use of drugs from other high school seniors; while they were somewhat more likely to smoke cigarettes, they were actually less likely to have used illicit drugs other than marijuana. There are several possible reasons for the discrepancies between these findings and previous research associating military service and drug use. The earlier studies were made at a time of military conscription and war, while the present study was composed of persons planning to join the armed forces voluntarily in a time of peace. Also, the present study did not include high school dropouts, who are usually heavier users of drugs and more likely to enter military service. Finally, military service itself may have the effect of increasing drug use, although this has only been demonstrated for Vietnam war service.

AN: 167
AU: Orive, R.; Gerard, H.B.
TI: Personality, attitudinal, and social correlates of drug use
SO: International Journal of the Addictions, 15:869-881, 1980
IN: Department of Psychology, University of California, Los Angeles
RF: 17

SUMMARY TABLE

DRUG: multidrug
TYPE: adolescents
NUMBER: 106
SEX: male (65); female (41)
AGE: 14-22 years
ETHNICITY: Anglo (90); Chicano (9); black (7)
LOCATION: Los Angeles, California
METHODOLOGY: longitudinal, correlational survey
INSTRUMENT(S):   questionnaire; interview
CONDUCTED: not specified

PURPOSE

Recent studies concerning the personality correlates of drug use have failed to provide a clear picture of what types of individuals are more or less susceptible to peer group influence or drug use. An attempt was made to discover which, if any, personality traits, attitudes, or peer interactions led to drug use. Subjects (N=106) on whom data concerning personality factors had been obtained ten years earlier were interviewed and filled out questionnaires concerning their drug use, their personalities, and their interactions with parents and peers.

OPERATIONAL DEFINITIONS

Drug categories: cigarettes, alcohol, marijuana, hallucinogens.

FINDINGS

1. About two thirds of the participants had used alcohol, almost half had used marijuana at least once, and one fifth had used hallucinogens (p. 872).

2. Of those personality factors determined in an earlier survey, none were found to be systematically related to the use of marijuana. However, low anxiety and a high I.Q. tended to predict hallucinogen use (p. 872).

3. Drug users scored significantly lower in anxiety than nondrug users in the early measurements, while a nonsignificant tendency towards lower anxiety scores was found in the later interviews (p. 872).

4. No relationship was found between socio-economic status and drug use (p. 872).

5. Users of hallucinogens and marijuana tended to show a greater involvement with peers and less involvement with parents (p. 874).

6. Users of illicit drugs and alcohol participated in delinquent activities to a greater extent than did nonusers (p. 874).

7. As a reaction to the statement "people should be allowed to take drugs to get high," illegal drug users tended to agree more than nonusers, although less than half of the users agreed (p. 875).

8. Adolescents perceived the negative effects on health to be nearly twice as great for cigarettes and hallucinogens as for alcohol and marijuana (p. 875).

9. A large percentage of drug users from each drug category indicated that they were unsure they were doing the right thing when they first began using drugs (p.875)

10. For both present and former drug users, similar proportions of peers were using a particular drug at the time the subjects started use of that drug. For all drugs, over half of the peers had used the drug that the subjects were using or had been using (p. 877).

11. Initiation to drug use was found to be a group phenomenon, and the recruiter for most drugs was usually a friend or close friend who was a nonleader member of the group (p. 877).

12. Adolescents who used drugs were much more likely to have obtained their knowledge about them from peers than from parents or teachers, whereas nondrug users learned about drugs more often from adults than from peers (p. 873).

CONCLUSION

Results of the study indicated that the individual's peer group was the primary influence on the initiation to both licit and illicit drugs. The further away from parental control the subjects moved, the further they moved from the norms and influences of their parents. No differences in personality traits were found for users and nonusers, indicating that other factors play a major role in drug-use initiation. This implies that in future research the peer group should be used as the basic medium for changing drug-use behavior.

AN: 168
AU: Paton, S.M.; Kandel, D.B.
TI: Psychological factors and adolescent illicit drug use: Ethnicity and sex differences
SO: Adolescence, 13:187-200, 1978
IN: New York State Psychiatric Institute, and School of Public Health, Columbia University, New York, New York
RF: 33

SUMMARY TABLE

DRUG: multidrug
TYPE: high school students
NUMBER: 8,206
SEX: male and female
AGE: high school
ETHNICITY: white (5641); black (621); Puerto Rican (355)
LOCATION: New York State
METHODOLOGY: cross-sectional survey
INSTRUMENT(S):   questionnaire
CONDUCTED: 1971-1972

PURPOSE

This study attempted to clarify the relationship between four psychological factors (depressive mood, normlessness, sense of isolation from the world, and self-esteem) and drug use in a random sample of public high school students. The analysis was based on a sample of adolescents (N=8,206) at 18 public high schools in New York State. In the fall of 1971, structured, self-administered questionnaires were given to a random sample of homerooms in 13 schools and to the entire student body in 5 schools.

FINDINGS

1. A positive relationship was found between each of four psychological factors (depressive mood, normlessness, social isolation, and self-esteem) and illicit drug use, with the relationship being stronger for multidrug users (p. 191).

2. Depressive mood and normlessness were more important correlates of illicit drug use (other than marijuana) than social isolation and self-esteem (p. 193).

3. The relationship between depressive mood and multiple drug use was stronger for girls than for boys (p. 191).

4. The correlation between depressive mood and multiple drug use was strong for whites, but nonexistent for blacks and Puerto Ricans (p. 194).

5. White teenagers who were depressed were more likely to be multidrug users than those who were not depressed, with the effect being stronger among girls than among boys (p. 194).

6. Both black and Puerto Rican boys were more likely to use multiple drugs when they were not depressed than when they were depressed (p. 195).

7. Black and especially Puerto Rican girls were more likely to use multiple drugs when they were depressed (p. 195).

CONCLUSION

The psychological factors of depressive mood and normlessness had a positive relationship with the use of illegal drugs (other than marijuana) among high school students. Normlessness and depressive mood had strong associations with drug use, while social isolation and self-esteem had weaker associations. The association of depressive mood and normlessness with illegal multiple drug use varied by ethnicity and sex, being more pronounced among girls and among whites. Among girls, depressive mood was positively related to multiple use regardless of race, but among boys, it was positively related to multiple drug use only for whites. Depressive mood was negatively related to multiple drug use for black and Puerto Rican boys. These findings ought to be interpreted with caution, since it is not clear whether the psychological states discussed preceded the use of illicit drugs or were consequences of such use.

AN: 169
AU: Paton, S.M.; Kessler, R.; Kandel, D.B.
TI: Depressive mood and adolescent illicit drug use: A longitudinal analysis
SO: Journal of Genetic Psychology, 131:267-289, 1977
IN: New York State Psychiatric Institute, and School of Public Health, Columbia
     University, New York, New York
RF: 50

SUMMARY TABLE

DRUG: multidrug
TYPE: high school students
NUMBER: 8,206
SEX: male and female
AGE: high school
ETHNICITY: [black; white]
LOCATION: New York State
METHODOLOGY: longitudinal panel survey
INSTRUMENT(S):   questionnaire
CONDUCTED: 1971-1972

PURPOSE

Previous studies have provided inconclusive evidence on the role of psychological factors in illicit drug use. In order to further understand this subject, the technique of Goodman's log linear method was applied in an analysis of longitudinal data to clarify the relationship between depressive mood and illicit drug use among youths. The following questions were explored: Is depressive mood related to the use of marijuana and other illicit drugs in a random population of high school students? Does the use of drugs result in depressive mood? Does depressive mood result in experimentation with drugs? Are the same processes involved in the use of marijuana and of other illicit drugs? Questionnaires were administered to a random sample of students in New York public high schools during fall 1971 and spring 1972.

OPERATIONAL DEFINITIONS

Time 1: fall 1971.

Time 2: spring 1972.

FINDINGS

1. In the total sample of students surveyed, depressive mood was positively associated with illicit drug use, especially with the use of drugs other than marijuana (p. 275).

2. At Time 1, the percentage of adolescents who were depressed was similar among those who did not use drugs and those who used marijuana only (44% vs 47%) (p. 275).

3. At Time 1, the percentage of students using illicit drugs other than marijuana who were depressed was higher than among marijuana users (57% vs 47%) (p. 275).

4. There seemed to be no causal influence between depressive mood and marijuana use during the five- to six-month period studied (p. 276).

5. Depression was positively (but not strongly) related to the initiation of marijuana use by youths who previously had not used any illicit drugs; depression was negatively related to continued use of marijuana (p. 280).

6. Depressive mood was significantly related to subsequent multiple drug use. Marijuana users who were depressed at Time 1 and who were not using other illicit drugs were more likely to start using drugs by Time 2 than those who were not depressed. Also, depressed marijuana users who were already using other illicit drugs were more likely to continue using these drugs than those who were not depressed (p. 282).

7. There was a strong interaction between relief of depressive mood among adolescents and stability of the use of drugs other than marijuana. Apparently, the use of illicit drugs other than marijuana was related to the relief of depression for some adolescents. These adolescents had a particularly high probability of continuing the use of these drugs compared to other users (p. 284).

8. Depressive mood among adolescents was slightly related to the termination of marijuana use and more strongly related to the initiation of the use of other illicit drugs (p. 284).

9. Depressive mood was related to progression in the use of other illicit drugs only among adolescents who were current users of marijuana (p. 285).

CONCLUSION

It was found that an interaction between depressive mood and illicit drug use in a random sample of high school students depended upon the drug in question, and may have been different over a period of time. Thus, for marijuana, depressive mood was clearly associated with the initiation of use among previous nonusers and somewhat associated with the cessation of use among users within the follow-up interval. For other illicit drugs, depressive mood at Time 1 predicted the use of such drugs by Time 2 among prior marijuana users, and the continued use of these illicit drugs over time by previously depressed users was related to a decrease in depressive mood by Time 2. These findings should not be interpreted as meaning that depressive mood causes drug use; depression was only one of the reasons a student might have had for using drugs.

AN: 170
AU: Robles, R.R.; Martinez, R.; Moscoso, M.
TI: Drug use among public and private secondary school students in Puerto Rico
SO: International Journal of the Addictions, 14:243-258, 1979
IN: University of Puerto Rico, San Juan, Puerto Rico
RF: 16

SUMMARY TABLE

DRUG: multidrug
TYPE: high school students
NUMBER: 18,562
SEX: male and female
AGE: high school
ETHNICITY: Puerto Rican
LOCATION: Puerto Rico
METHODOLOGY: cross-sectional survey
INSTRUMENT(S):   questionnaire
CONDUCTED: 1974-1975

PURPOSE

A two-wave panel study was carried out in Puerto Rico in order to investigate factors related to adolescent drug use. This report presents the results from the first wave of the survey. Since one purpose of the study was to compare the results with the patterns of drug use found in New York state by Kandel and her associates (see AN 161), the items in the structured, self-administered questionnaire were similar to or identical with those in the Kandel questionnaire, although questions were added to measure other variables. The questionnaire was administered to a stratified random sample of students attending public and private secondary schools in Puerto Rico.

FINDINGS

1. In 1974, nearly one in eight Puerto Rican students (11.8%) had ever used one or more illicit drug (p. 246).

2. The illicit drug most frequently used by Puerto Rican students was marijuana (7%) (p. 246).

3. The percentage of reported ever-use of illict drugs by the Puerto Rican adolescents (11.8%) was lower than that of New York State adolescents in 1971 (34.7%) (p. 246).

4. Reported marijuana use for New York State adolescents (29.5%) was more than four times that of their Puerto Rican peers (7%) (p. 246).

5. More than three times as many Puerto Rican students used alcohol and tobacco as used any of the illegal drugs: 40.5% vs 11.8% (p. 246).

6. The use of alcohol among Puerto Rican adolescents was lower than that of adolescents in the United States (p. 246).

7. Two of every three Puerto Rican students in private schools had ever used drugs, and one in every two students in public school had ever used drugs (p. 248).

8. More males than females reported significantly higher rates of use of illicit drugs in both private and public Puerto Rican schools (pp. 248-249).

9. Males in private schools in Puerto Rico were heavier drug users than males in public schools (20.8% vs 15.6%) (p. 249).

10. Puerto Rican females in private schools were more likely to report illicit drug use (11.9%) than were their peers in public schools (7%) (p. 249).

11. Puerto Rican males in private schools were the heaviest alcohol users and were more similar to their female peers in private schools than to males in public schools (p. 250).

12. Puerto Rican adolescents who used drugs associated with other adolescent drug users; students in private schools were slightly more likely than students in public schools to have friends who used illicit drugs (p. 250).

13. In both private and public Puerto Rican schools, illicit drug use was more frequent among students with lower scholastic averages than among those with higher averages (p. 251).

14. Three times as many adolescent illicit drug users in Puerto Rican private schools reported never attending church as those who reported attending often, with the ratio for drug users in public schools being slightly lower (p. 252).

15. Private school students in Puerto Rico were more likely than public school students to use both illicit and licit drugs regardless of the size of their community (p. 252).

16. There was a high frequency of illicit drug use among those adolescents who had once lived outside of Puerto Rico (p. 252).

CONCLUSION

Private school students in Puerto Rico were heavier users of both licit and illicit drugs than public school students. The difference in alcohol use between private and public school students may be explained by their different lifestyles, and not only by their different incomes. A significant finding is that Puerto Rican adolescents who had lived in the mainland of the United States had higher rates of drug use than those who had lived all their life in Puerto Rico. The finding that private school students used drugs in greater numbers than public students suggests that higher socio-economic status does not prevent drug use. Hence, efforts to stop drug use should not be limited to public schools only, but must be expanded to private schools as well.

```
AN:  171
AU:  Rosenberg, J.S.;  Berberian, R.M.
TI:  A report on the dropout study
SO:  Unpublished paper, Yale University School of Medicine, 1975.  45 pp.
IN:  Yale University School of Medicine, New Haven, Connecticut
RF:  0
```

SUMMARY TABLE

```
DRUG:           multidrug
TYPE:           high school dropouts and students
NUMBER:         554 (110 dropouts;  444 students)
SEX:            male;  female
AGE:            16-18 years
ETHNICITY:      white;  black;  Puerto Rican
LOCATION:       [Greater New Haven, Connecticut]
METHODOLOGY:    comparative survey
INSTRUMENT(S):  interview
CONDUCTED:      1971-1973
```

PURPOSE

Little is known about drug use among high school dropouts. What is known comes almost exclusively from adolescents attending school. In order to enlarge the small body of existing information concerning the drug use of dropouts, this study examined the socio-demographic characteristics of a population of dropouts, compared drug use among dropouts with that of nondropouts, sought to explain any differential drug use between dropouts and students, and tried to determine whether drug use is related to the dropping-out process. The data were gathered through personal interviews with randomly selected dropouts.

FINDINGS

1. For every drug, dropout females had a higher ever use rate than did in-school females, and these differences were substantial for most of the drugs studied (p. 9).

2. Male dropouts had signficantly higher ever use rates for only three drugs (marijuana, hashish, and heroin) when compared to in-school males (p. 9).

3. Dropout females had higher current use rates for only two drugs (marijuana and hashish) when compared to in-school females (p. 9).

4. Male dropouts showed higher current use of seven drugs (marijuana, hashish, amphetamines, mescaline, LSD, cocaine, and heroin) compared to in-school males (p. 10).

5. Dropout males and females used more beer and liquor outside their homes with friends and were more often regular cigarette users compared with in-school males and females (p. 10).

6. The main drug use differences (both ever use and current use) between dropouts and continuing students showed male and female dropouts dominating in the use of marijuana and hashish (p. 10).

7. Male dropouts had significantly greater heroin use than in-school males (p. 10).

8. More dropout females than in-school females reported the ability to procure all of the drugs inquired about (p. 11).

9. More dropout males reported the ability to obtain only three (marijuana, hashish, and glue) of the drugs studied when compared to in-school males (p. 11).

10. Compared to dropouts, more in-school students of both sexes believed that either negligible or the most severe consequences would follow being caught for drugs (p. 12).

11. Of the dropout males studied, almost 75%, compared to about 58% for the in-school males, felt they would have to serve time in a penal institution, suggesting that fear of jail was not a major deterrent to heroin use in males, since four times as many dropouts used it as did in-school males (p. 12).

12. Nearly 82% of the dropout males who used heroin had friends who also used heroin, compared to only 10% for the in-school males (p. 13).

13. For both sexes, dropouts were more likely than students to have friends who used drugs (p. 13).

14. The strength of association between the alcohol use of parent and child was much higher for dropouts than for the in-school group; proportionately more parents of dropouts used beer, wine, and liquor than did parents of students (p. 15).

15. More dropout males than in-school males began using heroin because they were troubled; in-school males were more likely than dropout males to report that they began heroin use "to see what it was like" (p. 16).

16. Dropouts in general and dropouts who used drugs had more drug education than students in general or students who used drugs (p. 16).

CONCLUSION

The following significant differences in the use of drugs between dropouts and the in-school group were found: male and female dropouts dominated in the use of marijuana, hashish, cigarettes, and beer; more male dropouts used heroin; more male and female students used wine; and more female dropouts used liquor. Differences in the use of drugs between dropouts and students may possibly be related to several factors: dropouts started marijuana and hashish use earlier than students, more reported the ability to obtain these drugs safely, more reported offers to share the drugs, fewer dropouts believed they would serve time in penal institutions for drug offenses, and more had particpated in drug education. The main reasons that male dropouts had a higher rate of heroin use than students include earlier onset of use, greater peer pressure, and a greater need to escape from problems. The findings suggest that illicit drug use contributes little to dropping out.

AN: 172
AU: Rosenberg, J.S.; Kasl, S.V.; Berberian, R.M.
TI: Sex differences in adolescent drug use: Recent trends
SO: Addictive Diseases: An International Journal, 1:73-96, 1974
IN: Center for Survey Research, Yale University, New Haven, Connecticut
RF: 25

SUMMARY TABLE

DRUG: multidrug
TYPE: junior and senior high school students
NUMBER: 4,500 first year; 4,500 second year
SEX: male (50%); female (50%)
AGE: junior and senior high school
ETHNICITY: white; black
LOCATION: [Greater New Haven, Connecticut]
METHODOLOGY: longitudinal, comparative survey
INSTRUMENT(S):   questionnaire
CONDUCTED: 1970-1972

PURPOSE

Previous studies on adolescent drug abuse did not differentiate between boys and girls. They simply ascribed characteristics of male users to adolescents in general. This study investigated the differences and similarities between boys' and girls' experiences with illicit drugs as well as with cigarettes and alcohol over a two-year period. It sought to confirm the hypothesis that differential changes in girls' drug use described in previous studies are not simply local phenomena but can be replicated elsewhere. It also elaborated more fully on sex differences in drug use by studying their relation to grade in school, race, school type, and type of use. The data for this study were collected by administering questionnaires to the students of 33 junior and senior high schools from 12 city and town areas in New England. The sample of respondents was selected randomly.

OPERATIONAL DEFINITIONS

Year One: first year of study (1970-1971).

Year Two: second year of study (1971-1972).

FINDINGS

1. The number of students using drugs was increasingly progressive with school grade. The association between use and school grade was stronger for males than for females (p. 80).

2. In Year One, males reported significantly greater frequency of drug use than females, except for amphetamines and barbiturates (p. 80).

3. In Year Two, males used drugs significantly more frequently than females in only four (amphetamines, barbiturates, LSD, and heroin) of the nine illicit drugs considered (p. 80).

4. Both females and males showed an increase in use from Year One to Year Two for all categories of drugs, except for heroin among males (p. 81).

5. From Year One to Year Two, females showed larger increases in drug use (except for marijuana and hashish) than did males (p. 82).

6. The more popular drugs had greater percentages of users who reported higher frequencies of use (p. 83).

7. During Year One, males reported greater frequency of current use of all drugs than did females, except for barbiturates and amphetamines (p. 84).

8. By Year Two, females reported significantly more current use of amphetamines and barbiturates than did males, and males reported significantly more current use of hashish than did females (p. 84).

9. The prevalence of current users among those who had tried a drug decreased between Year One and Year Two. The male-female differences were nonsignificant (p. 84).

10. The proportion of experimental users (those who had tried a drug but were not current users) did not remain constant over two years, but may have fluctuated independently of the trends in ever use (p. 84).

11. There were substantial and highly significant increases in current use of alcohol from Year One to Year Two for males and females. Males showed significantly greater frequency of use than did females during both years (p. 86).

12. The popularity of cigarettes declined for both sexes from Year One to Year Two (p. 87).

13. Whites exceeded blacks in ever use for most drugs (exceptions were cocaine and heroin for both sexes in Year One, but only for males in Year Two, and males' use of marijuana in both years) (p. 88).

14. Greater race differences in drug use existed between males than between females, especially during Year One (p. 88).

15. Sex differences in drug use were more prominent among blacks than whites (p. 88).

16. Between Year One and Year Two, black females were "catching up" to white females in marijuana and hashish use, but many of the other differences were maintained (amphetamines, barbiturates, glue, mescaline, LSD) (p. 88).

17. Black males were closer to white males in drug use during Year Two than Year One, with the exception of hashish (p. 88).

18. No significant race differences were seen regarding alcohol use (p. 88).

19. Black males exceeded white males on past or present regular cigarette use (35% vs 29%) (p. 88).

20. Associations between school grade and ever use of different drugs were highly similar for black and white females (p. 88).

21. The percentages of females and males attending religious schools who had ever used drugs were lower in comparison with their counterparts from other types of schools (p. 90).

22. The largest increase in the percentages of those who ever used a drug was experienced by females in large public schools (p. 90).

23. Males from religious schools showed greater increases than other males in drug use between Year One and Year Two in all drug categories, except for hashish (p. 90).

24. Between Year One and Year Two, females in the large public schools showed the largest increases in the ever used drug category and males the smallest (p. 91).

CONCLUSION

Although both adolescent boys and girls showed an increase in illicit drug use between survey years, the females' use showed larger changes than the males'. This was equally true for blacks and whites and was more pronounced in large public and religious schools. Past or present regular cigarette use declined among females attending large public and religious schools. The use of alcohol "outside your home with friends" was on the increase except for private school females, large public school males, and black males. Alcohol was the most popular substance for both sexes, although many more males than females used alcohol. Drug use, whether current or ever use, tended to be greater for students of both sexes in higher grades.

AN: 173
AU: Single, E.W.; Kandel, D.B.
TI: The role of buying and selling in illicit drug use
SO: In: Treback, A., ed. Drugs, Crime and Public Policy. New York: Praeger,
     1978. pp. 118-128
IN: Columbia University, New York, New York
RF: 12

SUMMARY TABLE

DRUG: multidrug
TYPE: high school students
NUMBER: 8,206
SEX: male and female
AGE: high school
ETHNICITY: white; black; Puerto-Rican
LOCATION: New York State
METHODOLOGY: cross-sectional survey
INSTRUMENT(S):   questionnaire
CONDUCTED: 1972

PURPOSE

It has been proposed by Goode and by Johnson that escalation from marijuana to
other drugs results not from any intrinsic property of marijuana itself but from
the marijuana user's participation in a drug-using subculture. This study tested
three interrelated propositions derived from this theory: (1) Marijuana users
whose friends use drugs, particularly the so-called hard drugs, are more likely to
also use these other drugs than marijuana users whose friends do not use illicit
drugs; (2) Marijuana users acquire friends who use hard drugs primarily by buying
and selling drugs; (3) When involvement in illicit marketing and friends' drug
use are controlled for, adolescent marijuana use is not related to the use of
other illicit drugs. The data were obtained from a random sample of 8,206
adolescents from 18 high schools, representative of public secondary school
students in New York State, who completed questionnaires in the fall of 1971. In
five of the schools, the questionnaires were administered to the entire student
body, and it was possible to match adolescents with their best school friends on
the basis of self-generated identification numbers. Except for general data on
the overall relationship between marijuana use and the use of other illicit drugs,
the findings presented are based on the subsample of matched student-friend dyads.

FINDINGS

1. Marijuana users whose friends used drugs, particularly illicit drugs other
than marijuana, were more likely to use those other illicit drugs than adolescents
whose friends did not use drugs (p. 121).

2. Adolescents were least likely to use drugs other than marijuana, not when
their best school friend used none of the illicit drugs, but when their best
friend used cannabis only (p. 121).

3. Adolescents who used marijuana but whose friends did not use illicit drugs were almost as likely to be involved in other illegal drug use as those whose friends used drugs other than marijuana (p. 121).

4. Adolescents who were involved in drug trafficking were more likely to have friends who used illicit drugs, whether determined by the adolescent's own perception or by friends' self-reported behavior, than were adolescents not involved with drug trafficking (p. 124).

5. At each level of involvement in illicit drug marketing, the frequency of marijuana use was related to self-reported friends' drug use as well as to the perception that friends used other illicit drugs (p. 124).

6. Marijuana use was strongly related to the use of other illicit drugs. Furthermore, the greater the frequency of marijuana use, the more likely that the adolescent had used each of the classes of other illicit drugs (pills, psychedelics, and opiates) (pp. 120-121).

CONCLUSION

Findings of this study partially support the subcultural theory of drug escalation of Goode and Johnson. Marijuana users whose friends used illicit drugs, particularly drugs other than marijuana, were more likely to use these drugs themselves than adolescents whose friends did not use such drugs. Furthermore, marijuana users who were involved in drug dealing most frequently had friends reporting other illicit drug use, and they themselves used drugs other than marijuana. But even when friends' illicit drug use and illegal marketing are controlled, the frequency of marijuana use was still independently related to the use of other drugs. The policy implications of these findings seem to indicate that legalization of marijuana would not prevent drug use, although it would reduce youth's use of other illicit drugs and involvement in illicit dealing.

AN: 174
AU: Single, E.W.; Kandel, D.B.; Faust, R.
TI: Patterns of multiple drug use in high school
SO: Journal of Health and Social Behavior, 15:344-357, 1974
IN: New York State Department of Mental Hygiene, and School of Public Health,
       Columbia University, New York, New York
RF: 41

SUMMARY TABLE

DRUG: multidrug
TYPE: high school students
NUMBER: 8,206
SEX: male and female
AGE: high school
ETHNICITY: black; white
LOCATION: New York State
METHODOLOGY: cross-sectional, correlational survey
INSTRUMENT(S):   questionnaire
CONDUCTED: 1971

PURPOSE

In order to examine inter-relationships in patterns of drug use among adolescents,
especially as regards marijuana and heroin, and to assess through scalogram
analysis whether drug use follows a unidimensional model, the researchers
conducted a large-scale investigation of drug use by high school students. The
data were based on a multiphasic representative sample of adolescents in New York
State high schools. The sample was drawn from 18 schools according to a two-stage
procedure involving the selection of (1) a sample of high schools; and (2) a
sample of students clustered by homerooms and stratified to represent the
different grades within each school.

FINDINGS

1. The most frequently used illicit drugs by high school students were marijuana
(28%) and hashish (21%), while amphetamines (14%) and barbiturates (12%) followed
next in popularity; about 8% of the students reported use of LSD or other
psychedelics, 4% cocaine, and 3% heroin. Two-thirds of the students smoked
cigarettes, or drank hard liquor, beer, or wine (p. 346).

2. The majority (70%) of students who used illicit drugs were multiple drug users
(p. 346).

3. Relative to other drug users, marijuana users were less likely to be users of
other illicit drugs (p. 346).

4. The overwhelming majority of illicit drug users had used beer or wine (94%),
hard liquor (90%), or tobacco (89%) (p. 346).

5. The users of any drug, whether legal or illegal, were more likely than
nonusers to use any other drug (p. 346).

6. Of legal drugs, tobacco showed the highest association with the use of the illicit drugs (p. 346).

7. Correlations between drugs used by high school students were generally higher between pairs of drugs which were similar in being legal or illegal; also, correlations between legal drugs and illegal drugs were lower than those between illegal drugs (p. 346).

8. A significant proportion of the adolescents who had used marijuana 60 or more times had used other drugs, and, conversely, most students who had used other drugs had also used marijuana. Few students who had used marijuana only once or twice reported the use of other illicit drugs (p. 349).

9. Daily drinking of hard liquor increased in direct proportion to the frequency of current marijuana use (p. 349).

10. If there is any progression in drug use, the first drug in the process is not marijuana, but beer/wine, or liquor, or tobacco (p. 354).

11. Blacks were more likely to use heroin than whites (7% vs 2%) and less likely to use psychedelics (3% vs 11%) (p. 354).

12. If drug use is taken to include both legal and illegal drugs, then 10% of the students were nonusers, 35% had used legal but no illegal drugs, 11% had used marijuana or hashish and legal drugs, but no other illegal drugs, and 19% had used legal and illegal drugs (p. 355).

CONCLUSION

The use of any drug, legal or illegal, was positively correlated with the use of any other drug. Illicit drug use rarely took place without marijuana use. The heavy marijuana users did not reduce their use of alcohol, hence it is doubtful whether legalizing marijuana would reduce the rates of alcohol use. Adolescent drug use tended to be cumulative; it began not with marijuana but with legal substances such as alcohol and tobacco. Persons who used higher ranking drugs had also used all lower ranking drugs. Concern with adolescent drug use should not be limited to illicit drugs only, but should also include the substances socially accepted by adults.

AN: 175
AU: Smith, G.M.; Fogg, C.P.
TI: Teenage drug use: A search for causes and consequenses
SO: In: Lettieri, D., ed. Predicting Adolescent Drug Abuse: A Review of
     Issues, Methods and Correlates (National Institute on Drug Abuse, Research
     Issues Series 11). Washington, D.C.: Government Printing Office, 1975. pp.
     279-282.
IN: Harvard Medical School, and Massachusetts General Hospital, Boston,
     Massachusetts
RF: 6

SUMMARY TABLE

DRUG: multidrug
TYPE: junior and senior high school students
NUMBER: 542
SEX: male; female
AGE: junior and senior high school
ETHNICITY: white
LOCATION: Boston, Massachusetts
METHODOLOGY: longitudinal cohort survey
INSTRUMENT(S):   questionnaire
CONDUCTED: 1969-1973

PURPOSE

In order to determine the relationship between early nondrug measures (grade-point
average, cigarette smoking, attitudes toward cigarette smoking, and personality)
and later use of illicit drugs, 542 students were selected from one of six
suburban Boston school systems participating in a larger study. The respondents
were 7th and 8th graders in Year 1 of the study and 11th and 12th graders in Year
5. The results reported were concerned with the predictive relationship between
the nondrug variables measured in Year 1 and drug use reported in Year 5.

FINDINGS

1. In 1973, of 542 students, 104 reported use of one of the following classes of
"hard" drugs at least once: opiates, hallucinogens, stimulants, and depressants;
216 reported use of marijuana but not "hard" drugs; and 222 said they had never
used any illicit drug (p. 279).

2. In comparison with users, nonusers of any illicit drug scored high on
grade-point average, low on cigarette smoking, high on each of seven measures of
negative attitudes toward smoking, low on the self-report measure of
"rebelliousness," high on each of the other seven personality questionnaire
measures (hardworking, ambitious, self-reliant, feels capable, feels accepted,
feels confident academically, likes school), high on peer ratings of "obedience,"
"works hard," "orderly," and low on peer ratings of "untrustworthy," "sociable,"
and "impulsive" (p. 280).

CONCLUSION

Membership in teenage groups, classified by self-report drug use, was
significantly predicted from nondrug variables measured four years prior to
assessment of drug use. The significant predictors were grade-point average,
cigarette smoking, attitudes toward cigaretts smoking, and several aspects of
personality.

AN: 176
AU: Smith, G.M.; Fogg, C.P.
TI: Psychological predictors of early use, late use, and nonuse of marijuana
     among teenage students
SO: In: Kandel, D.B., ed. Longitudinal Research on Drug Use: Empirical
     Findings and Methodological Issues. Washington, D.C.: Hemisphere Publishing
     Corp., 1978. pp. 101-113.
IN: Harvard Medical School, and Massachusetts General Hospital, Boston,
     Massachusetts
RF: 24

SUMMARY TABLE

DRUG: marijuana
TYPE: junior and senior high school students
NUMBER: 651
SEX: male; female
AGE: junior and senior high school
ETHNICITY: white
LOCATION: Boston, Massachusetts
METHODOLOGY: longitudinal cohort survey
INSTRUMENT(S): questionnaire
CONDUCTED: 1969-1973

PURPOSE

This study addressed the following questions: Which preuse psychosocial variables
differentiate among three groups of students, "early users" of marijuana, "late
users," and "nonusers"? And how successfully? The data were obtained from a
five-year longitudinal study of nine cohorts from six participating school
systems. Analysis attempted to predict the precocity of marijuana use in a sample
of 651 students. They were 7th or 8th graders in 1969 and 11th or 12th graders in
1973. All reported to be nonusers of marijuana in 1969. The comparisons were
made among junior high school initiates ("early users"), high schol initiates
("late users"), and students who remained nonusers through the five-year period of
the study.

OPERATIONAL DEFINITIONS

Early users: students who initiated marijuana use in 9th grade or earlier.

Late users: students who initiated marijuana use in 10th grade or later.

Nonusers: students who remained nonusers of marijuana thoughout the five years of
the study.

FINDINGS

1. Early users of marijuana were more emotional than late users or nonusers
(p. 104).

2. For both sexes, nonusers were rated as significantly less sociable than either late users or early users (p. 104).

3. Rebelliousness, poor academic performance, cigarette smoking, and favorable attitudes toward cigarette smoking distinguished among (1) nonusers of marijuana who were destined to begin marijuana use before entering high school, (2) nonusers who would begin use after entering high school, and (3) students who would remain nonusers (p. 112).

CONCLUSION

Precocity of marijuana use can be predicted from psychosocial variables that are similar to those that predict the degree of subsequent drug involvement. Earliest use of marijuana was associated with low scores on preuse measures of personal competence, social responsibility, and academic performance, and with high scores on preuse measures of emotionality, cigarette smoking, and favorable attitudes toward cigarette smoking.

AN: 177
AU: Soskin, W.F.; Stein, K.B.; Korchin, S.J.
TI: Project Community: Therapeutic Explorations with Adolescents
SO: Final Report, NIDA Grant, R01DA00066, 1976. 74 pp.
IN: University of California, Berkeley
RF: 17

SUMMARY TABLE

DRUG: multidrug
TYPE: high school students
NUMBER: 57 first year; 39 second year; 29 third year; 57 controls
SEX: male (37%); female (63%)
AGE: 14-18 years (mean: 16 years)
ETHNICITY: predominantly white
LOCATION: Berkeley, California
METHODOLOGY: experimental research
INSTRUMENT(S):   questionnaires; tests; scales; inventories
CONDUCTED: 1971-1974

PURPOSE

Project Community was a study designed to answer the following questions: What
are the personality and behavioral characteristics of drug-using adolescents?
Which needs of these adolescents are not met by existing social institutions?
What effect will a supportive institution and an educational program focused on
self-understanding have on the characteristics of adolescents and on their drug
use? To answer these questions, an experimental therapeutic-educational
after-school program for adolescents was created. Analysis was made of the
program's impact on personality and behavioral change and of the characteristics
of the students who were attracted to the program. A project house located near
the Berkeley campus served as the physical space for the experiment. In-school
programs were conducted at various school sites. Participants were tested when
they entered the program in the fall; those who remained until June and who
completed a second questionnaire constituted the subjects for the study. Two
replications (in 1972-1973 and 1973-1974) were carried out after the original
study (1971-1972). Data collection instruments included well-established as well
as newly developed tests, scales, and inventories. Data in the following areas
were generated: parent and adult relations, self- and ideal self-concept, peer
relations, drug use and antisocial behavior, school attitude, activity interest,
biographical information, and other data. Only results related to drug use are
listed in the Findings.

OPERATIONAL DEFINITIONS

Project Community after-school program: a set of experiences designed to increase
self-understanding, contribute to a sense of competence, provide opportunities for
informal contacts with young adults, promote exploration of values, provide group
emotional support, and create a sense of membership in a small group. Project
Community in-school program: a program with some of the experiences of the
after-school program integrated into the normal school curriculum and conducted
during school time.

FINDINGS

1. In the original study conducted in a neighborhood project house, drug use generally became stable, with the heaviest marijuana users tending to decrease their use (p. 3).

2. Drug use in the in-house Project Community programs stabilized, while it increased for the controls (p. 4).

3. A comparison of the amount of drug use between the Project Community members and the more conventional controls in three different school settings--urban, suburban, and private residential--found differences in the urban and suburban samples, but not in the private school sample (p. 4).

4. Change in marijuana use among Project Community members viewed from the perspective of past, present, and future use revealed a decrease in heavier use (p. 4).

5. Marijuana users in Project Community described themselves as more dominant, more competent in relating to the opposite sex, and more self-accepting at the end of the school year than at the beginning (p. 35).

6. After participation in Project Community, subjects who used marijuana became more negative towards their parents, particularly the father, whereas nonusers moved toward a more positive attitude towards both parents (p. 36).

7. Participants in Project Community who did not use marijuana came to have greater agreement with parental attitudes and values; they also moved towards more enjoyment of family activities (p. 36).

8. Although the nonusing marijuana participants in Project Community became more negative towards the criminal justice system and towards school, they increased their belief in democratic social change and became less sympathetic with revolution and rebellion (p. 34).

CONCLUSION

A significant number of high school adolescents are dissatisfied with various American social institutions and these youth use drugs as a means of coping with personal frustrations. Growth-inducing programs such as those designed for Project Community can attract and influence adolescents toward positive changes in personality and behavior. Preliminary experimentation has indicated that Project Community can be successfully operated as an in-school program. Such a program integrated into the school curriculum increases the number of students that can be reached, and can be economically feasible.

AN: 178
AU: Wingard, J.A.; Huba, G.J.; Bentler, P.M.
TI: The relationship of personality structure to patterns of adolescent substance
     use
SO: Multivariate Behavioral Research, 14:131-143, 1979
IN: Department of Psychology, University of California, Los Angeles
RF: 38

SUMMARY TABLE

DRUG: multidrug
TYPE: junior high school students
NUMBER: 1,634
SEX: male (35.6%); female (64.4%)
AGE: 13.4 years (average)
ETHNICITY: white (56.4%); Spanish (14.8%); black (23.6%); Asian (5.2%)
LOCATION: Los Angeles, California
METHODOLOGY: cross-sectional, correlational survey
INSTRUMENT(S):   questionnaire; Bentler Psychological Inventory
CONDUCTED: not specified

PURPOSE

Many recent studies have concluded that a relationship exists between the
personality traits of an individual and the likelihood of his being a user or
nonuser of drugs. However, few studies have indicated the extent to which these
two areas overlap. To determine the degree of overlap, data were collected from
1,634 students in eleven junior high schools in metropolitan Los Angeles,
California, on current use patterns of 13 substances and on 26 dimensions of
personality, interests, and attitudes.

FINDINGS

1. The substance category with the greatest use rate was beer, followed in
decreasing order by wine, cigarettes, liquor, marijuana, drug store medicines,
inhalants, hashish, amphetamines, tranquilizers, cocaine, hallucinogens, and
heroin (pp. 133-134).

2. Less than 10% of the students reported having experience with drugs that
involve severe legal penalties for possession (i.e., cocaine, barbituates, heroin,
hallucinogens, and amphetamines) (p. 134).

3. The overall association between the variables in the substance use domain and
those in the personality domain was highly significant (p. 136).

4. There was a positive relationship between general substance use in adolescence
and a personality marked by liberalism, nonabidance with the law, leadership,
extroversion, and lack of diligence or deliberateness (p. 139).

5. Among the students studied, the general overlap between drug use and
personality domains was moderately high; however, the ability of personality to
account for variations in substance use was relatively low (p. 140).

CONCLUSION

A general rate of substance use was found to be related to a diversified group of personality traits and attitudes rather than to any one specific personality trait. This conclusion can be interpreted in terms of an interactionist-socialization theory. This view would posit that interaction with nontraditional socialization agents will facilitate personality development along nonconventional, although not necessarily pathological, lines. Although this could possibly include further drug-involved behavior and peer associations, it appears that this differentiation had not yet occurred by the ninth grade, when this study was conducted.

VIII. DRUG USE AMONG COLLEGE STUDENTS AND YOUNG ADULTS

AN: 179
AU: Clayton, R.R.; Voss, H.L.
TI: Shacking up: Cohabitation in the 1970s
SO: Journal of Marriage and the Family, 39:273-283, 1977
IN: Department of Sociology, University of Kentucky, Lexington, Kentucky
RF: 11

SUMMARY TABLE

DRUG: multidrug
TYPE: nationwide sample of young men
NUMBER: 2,510
SEX: male
AGE: 20-30 years
ETHNICITY: white (84%); black (12%); other (4%)
LOCATION: United States (cross-sectional)
METHODOLOGY: cross-sectional survey
INSTRUMENT(S):   interview
CONDUCTED: 1974-1975

PURPOSE

In order to study the alternative lifestyle of cohabitation (nonmarital,
heterosexual living arrangements), data obtained from a nationwide random sample
of 2,510 young men born in the years 1944 through 1954 were analyzed to determine
current and lifetime prevalence of cohabitation as well as some correlates of
cohabitation, including nonmedical use of drugs. Only results related to drug use
are reported in the findings.

FINDINGS

1. There were only minimal differences between young men who had and those who
had not cohabited in their use of tobacco and alcohol (p. 281).

2. Young men who had ever cohabited were more likely than those who had not to
have ever used marijuana, psychedelics, stimulants, sedatives, heroin, opiates, or
cocaine (p. 281).

3. Young men who were cohabiting at the time of the study were more likely to use
illicit drugs than those who were married, living independently, or with parents.
Illicit drug use was lowest among currently married men (p. 281).

4. Young men who had ever cohabited or were currently cohabiting were more likely
to be currently using illicit drugs and to have a heavier or more extensive use of
these drugs than men who had never cohabited or who were not presently cohabiting
(p. 281).

CONCLUSION

Cohabitation seems to be correlated to other types of behavior that are defined as
unconventional, such as use of illicit drugs, study of eastern religion or
philosophy, and early sexual intercourse. Drug use was more likely among men who

had cohabited than among those who had not. Of the 2,510 young men studied in this nationwide random sample, 18% had cohabited for six months or more, but 65% had done so with only one partner. Furthermore, at the time of the interviews, only 5% of the men were cohabiting, suggesting that most young men in the United States are conventional in terms of serious heterosexual relationships.

AN: 180
AU: Clayton, R.R.; Voss, H.L.
TI: Young Men and Drugs in Manhattan: A Causal Analysis
SO: National Institute on Drug Abuse, Research Monograph 39. Washington, D.C.:
     Government Printing Office, 1981. 187 pp.
IN: Department of Sociology, University of Kentucky, Lexington, Kentucky
RF: 170

SUMMARY TABLE

DRUG: multidrug
TYPE: young men
NUMBER: 294
SEX: male
AGE: 20-30 years
ETHNICITY: black; white; other
LOCATION: Manhattan, New York
METHODOLOGY: cross-sectional survey
INSTRUMENT(S):   interview
CONDUCTED: 1975

PURPOSE

In 1973, the Special Action Office for Drug Abuse Prevention (SAODAP) funded a
study of drug use in the general population of young men in order to obtain
national estimates of incidence and prevalence for the use of illicit drugs (see
AN 200). Because the national sample would produce too few heroin users to
provide adequate information about the etiology and natural history of heroin use,
a smaller sample of young men living in an area of high drug use was also studied.
The target sample consisted of 540 young men chosen randomly from Selective
Service Boards serving those areas in Manhattan having high rates of opiate users;
the men were born in the years from 1944 to 1954. However, only 294 of these men
could be located for interviews in 1975; it also became apparent that many of
these men were not residents of Manhattan but had simply registered there.
Therefore, the sample was not representative of the population of young men in
Manhattan, although it did provide data on a group of young men which included a
significant percentage of heroin users who were not in treatment or incarcerated.
Data from the Manhattan sample were analyzed with regards to lifetime prevalence
and correlates, incidence and the drug epidemic, and multiple drug use. A
composite index of illicit drug use was constructed on the basis of seven national
data sets, with weights for each drug established according to extent of use;
this index was then used to analyze data from the Manhattan and national samples.
Finally, various predictors of illicit drug use were examined, and the technique
of path analysis was used to test causal models of illicit drug use.

FINDINGS

1. In the national sample and the Manhattan sample of young men, lifetime
prevalence rates for use of nine drugs were comparable except for these sizable
differences: marijuana (55% in national sample; 75% in Manhattan sample), heroin
(6%; 26%), and cocaine (14%; 37%) (p. xiii).

2. In the national and the Manhattan samples of young men, blacks were more likely than whites or other ethnic groups to have used marijuana, heroin, and cocaine. In the Manhattan sample, the lifetime prevalence of use of these drugs for blacks, whites, and others was: marijuana, 82%, 74%, and 53%; heroin, 39%, 11%, and 21%; and cocaine, 56%, 26%, and 30% (p. xiii).

3. About 60% of the black high school dropouts in the Manhattan sample of young men had used heroin, but only 1 of the 11 black college graduates had done so (p. xiii).

4. For young white men in the Manhattan sample, the percentage of drug users increased from the older to the younger age groups for psychedelics, sedatives, and, to a lesser extent, cocaine. However, among blacks there was a U-shaped curve with the percentages of illicit drug users higher in the two middle age groups (men born between 1947 and 1949 and between 1950 and 1952) than in the oldest (men born between 1944 and 1946) and the youngest (men born between 1953 and 1954) (p. 23).

5. In Manhattan, tobacco and heroin were used less frequently by the young men with more education. There were no consistent patterns associated with educational level for other drugs, but (except for minimal differences for psychedelics and stimulants) the lowest percentages were found among college graduates (p. 73).

6. When illicit drug use was correlated with the prestige level of father's occupation ranked from 1 (low) to 4 (high), among whites the lowest percentages of users were found in category 1 (except for users of heroin and opiates) and the higher percentages occurred in categories 2 and 3. For blacks, the highest percentages of marijuana, psychedelics, opiates, and cocaine users were found in category 3, and the highest levels of stimulant and sedative users were found in category 4. Only one-third of the black men who did not describe their father's occupation or whose father had a low prestige job used heroin, whereas almost one-half of the men in the other prestige categories had tried it (pp. 16-17).

7. There appeared to be an inverse relationship between lifetime prevalence of illicit drug use and occupational prestige of current employment for young men in Manhattan (p. 16).

8. For young white men in Manhattan, the highest percentage of lifetime prevalence for every drug (except heroin) was found among men who were coupled (cohabiting); the highest percentage of heroin users still lived with their parents. The lowest percentages of drug users among white males were found among married men. For blacks, the highest percentage of use for each drug was found among men who were coupled; men who lived independently ranked second in the use of psychedelics and opiates, while men who were married ranked second in the use of marijuana and stimulants (p. 20).

9. Among young white men in Manhattan, the percentages of those who had ever used marijuana, stimulants, and sedatives were highest among the unemployed, while the percentages of the use of psychedelics, heroin, opiates, and cocaine were higher among those who were students or worked part-time. For blacks, the highest prevalence of the use of sedatives, heroin, opiates, and cocaine was found among the unemployed, but the highest percentage of marijuana users were employed full-time (pp. 20-23).

10. A higher proportion of men in the younger age groups in the Manhattan sample had used opiates by the age of 20 than the older men; the percentages of use by age 20 were as follows: for men born between 1944 and 1946, 27%; between 1947 and 1949, 35%; between 1950 and 1952, 40%; and between 1953 and 1954, 35%. The age at first use of opiates, as well as of marijuana, was lower in the younger cohorts, suggesting an epidemic of drug use in Manhattan in the late 1960s and early 1970s (pp. xiii-xiv).

11. The annual prevalence of heroin-opiate use reached a peak of 20% among young men in Manhattan in 1970. This contrasts with findings from the national sample of young men that annual prevalence of heroin never exceeded 2% and that annual prevalence of opiates other than heroin reached 10% in only one year, 1974 (p. xiv).

12. There was more regular daily use of opiates by young men in Manhattan in 1968 than in 1973; 59% of opiate users reported daily or more frequent use in 1968 compared to 37% in 1973, while 20% reported opiate use once or twice a month or less in 1968 compared to 41% in 1973 (p. xiv).

13. Almost two-fifths of the young men from Manhattan who did not use marijuana reported that more than a few of their friends currently used marijuana, and almost half of the men who had used marijuana most frequently reported that they had friends who were currently using cocaine (p. xiv).

14. Marijuana seemed to be the key gateway drug for understanding multiple drug use. Of the young men from Manhattan who used marijuana, 37% had also used psychedelics and 49% had also used cocaine, while none of the nonusers of marijuana had used either drug. The figures for the use of other drugs by marijuana users and nonusers, respectively, are as follows: stimulants, 36%, 4%; sedatives, 35%, 3%; heroin, 34%, 1%; opiates, 36%, 5% (pp. xiv, 50).

15. The young men in the Manhattan sample who used marijuana were more likely to have used heroin and cocaine than their national counterparts; 34% reported use of heroin and 49% used cocaine, compared to 11% and 25%, respectively, in the national sample (p. xiv).

16. Heroin use was strongly correlated with the extent of marijuana use. In the national sample, only 1 young man who had not used marijuana had used heroin, while 33% of those who had used marijuana 1,000 times or more had done so. In the Manhattan sample, the percentage of heroin users ranged from 1% among nonusers of marijuana to 56% among those who used marijuana 1,000 times or more (pp. xiv-xv).

17. On a composite index of illicit drug use, the overall mean for young men in the Manhattan sample was 470 compared to 105 for the national sample; in Manhattan, the mean was 223 for whites and 737 for blacks (p. xv).

18. In the Manhattan sample, 33% of the young men had sold drugs compared to 17% of the national sample (p. xv).

19. In the Manhattan sample, 10% of the young men had sold heroin as compared to 2% in the national sample. Among the Manhattan drug sellers, 24% had sold heroin as a favor, 27% had sold heroin to purchase their own supply, and 28% had sold heroin for profit (p. xv).

20. Using path analysis to test causal models of illicit drug use, it was determined that selling drugs was the key variable in explaining illicit drug use (p. xv).

CONCLUSION

Young men in Manhattan reported higher percentages of illicit drug use than young men interviewed in a national study, particularly for the use of marijuana, heroin, and cocaine; drug use was greater among blacks than whites in both samples. In general, overlooking some differences observed in patterns for blacks and whites, a higher lifetime prevalence of illicit drug use was correlated with the younger birth cohorts (those men born in the early 1950s), with low prestige occupations, and with cohabitation (living with a woman without legal marriage). Heroin was used more frequently by both black and white men with lower educational attainment levels and by unemployed blacks. The findings indicate an epidemic of drug use in Manhattan, particularly of heroin and opiates, which peaked in 1970. Marijuana was pinpointed as a key gateway drug for understanding multiple drug use, since marijuana users were much more likely to have used all other drugs than nonusers. Scores on a composite index of illicit drug use revealed a higher overall mean for blacks than for whites in Manhattan. Various causal models of illicit drug use were tested through path analysis using data from this study; different models were developed for blacks and whites, but the key variable in the explanation of illicit drug use for both groups was found to be involvement in drug sales.

AN: 181
AU: Clayton, R.R.; Voss, H.L.
TI: Smoking and health, marijuana and use of other illicit drugs: Causal
       relationships
SO: Paper presented to the National Institute on Drug Abuse National Advisory
       Council, Bethesda, MD, January 1982. 51 pp.
IN: Department of Sociology, University of Kentucky, Lexington, Kentucky
RF: 31

SUMMARY TABLE

DRUG: marijuana; heroin; cocaine
TYPE: young men; young men (Manhattan); young adults; veterans
NUMBER: 2,406; 223; 413; 2,044
SEX: male and female
AGE: 18-30 years
ETHNICITY: white; black
LOCATION: United States (cross-sectional)
METHODOLOGY: statistical analysis
INSTRUMENT(S):   interview; questionnaire
CONDUCTED: 1981

PURPOSE

The stepping-stone hypothesis (the idea that marijuana use is usually related to
use of other illicit drugs, such as heroin and cocaine) has been discarded since
its rejection by the National Commission on Marihuana and Drug Abuse in 1973.
However, the relationship between cigarette smoking and lung cancer, which is
generally accepted by the public, is based on the same reasoning as the
stepping-stone hypothesis, namely (a) evidence that the variables are
statistically associated, (b) evidence that the causal variable is antecedent to
the effect variables, and (c) evidence that the relationship is not spurious. In
order to test the stepping-stone hypothesis for marijuana use, these three
criteria were examined using data from four studies: (1) Young Men and Drugs (see
AN 200), a nationwide sample of 2,510 young men between ages 20 and 30; (2) Young
Men and Drugs in Manhattan (see AN 180), a sample of 294 young men between ages 20
and 30 from high drug-using areas in Manhattan; (3) Vietnam Drug User Returns,
two studies of 451 returning Vietnam veterans and 494 returning veterans
classified as drug users; and (4) the 1979 NIDA National Survey, a nationwide
sample which included 2,044 young adults between ages 18 and 25. For the first
three samples, only results for whites and blacks were analyzed.

FINDINGS

1. There was a strong correlation between use of marijuana and use of heroin and
cocaine in the four sets of data examined; the probability of the use of heroin
and cocaine increased linearly with the extent of the use of marijuana regardless
of sex or race for all the samples. In the nationwide sample of young men, almost
one-third of the men who had used marijuana 1,000 times or more reported use of
heroin, and almost three out of four had used cocaine. In the Manhattan sample,
half of the men who had used marijuana 1,000 times or more had used heroin and
over 80% had used cocaine. Three-fourths of the white Vietnam veterans and close
to nine-tenths of the blacks who had used marijuana 25 or more times prior to

Vietnam reported heroin use while in Vietnam. Finally, for the nationwide sample of young adults, the percentage of persons reporting use of cocaine increased linearly in association with the extent of marijuana use (pp. 9-14).

2. For the vast majority of persons who used the drugs, the onset of marijuana use occurred prior to the use of either heroin or cocaine. The percentages of persons reporting marijuana use prior to the use of heroin and cocaine were as follows in the various studies: young men/national sample, 90%--heroin, 96%--cocaine; young men/Manhattan sample, 79%--heroin, 92%--cocaine; national sample of young adults, 95%--heroin, 94%--cocaine (pp. 13, 15).

3. When data from the nationwide survey of young men were used to compute the mean number of years between onset of marijuana use and first use of heroin, it was found that the first use of marijuana for whites occurred 3.4 years prior to first use of heroin, and marijuana was used on an average of 348 separate occasions before initial heroin use. The comparable figures for blacks were 3.23 years and 219 occasions of use. The figures for first use of marijuana and first use of cocaine were 3.62 years and 326 separate occasions for whites, and 3.55 years and 302 separate occasions for blacks. The average number of occasions of marijuana use for young men who had tried marijuana but not heroin were 273 for whites and 437 for blacks, while the figures for those who had used marijuana but not cocaine were 283 for whites and 534 for blacks (pp. 16-18).

4. The relationships between marijuana/heroin and marijuana/cocaine were not spurious in the nationwide sample of young men when tested for thirteen antecedent variables (early deviance, social controls at age 16, peer behavior at age 16, tobacco use, extent of alcohol use, birthyear, father's education, mother's education, father's drinking pattern, mother's drinking pattern, military service, major in college, and religion). Similarly, lack of spuriousness was also found in the Manhattan sample of young men and in the sample of Vietnam veterans (although somewhat different antecedent variables were used in each study) (pp. 20-22).

5. Given the three criteria used to determine causality (strong association between variables, causal variables antecedent to effect variables, and evidence that the relationship was not spurious), it was determined that marijuana use was a cause of the use of other illicit drugs such as heroin and cocaine (p. 25).

6. Involvement in the drug subculture as measured by involvement in drug sales was an intervening variable between marijuana use and heroin use, as demonstrated by Johnson in his study of New York college students. Prevalence of heroin use was extensive only when selling was combined with at least weekly marijuana use. Buying and selling drugs intervened between marijuana use and the use of other drugs (pp. 28-31).

CONCLUSION

Since the relationship between marijuana use and use of other illict drugs fulfills the three criteria of causality defined by this study, marijuana use is a cause of the use of other illicit drugs, such as heroin and cocaine. The Marihuana Commission's rejection of the stepping-stone hypothesis was based partly on errors in interpretation of data and partly on a political climate in which it was feared that adoption of the hypothesis would lead to severely repressive policies regarding marijuana. Once having accepted the stepping-stone hypothesis as correct, various public policies regarding marijuana use can be reexamined and

reassessed. Prohibition seems impractical and politically unfeasible.
Decriminalization has been seen as attractive because it reduces governmental
costs and does not lead to greater use of marijuana by nonusers. However, since
the source of the drug remains illegal, decriminalization does not change a key
reason that marijuana use leads to the use of other illicit drugs--involvement in
drug sales. Legalization would remove this contact with criminal activity,
increase tax revenues, regularize the product, and monitor access. But since
marijuana use is similar to cigarette smoking in its effects on health,
legalization would be inconsistent with the government's responsibility to protect
the general welfare and would lead to serious long-term health effects and social
costs. The only feasible policy option regarding marijuana is prevention, as has
been used in the campaign against cigarette smoking. This effort requires a
national commitment, a major financial investment, continuing basic research on
the epidemiology and etiology of drug use, the development of innovative treatment
approaches, and evaluation of prevention strategies.

AN: 182
AU: Davidson, S.T.;   Mellinger, G.D.;   Manheimer, D.I.
TI: Changing patterns of drug use among university males
SO: Addictive Diseases: An International Journal, 3:215-234, 1977
IN: Institute for Research in Social Behavior, Oakland, California
RF: 12

SUMMARY TABLE

DRUG: multidrug
TYPE: college students
NUMBER: 960
SEX: male
AGE: college/university
ETHNICITY: white (82%); Asian (12%)
LOCATION: Berkeley, California
METHODOLOGY: longitudinal survey
INSTRUMENT(S):   interview; questionnaire
CONDUCTED: 1970; 1973

PURPOSE

Is the phenomenon of youthful drug use transitory or enduring? In an examination of the extent to which different patterns of drug use were adopted and maintained over time, the investigators surveyed the use of various drugs by a student population at two points in time and the initiation and persistence of use over time. The data were collected first in late 1970 and early 1971 and again in 1973 as a part of a longitudinal study of the life styles and values of male entering freshman and graduating seniors at the University of California, Berkeley. A combination of personal interview and self-administered questionnaire was used for the initial data collection phase. A mail questionnaire was used for the second wave of data collection and was completed by 87% of the 1970 respondents (N=960).

FINDINGS

1. The majority of students who reported drug use in 1970 had used drugs before entering college (p. 220).

2. Initiation to drug use after arriving at the university generally occurred during the first year of college (p. 220).

3. By spring 1973, three-quarters of the students had used marijuana at least once, one-third had used psychedelics and stimulants, one-fifth had tried cocaine, one-seventh had tried sedatives and opium, less than a tenth had used inhalants and opiates other than opium and heroin, and less than 2% had tried heroin (pp. 220-221).

4. Between fall 1970 and spring 1973, the significant increases in drug use among college students were marijuana, 18%; psychedelics, 15%; stimulants, 17%; and cocaine, 16% (p. 221).

5. In general, the prevalence of use of each drug class among college students in 1973 was quite similar to the prevalence of use in 1970 (p. 222).

6. The proportions of students who persisted in their use of each of the drug classes ranged from four-fifths of the 1970 recent users of marijuana to none of the two 1970 users of heroin (p. 223).

7. Use of marijuana among college students was widespread and persistent in both 1970 and 1973 (p. 223).

8. In the years 1970 and 1973, the use of drugs other than marijuana by college students was very infrequent; frequency of drug use was less in 1973 than in 1970, particularly among recent users of psychedelics (p. 225).

9. The frequency of use among recent users of marijuana showed little change between 1970 and 1973: in both years one-quarter of the recent users were using it on the average of twice a week or more. Marijuana was the only drug to be used on the average of once a week or more (p. 225).

10. In 1970, a large marjority of students in the sample had either never used drugs or had used only marijuana; by 1973, 43% had at some time used an illicit drug in addition to marijuana and 16% had used three or more drugs in addition to marijuana (p. 225).

11. Although there was a 15% increase in ever use by college students of drugs other than marijuana, the percentages of recent multiple drug use in 1970 and 1973 were fairly similar; in fall 1970, 19%, and in spring 1973, 22% (p. 225).

12. Over half (56%) of the students who never used drugs in 1970 were still nonusers in 1973 (p. 227).

13. Fifty-five percent of the marijuana only users and 57% of the multiple drug users in 1970 were in the same category of use in 1973 (p. 227).

14. Of those students who had not recently used any drugs in 1970, 68% were in the same category of nonrecent use in 1973 (p. 227).

15. Use of drugs among college students was more persistent than nonuse of drugs between 1970 and 1973 (p. 227).

16. The level of drug use among college students in 1973 was highly related to the level of use in 1970 (p. 227).

17. Although multiple drug users did not use drugs other than marijuana very frequently, they were likely to use marijuana quite frequently (p. 228).

18. Among the recent multiple drug users in 1973, 62% used marijuana on the average of more than once a week, whereas 75% of the recent users of marijuana only used the drug less than once a week or not at all in the past two months (p. 228).

CONCLUSION

This research on drug use among college men provided a test of some of the conclusions of the National Commission on Marihuana and Drug Abuse. The

Commission concluded that "despite the increasing incidence of drug use, there is no indication that higher proportions of these ever users will escalate to higher frequency and intensities of drug use." In this sample, the frequency of use of most drugs decreased over the study period, particularly psychedelic use. Prevalence of recent drug use was similar in both years (1970 and 1973), since as many men had reduced or stopped drug use as had begun use during the two and one-half year interval. However, other Commission conclusions were only partly supported by this report's findings. For instance, the Commission concluded that most students confine their use to one type of drug and that most marijuana users do not progress to multiple drug use. Findings of this study showed that by 1973, 43% of the students had used an illicit drug other than marijuana. But prevalence data indicated that most users confined their use to one drug, marijuana. Whether students progress from marijuana to other drugs partly depends on the definition of "progression."

```
AN:  183
AU:  Dodge, D.L.
TI:  Survey of students and drugs at the University of Notre Dame:  An overview
SO:  Journal of the American College Health Association, 25:102-108, 1976
IN:  Department of Sociology and Anthropology, University of Notre Dame, Notre
     Dame, Indiana
RF:  15
```

SUMMARY TABLE

```
DRUG:          multidrug
TYPE:          college students
NUMBER:        134
SEX:           male
AGE:           college/university
ETHNICITY:     not specified
LOCATION:      Notre Dame, Indiana
METHODOLOGY:   cross-sectional survey
INSTRUMENT(S): questionnaire
CONDUCTED:     1972
```

PURPOSE

Previous studies at Catholic universities found that drug use was lower than at
other types of universities. The University of Notre Dame, however, has a student
population whose demographic characteristics differ from those at other Catholic
universities studied. A survey about drug use on the campus of Notre Dame
contained questions regarding student perceptions of drug use by college students,
student attitudes toward drug users, student beliefs about the consequences of
drug use, student assessment of the legal policies regarding marijuana, and
student appraisal of the sources of assistance for drug problems and abuse. A
stratified random sample of 134 students (2.1% of the undergraduate population)
completed questionnaires for analysis.

FINDINGS

1. A slight majority of Notre Dame students (52.5%) perceived most college
students in the United States as using marijuana occasionally rather than
frequently or never (p. 103).

2. Just over two-third (67.9%) of Notre Dame students were quite certain that
most students in the United States at least experimented with marijuana (p. 103).

3. A substantially greater percentage of drug nonusers (63.5%) than users (42.5%)
at Notre Dame did not view college students as frequent users of marijuana
(p. 103).

4. Although users and nonusers of drugs at Notre Dame thought most college
students used marijuana occasionally rather than frequently or never, users were
much more in agreement among themselves (62.5%) than were nonusers (38.4%)
(p. 103).

5. A majority (76.9%) of Notre Dame students did not consider drug use in general a problem on their campus (p. 103).

6. During the six months prior to completion of the questionnaires, Notre Dame students reported marijuana as the drug most frequently used at the university (55.2%), followed by psychedelics (12.9%), amphetamines (12.8%), barbiturates (10.5%), and heroin (1.5%) (p. 103).

7. Drug users at Notre Dame were much more inclined than nonusers to evaluate drug users as creative, sociable, and understanding of themselves and the world about them (p. 104).

8. Nonusers of drugs at Notre Dame tended to agree much more readily than users with the belief that drug users were very likeable people (p. 104).

9. Both users and nonusers of drugs at Notre Dame were more likely to indicate uncertainy or disagreement than agreement with the notions that users were more likeable, creative, sociable, and understanding of selves and the world than nonusers (p. 104).

10. Nonusers (76.9%) and users (95.0%) at Notre Dame alike felt that users "have what it takes to get ahead in the world" (p. 104).

11. The large majority (85.1%) of nonusers and all users of drugs at Notre Dame agreed with the statement that "marijuana users were not different from persons who don't use drugs or occasionally drink alcohol" (p. 104).

12. Notre Dame students did not regard drug users as a category of special persons, to be singled out from others (p. 104).

13. Few (7.7%) nonusers of drugs at Notre Dame saw marijuana as harmless compared with 46.3% of users who did so (p. 104).

14. Two percent of nonusers at Notre Dame as opposed to 31.6% of users believed that marijuana was beneficial (p. 104).

15. While 57.7% of nonusers of drugs at Notre Dame were uncertain regarding the harmlessness of marijuana and 34.6% disagreed, 37.5% and 16.3% of users, respectively, held these perspectives (p. 104).

16. Nearly half (49.0%) of nonusers at Notre Dame believed that marijuana was not beneficial or were uncertain, while 48.3% of users were uncertain whether marijuana was beneficial and 20.3% believed it was not (p. 104).

17. Four main reasons for using marijuana were cited by drug users at Notre Dame: enjoyment (56.9%), experimentation (17.8%), excitement (12.7%), and to relax/unwind (6.3%) (p. 104).

18. The primary reasons given by drug users at Notre Dame for involvement with drugs other than marijuana were as follows: amphetamines--"to help with work" (50%) or experimentation (49%); barbiturates--"to help unwind/relax" (36.4%), experimentation (27.3%), "help with work" (13.5%), or overcome depression (13.5%); psychedelics--enjoyment (44.0%), experimentation (32%), or excitement (24%); heroin--experimentation (100.0%) (p. 105).

19. Nearly four-fifths (79.1%) of respondents at Notre Dame said that they intended to use marijuana in the future; only 7.7% of current nonusers indicated that they intended to use marijuana in the future and only 12.7% of current users intended to stop use (p. 105).

20. There was little consensus, except in the case of heroin, among the respondents at Notre Dame concerning the ability of various drugs to create physical dependence. The respondents were generally certain that marijuana, barbiturates, amphetamines, psychedelics, and heroin, when used on a regular and extended basis, lead to psychological habituation (pp. 105-106).

21. Most (64.2%) students at Notre Dame wanted to legalize marijuana, with 65.7% believing it should have the same legal status as alcohol (p. 106).

22. Drug users were much more likely (78.8%) to favor legalization than nonusers (42.3%) (p. 106).

23. The most preferred sources of assistance in dealing with drug problems among Notre Dame students were the Student Drug Information Center (91.0%), Student Health Services (80.6%), known private physicians or psychiatrists (70.1%), and knowledgeable friends (64.9%) (p. 106).

CONCLUSION

A significant number of students at the University of Notre Dame were involved with drugs. This involvement was restricted primarily to marijuana and only marginally to other drugs excluding alcohol. The use of drugs at Notre Dame was commensurate with the national averages for colleges and universities; marijuana use exceeded the collegiate national averages. There is marked uncertainty and lack of knowledge among Notre Dame students (both users and nonusers) about various aspects of drugs and drug use. Elective courses on drugs developed in the sociology and psychology departments would appear appropriate in dealing with the problem. Distribution of relevant literature on the subject ought to be considered.

AN: 184
AU: Dodge, D.L.
TI: Dimensions of marijuana use in a midwest Catholic university: Subcultural
     considerations
SO: International Journal of the Addictions, 12:971-981, 1977
IN: Department of Sociology and Anthropology, University of Notre Dame, Notre
     Dame, Indiana
RF: 12

SUMMARY TABLE

DRUG: marijuana
TYPE: college students
NUMBER: 134
SEX: male
AGE: college/university
ETHNICITY: not specified
LOCATION: Notre Dame, Indiana
METHODOLOGY: cross-sectional survey
INSTRUMENT(S):   questionnaire
CONDUCTED: 1972

PURPOSE

The various accounts of the college marijuana scene depict it as largely a social
and recreational group activity with a subculture base. The subcultural values
and belief patterns, according to these accounts, differentiate it from the larger
society. The purpose of this research was to test these propositions: Are there
significant differences between college nonusers and college marijuana users? As
students become involved in marijuana use, do they manifest stronger commitment
to the values and beliefs of the drug subculture? The subjects of the study were
students at a private, all-male Roman Catholic university (Notre Dame). A random
sample of 134 students representing 2.1% of the total undergraduate population
completed a drug use questionnaire.

OPERATIONAL DEFINITIONS

Systematic users: those who used marijuana every week or two, primarily on
weekends.

Heavy users: those who used marijuana several times a week or daily.

FINDINGS

1. Fifty-nine percent of the students had "ever used" marijuana, while the
national college norm for the same time period (1972) was 51% (p. 974).

2. Over half (55.2%) of the students at the university used marijuana in the past
6-12 months, while the national college norm was 41% (p. 947).

3. Of the students who used marijuana within the past 6-12 months (55.2%), 62.2% used it every week or two or more frequently (p. 975).

4. There was no association found between marijuana user type (nonuser, systematic user, and heavy user) and year in school, college enrolled in, grade-point average, or residence (p. 975).

5. The Business College contained the highest proportion of systematic and heavy users in comparison with other colleges of the university (p. 976).

6. Off-campus residents had slightly more systematic users, while on campus residents had a greater proportion of heavy users (p. 976).

7. Fifty-five percent of the nonusers had a grade-point average of B or better, while 46% of the systematic users and heavy users had a grade average this high; 77% of the A students were nonusers, while only 8% of them were systematic users and 18% were heavy users (p. 976).

8. Users, unlike nonusers, tended to agree that marijuana use is harmless, beneficial, and does not lead to physical addiction (p. 976).

9. A significant proportion of users, particularly heavy users, were uncertain about the physical and/or psychological ramifications of consistent use (p. 976).

10. An overwhelming majority of the users believed marijuana ought to be legalized; users were much more strongly in favor of legalization than nonusers (pp. 976, 977).

11. The majority of users and nonusers either were uncertain or disagreed with the notion that legalization of marijuana would remedy its perception as a social problem (p. 978).

12. Thirty-two percent of current nonusers planned not to use marijuana; 68% planned at least to experiment with it in the future (p. 978).

13. All systematic users planned to use marijuana on occasion (54%) or perhaps regularly (46%) in the future (p. 978).

14. The vast majority of current heavy users intended to use marijuana at least occasionally (9%), but more likely regularly (91%) in the future (p. 978).

15. Forty-five percent of nonusers believed their friends had attitudes more lenient toward marijuana use than their own attitudes (p. 979).

CONCLUSION

The relatively small number of noticeable differences discerned between systematic users and heavy users provided only weak support for the notion that as one becomes more involved in a subculture, he tends to manifest subcultural values, attitudes, and behavior patterns. A refinement of nonuser and user categories is suggested for exploring the threshold variable and subculture intervention process.

AN: 185
AU: Dodge, D.L.
TI: The variation of a midwest Catholic university's drug use pattern from other Catholic university findings: Why?
SO: International Journal of the Addictions, 14:867-875, 1979
IN: Department of Sociology and Anthropology, University of Notre Dame, Notre Dame, Indiana
RF: 21

SUMMARY TABLE

DRUG: multidrug
TYPE: college students
NUMBER: 134
SEX: male
AGE: college/university
ETHNICITY: not specified
LOCATION: Notre Dame, Indiana
METHODOLOGY: cross-sectional survey
INSTRUMENT(S):   questionnaire
CONDUCTED: 1972

PURPOSE

Survey studies of drug use by college students have usually portrayed a lower pattern of drug use by students attending Catholic universities. However, a study of a large midwest Catholic university [Notre Dame] conducted by the author in 1972 showed a substantially higher involvement with all drugs, especially marijuana, than was usual for Catholic universities. This paper presented the data gathered in that study, derived from a drug-use questionnaire completed by 134 male university students. These findings were then compared with findings from other studies of drug use among college students. Various reasons for greater marijuana use at the particular college studied were then suggested.

FINDINGS

1. Students at a midwestern Catholic university reported greater marijuana use ("ever used") than students at a midwestern state university and college students surveyed in a national sample (p. 868).

2. Use of marijuana during the past year remained stable for students at a midwestern Catholic university but dropped off considerably among students at a midwestern state university and college students surveyed in a national sample (p. 868).

3. The percentage of students at a midwestern Catholic university who reported recent use (last 12 months) of drugs other than marijuana was noticeably higher than percentages among students at a midwestern state university but basically the same as that reported by college students in a national sample (p. 868).

4. The percentage of students at a midwestern Catholic university reporting recent use (last 12 months) of marijuana (55.2%) was exactly the same as that found in a study of students at 21 universities in New York City (p. 868).

5. The highest proportions of students at a midwestern Catholic university who had "ever used" marijuana were in the business (72.0%) and engineering (66.7%) college at the university (p. 869).

6. Of the 55.2% of students at a midwestern Catholic university who used marijuana, 47.8% did so rather extensively, which was comparable if not slightly greater than percentages of current regular use reported in other studies of college students during the same time period (p. 870).

CONCLUSION

Drug use, particularly marijuana use, by students of a large midwestern Catholic university was commensurate with, and even in some cases (such as current use patterns) greater than, drug use reported among college students in other studies, which was surprising since students at Catholic universities usually report lower than average drug use patterns. Several factors could account for this divergence from the usual pattern. Previous studies have indicated that males are more likely than females to experiment with and use marijuana, and since the university studied has an all-male student body, percentages of users would be expected to be higher than percentages reported by co-educational institutions. School residence has also been linked with marijuana use, and since 97% of the students attending the university studied resided on campus, the peer-culture could be expected to provide more opportunity for drug experimentation and use than among students at commuter colleges. Marijuana use has been shown to be linked with class background, and students at the university studied were more likely to come from middle- and upper-class families and to have two parents who were both college graduates. Studies have also linked the quality of the institution with marijuana use among students; students at the university studied had substantially higher SAT scores compared with students at other universities and colleges, had aspirations to more post-baccalaureate degrees, and more often cited the excellent academic reputation of the university as their reason for attending. It appears that the interaction of the above factors sufficiently offset the religious influence (usually associated with low drug use) so that students reported drug use patterns much greater than would normally be expected.

AN: 186
AU: Goldstein, J.W.
TI: Getting high in high school: The meaning of adolescent drug usage
SO: Paper presented at the Symposium on Students and Drugs, Annual Meeting of the
       American Educational Research Association, New York, New York, February 1971.
       12 pp. (ERIC ED 055 282)
IN: Department of Psychology, Carnegie-Mellon University, Pittsburgh,
       Pennsylvania
RF: 10

SUMMARY TABLE

DRUG: multidrug
TYPE: college students
NUMBER: 4,500
SEX: male and female
AGE: college/university
ETHNICITY: not specified
LOCATION: Pittsburgh, Pennsylvania
METHODOLOGY: longitudinal survey
INSTRUMENT(S):   questionnaire
CONDUCTED: 1968-1972

PURPOSE

This study presents data on patterns of drug use among college students,
relationships of use with attitudes of, and use by, one's friends, educational
level at the beginning of use, and attitudes and values related to use. The
entire student body of Carnegie-Mellon University was surveyed with a structured
questionnaire in 1968 and the Class of 1972 was resurveyed at several times during
their academic careers.

FINDINGS

1. Users of marijuana differed from nonusers in the following respects: users
were more likely to be from urban or suburban communities, to have educated
parents, to have a higher family income, to have a Jewish background or one with
little or no emphasis on formal religion, and to have liberal political views;
they prefered humanities or fine arts over other academic fields, and believed
that marijuana is not harmful and that marijuana laws are too harsh (p. 1).

2. No clear-cut relationships were found between marijuana use and sex of the
person, grades earned in school, or frequency of participation in extra-curricular
activities on or off campus (p. 2).

3. Most marijuana users intended to use marijuana again but not LSD or heroin
(p. 2).

4. Usually marijuana was the fourth or fifth psychoactive substance used of 17
drugs inquired about (p. 2).

5. The most frequently mentioned reasons for using marijuana were "to get high, feel good," "curiosity," and "to explore inner self" (p. 2).

6. Students who had decreased or stopped marijuana use indicated that they had done so because they did not desire to continue experiencing its effects or because of its illegality (p. 2).

7. Time of starting drug use for freshmen was: in elementary school, 7% had tried beer, 4% had tried hard liquor, and 12.5% had tried tobacco, but none had tried marijuana or LSD that early. In high school and after, but before college, an additional 63% had tried beer, 64% more had tried hard liquor, 44% more had tried tobacco, 17% had tried marijuana, and 2% had tried LSD (p. 3).

8. Upperclassmen and graduate students with one marijuana experience started using various drugs as follows: elementary school, 0%; high school or afterwards but before college, 5%; freshmen year, 24%; sophomore year, 26%; junior year, 24%; senior year, 6%; after college or in graduate school, 11% (p. 3).

9. Among upperclassmen and graduate students, users of stimulants, narcotics, hallucinogens, barbiturates, or tranquilizers who used at least one of these drugs at least 10 times started their drug use as follows: during elementary school, 0%; high school or immediately afterwards, 19%; freshman year, 19%; sophomore year, 13%; junior year, 7%; senior year, 5%; after college or in graduate school, 5% (p. 3).

10. Marijuana, amphetamine, and alcohol users differed from nonusers of these drugs in having a lower sense of well-being, and in being more nonconforming, more critical, more impulsive, more self-centered, less oriented toward achievement by conformity, more insecure, more pessimistic about their occupational futures, more disorganized under stress, more flexible in thinking, more rebellious toward rules and conventions, and more inclined toward aesthetic and social values and less toward economic, political, and religious values (p. 4).

11. The increase in any marijuana use among students at Carnegie-Mellon University was as follows: freshmen at the beginning of the academic year, 18%; end of first year, 28%; fall of junior year, 45% (p. 4).

CONCLUSION

As drug use becomes more widespread, the identification of special personality characteristics of users becomes less relevant. The problems related to the use of drugs have more to do with the social and cultural context of use than with the drug itself. One of the causes of drug use in schools is lack of trust between teacher and students. The problem can be alleviated by restoring this trust. In order to prevent self-destruction by the individual, the students should be encouraged to be their own clinical diagnosticians and their own first line of defense. The student should also monitor his own drug use.

AN: 187
AU: Goldstein, J.W.
TI: Motivations for psychoactive drug use among students
SO: In: Kleimuntz, B., ed. Readings in the Essentials of Abnormal Psychology.
     New York: Harper and Row, 1974. pp. 371-375.
IN: Department of Psychology, Carnegie-Mellon University, Pittsburgh,
     Pennsylvania
RF: 18

SUMMARY TABLE

DRUG: distilled spirits; marijuana; amphetamines
TYPE: college students (freshmen)
NUMBER: 752
SEX: male and female
AGE: college/university
ETHNICITY: not specified
LOCATION: Pittsburgh, Pennsylvania
METHODOLOGY: cross-sectional survey
INSTRUMENT(S): California Personality Inventory; Allport-Vernon-Lindzey Study of
                 Values
CONDUCTED: 1968

PURPOSE

In order to determine students' motivations for psychoactive drug use, detailed
data on amphetamine, marijuana, and hard liquor use by a university freshman class
(N=752), tested during their first days at college, were obtained as part of a
major all-university drug study. Scores and scale configurations on the
California Personality Inventory and the Allport-Vernon-Lindzey Study of Values
were analyzed to assess the pattern of motivation for users and nonusers of the
three drugs.

FINDINGS

1. "Curiosity" and a desire "to get high, feel good" were the most frequently
given reasons for marijuana, LSD, and mescaline use (p. 372).

2. University freshmen with any marijuana experience scored especially high on
the social presence and flexibility scales of the California Personality
Inventory, and especially low on the sense of well being, responsibility,
socialization, communality, and achievement via conformity scales (p. 373).

3. Most illicit drug use did not result in obvious deleterious effects to the
user. Only 7% of those who had used amphetamines recreationally 10 times or more
had a disturbing or upsetting experience with the drug, and only 1% of those who
had used marijuana at least ten times and 4% of the one-time marijuana "tasters"
had bad experiences with the drug (p. 374).

4. Novice drug users reported somewhat greater percentages of negative drug
experiences than did sophisticated users (p. 374).

CONCLUSION

Results indicate substantial agreement in the pattern of differences between users and nonusers of the three drugs studied. In order to anticipate which persons are likely to become abusers and to increase the effectiveness of therapeutic inventions with actual abusers, additional research is needed. There is great need for motivational analyses which would empirically differentiate between the person who uses psychoactive substances without harm to himself and the one whose use leads to personality disorders or medical problems. Since drug use in American society is widespread, all efforts intended to achieve abstinence are probably doomed to failure.

AN: 188
AU: Goldstein, J.W.
TI: Students' evaluations of their psychoactive drug use
SO: Journal of Counseling Psychology, 22:333-339, 1975
IN: Department of Psychology, Carnegie-Mellon University, Pittsburgh,
     Pennsylvania
RF: 23

SUMMARY TABLE

DRUG: multidrug
TYPE: college students
NUMBER: freshmen, 145; juniors, 229;   seniors, 250
SEX: male and female
AGE: college/university
ETHNICITY: white; minorities
LOCATION: Pittsburgh, Pennsylvania
METHODOLOGY: longitudinal survey
INSTRUMENT(S):   questionnaire
CONDUCTED: 1968-1972

PURPOSE

It has been suggested that drug use is related to users' evaluations of their drug
experience and to evaluations by friends. In 1968 the Carnegie-Mellon Drug Use
Research Project staff surveyed the drug use of the entire student body of
Carnegie-Mellon University using a questionnaire. The Class of 1972 was
resurveyed at the end of their freshman year (spring 1969), the beginning of their
junior year (1970), and the end of their senior year (spring 1972). The drug use
was categorized into eight groups (in order of frequency of use in 1968): beer,
hard liquor, tobacco, marijuana, tranquilizers and barbiturates, amphetamines,
hallucinogens, and narcotics.

FINDINGS

1. Most drug use was seen by the students as beneficial or as having no
particular effect (p. 337).

2. The more experience students had with drug use the more likely they were to
evaluate this use positively (p. 337).

3. Seniors in 1972 evaluated their experiences with marijuana, tranquilizers and
barbiturates, and hallucinogens as "very beneficial," while it was "no effect" for
other drugs (p. 335).

4. Among one-time drug users, the usual evaluation of drug impact was "no effect"
(p. 336).

5. In the university sample, most nonmedical psychoactive drug use was initiated
and carried out in the company of close friends (p. 338).

6. The percentage of students reporting unsatisfactory experiences was greater for hallucinogens (20%) than for any other drug studied (p. 336).

CONCLUSION

Evaluations of drug use are strongly determined by what one has heard from one's friends or has experienced oneself. Messages about drugs, like other messages, are evaluated against what the respondent already knows from personal experience or from his friends. To be effective, therapeutic efforts must take into account the fact that students' evaluations or expectations of drug impact are positive or neutral rather than negative.

AN: 189
AU: Goldstein, J.W.; Gleason, T.C.; Korn, J.H.
TI: Whither the epidemic? Psychoactive drug-use career patterns of college
      students
SO: Journal of Applied Social Psychology, 5:16-33, 1975
IN: Department of Psychology, Carnegie-Mellon University, Pittsburgh,
      Pennsylvania
RF: 27

SUMMARY TABLE

DRUG: multidrug
TYPE: college students
NUMBER: 3,100
SEX: male (66.6%); female (33.3%)
AGE: college/university
ETHNICITY: white (75%); minorities (25%)
LOCATION: Pittsburgh, Pennsylvania
METHODOLOGY: longitudinal survey
INSTRUMENT(S): questionnaire
CONDUCTED: 1968-1972

PURPOSE

In order to delineate the order of beginning drug use, the career patterns of use,
and the changes in these patterns, a sample of university students was surveyed
over the four years of their college education. All students were surveyed in
fall 1968; the freshmen were resurveyed in spring 1969, fall 1970, and spring
1972. A mail technique was used which preserved the anonymity of the respondent
while allowing identification of nonrespondents for follow-up and analysis
purposes.

FINDINGS

1. The earlier a drug had been used by students the more widely it was
experienced (p. 23).

2. The Class of 1968 displayed a growing interest in trying previously
unexperienced drugs; the Class of 1972 displayed a relative loss of interest in
progressing to new and less common drugs, despite an accumulated experience
(p. 30).

3. Findings did not support the common assertion that the use of the more common
psychoactive drugs causes use of the more extreme drugs (p. 29).

4. Three times as many of the seniors desired to regress as intended to progress
to new drugs (p. 25).

5. There is an ordering which is about the same for order of beginning use and of
commonness of use: beer, liquor, tobacco, cannabis, depressants, amphetamines,
hallucinogens, and narcotics. This ordering possesses Guttmann-Scale type
qualities: use of a later drug in the list implies use of a prior one at a beyond
chance level of probability (p. 26).

6. There were increases in the extent of use both over the four years and with increasing class year in 1968 (p. 27).

7. Comparisons of intentions for future use revealed that interclass differences were significant except for those between the freshmen in spring of 1969 and the sophomores of 1968 (p. 27).

8. The greatest discrepancies between the actual drug use and the predicted use based on students' intentions were a greater increase in liquor users (8%) and a lesser increase (5%) in hallucinogen users than intentions would predict (p. 23).

CONCLUSION

The data presented on changes in drug use support at least two conclusions: (1) Nonmedical drug use by students is a complex and dynamic but highly patterned behavioral process; (2) Drug use need not be the steadily increasing and ever more involving activity that it has been portrayed to be. Drug use in the population of students studied was self-limiting; results thus do not support fears of runaway escalation in drug use.

AN: 190
AU: Goldstein, J.W.; Korn, J.H.
TI: Judging the shape of things to come: Lessons learned from comparisons of
     student drug users in 1968 and 1970
SO: Carnegie-Mellon University, Department of Psychology Report No. 72-2,
     February 1972. 6 pp. (ERIC ED 083 509)
IN: Department of Psychology, Carnegie-Mellon University, Pittsburgh,
     Pennsylvania
RF: 0

SUMMARY TABLE

DRUG: marijuana; LSD
TYPE: college students
NUMBER: 4,500
SEX: male and female
AGE: college/university
ETHNICITY: not specified
LOCATION: Pittsburgh, Pennsylvania
METHODOLOGY: longitudinal, comparative survey
INSTRUMENT(S):   questionnaire; California Personality Inventory
CONDUCTED: 1968-1972

PURPOSE

In order to analyze the patterns of drug use over time, and the meaning of drug
use as it changes over time, in the Fall of 1968 the use of 17 psychoactive drugs
by students enrolled full-time at Carnegie-Mellon University was assessed. The
freshmen (the Class of 1972) were remeasured at the end of their freshmen year,
and at the beginning of their junior year. Data from 1968 juniors were used for
comparison.

FINDINGS

1. Users of marijuana differed from nonusers: they were more frequently from
upper-middle-class families, secular, liberal politically, and preferred
humanities, social sciences, and fine arts as academic majors (p. 2).

2. In comparing users and nonusers of marijuana, no relationship was found with
respect to sex of the person, grades in school, or frequency of participation in
extracurricular activities (p. 2).

3. On the California Personality Inventory, freshmen who used marijuana in 1968
were especially high on the social presence and flexibility scales, and especially
low on the sense of well-being, responsibility, socialization, communality, and
achievement via conformity scales (p. 2).

4. The growth rate for juniors between 1968 and 1970 in marijuana use was the
same for males and females (p. 3).

5. Comparison between juniors in 1968 and 1970 revealed sharp increases in the
percentages of those using marijuana 11 times or more who majored in humanities
and social science (from 19% to 46%) and in such formerly low-use fields as

mechanical, electrical, and chemical engineering (from 7% to 18%) (p. 3).

6. The currency of those using marijuana 11 times or more was high in 1968 (80% had used within the month) and remained high in 1970 (p. 3).

7. The currency of LSD use declined in the sample: 40% of the 1968 users had used LSD within the month and only 30% had not used the drug for at least six months; in 1970, only 25% had used within the month and 52% had abstained for six months or more (p. 3).

8. Respondents viewed marijuana and LSD experiences as much more beneficial than harmful or unpleasant and this belief was predominant among heavy users (p. 4).

9. The reasons given by nonusers in 1968 and in 1970 for not using marijuana were a lack of desire to experience the drug (60% and 56% respectively), concern over illegality of use and possible arrest (99% and 20% respectively), and concern over harmful effects (22% and 17% respectively) (p. 4).

10. In 1968, the responses of students asked to state why they used LSD fell into three categories: hedonistic, 20%; inner developmental, 66%; and instrumental (relieve sadness or depression, improve sex or learning, etc.), 14%. In 1970, the responses had shifted as follows: hedonistic, 44%; inner developmental, 46%; and instrumental, 10% (p. 5).

CONCLUSION

The findings suggest a process of the routinization of drug use. In 1970, as in 1968, marijuana use continued to permeate the same categories of students (e.g., humanities students). Reasons for failure to use or to continue to use marijuana shifted from those having to do with unsatisfactory experiences and difficulty getting the drug to increased concern over the illegality of use and the lack of desire for the drug. This suggests that later users had to overcome resistance toward drug use which prevented them from starting use as early as more liberal students.

AN: 191
AU: Goldstein, J.W.; Sappington, J.T.
TI: Personality characteristics of students who became drug users: An MMPI study
      of an avant-garde
SO: American Journal of Drug and Alcohol Abuse, 4:401-412, 1977
IN: Department of Psychology, Carnegie-Mellon University, Pittsburg, Pennsylvania
RF: 23

SUMMARY TABLE

DRUG: marijuana; hallucinogens
TYPE: college students
NUMBER: 66 (33 subjects; 33 controls)
SEX: male (27); female (6)
AGE: college/university
ETHNICITY: not specified
LOCATION: Pittsburgh, Pennsylvania
METHODOLOGY: comparative survey
INSTRUMENT(S):   Minnesota Multiphasic Personality Inventory
CONDUCTED: 1962-1965; 1974

PURPOSE

A psychometric study assessed the possibility of a pre-existing personality
configuration in students who became heavy drug users. Scores on the MMPI of
incoming freshmen at Carnegie-Mellon University were gathered during 1962-1965,
the period before the appearance of increasing drug use and the hippie subculture
in the Pittsburgh area. None of the subjects had used drugs at the time of the
test. The profiles of 33 students of Carnegie-Mellon University who used
marijuana and hallucinogenic drugs frequently and 33 peer control subjects were
compared.

OPERATIONAL DEFINITIONS

Preuser: a freshman who took the MMPI and almost certainly had no illegal drug
experience and who later became a heavy user of marijuana and hallucinogens.

FINDINGS

1. Preusers of drugs differed from the control group by being verbally skilled
and socially practiced individuals (p. 406).

2. The data did not support the proposition that psychopathology is a typical
antecedent to drug use in a college population (p. 407).

3. The nonusers of marijuana and hallucinogens were achievement and study
oriented, had a father-dominated family, lacked social skills, and exhibited
vacillation and immaturity (p. 409).

4. The personalities of drug users-to-be differed from those of the control group
by impulsiveness, gregariousness, and resistance to social norms (p. 409).

5. Nonusers of marijuana and hallucinogens displayed superior general adjustment to users of these drugs (p. 409).

6. Predrug use and prealcohol use profiles were virtually the same, suggesting a common motivation underlying the use of drugs in college populations, rooted in a certain spontaneous, uninhibited, independent, and hedonic perception (p. 410).

7. Ego strength was substantially superior among nonusers of marijuana and hallucinogens when compared to users of these drugs (p. 410).

CONCLUSION

Any application of this data in attempting to identify future drug abusers should be cautious. Overlap on key scales was considerable between the preuse avant-garde and the control group. Moreover, preusers were not characterized by psychopathology. Even differences on ego strength did not indicate preusers since their scores were average. Finally, the technical and professional nature of Carnegie-Mellon University may have exerted some influence on the kind of person who would choose it, thus biasing the collective traits of the control and drug-using groups.

AN: 192
AU: Huba, G.J.; Segal, B.; Singer, J.L.
TI: Organization of needs in male and female drug and alcohol users
SO: Journal of Consulting and Clinical Psychology, 45:34-44, 1977
IN: Department of Social, Psychological, and Philosophical Foundations of
     Education, University of Minnesota, Minneapolis
RF: 29

SUMMARY TABLE

DRUG: multidrug; alcohol
TYPE: college students
NUMBER: 1,095
SEX: male (498); female (597)
AGE: college/university
ETHNICITY: not specified
LOCATION: New Haven, Connecticut; Murray, Kentucky
METHODOLOGY: correlational survey
INSTRUMENT(S):   Personality Research Form; questionnaire
CONDUCTED: 1973-1974

PURPOSE

Previous investigations have demonstrated consistent quantitative differences on
measures of personality between users and nonusers of drugs and alcohol. It is
hypothesized that there may also be qualitative differences, specifically a
different organization of personality variables. Using factor analysis and a
subset of the basic needs postulated by Murray, personality variables were studied
in a sample of college students. Subjects were classified as male or female and
as nonusers, users of alcohol only, users of marijuana only, or polydrug users.
Personality Research Form (PRF) data were analyzed to determine whether needs
showed a stable organization across individuals.

FINDINGS

1. The dimensions of personality measured by the PRF were qualitatively the same
in groups classified either by drug and alcohol use or by sex (p. 42).

2. The generalized achievement motivation and playfulness dimensions of the PRF
were qualitatively different for individuals who did not use alcohol or drugs, and
were related to the need for order, nurturance, and understanding (p. 42).

3. The measure of playfulness in nonusers of alcohol or drugs was positively
related to the need for impulsivity and order and negatively related to the need
for endurance (p. 42).

4. Little difference was found between users and nonusers of alcohol and drugs
with regard to organization of motivations (p. 43).

CONCLUSION

The study demonstrates that the use of alcohol and drugs by young adults, sampled from a college population, is not associated with the reorganization of motivational patterns. With subjects classified as users and nonusers and as male and female, very little difference was found by group in the way in which motivations were organized. The findings cannot be generalized to an older population or to comparisons of nonusers with chronic users of alcohol and drugs.

AN: 193
AU: Kay, E.J.; Lyons, A.; Newman, W.; Mankin, D.; Loeb, R.C.
TI: A longitudinal study of the personality correlates of marijuana use
SO: Journal of Consulting and Clinical Psychology, 46:470-477, 1978
IN: Lehigh University, Bethlehem, Pennsylvania
RF: 14

SUMMARY TABLE

DRUG: marijuana
TYPE: college students
NUMBER: 251
SEX: male
AGE: college freshmen
ETHNICITY: not specified
LOCATION: Bethlehem, Pennsylvania
METHODOLOGY: longitudinal, correlational survey
INSTRUMENT(S): questionnaire; California Psychological Inventory; Adjective
               Check List
CONDUCTED: 1971-1973

PURPOSE

Each fall, during the years 1971, 1972, and 1973, 200 randomly chosen male
freshmen entering Lehigh University were asked to participate in a study of the
personality characteristics of marijuana users and nonusers. The various groups
of students were then contacted for follow-up studies in the spring of each year.
During test sessions, three instruments were completed: a drug questionnaire, the
Adjective Check List, and the California Psychological Inventory. Only those
students who remained three years at Lehigh University and completed all tests
were included in the final sample.

FINDINGS

1. The personality correlates of marijuana among the reputedly "straight"
apathetic, job-oriented college youth of the early 1970s were similar to the
personality correlates associated with marijuana use among the "hippie" college
youth of the late 1960s (p. 475).

2. The personality characteristics associated with marijuana use and nonuse did
not change over the years of the study (p. 475).

3. Certain people with specifiable personality traits fell into the three
categories of marijuana users, continued nonusers, and switched nonusers (p. 475).

4. Nonusers of marijuana tended to score higher than users on indices of
conformity (responsibility, socialization, self-control) (p. 475).

5. Marijuana users scored higher than nonusers on indices of nonconformity
(relative irresponsiveness, rebelliousness, hostility towards rules and
conventions) (p. 475).

6. Nonusers of marijuana scored relatively high on indices of efficiency, organization, and industriousness (p. 475).

7. Subjects who began the study as nonusers of marijuana but switched to use during the period of the study had personality characteristic scores that fell between nonusers and users prior to their initiation to marijuana; once use began, their scores fell more towards those of users, that is, the group of switched nonusers was similar to the users in being outgoing, socially self-confident, and spontaneous (p. 476).

CONCLUSION

Nonusers of marijuana appear to be well-socialized; they conform to norms, respect authority, strive for traditional goals, and rarely act on impulse. Users are nonconforming, independent, adventurous, and spontaneous. These findings ought to be treated cautiously; as a result of self-reporting, they may reflect social expectations. Results of the study support the proposition that certain personality types gravitate to marijuana use, as opposed to the usual interpretation that marijuana use results in personality changes.

AN: 194
AU: Korman, M.;   Trimboli, F.;   Semler, I.
TI: A psychiatric emergency room study of inhalant use
SO: In: Sharp, C.W., and Carroll, L.T., eds. Voluntary Inhalation of Industrial
      Solvents. Rockville, MD: National Institute on Drug Abuse, 1978. pp.
      137-158.
IN: Department of Psychology, University of Texas Health Science Center, Dallas,
      Texas
RF: 27

SUMMARY TABLE

DRUG: volatile solvents
TYPE: inhalant users; polydrug users
NUMBER: 273
SEX: male and female
AGE: 21 years (mean)
ETHNICITY: black (24%); Mexican-American (10%); Anglo-American (66%)
LOCATION: Dallas, Texas
METHODOLOGY: comparative, correlational survey
INSTRUMENT(S):   structured interview
CONDUCTED: not specified

PURPOSE

A sample group of 91 inhalant users was compared with similar groups of 91
noninhalant polydrug users and 91 nondrug users who were admitted to a psychiatric
emergency room in Dallas, Texas. A statistical analysis was performed on data
derived from a structured interview in order to determine if there were
significant differences between inhalant users and the other groups on demographic
data such as age, sex, and ethnicity and on clinical variables such as appearance,
mood and affect, cognitive and intrapersonal difficulties, and danger to self and
others.

FINDINGS

1. Inhalant users were more likely to show poorer hygiene in their personal
appearance than noninhalant polydrug users, who, in turn, were more likely to show
poorer hygiene than nondrug users (p. 144).

2. Inhalant users rated higher on three variables (trouble with the law, school
problems, and family discord) than noninhalant polydrug users, who likewise rated
higher on these variables than nondrug users (p. 144).

3. Compared with noninhalant polydrug users and nondrug users, inhalant users
were more likely to show the following cognitive difficulties: abstraction
deficit, insight deficit, and judgment deficit (p. 144).

4. A significantly higher frequency of phobias was observed in Mexican-American
inhalant users than in black or Anglo-American inhalant users (p. 144).

5. Mexican-American inhalant users, who also used other drugs, reported a higher incidence of recent weight gain than did black or Anglo-American inhalant users (p. 144).

6. Anglo-American inhalant users were more likely to be considered a potential danger to themselves than were black or Mexican-American inhalant users (p. 147).

7. Both inhalant users and noninhalant polydrug users were more likely to be rated as a danger to themselves and others than were nondrug users, but inhalant users were demonstrably more prone to self- and other-directed aggressive behavior than were polydrug users (p. 147).

8. Polydrug users were more likely to have anxiety or fear, initial sleep disturbance, employment problems, and thoughts of suicide than were inhalant users or nondrug users, indicating intrapersonal difficulties, primarily of an acute emotional nature (p. 147).

9. Polydrug users were more likely to have loss of immediate recall than were inhalant users or nondrug users (pp. 147-148).

10. There was no difference between inhalant users, polydrug users, and nondrug users in their level of intellectual functioning (p. 148).

11. Inhalant users did not demonstrate greater emotional dyscontrol than polydrug users or nondrug users (p. 151).

12. Heavy users of inhalants were more likely than light users to demonstrate poor hygiene, inappropriate dress, flat affect, and soft and monotonic speech (pp. 149-150).

13. The average age of individuals reporting recent inhalant use was nearly identical with that of nonrecent inhalant users (20.9 and 21.2 years, respectively) (p. 154).

14. About a fourth of the inhalant users studied were females (p. 154).

15. The ethnic distribution of inhalant users was similar to the ethnic distribution in the community, with certain consistent but limited exceptions: blacks were under-represented and Mexican-Americans over-represented (pp. 154-155).

16. Inhalant use was found in all socio-economic groups (p. 155).

CONCLUSION

Inhalant users, when compared with similar groups of noninhalant polydrug users and nondrug users, showed more self- and other-directed aggressive behavior, a wider range of cognitive deficits, and greater social disruption. Inhalant users were not significantly different in emotional dyscontrol or intellectual functioning. Inhalant use was found at all socio-economic levels, in both males and females (at a ratio of 3:1), and among blacks, Anglo-Americans, and Mexican-Americans, though blacks were slightly under-represented compared to the community at large and Mexican-Americans were slightly over-represented. The Anglo-American inhalant users were more likely to demonstrate self-directed acting-out behavior, while Mexican-American inhalant users were characterized by phobic trends, suggesting that inhalant use results in an intensification of typical coping styles. Heavy users of inhalants were distinguished from light users in showing poor hygiene, inappropriate dress, flattened affect, and soft and monotonic speech, suggesting that extensive and chronic use of inhalants diminishes social contact and interest and results in lack of care for oneself.

AN: 195
AU: Korn, J.H.; Goldstein, J.W.
TI: Psychoactive drugs: A course evaluation
SO: Journal of Drug Education, 3:353-368, 1973
IN: Department of Psychology, Carnegie-Mellon University, Pittsburgh,
     Pennsylvania
RF: 13

SUMMARY TABLE

DRUG: multidrug
TYPE: college students
NUMBER: 136
SEX: male (83); female (38)
AGE: college/university
ETHNICITY: not specified
LOCATION: Pittsburgh, Pennsylvania
METHODOLOGY: experimental research
INSTRUMENT(S):   questionnaire
CONDUCTED: 1969

PURPOSE

This study presents an evaluation of a college-level course on drugs; the
objectives for the course had to do with knowledge about drugs and drug users and
sources of information about drugs. Along with other findings, student attitudes
toward drugs and intended drug use are reported. A structured questionnaire was
distributed to 136 students participating in the course; 134 filled out the
questionnaire at the beginning of the course; 129 at the end.

FINDINGS

1. Following a college course on psychoactive drugs, there was an 8.6% increase
in "very extensive" use of drugs from the beginning to the end of the semester,
although this was not a statistically significant change (p. 362).

2. Following a college course on psychoactive drugs, there was a significant
decrease in intent to use any tranquilizer (p. 362).

3. After a college course on psychoactive drugs, the students expressed higher
concern about close friends' use of drugs. The greatest increase in concern was
for heroin, with hard liquor second (p. 363).

4. The most frequently selected first choice for advice on drug use before a
college course on psychoactive drugs was a close friend; the university
counseling center and a physician were second choices. After the course, a close
friend remained the first choice, but the course instructors replaced the
counseling center as the most frequent second choice (p. 363).

CONCLUSION

When ratings before and after the course on psychoactive drugs were compared, there was no significant change in students' extent of experience with drugs. A nonsignificant change occurred in "very extensive" experience. Moreover, students indicated that their concern over friends' use of drugs (except marijuana) increased. The students in the course became more cautious towards drugs as a result of the course. Knowledge about drugs also increased.

AN: 196
AU: Mellinger, G.D.; Somers, R.H.; Bazell, S.; Manheimer, D.I.
TI: Drug use, academic performance, and career indecision: Longitudinal data in
       search of a model
SO: In: Kandel, D.B., ed. Longitudinal Research on Drug Use: Empirical
       Findings and Methodological Issues. Washington, D.C.: Hemisphere Publishing
       Corp., 1978. pp. 157-177.
IN: Institute for Research in Social Behavior, Oakland, California
RF: 32

SUMMARY TABLE

DRUG: multidrug
TYPE: college students
NUMBER: 834
SEX: male
AGE: college/university
ETHNICITY: Caucasian (82%); Asians (12%)
LOCATION: Berkeley, California
METHODOLOGY: longitudinal survey
INSTRUMENT(S):   interview; questionnaire; academic records
CONDUCTED: 1970; 1973

PURPOSE

The study sought to identify the adverse effects of illicit drug use among college
males. The search for negative consequences centered on three main outcome
criteria: (1) dropping out of school; (2) clarity of occupational goals; and
(3) academic performance as measured by grade-point average during the academic
year 1972-1973. The data for the study were gathered through questionnaires and
personal interviews with a selected sample of male students at the University of
California, Berkeley. The survey and personal interviewing were conducted in Fall
1970 and Spring 1973.

FINDINGS

1. Drug users were more likely than nonusers to come from relatively well-to-do,
liberal, and, probably, intellectually-oriented families (p. 168).

2. Drug users were more likely than nonusers to go into the social sciences or
humanities (p. 168).

3. Drug users were more likely than nonusers to be white and non-Latin (p. 169).

4. Drug users were more likely than nonusers to have had lower grades in high
school, but to have received high Scholastic Aptitude Test scores of verbal
aptitude (p. 169).

5. Drug users were significantly more likely than nonusers to be undecided about
their occupational goals (p. 169).

6. Drug use was found to have adverse consequences with respect to academic performance and decisions about occupational goals in only a small number of cases (p. 173).

7. There was no evidence showing that use of marijuana had any adverse consequences with respect to academic performance and decisions about occupational goals (p. 173).

8. For most drug users in the university setting, drug use (like drinking) was a social rather than a pathological phenomenon (p. 173).

CONCLUSION

In general, this study validated the sociogenic or subcultural theory of drug use. Variables reflecting the theory explained very well adverse outcomes involving the total group of multiple drug users. However, sociocultural variables of the theory did not explain those cases in which drug use was associated with favorable outcomes. The implications of these findings are limited because of the selected nature of the sample under study. These were students who were sufficiently talented and motivated to gain admission to a highly competitive university. Less motivated and talented students, who may have been involved in drug use, would not have been included in this sample.

AN: 197
AU: Mellinger, G.D.; Somers, R.H.; Davidson, S.T.; Manheimer, D.I.
TI: The amotivational syndrome and the college student
SO: Annals of the New York Academy of Sciences, 282:37-55, 1976
IN: Institute for Research in Social Behavior, Oakland, California
RF: 24

SUMMARY TABLE

DRUG: multidrug
TYPE: college students
NUMBER: 960
SEX: male
AGE: college/university
ETHNICITY: [Caucasian (82%); Asian (12%)]
LOCATION: Berkeley, California
METHODOLOGY: longitudinal survey
INSTRUMENT(S):   interview; questionnaire
CONDUCTED: 1970; 1973

PURPOSE

This study is concerned with the extent to which men at a major public university
are able to benefit from their academic experience and find self-fulfilling and
socially useful roles in society. It has been suggested that drug use impairs
this process by producing an amotivational syndrome of apathy, mental confusion,
and lack of goals. The study sought to test the hypothesis that drug use produces
amotivational symptoms that are serious and long lasting enough to be reflected in
the academic and career progress of drug users as compared with nonusers. The
data for this analysis were gatherd from a large-scale longitudinal study of
probability samples of two groups of male students at the University of California
at Berkeley.

FINDINGS

1. More than one half the sample population had used drugs before entering the
university (p. 42).

2. Almost one half (47%) of the sample used drugs at least once during the Fall
quarter (p. 42).

3. Multiple drug users as a group appeared to be substantially more involved in
drug use and in the drug subculture than were men who restricted their use of
illict drugs to marijuana (p. 43).

4. Compared with marijuana-only users, multiple drug users tended to use
marijuana more frequently, were more likely to have many friends who used drugs,
and were more likely to identify with drug users (p. 43).

5. Among marijuana-only users, 16% (47 men) had used marijuana 18 or more times
during the Fall quarter, i.e., an average of about twice weekly or more (p. 43).

6. The frequency of drugs other than marijuana was rather substantial given the greater potency of these drugs--almost half the men who had used drugs other than marijuana during the year before entering the university had done so seven or more times (p. 43).

7. Continuity of drug use (i.e., use during both the Fall quarter and during the year before entering the university) and multiple drug use were strongly related to frequency of marijuana use (p. 43).

8. Of the subjects who had never used marijuana, only 3% became permanent dropouts from college, as compared with 6% of the men who used only marijuana and 14% of those who used multiple drugs (p. 46).

9. Among freshmen whose academic motivation was high (62% of the total sample), there was no relation between drug use and becoming a permanent dropout from college (p. 46).

10. Among low motivation students (38% of the total sample), although there were no significant differences with regard to dropping out between those who had and those who had not used drugs, there was a high percentage of dropouts (53%) in a subgroup of multiple drug users who had low motivation and whose parents had never gone to college (p. 47).

11. College men who were using (or had used) drugs as freshmen were more likely than nonusers to become permanent dropouts (p. 49).

12. For most of the drug users in the sample, the likelihood of becoming a college dropout was no higher than one would expect, given their background characteristics, value orientations, and academic motivation as freshmen. The only significant exception to this finding were the continuing multiple drug users with less educated parents who showed a high rate of dropping out (p. 51).

13. Drug use among college men appeared to have little, if any, effect on dropping out of college by way of whatever effect it may have had on academic motivation (p. 51).

CONCLUSION

The investigators addressed two questions raised by earlier analysis: (1) Would multivariate analysis reveal that drug use had an indirect effect on dropping out by virtue of its relation to academic motivation? (2) To what extent can the combined direct and indirect effects of drug use on dropping out be explained by social and cultural characteristics that differentiate users and nonusers? Analysis of the data showed that the indirect effects of drug use on dropping out were negligible, and for most users, it appeared that other variables (family background, relationship with parents while in high school, social values) rather than drug use per se accounted for dropping out of school. The findings suggest that some illicit drug users are unable to cope and consequently impair their capacity for optimum-functioning. A good family relationship had been previously noted as one visible means for support and as such could realistically be used to minimize the destructive consequences of drug use.

AN: 198
AU: O'Donnell, J.A.
TI: Cigarette smoking as a precursor of illicit drug use
SO: In: Krasnegor, N.A., ed. Cigarette Smoking as a Dependence Process
     (National Institute on Drug Abuse, Research Monograph 23). Washington, D.C.:
     Government Printing Office, 1979. pp. 30-43.
IN: Department of Sociology, University of Kentucky, Lexington, Kentucky
RF: 22

SUMMARY TABLE

DRUG: cigarettes; multidrug
TYPE: nationwide sample of young men
NUMBER: 2,510
SEX: male
AGE: 20-30 years
ETHNICITY: white; black; Spanish
LOCATION: United States (cross-sectional)
METHODOLOGY: cross-sectional, correlational survey
INSTRUMENT(S):   interview
CONDUCTED: 1974-1975

PURPOSE

In order to determine whether cigarette use is a predictor, and possibly a cause,
of other forms of drug use, data derived from interviews with 2,510 young men
between the ages of 20 and 30 in a nationwide probability sample conducted in 1974
and 1975 were analyzed. Alcohol use and marijuana use were employed as
competitive predictors and causes.

FINDINGS

1. Alcohol, cigarettes, or marijuana were almost always used before the use of
any illicit drug, though none of the three was invariably first. For young men
who used both alcohol and other drugs, alcohol was used first in 71% of the cases,
while regular cigarette use normally preceded marijuana use (p. 32).

2. Among a nationwide sample of young men, when cocaine use was correlated to the
extent of lifetime use of alcohol and marijuana, the heavier the use of alcohol or
marijuana, the more likely the use of cocaine; the marijuana-cocaine relationship
was not reduced by control on the alcohol variable, while the alcohol-cocaine
relationship disappeared when controlled on the variable of marijuana use,
suggesting that marijuana use comes after alcohol use but before cocaine use in a
causal chain (p. 33).

3. Although both alcohol use and marijuana use among young men were associated
with the use of other drugs, the relationship was strongest for marijuana use,
suggesting that the effect of alcohol use is indirect, through marijuana, with
little or no direct effect (p. 33).

4. The earlier the young men in the sample began marijuana use, the more likely
they were to use heroin and other opiates, and other drugs, and to engage in
illicit drug sales and criminal behavior (p. 33).

5. Among a nationwide sample of young men, there was a weak association between heavy cigarette smoking and early age at first regular use of cigarettes and marijuana use (p. 37).

6. The use of illicit drugs was rare and minimal among young men who did not use marijuana (p. 37).

7. Among a nationwide sample of young men, cigarette use was correlated with the use of illicit drugs directly, as well as indirectly through marijuana use, but the correlation was weak (p. 40).

8. For a sample of young men, the earlier the use of alcohol, cigarettes, or marijuana, the earlier was the use of the other two substances, as well as the more likely the use of illicit drugs (p. 41).

9. The correlation between early onset of marijuana use and illicit drug use among young men was significant, while the correlation between early use of alcohol and drug use was somewhat lower but still significant; the correlation between early regular use of cigarettes and drug use was even smaller, but still significant, although the correlation disappeared when controlled on either the alcohol or marijuana variables (p. 41).

10. Of 299 young men in the sample who had never used tobacco, 27% had used marijuana, while among the 467 who used tobacco but not cigarettes, 48% had used marijuana, and for the 1,743 young men who used cigarettes regularly, 62% also used marijuana (p. 41).

                                    CONCLUSION

Cigarette use, though significantly correlated with marijuana use, is not a useful predictor of later drug use. Though the association may be partially a causal connection, it seems more likely to be greatly spurious, due to the fact that both cigarette use and marijuana use are connected with alcohol use and almost certainly with personality and social variables.

AN: 199
AU: O'Donnell, J.A.; Clayton, R.R.
TI: Determinants of early marihuana use
SO: In: Beschner, G.M., and Friedman, A.S., eds. Youth Drug Abuse. Lexington,
      MA: D.C. Heath, 1979. pp. 63-110.
IN: Department of Sociology, University of Kentucky, Lexington, Kentucky
RF: 41

SUMMARY TABLE

DRUG: marijuana
TYPE: nationwide sample of young men; New York City sample of young men
NUMBER: nationwide sample: 2,510; New York City sample: 294
SEX: male
AGE: 20-30 years
ETHNICITY: black; white
LOCATION: United States (cross-sectional); New York, New York
METHODOLOGY: correlational, comparative survey
INSTRUMENT(S): interview
CONDUCTED: 1974

PURPOSE

Previous studies on heroin addicts have been based on populations of known addicts
(such as those incarcerated or in treatment), although it is clear from other
research that large numbers of Americans have used heroin and other illicit drugs
occasionally or experimentally and that many heroin and other drugs users have
discontinued use of drugs on their own. Because it is easier to locate marijuana
users and because marijuana use precedes heroin use, any variables shown to be the
cause of marijuana use might also be inferred as causes of heroin use. This study
is based on path analysis, which uses words like cause, direct effect, and
indirect effect, although it is based only on correlational data, plus assumptions
about causal or temporal priority. The study focused on the causes, or
predictors, of marijuana use based on data from two samples: a nationwide
probability sample of 2,510 young men between the ages of 20 and 30 in 1974, and a
smaller probability sample of 294 young men in areas of New York City identified
as areas of high drug use. The paths by which young men progress toward illicit
drug use are described for blacks and whites.

OPERATIONAL DEFINITIONS

Labeling: predictions by friends, parents, and teachers of future trouble with
the law.

FINDINGS

1. There was a strong association between marijuana use and heroin use in both a
nationwide sample of young men and a sample of young men in New York City. In the
nationwide sample, 90%-93% of the men who used both drugs had used marijuana
first, and in the New York City sample, 75%-86% of the men who used both drugs had
used marijuana first. This association remained valid when analyzed for
spuriousness with controls on all available prior variables (pp. 69-70).

2. Age at first use of marijuana was earlier for a sample of young men in New
York City than for a nationwide sample of young men and was earlier for blacks
than for whites in both samples. Fourteen percent of the New Yorkers (22% of
blacks) began to use marijuana before age 15. Marijuana use began after age 20
for over 15% of the nationwide sample, but only a very small proportion of the New
York sample began this late. In the national sample, less than 40% of the older
cohorts, but over 60% of the youngest, had used marijuana, and the median age at
first use dropped from 25 in the oldest cohorts to 17 in the youngest, but in the
New York sample the percentage of users was high among all age groups, and early
onset was as common among the older cohorts as among the younger (pp. 71-72, 78).

3. The use of illicit drugs was higher in a sample of young men from New York
City than among those in a nationwide sample. Among whites, 44% of the New
Yorkers compared to 30% of the national sample were in the highest use categories
for illicit drugs; the corresponding figures for blacks were 49% and 36% and for
other ethnic groups, 32% and 24% (p. 72).

4. For young men in both a national and a New York City sample, the older a man
was when he began using marijuana, the less likely he was to use any other drugs,
and those who never used marijuana at all were least likely to use other drugs or
to use them extensively. Conversely, the earlier a man began to use marijuana,
the greater was the likelihood that he would use other drugs and that his use
would be extensive (p. 72).

5. For young men in both a national and a New York City sample, the younger the
age at first marijuana use the higher the probability of heroin or opiate use
(p. 74).

6. More than half of the young men in a New York city sample who used marijuana
more than 1,000 times were also heroin users (p. 75).

7. For whites and blacks, over 30% of the young men in a New York City sample
sold drugs as compared to less than 20% in the national sample. Thirty percent of
all marijuana users and 17% of all young men in the national sample had sold
drugs. The earlier the age of first marijuana use, the more likely were drug
sales, which were almost (though not completely) absent among young men who had
never used marijuana (p. 75).

8. For young men in both a national and a New York City sample, the earlier the
first use of marijuana, the more likely the user was to report involvement in
criminal behavior and involvement in the more serious crimes (p. 77).

9. Young black men in New York City were more likely than whites to report early
deviant behavior, peer delinquency, peer drug use, labeling, and perception of
drug availability (p. 82).

10. For both black and white young men in New York City, early age of marijuana
use was correlated significantly with early deviant behavior, peer delinquency,
peer drug use, labeling, and perception of drug availability. The correlation
between age at first use of marijuana and school adjustment and involvement in
conventional activities approached significance for whites, but only the
correlation with school adjustment approached significance for blacks (p. 83).

11. For blacks in New York City, early age of marijuana use was significantly
correlated with perception of the father as a role model; the degree of family
control and closeness to the father approached significance. For whites,

closeness to the mother and closeness to the father were both significantly correlated with early age of marijuana use and degree of family control, communication with parents, and father as a role model approached significance (p. 83).

12. Peer influence was the most important predictor of early age of marijuana use for New York City blacks, followed by perception of drug availability, early deviant behavior, family influence, and labeling, while perception of drug availability was most important for whites, followed by family influence and peer influence (p. 92).

13. Family influence had a direct effect upon age at first marijuana use for New York City whites, and an additional indirect effect, while there was no direct effect for blacks, but a strong indirect effect. Early deviant behavior had only indirect effects for both groups, although this seemed to be more important for blacks. Peer influence also appeared to have a greater effect for blacks than for whites. Labeling had no effect on age at first use of marijuana for whites, while it had a considerable direct effect for blacks (p. 93).

CONCLUSION

Age at first marijuana use is a variable which seems to predict later drug use and sales and is associated with crime, although it may not predict crime. Variables associated with age at first use of marijuana when analyzed statistically for black and white young men in New York City produce two different path models which describe the relative importance of the variables for each group. For whites, perception of drug availability and family influence have direct effects upon age at first marijuana use, while early deviant behavior and peer influence have indirect effects. For blacks, the model is more complex, with perception of drug availability, peer influence, and labeling having a direct effect upon age at first marijuana use, with early deviant behavior, family influence, and peer influence having indirect effects. Perception of drug availability is of more central importance for whites, since it acts as a filter through which most of the other variables act on age at first use, while for blacks these variables have additional direct or indirect paths. Blacks had higher perceptions of drug availability than whites, probably because both delinquency and drug use are higher and more closely associated for blacks in the sample, which may also explain the greater impact of labeling on blacks. Family influence seems to be more effective among whites in preventing or delaying marijuana use, while peer influence and early deviant behavior seem to have stronger effects on blacks, though these differences have to be discounted to some extent because the model for blacks accounts for more variance in the dependent variables than the model for whites.

AN: 200
AU: O'Donnell, J.A.; Voss, H.L.; Clayton, R.R.; Slatin, G.T.; Room, R.G.W.
TI: Young Men and Drugs--A Nationwide Survey
SO: Rockville, MD: National Institute on Drug Abuse (NIDA Research Monograph 5),
      1976. 144 pp.
IN: Department of Sociology, University of Kentucky, Lexington, Kentucky
RF: 11

SUMMARY TABLE

DRUG: multidrug
TYPE: nationwide sample of young men
NUMBER: 2,510
SEX: male
AGE: 20-30 years
ETHNICITY: white; black; Spanish
LOCATION: United States (cross-sectional)
METHODOLOGY: cross-sectional survey
INSTRUMENT(S): interview
CONDUCTED: 1974-1975

PURPOSE

In order to study drug use in the general population, 2,510 young men between the
ages of 20 and 30 were selected from Selective Service records to constitute a
stratified, nationwide probability sample and were interviewed during 1974 and
1975. The study focused on obtaining histories of drug use, estimating incidence
and prevalence with particular emphasis on cohort use, examining the question of a
drug epidemic, and exploring correlates and determinants of drug use.

FINDINGS

1. The following percentages of young men reported lifetime use and current use
of the following drugs: cigarettes, 70% (lifetime), 60% (current); alcohol, 97%,
92%; marijuana, 55%, 38%; psychedelics, 22%, 7%; stimulants, 27%, 12%;
sedatives, 20%, 9%; heroin, 6%, 2%; opiates, 31%, 10%; cocaine, 14%, 7%
(p. vii).

2. Half or more of the users of most of the illicit drugs indicated that they
used the drug less than 10 times; although use was not under medical direction,
some use of stimulants, sedatives, and especially opiates could be best described
as quasi-medical (p. vii).

3. Data from a nationwide sample of young men suggested that cigarette use was
declining; cigarette use was less common among the younger men (slightly over 60%
had used cigarettes) than among the older men (about 75%) (p. vii).

4. The peak periods of incidence (new cases of use) among young men for any drug
except alcohol were 1968-1972 and 1969-1973, suggesting that there was a drug
epidemic in the late 1960s. Larger proportions of men in the younger cohorts than
in the older cohorts used all drugs, except alcohol and tobacco; the younger
cohorts were larger in number; and the median age at onset of use was lower in
the younger than in the older cohorts. The data also indicated that when use of

drugs became more widespread in the younger cohorts, more men in older cohorts experimented with the drugs than would have been expected to do so (p. vii).

5. For a nationwide sample of young men, differences in drug use between blacks and whites diminished by 1974. Among whites, there was a strong inverse relationship between age and drug use except for alcohol and tobacco; more of the younger men had used drugs. But for blacks, smaller proportions of the younger than the older men used drugs. In the older birth cohorts, the percentages of users were higher for blacks than whites for most drugs, but in the younger cohorts the differences were negligible (p. vii).

6. For a nationwide sample of young men, there was no indication of any recent decline in the annual prevalence of the use of any drug, with the possible exception of psychedelics; for several drugs, particularly cocaine, use was increasing (p. viii).

7. Veterans, whether they had served only in the United States, overseas but not in Vietnam, or in Vietnam, showed no higher rates of current drug use than nonveterans. Rates of lifetime use of drugs by veterans were not significantly higher than those of nonveterans, except that marijuana and heroin use was higher in a few of the eleven birth cohorts (p. viii).

8. The use of any drug by young men was associated with the use of all other drugs. If tobacco is excluded, alcohol and marijuana were almost always the first and second drugs used respectively, and the use of other drugs was rare if alcohol and marijuana had not been used (p. viii).

9. Reports by young men of involvement in criminal behavior, arrests, appearances in juvenile courts, convictions, and prison sentences increased directly with drug use (p. viii).

10. Less than 3% of a national sample of young men reported treatment for drug use. The largest number sought treatment for alcohol use, but they constituted only a minute fraction of the alcohol users. The next largest number sought treatment for heroin use; they constituted 14% of all heroin users. One-third or more of the men who used heroin most extensively had been treated (p. viii).

11. For a sample of young men, both lifetime and current drug use were higher: the larger the city was in which the men lived to age 18; among the unemployed, or part-time employees; the less conventional the men were in terms of indicators of conventionality such as marital history, current living arrangements, and expressed attitudes; the lower the educational level achieved; and among men who entered college and reported the social sciences, fine arts, and humanities as their college majors (p. viii).

CONCLUSION

Drug use became more extensive during the late 1960s among a group of men who were ages 20 to 30 in 1974, and the prevalence of use did not seem to be declining in 1974, with the possible exception of the use of psychedelics. Cigarettes and alcohol were the licit drugs most commonly used and continuing to be used, although cigarette use was declining among the younger groups of men. There were higher percentages of users among blacks than among whites in the older birth cohorts, but younger white men were more likely than younger black men to use drugs, so that differences in the percentages of drug use based on ethnicity were

disappearing by 1974. Alcohol and marijuana were the first drugs used by nearly
all of the men, and those who did not use these drugs were very unlikely to use
other drugs. Drug use was associated with greater involvement in crime and was
correlated with such variables as residence in a large city, unemployment or
part-time employment, unconventional behavior and attitudes, lower educational
levels, and college majors in the social sciences, fine arts, and humanities.

AN: 201
AU: Segal, B.; Huba, G.J.; Singer, J.L.
TI: Prediction of college drug use from personality and inner experience
SO: International Journal of the Addictions, 15:849-867, 1980
IN: Center for Alcohol and Addiction Studies, University of Alaska, Anchorage, Alaska
RF: 33

SUMMARY TABLE

DRUG: alcohol; marijuana; multidrug
TYPE: college students
NUMBER: 1,095
SEX: female (597); male (498)
AGE: college/university
ETHNICITY: not specified
LOCATION: New Haven, Connecticut; Murray, Kentucky
METHODOLOGY: correlational survey
INSTRUMENT(S): Alcohol-Drug Use Research Survey; Personalty Research Form;
                Imaginal Processes Inventory; Sensation Seeking Scales; Locus of
                Control Scale
CONDUCTED: 1973-1974

PURPOSE

In order to examine the relationship between drug use and personality, college students at Murray State University (Kentucky) and Yale University were administered four psychometric instruments and a drug-alcohol use survey in 1973 and 1974. A total of 1,095 students participated in the study, 590 in 1973 and 505 in 1974. The four psychometric instruments were the Personality Research Form, which assesses needs, the Imaginal Processes Inventory, which assesses daydreaming and mental style, the Sensation Seeking Scales, which measure an individual's tendencies to seek out stimulation, and Locus of Control, which assesses an individual's perceptions of the source of reinforcements in the environment for specific behaviors. The college students were divided into four groups on the basis of their responses to the alcohol-drug use survey: Nonusers, Alcohol Only users, Marijuana Only users, and Polydrug users. Separate stepwise discriminant analyses were computed for males and females tested in each year in order to predict drug use pattern. The analyses were replicated, and the best set of predictor variables were used to predict classification in the different samples.

FINDINGS

1. It was possible to differentiate nonusers of drugs, alcohol only users, marijuana only users, and polydrug users among two samples of college students in a statistically reliable manner on the basis of four psychometric instruments with an accuracy of 60% to 65% (p. 864).

2. For both males and females, the Experience Sensation Seeking Scale (which represents a striving for a broad variety of experiences and unconventional behavioral styles oriented toward seeking such variety) was the single best discriminating variable associated with drug use among college students, followed

by the Disinhibition Sensation Seeking scale (which measures a fundamental hedonistic orientation involving strong social needs for "letting go" of oneself). For males, Heroic Daydreaming was also a consistently discriminating variable (p. 861).

3. The following variables from four psychometric instruments were the most predictive of drug use for college students: Experience Sensation Seeking, Disinhibition Sensation Seeking, General Sensation Seeking, and Thrill and Adventure Seeking from the Sensation Seeking Scales; the Night Dreaming Frequency, Need for External Stimulation, and Self Revelation scales from the Imaginal Processes Inventory, as well as the Personality Research Form scales for Autonomy, Impulsivity, Play, Understanding, Harm-avoidance, Achievement, Social Recognition, and Nurturance. Locus of Control also has some relation to drug use (p. 865).

CONCLUSION

It is possible to classify individuals into one of four drug and alcohol use categories on the basis of their scores on the theoretically based personality construct with a maximum of 60% to 65% accuracy. Since little true predictive covariance was lost to measurement error, the predictive accuracy estimate of 60% is taken to be an accurate estimate of the degree of overlap between drug and alcohol use among college students and general personality functioning. The most important variables in predicting drug use for both sexes were Experience Sensation Seeking and Disinhibition Sensation Seeking, both from the Sensation Seeking Scales. College students who use drugs are best differentiated from nonusers along a dimension which includes a life style characterized by the seeking of many varied and unusual experiences and a social pattern which is generally autonomous and lacking in concern for typical cultural expectations of success and recognition. It is not necessary, particularly in cases in which there is no emotional disturbance or addiction, to identify possible underlying motives for substance use, but rather to help drug users evolve alternative means of satisfying strong needs for new and exciting experiences.

AN: 202
AU: Segal, B.; Huba, G.J.; Singer, J.L.
TI: Reasons for drug and alcohol use by college students
SO: International Journal of the Addictions, 15:489-498, 1980
IN: Center for Alcohol and Addiction Studies, University of Alaska, Anchorage,
     Alaska
RF: 14

SUMMARY TABLE

DRUG:	alcohol; barbiturates; amphetamines; hallucinogens; marijuana
TYPE:	college students
NUMBER:	854
SEX:	male and female
AGE:	college/university
ETHNICITY:	not specified
LOCATION:	[New Haven, Connecticut; Murray, Kentucky]
METHODOLOGY:	correlational survey
INSTRUMENT(S):	Imaginal Processes Inventory; Personality Research Form; Sensation Seeking Scales; Locus of Control Scale; questionnaire
CONDUCTED:	1973-1974

PURPOSE

The study was undertaken with a sample of college students to examine the relationships between motives for alcohol/drug use and personality. Canonical correlation analysis was used to examine the interrelatedness of self-perceived reasons for alcohol and drug use and personality needs, daydreaming, mental style, optimal level of stimulation, and locus of control. Students also completed a drug use questionnaire.

FINDINGS

1. The overall multivariate relationship of alcohol use variables and the personality/daydreaming scales was found to be highly significant (p. 491).

2. On the first canonical dimension, high loadings were obtained for the use of alcohol in connection with hot weather and in order to have fun, with further substantial loadings for alcohol use following hard work and in order to feel better and happier. On the first dimension the two domains were linked in a pattern interpreted as normal for action-oriented male college students (p. 493).

3. On the second canonical dimension, alcohol was used to reduce loneliness, pressure, sadness, and problems, as well as a means to forget, to worry less, to increase confidence, and to compensate for low self-esteem. The second dimension is interpreted as a factor of alcohol use associated with the reduction of negative affect and neurotic daydreaming (p. 493).

4. On the third canonical dimension, alcohol was used to deal with problems and to cope with anger. The third dimension is viewed as a conforming type of social drinking by the individual with needs to belong to a group (p. 493).

5. The fourth canonical dimension had high loadings for the use of alcohol to cope with shyness, forgetfulness, low self-esteem, and to get along with others (p. 493).

6. In a canonical correlation analysis of marijuana use and personality/daydreaming variables, the highest loadings were on the use of marijuana to expand consciousness, to have new experiences, and to gain self-insight. The personality/daydreaming dimension, which correlated 0.45 with the enhancement of cognitive experiences through marijuana use, showed positive loadings for experience sensation seeking and for the needs for understanding and autonomy. The analysis is interpreted as suggesting a nonreckless use of marijuana associated with a general inquisitiveness and a desire for new cognitive experiences (p. 494).

7. Canonical correlation analysis showed a significant relationship between polydrug use and personality/daydreaming variables. The first canonical dimension suggests a pattern similar to that found for alcohol use and is interpreted as the linkage of a neurotic mental style with polydrug use to control maladaptive thoughts (p. 495).

8. A second canonical dimension for polydrug use had its highest loading for marijuana use together with a loading for amphetamine use and suggests that drug use is linked to the individual's tendency to seek pleasure in his own environment (p. 496).

CONCLUSION

The findings from canonical analysis suggest that there is a complex multidimensional relationship between drug use and personality. Studies based on a unidimensional drug/alcohol use continuum may not reveal the true nature of the relationship. Two distinctly different dimensions have been found. One dimension is a motive for substance use to increase positive affect, and the second is a motive for substance use to decrease negative affect. These dimensions have quite different patterns of personality and private experience correlates.

IX. DRUG USE AMONG ETHNIC MINORITY YOUTH

AN: 203
AU: Bonnheim, M.L.; Korman, M.
TI: Family interaction and acculturation in Mexican-American inhalant users
SO: Unpublished paper, 1978. 21 pp.
IN: Department of Psychology, University of Texas Health Science Center, Dallas, Texas
RF: 36

SUMMARY TABLE

DRUG: volatile solvents
TYPE: inhalant users and their parents
NUMBER: 20 (10 users; 10 controls)
SEX: male
AGE: 11-16 years
ETHNICITY: Mexican-American
LOCATION: Dallas, Texas
METHODOLOGY: comparative, correlational survey
INSTRUMENT(S):   questionnaire; structured interview
CONDUCTED: not specified

PURPOSE

In order to examine specific family attributes and interactions which may characterize the families of inhalant users, 20 three-person Mexican-American families consisting of a mother, father, and male adolescent were studied. In ten of these families, the child used inhalants, while in the other ten families, the child did not. The families were interviewed, and the interviews were assessed with respect to family organization, communication patterns, and individual characteristics. Each individual was also administered an acculturation questionnaire, since it was believed that inhalant use might be related to the level of acculturation of the individual family members, especially if the child's level of acculturation was very different from that of his parents.

FINDINGS

1. The families of inhalant users were more confused, negativistic, inconsistent, and internally conflicted than the families in which the child was not an inhalant user (p. 12).

2. Anxiety levels were high in the families of inhalant users and the families were more defensive than families without inhalant users (p. 12).

3. A marked generation gap was noted in the families of inhalant users (p. 12).

4. Communication was not goal-directed in the families of inhalant users, while communication was straightforward and goal-directed in families without inhalant users (p. 12).

5. Compared with families without inhalant users, families of inhalant users were more disorganized and family members were seen as being different from one another (p. 12).

6. In families of inhalant users, there was a trend for the father and child to be viewed as family scapegoats and for the child to act as if his parents were unimportant (p. 12).

7. While there were no strong coalitions between family members in the families of inhalant users, a strong and productive coalition was observed between the mother and father in the families with no inhalant users (p. 17).

8. While conflict between family members was evident in families with inhalant users, conflict was not as evident in families without inhalant users, and when conflict did occur, it was handled more supportively and with less criticism and divisiveness (p. 17).

9. Inhalant use was not found to be related to the acculturation levels of the father, mother, or child in the Mexican-American families studied (p. 14).

10. Mexican-American adolescents whose acculturation level was markedly different from that of their parents were not more likely to use inhalants than were adolescents with acculturation levels equal to those of their parents (p. 15).

11. The inhalant-using adolescents were withdrawn and noncommunicative with their parents, and seemed alienated from the family (p. 17).

CONCLUSION

Mexican-American families in which adolescent children used inhalants were less healthy and more conflicted than similar families in which adolescent children did not use inhalants. It is unclear whether or not there is a causal link between inhalant use and family interaction. Family conflict, inconsistency, and disorganization probably precede inhalant use by adolescents, but the child's use of inhalants may also exacerbate the family's problems. Adolescence is a time when the child must find his identity in the outside world, while at the same time retaining the support of his family. For the Mexican-American adolescent from an already conflicted family, the difficulty of asserting his identity in an Anglo-dominated society, combined with lack of support at home, heightens the stress of adolescence, and inhalants are used as one means of coping with this stress.

AN: 204
AU: Boyle, J.M.; Brunswick, A.F.
TI: What happened in Harlem? Analysis of a decline in heroin use among a
     generation unit of urban black youth
SO: Journal of Drug Issues, 10:109-130, 1980
IN: Columbia University, New York, New York
RF: 12

SUMMARY TABLE

DRUG: heroin
TYPE: heroin users
NUMBER: 535
SEX: male (52%); female (48%)
AGE: 18-23 years
ETHNICITY: black
LOCATION: New York (Harlem), New York
METHODOLOGY: retrospective survey
INSTRUMENT(S):   interview
CONDUCTED: 1975-1976

PURPOSE

The annual prevalence of heroin use among black adolescents and young adults in
Harlem declined from 8% in 1970-1971 to about 3% in 1975-1976. The reasons for
this decline were analyzed from interviews with a representative community sample
of young black men and women whose drug histories were compared to various factors
that may have influenced the decline, such as direct government policy in the
forms of supply variables, legal sanctions, and treatment efforts. To assess the
influence of broad social changes on heroin use, the sample was divided into six
cohorts by age of birth, and the drug histories and the reasons given for nonuse
or cessation of use of heroin were also compared.

FINDINGS

1. Heroin use among young black men and women in Harlem declined by more than 50%
from the early 1970s to 1975 (p. 113).

2. The decline in heroin use among young adults in Harlem showed no close
association with changes in the supply of the drug as measured by price and purity
(p. 118).

3. Opiate arrests in Harlem declined during the same period (1971-1974) that
heroin use was declining, indicating that arrest rates were reflecting rather than
causing the change in heroin prevalence (p. 118).

4. Drug treatment did not explain the major source of decline in heroin use in
Harlem in the early 1970s; the percentage of current users was virtually
identical among heroin users who had been in treatment and those who had not
(p. 118).

5. When a sample of young adults in Harlem was divided into six birth cohorts (those born in 1952, 1953, 1954, 1955, 1956, and 1957), it was found that heroin use declined progressively from 24% in the oldest cohort to 3% in the two youngest; when heroin use for all cohorts through age 18 was considered, the same pattern of progressive decline held true. The rate of current heroin users compared to lifetime users increased from older to younger across the four older cohorts: 8%, 17%, 29%, and 50%. But in the two youngest cohorts, the proportion of current users dropped to 33% and then to zero (p. 120-121).

6. Most of the young adults in Harlem who had used heroin discontinued use within a limited span of time, approximately four years. The youngest individuals studied (those born in 1956 and 1957) terminated use even more quickly than this (p. 122).

7. When asked what issues influenced their decision not to use drugs or to increase use of drugs, young adults in Harlem rarely offered cost or legal sanctions as reasons (p. 122).

8. When asked what deterred them from using drugs or using them more, young adults in Harlem most often cited observation of the consequences of drug use on others, a concern for self-control, and a concern about health consequences (pp. 122, 125).

9. The most common reason given by young adults in Harlem for stopping heroin use was having a bad experience with drugs (82% males, 87% females); the least common reason was cost (51% males, 53% females) (p. 125).

10. The general sample of youth in Harlem was less likely to agree that trouble with the law was an important reason for stopping drug use (59% males, 49% females) than were the heroin users among the sample (71% males, 64% females). Male heroin users indicated trouble with the law as the second most common reason for stopping use (p. 125).

11. Among this sample of young adults in Harlem, younger men were more likely than older men to cite as reasons for not using heroin: family opposition (72% younger, 52% older), its effects on health (77%, 63%), and its effects on employment (59%, 45%) (p. 125).

12. Young adults from Harlem learned about drugs more from peers (53%), other people who used drugs (52%), and their own experience with drugs (25%) than from the media (18%) or education in schools (12%) (p. 128).

CONCLUSION

There is no apparent correlation between direct government policy in the form of supply variables, legal sanctions, or treatment efforts and the decline of heroin use found among a sample of 18-23 year old black youths in Harlem. However, there is evidence to suggest that broad social and contextual changes affected the decline, so that those persons born in 1957 were less likely to initiate use and were more likely to discontinue use rapidly than those born in 1952. Responses to interview questions reveal a growing concern with the undesirable health, social, and economic consequences of heroin use. These findings suggest that for most individuals, the actions of initiating and discontinuing heroin use appear to be a product of rational choice, based on weighing perceived benefits with estimated costs. This change in attitude was effected through the changed content of the information environment in the late 1960s. Both government policy (the Rockefeller law in 1973 and the subsequent publicity on increased penalties) and, more probably, changes in social and community context, such as new community organizations, Black Muslims, neighborhood self-help activities, and the like, all of which advocated ethnic pride and responsibility, are partially responsible for the change in heroin use. However, the effects of direct observation and personal experience appear to be the strongest deterrents to drug use.

AN: 205
AU: Brunswick, A.F.
TI: Health and drug behavior: A study of urban black adolescents
SO: Addictive Diseases: An International Journal, 3:197-214, 1977
IN: Columbia University, New York, New York
RF: 15

SUMMARY TABLE

DRUG: multidrug
TYPE: drug users
NUMBER: 19 (total sample 752)
SEX: male and female
AGE: 12-17 years
ETHNICITY: black
LOCATION: New York (Harlem), New York
METHODOLOGY: comparative survey
INSTRUMENT(S):   interview; school records; medical records
CONDUCTED: 1968-1970

PURPOSE

The study explores the relationships between health and drug behavior. The
following interrelationships were analyzed: physical and emotional health status
and drug use, physical development patterns and drug use, mental health and drug
use. The study also compared drug users with drug nonusers on a wide range of
psychosocial and background factors such as feelings of competency, achievement in
school, occupational aspiration, etc. The findings were based on interviews with
19 drug-using young people selected from a larger study population of 752,
consisting mainly of black adolescents (12 to 17 years) from one health district
in New York. The smaller drug-using group was compared with the total sample on
various attitudes, behaviors, and characteristics.

OPERATIONAL DEFINITIONS

Older drug users: adolescents 16 to 17 years old.

Younger drug users: adolescents below age 16.

Total sample: 752 black adolescents from which the 19 drug users were drawn and
with whom the latter were compared.

FINDINGS

1. Drug users differed from the total sample on three self-reported indicators of
general health status: total number of health problems, limitation on activities
in or out of school, and days absent from school for health reasons (p. 205).

2. Drug users, regardless of age, were more likely to be in poorer health than
their age peers (p. 205).

3. Approximately four in five older drug users had a futile or depressed attitude (p. 205).

4. The older drug users more frequently reported feelings of estrangement or loneliness, even when among friends, than did their peers in the total sample (p. 205).

5. Almost twice as many older users as others in the sample reported "a lot" of worry about the future (p. 205).

6. Known drug users, regardless of age, were much more likely to smoke cigarettes than were nondrug users of similar age (p. 205).

7. Drinking was significantly related to drug use only in the younger drug users. Among older drug users, drinking was as common as among other young people of similar age (p. 209).

8. No drug user had obtained a grade average of C or better during the preceding school year, whereas slightly more than four in ten in the total sample had (p. 209).

9. Most drug users (nine out of ten) of both age levels, but particularly those ages 16 to 17, said that they spent most of their time with friends, compared with about half for the total sample (p. 209).

10. Drug users were less likely to attend church than their peers (p. 209).

11. Drug users had higher occupational aspirations than their peers, but the discrepancy between their aspirations and expectations was greater (p. 209).

12. More than half of the older drug users (compared with a quarter of the younger users and a quarter of the total sample) expected to be dead before age 60 (p. 210).

CONCLUSION

Drug users in this sample of black adolescents smoked more than their peers, had lower school grades, were more often neither in school nor working, more often aspired to some professional occupation, and exhibited a greater gap between professional aspiration and expectation. Selection into drug use was not accidental; rather, it was contingent upon general health status, developmental patterns, and psychological and demographic variables. The findings regarding social structural or demographic variables fit in with theories of status incongruency and social stress as factors in the etiology of drug use among young black people. The findings revealing differences between older and younger drug users suggest that different norms may operate within different age groupings of adolescent drug users. But more research is needed to distinguish between those differences that result from developmental progression with age and those that result from changes in historical context.

```
AN:  206
AU:  Brunswick, A.F.
TI:  Black youths and drug-use behavior
SO:  In: Beschner, G., and Friedman, A., eds.  Youth Drug Abuse.  Lexington, MA:
     D.C.  Health, 1979.  pp.  443-490.
IN:  Columbia University, New York, New York
RF:  44
```

SUMMARY TABLE

```
DRUG:             multidrug
TYPE:             black youths
NUMBER:           535
SEX:              male (52%);  female (48%)
AGE:              18-23 years
ETHNICITY:        black
LOCATION:         New York (Harlem), New York
METHODOLOGY:      cross-sectional, descriptive survey
INSTRUMENT(S):    interview
CONDUCTED:        1975-1976
```

PURPOSE

In order to examine nonmedical substance use by a sample of black youths from the
Harlem section of New York City, the extent and nature of drug use and the
characteristics of different drug users were studied from an epidemiological or
population perspective. The data for this report came from the second wave of a
prospective health study of urban black adolescents ages 18 to 23. The study
group was drawn in the late 1960s on the basis of a stratified community
probability sample of households located in a single inner-city health district,
Central Harlem, New York City. The follow-up, on which the findings in this
report are based, was conducted in 1975-1976.

FINDINGS

1. The rate of current (past month) marijuana use (56%) among black young males
was about the same as that reported for cigarette smoking (57%) and only slightly
less than the rate of current alcohol drinking (63%) (p. 448).

2. Rates of drug use for black males were generally higher than for females on
all illicit drugs, although females showed more experimentation with marijuana and
an equal percentage of methadone use (nonexperimental). The two drugs black men
used most heavily were marijuana, first, and then heroin, with methadone a distant
third. Among women, the most heavily used drug was heroin, with methadone and
marijuana following with almost equivalent frequencies (pp. 448-450).

3. When compared with figures on drug use from a national sample (see AN 200),
the rates of use of illicit drugs in this low-income black community were higher,
especially for the use of marijuana, heroin, and cocaine (p. 451).

4. A comparison of lifetime use and past-year use showed that not all black
youths who began use of a drug continued to use it (p. 451).

5. Alcohol was the earliest used drug among black youth. For males, it preceded marijuana use by a year on the average; for females, who were most likely to use heroin next, the interval was slightly more than a year. Psychedelics were the last drug to be used and the most likely to be used experimentally. Cocaine use also started later than marijuana and heroin use, but its lifetime prevalence was second only to marijuana (p. 460).

6. The major life activity at the time of initiation to use of any drug among black youth was "going to school" (p. 460).

7. Heroin was used with greatest frequency by black youth, followed by alcohol and marijuana. Only a small number of cocaine or psychedelic users took those substances on a weekly basis, with psychedelics used least frequently (p. 460).

8. Duration of use of any substance correlated with age at onset among black youth. Alcohol and marijuana were the longest-used drugs, heroin was third, while psychedelics had been used over the shortest period of time. Data on recency of last use indicated that a large percentage of the subjects (77%) had stopped using heroin (no use in the past year) (p. 460).

9. There was a weak but statistically reliable association between early alcohol drinking and the use of illicit drugs among black youth, with the strongest relationship being between early use of alcohol and male cocaine use (p. 461).

10. For black youths, there was a strong association between early onset of heroin use and its frequent use. To a lesser extent, early marijuana use also was associated with more frequent marijuana use. Males' (but not females') early alcohol use had a weak (but reliable) association with frequent use. Frequency of heroin use showed a strong association with duration of use among males. Frequent marijuana use was associated with longer use among both sexes. Frequent alcohol use had a weak but significant association with duration among females only (p. 461).

11. About four in ten females and six in ten males in this sample of black youths had used two or more drugs during the past year. The most common combination was alcohol and marijuana (36%), followed by the three-drug combination of alcohol, cocaine, marijuana (9%) and the four-drug combination of alcohol, marijuana, heroin, cocaine (6%). Females were twice as likely as males to use just one drug, while males were twice as likely as females to use as many as three, four, or five drugs. Psychedelics were most often used by polydrug users and were used most frequently in the four-drug combination which excluded heroin (pp. 462-463).

12. About three-quarters (72%) of young black males and one-half of young black females used both alcohol and marijuana nonexperimentally (p. 462).

13. Heavy alcohol use increased with hard-drug use; heroin users of both sexes were the heaviest drinkers (p. 462).

14. Marijuana was the only one of the illicit drugs studied for which the majority of young black users did not progress to the use of any harder drug (p. 466).

15. Heroin and cocaine users among black youth almost always also used marijuana. Most heroin users were also cocaine users (p. 466).

16. There was a substantially greater use of all drugs (but especially heroin) among black females born between 1952 and 1954 than among the younger women in the study. Most black male heroin users in this sample were born between 1953 and 1955 and very few younger black men used heroin (pp. 466-467).

17. Both male and female heroin users completed less education than other black youth (p. 467).

18. Male heroin users were less likely than other young black males to be employed; female heroin users were twice as likely to stay home as other black females (p. 471).

19. Considerably more female heroin users were married than the other young black women in the sample. Parenthood status was highly associated with heroin use for both men and women; 49% of the male heroin users and 74% of the female users reported having one or more children (pp. 469-471).

20. There was no association between drug use and migrational-generational status among young black males, but female hard-drug users were less likely to be first generation immigrants (mother and daughter both born in the South) than their peers (p. 469).

21. Maternal school attainment was generally below high school completion and the rate was slightly higher for heroin-using black youths (p. 471).

22. Hard drug users were more likely than other young blacks to have more drug-using friends, with the exception of female heroin users, whose proportions of drug-using friends were not greater than among alcohol- or marijuana-using females (p. 470).

23. Approximately 21% of the young black males and females who drank or used illicit drugs reported some problems (cognitive, perceptual, emotional) stemming from the use of one or another of these substances. Alcohol was the drug most often cited as resulting in problems (by 33% of the males and 44% of the females who had problems) and heroin was second, cited by about one in five of each sex (p. 472).

24. Although only small percentages of the total group of black youth had been in heroin treatment (9% of the males and 7% of the females), approximately half of all those who had ever used heroin (45% of the males, 53% of the females) had been treated (p. 472-473).

25. Young black female heroin users were more likely to go into a treatment program and to remain in treatment for longer periods than males, but females had generally used heroin longer (four years or more) before entering treatment than males (p. 473).

26. The most frequently given reason for entering a heroin treatment program was "wanting it" (cited by 78% of black female heroin users and 48% of the males); the second most common reason, given by 30% of the males, was "to please others" (p. 475).

27. Young black female heroin users were more likely to be treated in a methadone clinic (61%) than were males (23%), while male heroin users were more likely to go to a nonmethadone clinic or hospital service. About one third of both sexes had had some experience in residential treatment. More female heroin users received

methadone therapy than males (74% and 50%, respectively); personal therapy was
the second most common service (57% for females, 44% males) (p. 475).

28. Young black heroin users of both sexes who were currently or had been in
treatment had used heroin longer than those never treated (p. 475).

29. Young black heroin users who had been in a treatment program were less
educated than those never treated and were less likely to be working (p. 476).

CONCLUSION

The major illicit drugs used by black youths were marijuana, heroin, and cocaine,
in that order. Marijuana use among males was close to the rates of use of tobacco
and alcohol. Males used illicit drugs more often than females. Heavy drinking
was associated with illicit drug use, particularly heroin. Marijuana and cocaine
were the drugs of more enduring use, while many heroin users had stopped using
heroin; further study is needed to determine the factors which support or
encourage termination of heroin use. Most black youths used more than one drug,
with alcohol and marijuana the most frequent combination. Most marijuana users
did not become users of other illicit drugs, suggesting that the transition from
marijuana use to the use of hard drugs should not be assessed in a linear way.
When personal characteristics of drug users were compared, only heroin users were
consistently different; differences were greater for females than for males.
Heroin users were less educated, more likely to stay at home, to be unemployed,
and to have children. Female heroin users were more likely than male heroin users
to have entered treatment and to have remained in treatment longer; they also had
used heroin longer before entering treatment. Heroin users in treatment were more
likely to have used heroin longer, had completed less education, had less
employment, and were more likely to continue using heroin than those not in
treatment. Because illicit drug use is (statistically) more norm violating for
young women than young men, women who use heroin show a greater commitment to its
use with more serious life outcomes than men, suggesting the need for further
research on female heroin users and a recognition in policy formulation and
treatment plans of their specific problems.

AN: 207
AU: Brunswick, A.F.; Boyle, J.M.
TI: Patterns of drug involvement: Developmental and secular influences on age at
     initiation
SO: Youth and Society, 11:139-172, 1979
IN: Columbia University, New York, New York
RF: 29

SUMMARY TABLE

DRUG: multidrug
TYPE: black youths
NUMBER: 535
SEX: male (52%); female (48%)
AGE: 18-23 years
ETHNICITY: black
LOCATION: New York (Harlem), New York
METHODOLOGY: correlational survey
INSTRUMENT(S):   interview
CONDUCTED: 1975-1976

PURPOSE

The study focused on observed changes in the incidence and prevalence of drug use.
Patterns of drug involvement are considered in terms of development/maturational,
sociohistorical, and situational factors. The data were drawn from a longitudinal
survey in which respondents were first identified and interviewed in 1968-1970 at
ages 12 through 17, and reinterviewed six to eight years later (1975-1976) at ages
18 through 23. Results reported are from the second set of interviews. The
following research questions were posed: Is there a developmental pattern for
drug initiation? Is there a birth-cohort effect on drug initiation? Is there a
chronological effect on drug initiation? Can secular and/or historical effects be
rejected as artifacts of the developmental process or do they have independent
explanatory roles?

FINDINGS

1. The relative order of lifetime prevalence for the various drugs studied were
(from high to low): alcohol, marijuana, cocaine, psychedelics, heroin,
amphetamines, barbiturates, inhalants. Psychedelics were used more often than
heroin experimentally, but the reverse was true for nonexperimental use (p. 145).

2. Twenty-two percent of women in the sample and 37% of men reported the use of
some illicit drug "harder" than marijuana on more than an experimental basis
(p. 145).

3. The prevalence of current use of all drugs studied was lower than lifetime
nonexperimental use, indicating that nonmedical drug use can be stopped by some
people (p. 147).

4. Marijuana and cocaine were the most "currently" used drugs, followed by
methadone (p. 147).

5. Heroin, barbiturates, and amphetamines showed the highest rates of discontinuance; current use was less than a fourth of lifetime nonexperimental use (p. 147).

6. Among four drugs (marijuana, heroin, cocaine, psychedelics), marijuana and heroin use began earliest. Use of marijuana and heroin began between ages 13 and 16; use of cocaine and psychedelics began later, usually between ages 15 and 20 (pp. 147-148).

7. Except for psychedelics, rates of initiation to drugs peaked to varying degrees between ages 16 and 18 (p. 150).

8. Prevalence of heroin use showed the strongest cohort association; it dropped sharply from the oldest to the youngest cohort. Marijuana use showed a less marked (than heroin) association, with younger cohorts attaining higher prevalence of use before age 19 than did older cohorts (p. 152).

9. The mean ages at first use in younger and older cohorts were surprisingly constant for each drug (marijuana, heroin, cocaine, psychedelics) (p. 154).

10. Marijuana, heroin, and cocaine initiation showed no significant association with calendar year beyond what was explained by developmental age. Of the drugs studied, situational factors, expressed by calendar year, had some effect on initiation of psychedelic use alone (p. 157).

CONCLUSION

The analysis was intended to explore the relative effect of age, birth cohort, and calendar year on time of initiation of drug use. The major findings were the following: developmental age had a clear effect on initiation of drug use; differential social norms and outlooks (as reflected by birth cohort variations) had some effect on lifetime prevalence rates for individual drug use; situational factors such as drug availability, which would be reflected in calendar year of onset, showed little effect independent of developmental age. Furthermore, it was found that there was little change in age risk for initiation in successive age cohorts within the time period and for the population studied

AN: 208
AU: Caplovitz, D.
TI: Youngsters Experimenting with Drugs
SO: New York: Graduate School and University Center, City University of New
     York, 1980. 150 pp.
IN: Graduate School and University Center, City University of New York
RF: 0

SUMMARY TABLE

DRUG: multidrug
TYPE: adolescents
NUMBER: 609 total (subsample of 394 interviewed at 3 points in time)
SEX: male
AGE: 10-15 years
ETHNICITY: Hispanic (69%); black (21%); white (7%); Oriental (3%)
LOCATION: New York (Lower East Side), New York
METHODOLOGY: longitudinal panel study
INSTRUMENT(S):   interview
CONDUCTED: not specified

PURPOSE

Since illicit drug use, particularly of marijuana, has become increasingly common
in younger age groups, a longitudinal panel study of 10-13 year old boys was
conducted to determine the extent of experimentation with illicit drugs and some
factors associated with use. Because drug use is especially prevalent in
low-income communities, subjects were located through canvassing of families
living in low-income housing projects on the lower East Side of New York City.
Initial interviews (Wave I) were conducted with 543 boys and their mothers;
eleven months later (Wave II), 443 boys (82%) of the original sample were
reinterviewed as well as 40 new boys and their mothers. At the time of the third
and final wave of sampling, eleven months later, 26 new boys and their mothers
were interviewed, while boys who had been interviewed on either Wave I or Wave II
or both were reinterviewed. Most of the findings are reported for the 394 boys
who were interviewed on all three waves; however, when drug use patterns were
observed for both the entire sample of 609 and the subsample of 394, the results
were comparable. Although nearly equal numbers of 10, 11, 12, and 13 year olds
were interviewed on Wave I, the oldest boys were the most difficult to locate for
reinterviewing and their rate of response fell off sharply. Data on drug use and
the influences of family, peer group, school, values, attitudes, and personality
were described from the information gathered in the interviews; some
contradictions and errors, especially in the reporting of drug use occurred,
perhaps because of the influence of the setting of the interview, which was
sometimes in the home and sometimes in the presence of the mother.

FINDINGS

1. Alcohol, especially in the forms of beer and wine, was the only drug used with
any frequency (26%) among lower-income 10-13 year old boys, and alcohol use
increased to 45% by the time the boys were 12-15. Marijuana use increased over
the same time period from 8% to 18% as did use of hard liquor (3% to 16%). Only
about 1% of the youngsters reported using other illicit drugs at any point in

time, with the highest rate being 2% for cocaine when the boys were 12-15; the use of angel dust (PCP) and pills (amphetamines or barbiturates) declined over the period of the study (pp. 9-12).

2. Older boys were more likely to use wine, beer, hard liquor, and marijuana and to report that their friends did so than the younger boys. The same trends were apparent for other illicit drugs, although only small percentages reported the use of angel dust and pills; cocaine was the most popular illicit drug after marijuana, with 8% of 15 year olds reporting use (pp. 12-17).

3. In a group of lower-income boys, over three-quarters reported no use of marijuana, while one-tenth reported one use only and another tenth reported current use. The percentages of boys who reported using marijuana once and then stopping (ex-users) exceeded the percentages of current users in every age group, except that of 13 year olds (pp. 25, 27).

4. For 10-15 year old boys, there were no major differences in drug involvement among the three major ethnic groups (whites, blacks, and Spanish-speaking), although blacks seemed somewhat more likely and whites somewhat less likely to use marijuana; none of the 11 Oriental boys used marijuana or any other illicit drug, whereas approximately a quarter of the boys in the other ethnic groups reported such drug use (pp. 30-31).

5. The findings on the relationship between source and level of family income and drug involvement for 10-15 year old boys were contradictory. Although boys from families with incomes over $15,000 reported more use of illicit drugs than boys from families with lower incomes, when source of income was examined, boys from families supported by social security were most likely to use illicit drugs (42%), followed by boys from welfare families (29%), and finally boys whose parents worked (19%) (pp. 32-33).

6. Family stability (broken home vs intact home) had no bearing on drug involvement for low-income boys; sons of divorced mothers had the lowest rates of marijuana and illicit drug use (12%) and sons of widows had the highest (40%) (pp. 33-34).

7. Close familial relationships, close supervision, and readiness to punish the child for wrongdoing were strong deterrents to drug use, particularly marijuana use, among low-income boys (pp. 50-51).

8. Family exposure to addicts, use of drugs by family members, and mother's permissive attitudes toward drugs were powerful influences leading to drug involvement on the part of low-income boys (p. 51).

9. Although the quality of family relations was an important influence on marijuana use for the boys in the sample, it did not affect the decision to stop use, suggesting that the family plays only a deterrent role, but that once a boy uses marijuana, his decision to give it up or continue is not influenced by his family (p. 50).

10. Low-income boys were more likely to report that their friends used drugs than that they themselves used drugs, but whereas self-use of drugs sharply increased as the youngsters got older, data on drug use by friends did not show a similar trend. Only about one-fourth (26%) said their friends never used any drugs including alcohol; the majority of the boys belonged to peer groups in which illegal drugs were part of the group culture (pp. 52-53).

11. Membership in a peer group, especially in a peer group with a name (a gang) or a peer group that was "tough" and prone to delinquent behavior, was related to more drug involvement, particularly with illicit drugs. Some peer group influences were positive and contributed to avoidance of drugs, but boys who identified themselves as leaders of a group were more likely to use drugs than nonleaders (pp. 54-58).

12. When the influences of family and peer groups upon drug involvement were examined for a group of early adolescent boys, involvement with peers and types of peer groups were more important influences than the quality of family relations (p. 68).

13. Low commitment to school, as measured by frequent absences, tardiness, neglect of homework, leaving school without permission, and expressed dislike for school, was highly related to drug involvement, especially marijuana use, for low-income boys. Boys who did not have good relations with their teachers were more likely to use illicit drugs, and boys who said that their teachers yelled at and made fun of students were also more deeply involved with drugs. Good school performance was related to less use of drugs, while frequent bad experiences in school (such as thefts and fights) were related to higher use of illicit drugs (pp. 111-112).

14. Negative peer influences were found to be more influential in terms of drug involvement among low-income boys than were variables relating to school commitment, performance, and bad school experiences (p. 89).

15. Delinquent behavior among young adolescent boys was highly related to drug use, especially use of illicit drugs (p. 91).

16. Signs of insecurity (such as not being popular, being ridiculed, etc.) were not related to drug use by 10-15 year old boys. Boys out of step with the majority (in terms of being good at sports and liking to fix things) were somewhat more likely to use illicit drugs, but the minority of boys who said they tried hard to be like others avoided drug use. Finally, boys who did not see themselves as calm and relaxed, who did not feel happy, and who got angry easily were much more likely to use drugs, especially illicit drugs, than boys who did not have these traits (pp. 90-93).

17. Low-income boys who did not respect the law, who felt they were victims of prejudice, and who were tolerant of drug use were much more likely to use illicit drugs than boys who held the opposite views (pp. 93-98).

18. For a group of low-income boys, those who planned to go to college were only slightly less likely to use drugs than those who did not want to go to college, but the small minority of boys who thought they would not be able to attend college were much more likely to use drugs than the others, perhaps reflecting a pessimism about their opportunities. When asked about occupational aspirations, boys who wanted to be doctors reported little use of illicit drugs (8%), while 42% of the boys who wanted to be artists used such drugs. The percentages of boys aspiring to other occupations who used illicit drugs fell between 21% (military) to 30% (lawyers) (pp. 100-101).

19. For low-income boys, indications of personality problems and disrespect for the law influenced drug involvement, even when other variables (family, peer group, and school influence) were held constant, but perception of prejudice and tolerance of drug use had only a weak effect on drug involvement when the other

variables were considered (p. 108).

CONCLUSION

Only a quarter of low-income boys had used marijuana or harder drugs by the end of
a two-year study period when the boys ranged in age from 12 to 15. Illicit drug
use increased with age, from 3% of the 10 year old boys interviewed at the start
of the study, to 42% of the 15 year olds interviewed two years later. Certain
factors were found to be associated with drug use. Boys who were closely
supervised, who felt they had close relationships with their parents, and who were
disciplined when they got in trouble were much less likely to use drugs,
especially marijuana, than boys who were seldom supervised, who had distant or
troubled relationships with their parents, and who were seldom punished. Peer
groups also had a strong influence on drug use: boys who belonged to "tough" peer
groups, especially gangs, were more likely to use drugs than boys who belonged to
peer groups with a positive influence; boys who were leaders of their peer groups
were more likely to use drugs than nonleaders. School also played a major role in
drug involvement; boys who were deeply committed to school were much less likely
to use drugs, especially marijuana. Good school performance was associated with
less drug use. Finally, attitudes and values had an influence on drug use, with
boys who reported delinquent behavior, little respect for the law, tolerant
attitudes toward drug use, and personality problems, and those who felt they were
the victims of prejudice being more likely to use illicit drugs than their peers.
These findings have implications for drug prevention. Certain child-rearing
practices (such as close supervision and strict discipline) serve as deterrents to
drug use. Schools can also deter drug use if teachers are trained to be
considerate of students and if students are encouraged to make a commitment to
school through the development of interesting and exciting programs. Even peer
groups, if directed toward positive activities such as sports and community
betterment, might contribute to drug prevention.

AN: 209
AU: Ensminger, M.E.; Brown, C.H.; Kellam, S.G.
TI: Sex differences in antecedents of substance use among adolescents
SO: Journal of Social Issues, 38:25-42, 1982
IN: Social Psychiatry Study Center, Department of Psychiatry, University of
     Chicago, Chicago, Illinois
RF: 30

SUMMARY TABLE

DRUG: marijuana; alcohol; cigarettes
TYPE: adolescents (ten-year follow-up of 1966-1967 first graders)
NUMBER: 705
SEX: male (345); female (360)
AGE: 16-17 years
ETHNICITY: black
LOCATION: Chicago (Woodlawn), Illinois
METHODOLOGY: prospective longitudinal survey
INSTRUMENT(S):   questionnaire; Metropolitan Readiness Test; Teacher's Observation
                  of Classroom Adaptation
CONDUCTED: 1966-1967; 1975-1976

PURPOSE

The research focused on sex differences in teenage marijuana, alcohol, and
cigarette use in a population of 705 adolescents of a poor, black community who
had been assessed in first grade and were reassessed ten years later. Sex
differences were examined from the theoretical perspectives of social adaptation
and social bonds. Social adaptation is defined as the success or failure of the
individual in meeting social task demands in a specific social field at a specific
stage of life. Social bonds refer to the attachment and commitment of the
individual to family, school, and peers. Social adaptation was measured by the
first-grade teacher using the Teacher's Observation of Classroom Adaptation and by
the child's score on the Metropolitan Readiness Test. As adolescents, the
subjects completed a questionnaire asking about drug use and social attachments
with family, school, and peers.

FINDINGS

1. Males reported significantly more beer or wine, liquor, and marijuana use than
females, but there were no significant differences between sexes in the rates of
cigarette use (p. 32).

2. Ratings of males as aggressive in first grade were associated with heavy
substance use ten years later; shy first-grade males had significantly less
marijuana and cigarette use as teenagers, but those who were both shy and
aggressive had the highest levels of substance use as teenagers. Early shyness
and aggression in females showed no significant relationship to later substance
use (p. 32).

3. Scores on the Metropolitan Readiness Test in first grade were positively
related to heavy substance use by both males and females (p. 34).

4. A female with low family bonds was four times more likely to use alcohol, and two times more likely to use marijuana than a female with high family bonds. For males, the association between family bonds and substance use was weak (p. 36).

5. A male or female with only weak bonds to school was four times more likely to use marijuana than an individual with strong school bonds. The association between weak school bonds and male cigarette and alcohol use was similar to that for marijuana; the association for females was somewhat weaker (p. 36).

6. Attachment to peers was very important for males' substance use, with high peer bonds associated with heavier drug use. The relation between peer bonds and female substance use was in the same direction as that for males, but was nonsignificant (p. 36).

7. Gender was found to be significant in accounting for frequency of use for beer, hard liquor, and marijuana, but not for cigarettes (p. 37).

CONCLUSION

Sex differences in substance use may occur because of different variables, because the same variables operate in different ways for males and females, or because males and females have different distributions on the predictor variables. Early shyness and aggressiveness were found to be important for later substance use by males but not by females. Metropolitan Readiness Test scores and social bonds were important in terms of substance use for both sexes. For males, substance use was primarily accounted for by peer attachment and school bonds, while for females, family bonds and school bonds were important. There was relatively little significant interaction of predictor variables and gender, but there were important differences by sex in the distribution of predictors.

AN: 210
AU: Goldstein, G.S.
TI: Inhalant abuse among the Pueblo tribes of New Mexico
SO: In: Sharp, C.W.; Carroll, L.T., eds. Voluntary Inhalation of Industrial
     Solvents. Rockville, MD: National Institute on Drug Abuse, 1978. pp.
     90-94.
IN: Department of Hospitals and Institutions for the State of New Mexico
RF: 0

SUMMARY TABLE

DRUG: inhalants
TYPE: Native American adolescents
NUMBER: 2,200
SEX: male (50%); female (50%)
AGE: junior and senior high school
ETHNICITY: Native American
LOCATION: New Mexico
METHODOLOGY: descriptive, comparative survey
INSTRUMENT(S): questionnaire
CONDUCTED: 1975

PURPOSE

In the process of collecting information on substance abuse among Native American
adolescents, data on inhalant use were isolated and studied. Questionnaires on
drug use were given to 2,200 Native American children of junior and senior high
school age in five of the pueblos in New Mexico. Of these, 17.2% (374) had used
or experimented with inhalants, and this subsample was compared to the larger
sample on variables such as sex, religion, age, accessibility of inhalants,
frequency of use, reasons for use, attitudes about and participation in Indian
culture, and peer encouragement and use. Data for this sample were also compared
to data gathered in a Columbia University study of a nationwide sample of
adolescents conducted in 1973 (see AN 138).

FINDINGS

1. In a group of 2,200 Native American adolescents in New Mexico, 17.2% had used
or experimented with inhalants and 13.9% were current users (p. 91).

2. Female Native American adolescents were more likely than males to use
inhalants, apparently because males had greater access to other substances;
although females represented approximately 50% of the total sample, they
constituted 65% of the inhalant users (p. 91).

3. Inhalant users among Native American adolescents were more likely to be
Protestant or Catholic and less likely to belong to the Native American Church
than noninhalant users (p. 91).

4. In a group of Native American adolescents, 13% of those who came from homes
where the Indian language was spoken exclusively used inhalants, while 34.8% of
those who came from homes where only English was spoken used inhalants (p. 91).

5. The mean age of Native American adolescents who used inhalants (14.5 years) was not significantly different from the mean age of those who used other drugs, but the age at which children first used inhalants was significantly lower than the age at which they first used other substances (p. 91).

6. Inhalant use among Native American adolescents was more common in boarding and mission schools in remote or captured environments, probably because of lack of accessibility to other drugs (pp. 91-92).

7. When Native American adolescents were asked how easy it would be to get inhalants, 17.4% said it would be very easy, 14.9% said fairly easy, 10% said difficult, and 57% said impossible; these figures were consistent across all tribes, with the exception of one extremely remote and closed tribe in which 81% of the adolescents said it would be difficult or impossible to secure inhalants (p. 92).

8. Among Native American adolescent inhalant users, 0.3% identified themselves as heavy users, 9.2% as light users, and 0.8% as moderate users; 89.6% were experimenters or nonusers (p. 92).

9. When asked to select from a list of possible reasons for drug misuse, inhalant users among a group of Native American adolescents were more likely to indicate "do not care what happens to me" than nonusers or users of other drugs, with the exception of heavy and addicted drug users. When asked about the prospect of a good future, young inhalant users rated their chances lower than nonusers, light users, and even heavy users of other drugs (p. 92).

10. Native American adolescents who used inhalants were as likely as nonusers to feel that Indian culture was important and to participate in the tribe (p. 92).

11. Among a group of Native American adolescents, inhalant users were more likely than others to feel that they and their parents were not as successful in the Indian way (p. 93).

12. Young Native Americans were more often encouraged by friends to use inhalants than any other drug, including alcohol, with the exception of friends of heavy "dangerous" drug users, who were encouraged to use those drugs about as often as friends of inhalant users were encouraged to use inhalants; there was also a poorer chance that friends of heavy drug or inhalant users would try to stop the use of these substances (p. 93).

13. Native American adolescents who were heavily involved with "dangerous" drugs and glue were more likely to begin using inhalants earlier than other drug users (mean age of 11 and 13, respectively) (p. 93).

14. When compared to a national sample of junior and senior high school students, Native American adolescents showed a higher percentage of inhalant use (17.2% compared to 11.1%) and current use (6.3% compared to 1.7%), although both groups had the same percentages of frequent users (pp. 93-94).

CONCLUSION

Inhalant use is a significant problem among Native American adolescents in the pueblos. Although not the drug of choice, inhalants are easily accessible, particularly to young children and females. Inhalant users often feel less successful in the Indian way of life than nonusers, are more likely to come from homes where English is spoken, and are less likely to belong to the Native American church. Young inhalant users are more likely to be pessimistic about their futures. Peer encouragement towards inhalant and heavy "dangerous" drug use is stronger than for other drugs and alcohol, and early inhalant use is associated with later heavy involvement with "dangerous" drugs and glue. On a number of social questions, inhalant abusers are more like heroin, cocaine, and heavy alcohol users than any other drug users, suggesting that inhalant abuse is not culture specific but is related to poverty and unavailability of other substances.

AN: 211
AU: Goldstein, G.S.; Oetting, E.R.; Edwards, R.; Garcia-Mason, V.
TI: Drug use among Native American adults
SO: International Journal of the Addictions, 14:855-860, 1979
IN: Department of Psychology, Colorado State University, Fort Collins, Colorado
RF: 4

SUMMARY TABLE

DRUG: multidrug
TYPE: young adult Native Americans
NUMBER: 276
SEX: male (127); female (149)
AGE: 21 years (mean)
ETHNICITY: Native American
LOCATION: not specified
METHODOLOGY: descriptive survey
INSTRUMENT(S):   questionnaire
CONDUCTED: 1975

PURPOSE

Although the use of alcohol by young Native Americans has been studied, there has been little study of the extent of use of other drugs. In order to provide this data, a drug use survey was administered to 127 male and 149 female students at an urban, post-high school institution that provided training in arts and technical skills for young Native Americans from various reservations all over the country.

FINDINGS

1. For young Native American adults, beer, liquor, and marijuana were the most popular drugs (p. 856).

2. In a group of young Native American adults, 41% considered themselves moderate to heavy users of beer, 20% considered themselves moderate to heavy users of liquor, and 42% reported having gotten really drunk at least once (pp. 856-857).

3. In a group of young Native American adults, 70% had tried marijuana, 59% had used it in the past two months, and 27% considered themselves moderate to heavy users (pp. 856-858).

4. One out of five young Native American adults had used amphetamines in the past two months and 6% considered themselves moderate to heavy users (p. 858).

5. Almost a third (31%) of Native American young adults had tried inhalants, but only 4% had used inhalants in the past two months (p. 858).

6. Native American young adults reported having tried cocaine (13%), heroin (6%), barbiturates (22%), and hallucinogens (21%), but smaller percentages reported use during the past two months of cocaine (5%), heroin (1%), barbiturates (8%), and hallucinogens (6%), and no moderate to heavy use was reported for any of these drugs, except for 1% who considered themselves moderate to heavy users of hallucinogens (p. 857).

7. Half of the Native American young adults who had tried amphetamines used them only once or twice, but the others who used amphetamines (about 10% of the total group) were also heavily involved with other drugs, accounting for most of the use of cocaine and barbiturates and about half of the hallucinogen use (p. 859).

8. Three-fourths of the Native American young adults had some problem with school authorities because of alcohol use and one-fourth because of drug use. Eight percent said drinking and 54% said drug use had prevented them from doing something they wanted to do (p. 859).

9. Native American young adults who were not part of an intensive multidrug using subgroup and who used hallucinogens just to get high were occasional users who limited their hallucinogen use almost entirely to weekends or holidays (p. 859).

10. Native American young adults when compared to other young adult populations reported higher percentages for the use of every drug, particularly for the use of inhalants (31% compared to between 2% and 4% in the general population) (p. 857).

CONCLUSION

Young adult Native American students at a postsecondary educational institute showed a very high level of use for all drugs when compared with other samples of college-age youth. Alcohol, marijuana, and amphetamines were drugs of choice; 31% had tried inhalants, although there was little current use; 10% were involved in a drug subculture, using multiple drugs relatively heavily. Unless this particular institution attracts a high percentage of drug users, these findings indicate that Native American young adults are more likely to experiment with and use drugs than are other young adults, a tendency which may be exacerbated when they leave relatively isolated environments reservations and move into an urban area where drugs are more readily accessible.

AN: 212
AU: Kellam, S.G.; Brown, C.H.; Fleming, J.P.
TI: Longitudinal community epidemiological studies of drug use: Early
     aggressiveness, shyness, and learning problems
SO: In: Robins, L.N., ed. Studying Drug Use and Abuse. New Brunswick, NJ:
     Rutgers University Press, in press.
IN: Social Psychiatry Study Center, Department of Psychiatry, University of
     Chicago, Chicago, Illinois
RF: 50

SUMMARY TABLE

DRUG: multidrug
TYPE: adolescents (ten-year follow-up of 1966-1967 first graders)
NUMBER: 705
SEX: [male (345); female (360)]
AGE: 16-17 years
ETHNICITY: black
LOCATION: Chicago (Woodlawn), Illinois
METHODOLOGY: prospective longitudinal survey
INSTRUMENT(S):   questionnaire; Teacher's Obervation of Classroom Adaptation;
                 Mother Symptom Inventory
CONDUCTED: 1966-1967; 1975-1976

PURPOSE

In order to study the antecedents of teenage use of licit and illicit drugs,
prospective data were gathered in 1966-1967 on the total population of first-grade
children in Woodlawn, a poor, black Chicago community. The children were assessed
for psychological well-being and social adaptational status and were followed up
ten years later. Families of this cohort were also assessed at the same time
periods. Outcomes were broadly conceptualized for study in terms of social role
performance and psychological status. At the first-grade level, interviews were
conducted with mothers, and teachers rated each child on performance of social
tasks. Ten years later, interviews and assessments were repeated for those
respondents who could be located and who consented to participate.

FINDINGS

1. The pattern of drug use among Woodlawn teenagers was heavily centered on beer
or wine, liquor, marijuana, and cigarettes; males used significantly more beer or
wine, liquor, and marijuana than females (p. 25).

2. More than one-third of the males and about one-sixth of the females reported
using beer or wine and marijuana twenty times or more; fewer used liquor and use
rates for other illicit drugs were low (p. 25).

3. Three characteristics observable in first grade were associated with
adolescent drug use: (1) Higher first-grade IQ test scores predicted more beer or
wine use, and school readiness scores predicted more frequent marijuana and
alcohol use. (2) Males used drugs and alcohol (not cigarettes) more often than
females, and antecedents of later drug use were clearer for males. (3) Children
whose first-grade teachers rated them as shy used drugs less often ten years

later; aggressive first graders used drugs most often ten years later; adapting first graders and those with learning problems became moderate substance users. These findings held more strongly for males than females (pp. 28-29).

4. Shyness and aggressiveness in first-grade females were not related to their drug use in adolescence (p. 31).

5. Aggressiveness in males in first grade led to one and a half times more use in adolescence of beer or wine, hard liquor, marijuana, and cigarettes compared to not-aggressive males (p. 31).

6. Shyness wthout aggression in first grade was found to produce an inhibition of both cigarette and marijuana use in adolescence, with trends in this direction for liquor and beer or wine (p. 31).

7. For cigarette use among adolescents, the difference between the frequency of heavy use in not-aggressive and aggressive children (measured in first grade) was greater among shy children than among not-shy children; i.e., shyness without aggression appeared to decrease the use of cigarettes, but shyness with aggression seemed to enhance use (p.32)

8. Shyness in first grade, whether with or without aggression, inhibited the use of marijuana in adolescence (p. 32).

9. Heavy use by teenagers of beer or wine, liquor, and marijuana was found to be positively related to Metropolitan Readiness Test scores and IQ scores taken in first grade (p. 32).

10. Aggressiveness was found to be the most consistent first-grade antecedent of drug use ten years later (p. 34).

11. School performance in first grade was associated with adolescent drug use, but learning problems were not the important factor; rather, the aggressiveness which tends to be associated with learning problems accounted for the relationship between poor school performance and later drug use (p. 36).

CONCLUSION

Predispositions to drug use are laid down early in childhood, and the antecedents of social adaptational status early in school lead to different outcomes, with some children evolving toward drug use, while others evolve toward psychiatric symptoms and still others to good adjustment. The Woodlawn data confirm the importance of aggressiveness among males as a predictor of drug use. Shyness, on the other hand, acts to inhibit the use of cigarettes and decreases the likelihood of trying marijuana. Shyness and aggressiveness are interpreted as maladaptive responses to the social demand to interact with others and to obey rules. Early psychological status is not a consistent predictor of drug use. It is concluded that drug use is multi-determined. Prevention models must integrate social structural, social adaptational, psychological, and biological determinants.

AN: 213
AU: Kellam, S.G.;   Ensminger, M.E.;   Simon, M.B.
TI: Mental health in first grade and teenage drug, alcohol, and cigarette use
SO: Drug and Alcohol Dependence, 5:273-304, 1980
IN: Social Psychiatry Study Center, Department of Psychiatry, University of
      Chicago, Chicago, Illinois
RF: 42

SUMMARY TABLE

DRUG: multidrug
TYPE: adolescents (ten-year follow-up of 1966-1967 first graders)
NUMBER: 705
SEX: [male (345);   female (360)]
AGE: 16-17 years
ETHNICITY: black
LOCATION: Chicago (Woodlawn), Illinois
METHODOLOGY: prospective longitudinal survey
INSTRUMENT(S): questionnaire;   IQ test;   Metropolitan Readiness Test;   Teacher's
                Observation of Classroom Adaptation;   Mother Symptom Inventory;
                clinical observation
CONDUCTED: 1966-1967;   1975-1976

PURPOSE

In 1976, the investigators reassessed teenagers who had been studied as first
graders in 1966-1967 in Woodlawn, a poor, black Chicago neighborhood. The data
derived from the earlier study on the first graders included results of the
Kuhlmann-Anderson IQ test and the Metropolitan Readiness Test, evaluations of
social adaptational status as measured by the Teacher's Observation of Classroom
Adaptation, and assessment of psychological well-being based on direct clinical
observation and the Mother Symptom Inventory. The 705 teenagers from the original
study group who were relocated completed a self-report questionnaire on drug use,
social involvement scales, and antisocial measures. The two sets of data were
then compared. The focus of the article is upon the relationship between the
psychological and social variables measured in 1966-1967 and drug use ten years
later.

FINDINGS

1. Adolescent males and females reported frequent use of drugs, particularly
alcohol, marijuana, and tobacco, with males reporting more use than females
(p. 280).

2. First-grade teachers' ratings of social adaptational status were related to
teenage drug use for males. Males who were shy in first grade used drugs less
frequently ten years later, while aggressive and shy-aggressive first-grade males
used drugs more often, with adapting males and those with learning problems
falling in the middle range of teenage drug use (p. 289).

3. First-grade teachers' ratings of social adaptational status were related only
to adolescent marijuana use among females;   girls rated as moderate or severe
shy-aggressive in first grade were more likely to use marijuana as adolescents,

while those rated moderate or severe shy in first grade were less likely to use marijuana (p. 289).

4.   Both male and female children who scored high on the first-grade Metropolitan Readiness Test were more likely to use drugs ten years later than those with lower scores (p. 289).

5.   For both males and females, first-grade IQ was related to teenage drug use, with high IQ males and medium and high IQ females more likely to use drugs, particularly beer and wine, than those with low IQs (p. 289).

6.   First-grade psychological well-being was not strongly related to teenage drug use;   those few children who were evaluated as symptomatic in first grade were less likely to use drugs as teenagers than nonsymptomatic children (p. 291).

7.   Teenage antisocial behavior was strongly related to drug use for both males and females;   females reported less antisocial behavior than males, but there was a stronger correlation between antisocial behavior and drug use for females than for males (p. 293).

8.   Teenage social involvement was not related to drug use by females, but was strongly associated with alcohol use by males, and somewhat less so with marijuana and cigarette use (p. 293).

9.   Males who were shy in first grade used drugs less as teenagers than their peers, whether or not they later became more socially involved or more antisocial (p. 295).

10.   For males rated aggressive in first grade, teenage drug use was correlated with teenage antisocial behavior but not with social involvement;   they used beer/wine and marijuana less often if they were less antisocial as teenagers and more often if they were more antisocial, although the use of hard liquor and cigarettes was high for this group regardless of the level of teenage antisocial behavior (p. 298).

11.   For males rated shy-aggressive in first grade, teenage drug use, especially of alcohol and opiates, was strongly correlated with antisocial behavior (p. 297).

12.   Males evaluated as adapting in first grade used drugs less as teenagers if they were low in social involvement and more if they were antisocial (p. 298).

13.   For females, there was no evidence that teenage social involvement or antisocial behavior mediated the relationship between first-grade social adaptational status and teenage drug use (p. 294).

CONCLUSION

In a poor, black, urban community, both male and female teenagers reported frequent drug use, especially of alcohol, marijuana, and tobacco, with males using drugs more frequently than females. First-grade characteristics of shy, shy-aggressive, high IQ, and school-readiness were associated with teenage drug use. Psychological well-being at the first-grade level, as measured in this study, was not strongly related to later drug use. Antisocial behavior by teenagers was associated with drug use, as was social involvement for males only. Stronger correlations were found between first-grade social adaptation and later

drug use for males than for females, suggesting that early shy or aggressive
behavior has less impact for a female on her later social behavior. The
correlation between first-grade shyness and aggressiveness and teenage drug use
requires further study; it may be due to a psychological factor, such as
willingness to take risks. It is not known whether the findings of this study can
be generalized to other populations, but they do suggest that among similar
groups, teenage drug use is associated with early signs of intelligence, readiness
for school, social maladaptative behavior, and signs of trouble with authority as
adolescents.

AN: 214
AU: Oetting, E.R.;   Edwards, R.;   Goldstein, G.S.;   Garcia-Mason, V.
TI: Drug use among adolescents of five Southwestern Native American tribes
SO: International Journal of the Addictions, 15:439-445, 1980
IN: Department of Psychology, Colorado State University, Fort Collins, Colorado
RF: 7

SUMMARY TABLE

DRUG: multidrug
TYPE: Native American adolescents
NUMBER: 1,744
SEX: male (839); female (905)
AGE: 12-18 years
ETHNICITY: Native American
LOCATION: Southwest
METHODOLOGY: descriptive survey
INSTRUMENT(S):   questionnaire
CONDUCTED: [1975]

PURPOSE

In order to collect information about drug use among Native American adolescents, a drug questionnaire was administered to adolescents from five different but culturally related Native American tribes in the Southwestern United States. The final sample consisted of 1,744 adolescents, approximately 52% of all adolescents between ages 12 and 18 on the rolls of these tribes. The data collected about drug use patterns were compared with data from a nationwide survey of American adolescents in 1973 (see AN 138).

FINDINGS

1. Native American adolescents showed higher use of alcohol, marijuana, and inhalants but lower use of barbiturates than adolescents in a nationwide sample; there were no significant differences in the proportions who had experimented with other drugs (p. 441).

2. Alcohol and marijuana were the drugs of choice of Native American adolescents beginning at the 7th or 8th grade level, and the number of users increased with age. This was the same for adolescents in a nationwide sample, but Native American adolescents maintained significantly higher levels of use at all ages (p. 441).

3. Some Native American adolescents were heavily involved with alcohol; 2.2% listed themselves as heavy or very heavy drinkers; and 17.3% reported having blacked out more than once, suggesting that "binge" drinking is a common pattern (p. 442).

4. Three percent of Native American adolescents reported heavy use of marijuana; they used it during both the week and on the weekends, and had used it more than ten times in the previous two months. Nearly all reported daily use (p. 442).

5. Native American adolescents who had taken LSD were likely to use peyote but also to use amphetamines, cocaine, or heroin, while those who had used peyote but not LSD were very unlikely to use any other drugs except alcohol and marijuana (p. 442).

6. A small percentage of Native American adolescents (2.2%) were actually part of a drug subculture involving the heavy use of amphetamines (or for a few, barbiturates) and the use of at least one other drug: LSD, peyote, cocaine, or heroin, in addition to alcohol and marijuana (pp. 442-443).

7. By the time they were in 7th grade, 15.37% of Native American adolescents were using inhalants, typically airplane glue, but when that was unavailable they also used gasoline, paint, paint thinner, magic marker pens, deodorants, hair spray, and other substances (p. 443).

CONCLUSION

Native American adolescents reported higher use of alcohol, marijuana, and inhalants than adolescents in a national sample. The higher level of inhalant use may relate to higher peer pressure to use drugs or to relative lack of peer sanctions. Cultural characteristics, for example, relative poverty and perceived lack of future opportunities, may make young Native Americans more likely to experiment with drugs. Drug use can also be viewed as a method of self-medication for emotional states such as depression and anxiety. Further study is required to determine the social, cultural, and attitudinal characteristics associated with use of drugs by Native American children. Culturally relevant intervention strategies, such as bringing young drug users into closer contact with their cultural roots or modelling of counterdrug values by a charismatic figure, should be developed and tested.

AN: 215
AU: Oetting, E.R.; Goldstein, G.S.
TI: Drug use among Native American adolescents
SO: In: Beschner, G.M., and Friedman, A.S., eds. Youth Drug Abuse: Problems,
       Issues and Treatment. Lexington, MA: Lexington Books, 1979. pp. 409-441.
IN: Department of Psychology, Colorado State University, Fort Collins, Colorado
RF: 18

SUMMARY TABLE

DRUG: multidrug
TYPE: Native American adolescents
NUMBER: 1,844
SEX: male and female
AGE: junior and senior high school
ETHNICITY: Native American
LOCATION: Southwest
METHODOLOGY: descriptive, correlational survey
INSTRUMENT(S):   questionnaire
CONDUCTED: 1975

PURPOSE

In order to study drug use among Native American youth, data were collected in
1975 through a survey administered to 1,844 7th through 12th graders from five
different but culturally related Native American tribes in the Southwest. Results
from this survey were compared with results on drug use from a large-scale study
of adolescents done at Columbia University in 1973 (see AN 138) and also with
results of a drug survey given to Native American young adults who were attending
a postsecondary technical institute. Problems common to Native American youth
such as poverty, isolation, and cultural conflict were examined. Patterns of drug
use among Native Americans were defined, and other variables such as age, sex,
school success, and peer attitudes were correlated with drug use.

FINDINGS

1. More young Native Americans had tried alcohol, glue or other inhalants, and
marijuana than a sample of young Americans surveyed in a Columbia University
study; the Columbia sample reported more barbiturate use; statistical
differences in the use of other drugs were not significant (pp. 414-416).

2. Alcohol was the drug of preference for Native American youth; almost 90% had
tried it by 12th grade. For both Native American youth and a national sample of
adolescents, alcohol use was prevalent by the 7th grade, with another large
increase in use among 9th graders, and again among 11th graders; at every grade
level, more Native American youth used alcohol than adolescents in the national
sample (p. 416).

3. Marijuana was the second drug of preference, following alcohol, for Native
American youth, with 62% having tried it by the 12th grade. For both Native
American youth and adolescents in a national sample, marijuana use was prevalent
by the 7th and 8th grades, and increased in use for each subsequent grade level,
with Native Americans showing greater use than the national sample (p. 416).

4. Inhalant use among Native American youth was present at close to its highest level by the 7th and 8th grades, increased slightly during the next couple of years, and then stabilized; inhalant use was higher at every grade level among Native American adolescents than among adolescents in a national sample (p. 416).

5. Native American young adults at a technical institute reported higher percentages for the use of all types of drugs than Native American high school students, although there were no differences in greater prevalence of current use of drugs such as heroin and cocaine, suggesting more experimentation but not necessarily greater involvement for those two drugs. However, there was a higher prevalence rate for current use of alcohol, amphetamines, and marijuana for the young adults than for the adolescents (pp. 417-418).

6. Only 12 out of almost 1,800 Native American high school students were considered to be addicted or drug dependent; 3 used amphetamines daily, 2 used barbiturates daily, and 7 were heavy and daily users of alcohol (pp. 419-420).

7. About 1% of the Native American adolescents studied were heavily involved with several dangerous drugs; about half of this group had used heroin and all used multiple drugs (p. 420).

8. Drug use increased over time both in the types of substances used and in the degree of use for Native American high school students, with the exception of inhalant use, which occurred primarily among younger children (p. 424).

9. The median age for first use of any drug by Native American high school students, including marijuana, was over 14, with the exceptions of alcohol and inhalants, which were more readily available and used earlier than other drugs. Half of those who used beer and half of those who used inhalants had first tried these substances before they were 13. Those adolescents who became heavy users of dangerous drugs began drug use earlier than the average, and for those of this group who used inhalants, half began using inhalants before age 11 (pp. 424-245).

10. More boys than girls among a group of Native American adolescents had tried or used alcohol and marijuana, but the heavy drug-use groups included equal numbers of boys and girls. While more boys than girls experimented with inhalants or used them lightly, two-thirds of the group that used inhalants moderately to heavily were girls (p. 425).

11. Among a group of Native American high school students, those who came from the tribe in which the tribal leaders punished children most severely for drug use had the highest percentage of very heavy drug users (p. 426).

12. Young Native Americans who believed in traditional Native American values such as speaking a Native American language, learning legends and tribal stories, and participating in traditional practices were as likely to use drugs as those who felt such things were unimportant (p. 426).

13. High school students from Native American tribes that provided alternative activities for adolescents reported less use of the most dangerous drugs, but used as much alcohol and marijuana as their peers. Just less than half of the drug users said that one reason they used drugs was that there was "nothing else to do around here" (p. 426).

14. Native American adolescents from broken homes, and especially from homes in which the mother was absent, were more likely to use drugs than those from intact homes; among nonusers or moderate alcohol users, 75% had married parents, while only 50% of those who used dangerous drugs had married parents (p. 426).

15. Native American adolescents who felt that their families were less successful "in the Indian way" were more likely to be heavily involved with drugs than their peers (p. 426).

16. When asked about their parents' feelings on drug use, most Native American adolescents who used drugs heavily said "They don't care what I do" (p. 426).

17. For a group of Native American adolescents, greater involvement with drugs usually corresponded with poorer grades in high school, although some of the students who were most heavily involved with drugs had good grades (p. 428).

18. Native American high school students who were more involved with drugs had a lower expectancy of doing well in school than those less involved, and inhalant users had the lowest expectancy of all (p. 428).

19. Peer attitudes among Native American adolescents were strongly related to drug use; friends of drug users were likely to be users, to encourage use, and to apply few sanctions against use, while friends of nonusers were likely to be nonusers, to discourage use, and to apply sanctions against drug use (p. 428).

20. Native American high school students who used drugs did not report as much need for social respect as did nonusers; for nonusers of drugs and alcohol, the need to be a good person or a good student was found to be more closely related to family attitudes than to the attitudes of their friends, which was not true for drug users (p. 433).

21. Native American adolescents who attended religious ceremonies regularly or often or who perceived themselves as being religious were less involved with drugs than their peers (p. 433).

22. Native American adolescents who used drugs were more tolerant of deviant behavior than their nonusing peers, and they were more likely than nonusers to have talked back to their teachers, cheated on tests, or damaged property (p. 433).

23. Native American adolescents who were most heavily involved with drugs had lower expectations of meeting their life goals, and inhalant users had the lowest expectancy of all (pp. 433, 437).

CONCLUSION

Native American adolescents, when compared to other adolescents in a national sample, were more likely to use alcohol, inhalants, and marijuana. Use of beer and inhalants usually began before age 13, and for some adolescents who became heavily involved with dangerous drugs, before the age of 11. A survey of a group of Native American young adults at a postsecondary technical institute showed that drug use and drug experimentation continued to increase after high school. Young Native American drug users were more likely than nonusers to be alienated from the Indian way of life, to come from broken homes, to be less religious, to have less need for the respect of others, to be more tolerant of deviant behaviors, and to engage in more deviant behaviors. They were very likely to have friends who were also drug users and who encouraged drug use. The high percentage of inhalant use among young Native Americans is of particular concern because of the very young age of those who use inhalants, because of the dangers of the substances, and because inhalant use is associated with low expectancy of meeting any life goals.

AN: 216
AU: Oetting, E.R.; Goldstein, G.S.; Garcia-Mason, V.
TI: Native American Drug Use: Drug Abuse Among Indian Adolescents
SO: Final Report, NIDA Grant R01DA01054, 1978. 88 pp.
IN: Department of Psychology, Colorado State University, Fort Collins, Colorado
RF: 6

SUMMARY TABLE

DRUG: multidrug
TYPE: Native American children and adolescents
NUMBER: adolescents: 2,904; children: 401
SEX: adolescent: male (47.9%), female (52.1%); children: male
                  (58.1%), female (41.9%)
AGE: 8-18 years
ETHNICITY: Native American
LOCATION: United States (cross-sectional)
METHODOLOGY: descriptive, correlational survey
INSTRUMENT(S):   questionnaire
CONDUCTED: 1976-1977

PURPOSE

In the course of developing a survey instrument which could provide accurate information on drug use among Native American adolescents, data on drug use and correlates of drug use were also collected. Questionnaires were given to 2,904 students between the ages of 12 and 17 on reservations in seven different areas across the United States. The adolescents listed 201 different tribes or tribal combinations, with the highest percentages being Navajo (26.4%) and Sioux (12.0%). The sample was not intended to be representative of Native American adolescents in general, but the findings are probably similar to those which would be found if such a survey were conducted. Data derived from these questionnaires were correlated with data obtained from a Columbia University study of drug use among a national sample of adolescents in 1973 (see AN 138). al. 1977). Because many Native American adolescents begin using drugs before the age of 12, a second questionnaire on drug use was administered to a pilot group of 401 children between the ages of 8 and 13. Data from this pilot study were also presented.

FINDINGS

1. Native American adolescents heavily involved with dangerous drugs were more likely to be from broken homes, to have negative attitudes toward school, less need for social respect, and less care about what others, particularly teachers, thought of them; strong religious identification was associated with lower drug use (p. 9).

2. Peer encouragement was highly related to drug use among Native American adolescents, and peer sanctions were related to less use of drugs (p. 9).

3. Native American adolescents who were more involved with drugs were also more tolerant of deviance, more likely to cheat on tests or damage property, and had a lower expectancy of meeting life goals than their peers. Inhalant users tended to be younger than other drug users and had a particularly low expectancy of meeting

life goals, such as earning a living or being respected by others when they became adults (p. 10).

4. Native American adolescents had a far higher rate of experimentation with drugs than adolescents from a national sample. Marijuana and alcohol were the most common drugs used by both groups, but 78.3% of Native American youth had tried alcohol compared to 52.6% of the national sample and 46.4% of Native American adolescents tried marijuana compared to 28.2% of the national sample. For other drugs, Native Americans ranged from double to more than triple the percentages of other youths who had tried a drug (pp. 11-12).

5. Native American adolescents were more likely to have tried inhalants than adolescents in a national sample (22.8% compared to 9.0%) and reported more recent use (15.5% had used inhalants in the past two months compared to 0.7% of the national sample reporting use in the past month), suggesting a high continuing use of inhalants among Native Americans (p. 34).

6. By the age of 17, 85% of Native American adolescents had tried alcohol, 57% had tried marijuana, and about 20% had tried inhalants (p. 34).

7. Alcohol was the drug most frequently used by young Native Americans; by the age of 11, nearly a third had tried it (p. 35).

8. For young Native Americans, marijuana use increased over time, both in numbers of children using marijuana and earlier age at first use (p. 36).

9. Inhalant use among young Native Americans began at an early age and increased steadily with age for every age group; nearly 20% of the children under 12 had tried inhalants (pp. 37-38).

10. Among a group of 4th- to 6th-grade Native American children, 29.7% had tried alcohol (mostly beer), 6.8% had tried inhalants (mostly paint and gasoline), and 2.5% had tried "pills" (p. 40).

11. Access to alcohol and encouragement to drink, from siblings as well as friends, were important correlates of alcohol use among Native American children ages 8 to 13 (p. 44).

12. Deviant behavior was only slightly correlated with alcohol use for Native American children (p. 44).

13. Use of inhalants was correlated with alcohol use for Native American children; those who did not use alcohol were more likely not to use inhalants (p. 44).

14. Negative feelings and low self-esteem were not correlated with the use of alcohol and inhalants by Native American children (p. 45).

15. For Native American children, social sanctions against drug use correlated closely with feelings that drugs were dangerous (p. 47).

16. For Native American children, the fewer perceived sanctions against drug use, the higher was the use of both alcohol and inhalants, as well as cigarette smoking (p. 47).

CONCLUSION

There is a high level of drug use among Native American adolescents, which most often begins during adolescence and increases during that period in both the number of those who experiment and the extent of drug use by individuals. Experimentation with three classes of drugs--alcohol, marijuana, and inhalants--often begins before 7th grade. Among the younger children, substance use involves high social pressure. It may not be related to personal problems, and children who do not show signs of personal, family, or social stress may still use drugs. Inhalant abuse, in particular, presents serious health problems as well as social and psychological problems for those adolescents who have low expectancy that their future goals will be met and who seem alienated from social structures such as home, religion, school, and tribe. Early inhalant use may be a precursor of later heavy drug involvement and requires further study to provide more information regarding the development and correlates of its use.

X. STUDIES ON MARIJUANA AND HALLUCINOGENS

AN: 217
AU: Comitas, L.
TI: Cannabis and work in Jamaica: A refutation of the amotivational syndrome
SO: Annals of the New York Academy of Sciences, 282:24-32, 1974
IN: Department of Philosophy and the Social Sciences, Teachers College, Columbia
     University, New York, New York
RF: 10

SUMMARY TABLE

DRUG: cannabis
TYPE: Jamaican workers
NUMBER: 60 (clinical); 159 (observed workers)
SEX: male
AGE: not specified
ETHNICITY: Jamaican
LOCATION: Jamaica, West Indies
METHODOLOGY: clinical; ethnographic observation
INSTRUMENT(S): clinical observation; verbal reports
CONDUCTED: 1970-1972

PURPOSE

The amotivational syndrome has been defined as "a set of symptoms including
apathy, ineffectiveness, and non-productiveness, considered to reflect a deficit
in general motivation." It has been implied that this syndrome is possibly the
result of the chronic use of particular drugs. An attempt was made to test this
theory by investigating a population of Jamaican workers who were chronic users of
cannabis. In Jamaican society cannabis use is thought to have motivational
effects and has been an acceptable practice for many years. A social science team
investigated the patterns of cannabis use among the Jamaican working class, and a
clinical team conducted medical and psychological testing on 60 subjects chosen
from the Jamaican population.

FINDINGS

1. Cannabis users in the study communities almost unanimously stated that
cannabis enhanced their ability to perform hard work (p. 26).

2. Of the 27 out of 30 smokers in the clinical phase of the study who were asked
about their alcohol/ganja preferences, 25 preferred cannabis to alcohol (p. 27).

3. No significant difference was found in the number of school years completed by
cannabis smokers and nonsmokers or in their current and past occupations (p. 27).

4. Although nonsmokers of cannabis were more inclined to state that they changed
jobs to better themselves and smokers indicated a dislike for the job or
co-workers, the difference was not significant (p. 28).

5. There was no difference between smokers and nonsmokers of cannabis in
ownership and control of property or in income (p. 28).

6. Results from the actual observation of workers indicated that ganja smoking was related to changes in the rate and organization of body movement and the expenditure of energy (p. 28).

7. Both moderate and heavy cannabis smoking were found to reinforce social cohesiveness during work in group situations (p. 28).

8. Behavioral changes related to light or moderate cannabis smoking were not significant in agricultural work over extended time periods, although the behavioral changes in heavy smokers were significant (p. 29).

9. No significant differences were found in the work productivity of ganja smokers and nonsmokers. No direct relationship was found between heavy cannabis use and decreased production (p. 30).

CONCLUSION

The results support a refutation of the amotivational syndrome in cannabis users in Jamaica. No significant differences were found between the population of users and nonusers on their work productivity. Cannabis was actually associated in the minds of Jamaican workers with a motivational rather than an amotivational syndrome. It was believed to decrease fatigue during hard work and increase the duration and intensity of work.

AN: 218
AU: du Toit, B.M.
TI: Ethnicity and patterning in South African drug use
SO: In: du Toit, B.M., ed. Drug, Rituals, and Altered States of Consciousness.
      Rotterdam: A.A. Balkema, 1977. pp. 75-99.
IN: University of Florida, Gainesville
RF: 35

SUMMARY TABLE

DRUG: multidrug
TYPE: cannabis users
NUMBER: 494
SEX: male (88%); female (12%)
AGE: below 17 (11%); 18-23 (46%); 24-29 (27%); over 30 (15%)
ETHNICITY: African (40%); Coloured (25%); Indian (11%); White (24%)
LOCATION: South Africa
mETHODOLOGY: cross-sectional survey
INSTRUMENT(S):   interview
CONDUCTED: 1972-1974

PURPOSE

The use of mind-altering substances must be studied in specific socio-cultural
settings before reliable comparisons of cross-cultural or cross-disciplinary
studies can be carried out. This paper analyzes the use of various kinds of
mind-altering substances in South Africa. The research was concentrated on two
samples of Zulu-speaking Africans, and samples of Coloureds, Whites, and Indians.
The criterion for including the subjects into study samples was their use of
cannabis. The paper combines two major concepts, namely altered states of
consciousness and ritual.

OPERATIONAL DEFINITIONS

Ethnic groups studied: African, Coloured, Indian, White.

FINDINGS

1. For the under 17 year old category, 42.6% had tried other drugs than cannabis,
in contrast with only 11.0% for the over thirty category (p. 85).

2. Persons below age 24 contrasted with the older categories in rates of use of
non-cannabis drugs by 23.5% to 8.6% (p. 87).

3. The greatest amount of experimentation was with LSD: 33 persons (6.7% of the
total sample) had used it; 45.5% (15 persons) of those who had tried LSD
discontinued its use, while 18 or 54.4% were still using it (p. 87).

4. Twenty-seven persons (5.5%) of the total sample used Mandrax (methaqualone).
Of those who had tried Mandrax, 22.2% had discontinued use and 77.8% still used it
regularly (pp. 87-88).

5.   Forty-five persons (9.1% of the sample) had used benzene and petrol, and 15.6% of them had discontinued their use, leaving 84.4% who still used these substances (p. 88).

6.   Opium was smoked by 12 persons (2.4% of the sample) (p. 88).

7.   Purple hearts, glue sniffing, and Dexedrine experimenters each represented between 1.5% and 1% of the total sample (p. 88).

8.   Triers and users of LSD were mostly Whites and Coloureds in equal proportions, with a complete absence of Africans and Indians (p. 88).

9.   Mandrax had the widest ethnic distribution of use among Whites, Coloureds, and Indians, while being completely absent among Africans (p. 88).

10.   Benzene use was almost exclusively found among the Coloured subjects of the sample (p. 88).

11.   Opium was in continued use among Coloureds and Indians, while one White had discontinued using it (p. 89).

12.   Only 2.6% of Whites and 5.4% of Coloureds did not use alcohol, while 32.8% of Africans and 12.8% of Indians did not use alcohol; the rural older Africans said they did not drink alcohol because they used cannabis (p. 89).

13.   Use of African beer was almost exclusively restricted to Africans; its use was absent among Indians and Whites (p. 90).

14.   The large majority (81.1%) of Coloureds favored the use of liquor, while only 3.6% stated that they used wine (p. 91).

15.   For the under 17 category of all four ethnic groups, 45.2% used alcohol as their first drug, and 28.6% used petrol and benzene first (benzene was exclusively limited to Coloureds) (p. 92).

16.   Whites used alcohol as their first drug (85.7%), and 42.6% of Coloureds used benzene as their first drug (p. 92).

17.   Two-thirds (67.4%) of the 18-23 year old category of all four ethnic groups began using alcohol as their first drug; among 18-23 year olds, 88.7% of Whites and 63.3% of Indians began using alcohol as their first drug (p. 92).

18.   In the 24-29 year old category of all four ethnic groups, 56.3% began using alcohol as their first drug and 38.8% cannabis (p. 93).

19.   In the over 30 year old category of all four ethnic groups, 48.9% began using alcohol as their first drug and 36.7% cannabis (p. 94).

CONCLUSION

This paper attempted to establish the patterns of drug use among four ethnic groups in South Africa: Whites, Coloureds, Africans, and Indians. Because of the ethnic complexity, it was almost impossible to generate hypotheses concerning use of drugs. However, some valuable conclusions were arrived at. It was established that all ethnic groups use certain drugs not because of their economic status, as some have argued, but because of a long-standing socio-cultural tradition. The "problem" of drug use can be well defined once cultural setting, substances employed, and reasons for use are known. Knowledge of these factors is particularly valuable in cases where rehabilitation is necessary.

AN: 219
AU: Fisher, S.; Pillard, R.C.; Botto, R.W.
TI: Hypnotic susceptibility during cannabis intoxication
SO: In: Psychopharmacology, Sexual Disorders and Drug Abuse. Prague, Avicenum:
     Czechoslovak Medical Press, 1973. pp. 699-700.
IN: Psychopharmacology Laboratory, Division of Psychiatry, Boston University
     School of Medicine, Boston, Massachusetts
RF: 2

SUMMARY TABLE

DRUG: marijuana
TYPE: marijuana users
NUMBER: 20
SEX: male
AGE: 21 years and older
ETHNICITY: not specified
LOCATION: Boston, Massachusetts
mETHODOLOGY: experimental research
INSTRUMENT(S):   Stanford Scale of Hypnotic Susceptibility
CONDUCTED: not specified

PURPOSE

In an attempt to determine whether hypnotic susceptibility is modified during
marijuana intoxication, 20 male volunteers were selected using the following
criteria: (1) over age 21, (2) prior experience with marijuana, and (3) record of
stable hypnotic susceptibility scores. Subjects were tested using the Stanford
Scale of Hypnotic Susceptibility in three sessions: (1) a baseline period with no
marijuana, (2) about two weeks later, following "ad lib" smoking of marijuana, and
(3) a second control session between two and four weeks later involving a third
administration of the Stanford Scale.

FINDINGS

1. No evidence was found of any systematic influence of marijuana upon hypnotic
susceptibility (p. 700).

CONCLUSION

Twenty participants were selected to test whether hypnotic susceptibility is
modified by marijuana intoxication. They were put through three sessions in which
their susceptibility was tested with and without marijuana intoxication. Those
who were resistant to the hypnotic suggestions without use of marijuana were
equally resistant with the use of marijuana.

AN: 220
AU: Huba, G.J.; Bentler, P.M.
TI: Phencyclidine use in high school: Tests of models
SO: Journal of Drug Education, 9:285-291, 1979
IN: Department of Psychology, University of California, Los Angeles
RF: 8

SUMMARY TABLE

DRUG:	phencyclidine; marijuana; alcohol
TYPE:	tenth-grade students
NUMBER:	49
SEX:	male (62.5%); female (37.5%)
AGE:	16.2 years (average)
ETHNICITY:	Anglo (87%); Hispanic (6.5%); Asian (2.2%); other (4.3%)
LOCATION:	Los Angeles, California
METHODOLOGY:	cross-sectional survey
INSTRUMENT(S):	questionnaire; interview
CONDUCTED:	not specified

PURPOSE

An attempt was made to ascertain whether the use of phencyclidine (PCP) is a relatively autonomous behavior or whether some individuals are more prone to use of this drug than others. Rates of use for marijuana, alcohol, and PCP, attitudes toward the drug, perceived norms among significant others, and intentions to use the drugs in the future were assessed and related. Students (N=49) from two high schools in suburban Los Angeles, California, were interviewed and completed questionnaires concerning their attitudes towards drug use.

FINDINGS

1. Beer was used by 83.7% of the high school students at least once in the last six months, while marijuana (65.3%), cigarettes (57.1%), and PCP (14.3%) were used progressively less (p. 286).

2. All of the high school students stated that they believed using PCP was a bad idea (p. 288).

3. Some (20.4%) of the high school students thought the significant others in their lives approved of alcohol use, and 12.2% thought their significant others approved of marijuana use. No students thought their significant others approved of PCP use (p. 288).

4. With regard to the high school students' intentions to use drugs in the future, 8.2% were definitely sure they would not use alcohol; while the percentages for PCP and marijuana were 85.7% and 26.5%, respectively (p. 288).

5. Use of a drug, intentions about future use, and general attitudes about that drug were related for marijuana, alcohol, and PCP (p. 288).

6. A causal or "stepping-stone" model of drug use was supported concerning PCP attitudes, intentions, perceived norms, and behaviors (p. 290).

7. Although not all individuals who used marijuana progressed to PCP, marijuana was found to be a necessary step within the current society for the potential PCP user (p. 290).

CONCLUSION

The overall pattern of results suggests that PCP use is dependent upon marijuana use. Furthermore, attitudes, norms, and intentions concerning PCP use seem to be explained by attitudes, norms, and intentions concerning marijuana and alcohol use. The results support a "stepping-stone" model for PCP attitudes, intentions to use, and perceived norms and behaviors that needs to be further investigated with larger samples of subjects in longitudinal research. Future programs for combating PCP abuse should focus on the marijuana-PCP linkage.

AN: 221
AU: Hudiburg, R.A.; Joe, G.W.
TI: Behavioral correlates and comparisons of current marijuana users, quitters
     and evasives
SO: Texas Christian University, Institute for Behavioral Research Report No.
     76-6, 1976. 26 pp.
IN: Institute of Behavioral Research, Texas Christian University, Fort Worth,
     Texas
RF: 11

SUMMARY TABLE

DRUG: marijuana
TYPE: marijuana users
NUMBER: 445
SEX: males and females
AGE: adults (18 years or older)
ETHNICITY: white; black; other
LOCATION: United States (cross-sectional)
METHODOLOGY: statistical analysis
INSTRUMENT(S):   interview; questionnaire
CONDUCTED: 1971

PURPOSE

In order to study discontinuance of marijuana use, data collected on 445 marijuana
users by Response Analysis Corporation as part of a 1971 study on public attitudes
towards marijuana were analyzed in a secondary investigation. Demographic and
background variables derived from interviews, including age, marital status, sex,
race, and area type, were analyzed, as were variables derived from a self-report
questionnaire relating to first use of marijuana, reasons for quitting marijuana
use, use of alcohol and other drugs, and current marijuana use.

OPERATIONAL DEFINITIONS

Evasives: individuals who failed to answer questions concerning their use of
marijuana on a self-report questionnaire (26.9%).

Quitters: persons who had discontinued marijuana use (42.8%).

Users: current users of marijuana (30.3%).

FINDINGS

1. Compared to evasives and quitters, current marijuana users were more likely to
be younger, single, and students in school (p. 21).

2. Current users were more likely than evasives and quitters to have first used
marijuana between the ages of 15 and 19, and a large majority used marijuana at
the first opportunity (p. 21).

3. In terms of drug use other than marijuana, current marijuana users had a percentage twice as large as that of quitters and four times as large as that of evasives (p. 21).

4. Evasives were more likely to be older and married than users or quitters, and were also less educated (p. 22).

5. Most of the present peer groups of quitters consisted of people who generally did not use marijuana (fewer than half or none at all) (p. 21).

6. Many quitters had used marijuana only once, perhaps quite unintentionally (p. 21).

7. Users gave more reasons for using marijuana than did quitters (p. 22).

8. When questioned about possible harmful effects of marijuana, evasives were most likely to agree that marijuana is harmful, while users were least likely to agree; quitters were more similar in their attitudes to evasives. When questioned about the pleasurable effects of marijuana and the use of marijuana by youth, users and quitters were more likely to agree while evasives showed the greatest disapproval (p. 22).

CONCLUSION

Profiles of three groups of marijuana users show that current users are likely to be young, single, and still in school; to associate with other marijuana users; to use other drugs frequently; and to have begun marijuana use at an early age (between 15 and 19 years) and at the first opportunity. Quitters, persons who have discontinued marijuana use, are slightly older than users, more likely to be married, less likely to use other drugs, and less likely to have friends who use marijuana; many have tried marijuana only once. Evasives, individuals who did not provide information concerning their use of marijuana, are more likely to be older, married, and less educated than the other two groups; they are also less likely to use other drugs. Users tend to be more socially deviant, outside the mainstream of society, and have more reasons for using marijuana. Quitters tend to reject deviant environments where marijuana is used, while evasives are the most integrated into "square" society. This may be the reason that the evasives failed to divulge information regarding marijuana use, although, since they are older, this lack of information may also be attributed to lack of recollection. When questioned about the effects of marijuana, evasives maintain that marijuana is harmful, while users disagree and instead stress the pleasurable effects of marijuana and sanction its use by youth. Quitters are more similar in their opinions to evasives when asked about harmful effects, but more similar to users when asked about the pleasurable effects of marijuana.

AN: 222
AU: James, J.; Andresen, E.
TI: Sea-Tac and PCP
SO: In: Feldman, H.W.; Ager, M.; Beschner, G., eds. Angel Dust: An
       Ethnographic Study of PCP Users. Lexington, Massachusetts: Lexington Books,
       1980. pp. 109-158.
IN: Department of Psychiatry, University of Washington, Seattle, Washington
RF: 4

SUMMARY TABLE

DRUG: phencyclidine (PCP)
TYPE: phencyclidine users
NUMBER: 31
SEX: male and female
AGE: 15-40 years
ETHNICITY: white; black
LOCATION: Seattle and Tacoma, Washington
 ETHODOLOGY: ethnographic, participant-observation study
INSTRUMENT(S):   interview
CONDUCTED: not specified

PURPOSE

The Seattle-Tacoma (Sea-Tac) area of Washington has been referred to as the PCP
(phencyclidine) center of the Northwest coast, second only to Hayward and San Jose
in California. In order to gain some insight into the patterns and motivations
for use of this drug, four groups of PCP users representing all ages and
socioeconomic status groups were studied using ethnographic techniques. The
groups were labelled Seattle adolescents (N=8), Seattle young adults (N=5), the
Tacoma network (N=16), and loners (N=2).

FINDINGS

1. From 1973 to 1976, five out of every eleven juveniles tested in Tacoma's drug
programs were found to have used PCP (p. 110).

2. For the Seattle groups, PCP was considered the drug of preference in the
predominately white schools, while marijuana and cocaine were the primary drugs in
schools with a majority of black students (p. 113).

3. None of the PCP users of the Tacoma network, except the teenagers, saw much
possibility for change in their lives for pursuing a profession (p. 119).

4. PCP never reached the prevalence in Seattle as in Tacoma, where it was the
number two street drug and third in terms of emergency room calls (p. 123).

5. The pattern of first use of PCP was the same for all PCP-using groups. The
experience was casual, unplanned, and part of a regular lifestyle of experimenting
with drugs, and was primarily related to the network of the teenage group
(p. 126).

6. All of the PCP users studied had used other drugs before their first experience with PCP (p. 127).

7. For the Seattle adolescents, there was a strong social motivation for taking PCP; it was a "group" drug. However, there were no specific patterns of motivation for adult PCP users (p. 129).

8. The heaviest PCP users in Seattle-Tacoma were primarily youths of white, middle- and lower-income, primarily from military and working-class families, and between the ages of 14 and 15 years (p. 157).

CONCLUSION

PCP is no longer the "in" drug in Seattle-Tacoma. It is considered dangerous, but not as bad as heroin. Although motivations were different for the different age groups, the primary purpose was the desire, regardless of the negative aspects, to change mental states or to be part of what was happening. Adolescent PCP users are not that different from the psychedelic drug users of the 1960s; their pressures and stresses are probably greater now. The same need for some escape exists, and PCP is an easy alternative.

AN: 223
AU: Joe, G.W.; Hudiburg, R.A.
TI: Behavioral correlates of age at first marijuana use
SO: Texas Christian University, Institute for Behavioral Research, Report No.
     76-1, 1976. 25 pp.
IN: Institute of Behavioral Research, Texas Christian University, Fort Worth,
     Texas
RF: 6

SUMMARY TABLE

DRUG: marijuana
TYPE: marijuana users; Vietnam veterans
NUMBER: 370
SEX: male
AGE: not specified
ETHNICITY: black (26.2%); white (67.6%); other (3%); unspecified (3.2%)
LOCATION: United States (cross-sectional)
METHODOLOGY: statistical analysis
INSTRUMENT(S):   questionnaire
CONDUCTED: 1971

PURPOSE

In order to investigate relationships between age at first use of marijuana and
selected behavioral measures such as education, employment, criminality, and drug
use, statistical analyses were performed on data derived from Robins' 1971 survey
of 370 returned Vietnam veterans who indicated use of marijuana prior to entering
the service. The subsample of marijuana users was also compared to the larger
sample of 933 returned Vietnam veterans.

FINDINGS

1. Veterans who began use of marijuana by age 15 or 16 were more likely to have
engaged in various deviant behaviors prior to entering military service than those
who began marijuana use at an older age (p. 9).

2. Veterans who began using marijuana by the age of 15 or 16 were more likely
than those beginning marijuana use at a later age to have completed less
education, less likely to have attended school regularly, less likely to have held
a full-time job, more likely to have been arrested, more likely to have become
drunk at an earlier age, more likely to have used marijuana, uppers, and downers
frequently, and more likely to have used opiates (p. 17).

3. Nearly 11% of the variance in the Drug Use factor and nearly 9% of the
variance in the School Dropout factor were predictable from age at initial
marijuana use. But only 1% of the variance in the Additional Propensity to
Delinquency factor was predictable from age at initial marijuana use (p. 21).

CONCLUSION

On the basis of data derived from a sample of returned Vietnam veterans regarding their marijuana use prior to entering the service, a positive correlation was found between early use of marijuana and socially deviant behavior in the areas of drug use, school delinquency, and other delinquent behaviors. Age at first marijuana use seems to be a useful indicator of a developing deviant lifestyle. Lack of socially structured means for achieving cultural goals, such as education and employment, can cause frustration and create further participation in a deviant subculture; thus, "social rehabilitation" programs may be helpful for persons lacking education and orientation to work.

AN: 224
AU: Johnson, W.T.; Petersen, R.E.; Wells, L.E.
TI: Arrest probabilities for marijuana users as indicators of selective law
     enforcement
SO: American Journal of Sociology, 83:681-699, 1977
IN: University of Illinois at Chicago Circle, Chicago, Illinois
RF: 28

SUMMARY TABLE

DRUG: marijuana
TYPE: marijuana users and arrestees
NUMBER: 1,859
SEX: male and female
AGE: 18 years and older
ETHNICITY: black; nonblack
LOCATION: Cook County, Illinois; Washington, D.C.; Omaha, Nebraska
METHODOLOGY: statistical analysis
INSTRUMENT(S):   interview; self-administered questionnaire; police log entries
CONDUCTED: 1971-1972

PURPOSE

Selective law enforcement ostensibly violates equal protection as specified by the
Fourteenth Amendment to the Constitution. A test of selective enforcement
requires a conceptual model, but in this context the null hypothesis, or the
no-difference model, which assumes that all persons and groups should have equal
frequencies of apprehension and sanctioning, is viewed as too simplistic. An
"explicable differences" model is proposed. The reported research examined
explicable differences in relation to arrest probabilities as a function of the
social characteristics of offenders and of the features of the jurisdiction of
arrest. The analyzed data were collected in two studies of marijuana users and
arrestees in three jurisdictions (Cook County, Illinois; Douglas County (Omaha),
Nebraska; Washington, D.C.).

FINDINGS

1. Marijuana arrest/use ratios, and thus the probability of arrest, were found to
be highest in Cook County, Illinois, and lowest in Washington, D.C., with Douglas
County, Nebraska, in an intermediate position (p. 689).

2. Males had substantially higher marijuana arrest/use ratios than females in all
three study jurisdictions, a difference attributable primarily to arrest rates
(p. 690).

3. Marijuana arrest/use ratios varied by occupation. The blue-collar group
showed the highest ratio due to high arrest rates coupled with low use rates.
Students also had a high arrest rate, but their high use rate yielded a lower
arrest/use ratio. The white-collar group had a moderately high use rate coupled
with the lowest rate of arrest (pp. 690-691).

4. Race effects were not found to be consistent across jurisdictions. The marijuana arrest/use ratio was at least twice as high for blacks as for nonblacks in Cook County. There were no appreciable differences by race in Washington, D.C., or Douglas County (p. 691).

5. Age effects were greatest in Cook County, where the marijuana arrest/use ratio was substantially higher for persons age 25 or younger than for persons older than 25. Age-related differences were smaller in the other two jurisdictions (p. 691).

6. The most frequently arrested groups generally had the highest estimated marijuana use rates, but differences in violation rates did not fully account for differences in arrest rates (p. 692).

7. In comparison with females, males were more often arrested for marijuana violations by general patrolmen, in vehicles, and alone, and more often had prior records (p. 693).

8. Marijuana arrests of students appear to involve routine encounters, often in connection with a vehicle stop (p. 693).

9. Persons age 25 and younger were more often arrested for marijuana violations in vehicles and in groups than were older arrestees (p. 693).

10. Racial differences were evident in the circumstances of marijuana detection in Cook County, where, in comparison to nonblacks, apprehension of blacks more often occurred in spontaneous contact, in the street setting (p. 694).

11. In each jurisdiction, marijuana arrests in the high arrest probability group, compared to the low arrest probability group, more frequently involved persons with a prior arrest record, less often resulted from prior investigation, more often involved a single apprehension in a street location, more often involved routine contact with police, and more often were carried out by general patrolmen (pp. 694-695).

CONCLUSION

Estimated arrest probabilities can be calculated by an analysis which combines arrest data and marijuana use estimates. The arrest probabilities for three jurisdictions show gender and occupation differences which cannot be explained by simple differences in violations. However, explanations based on differential enforcement and on differential visibility are both consistent with the data. The social location of marijuana use and the sociodemographic characteristics of users are tenable explanations of arrest probabilities.

AN: 225
AU: Khavari, K.A.; Mabry, E.; Humes, M.
TI: Personaltiy correlates of hallucinogen use
SO: Journal of Abnormal Psychology, 86:172-178, 1977
IN: Department of Psychology and Midwest Institute on Drug Use, University of
     Wisconsin, Milwaukee
RF: 21

SUMMARY TABLE

DRUG: marijuana; hashish; LSD; other hallucinogens
TYPE: marijuana users; hallucinogen users
NUMBER: 298
SEX: male and female
AGE: 18-40 years
ETHNICITY: not specified
LOCATION: not specified
METHODOLOGY: correlational survey
INSTRUMENT(S):   Eysenck Personality Inventory; Sensation-Seeking Scale;
                 Marlowe-Crowne Social Desirability Scale; Manifest Anxiety Scale;
                 Wisconsin Substance Use Inventory
CONDUCTED: not specified

PURPOSE

Although a number of investigators have examined the relationship between
personality and drug abuse, most studies have focused on opiates. Only recently
have studies been specifically addressed to the personality correlates of
hallucinogenic drug use. This study assessed the relationship of personality
variables and hallucinogenic drug use, using a battery of standard psychological
tests. The battery was administered to a nonrandom, volunteer sample of adult
union members.

FINDINGS

1. The use of hallucinogens, particularly marijuana, is associated with an
individual's need to seek new and unconventional experiences (p. 176).

2. Marijuana users are differentiated from users of other hallucinogic drugs by
their characteristic seeking of social approval and by their uninhibited modes of
self-expression (p. 176).

3. The use of hallucinogens other than marijuana is associated with anxiety and
with seeking of social stimulation (p. 176).

4. Marijuana users appear to be more gregarious, introspective, unconventional,
and rebellious than nonusers (p. 177).

5. Research dealing with stronger hallucinogens than marijuana suggests that
users are more likely to exhibit various forms of psychopathology than nonusers
(p. 177).

6. Marijuana use is associated with a different set of personality variables than use of other hallucinogens. Marijuana use is correlated with a need for social approval and with a desire to experience uninhibited modes of self-expression, whereas the use of other kinds of hallucinogens is correlated with manifest anxiety, a tendency to seek out social stimulation, and introversion/extroversion (p. 177).

7. Personality scales which measure sensation seeking, need for approval, anxiety, and extroversion/introversion are useful in predicting hallucinogenic drug use (p. 178).

8. Different categories of hallucinogenic drug use are associated with different personality variables; thus, personality variables are not equally suitable as predictors across types of drugs (p. 178).

CONCLUSION

Scores on a battery of psychological tests which measure personality variables differentiated marijuana users from users of other hallucinogens. This finding is consistent with reports from previous research that the personality attributes of marijuana users differ from the attributes of users of more powerful hallucinogens. The latter are more likely to manifest various psychopathologies, whereas marijuana users are more gregarious, introspective, unconventional, and rebellious than nonusers. Personality scales appear to be useful in predicting hallucinogenic drug use, but the various scales are differentially suitable, and a specific instrument cannot be used across all categories of drugs.

AN: 226
AU: Maksud, M.G.; Baron, A.
TI: Physiological responses to exercise in chronic cigarette and marijuana users
SO: European Journal of Applied Physiology and Occupational Physiology,
    43:127-134, 1980
IN: Exercise Physiology Laboratory, University of Wisconsin, Milwaukee, Wisconsin
RF: 27

SUMMARY TABLE

DRUG: tobacco; marijuana
TYPE: young adult blue-collar workers
NUMBER: 65
SEX: male
AGE: 23-27 years
ETHNICITY: not specified
LOCATION: Milwaukee, Wisconsin
METHODOLOGY: experimental research
INSTRUMENT(S):   questionnaire; measurements of physiological responses
CONDUCTED: not specified

PURPOSE

Although several clinical scientists have studied the physiological effects of cigarette smoking, there have been few studies of the chronic effects of drug use on physical performance. In order to measure various physiological responses to exercise, particularly physical work capacity and aerobic power, in chronic cigarette and marijuana smokers, 65 young adult male industrial cigarette and marijuana smokers from a large midwestern city were studied. On the basis of their responses to a questionnaire about drug use, the men were divided into four groups: 18 were cigarette and marijuana users, 13 were marijuana only users, 17 were cigarette only users, and 17 did not use either cigarettes or marijuana. Skinfold measurements, resting heart rate and blood pressure, and a blood sample for determination of hematocrit and hemoglobin were taken for each subject. After these procedures were completed, each subject participated in an exercise sequence on a bicycle ergometer. Each subject was encouraged to exercise to maximal effort, and the test was terminated when subjects were unable to maintain pedalling frequency, suggesting fatigue. During the exercise, heart rate was monitored, ventilation and oxygen consumption were measured, and oxygen and carbon dioxide concentrations of expired air were determined; each subject's perceived exertion was assessed using the Borg Perceived Exertion Scale. These data were analyzed using both univariate and covariate analyses of variance.

OPERATIONAL DEFINITIONS

Group I: current cigarette and marijuana users.

Group II: men who used marijuana but not cigarettes.

Group III: men who smoked cigarettes but not marijuana.

Group IV: men who had never used either cigarettes or marijuana.

FINDINGS

1. Although percentage body fat and lean body mass were lower and hematocrits
higher for the men who used marijuana (Groups I and II) than for the men who did
not (Groups III and IV), these differences disappeared when age, height, weight,
and race were controlled (pp. 129-130).

2. Men in Groups I and III were significantly different from men in Groups II and
IV on minute ventilation at 9 and 12 minutes of exercise; perceived exertion
values were also higher; no differences were observed for heart rate and oxygen
consumption (pp. 130-131).

3. The mean values for peak aerobic capacity and physical work capacity were
higher for the men in groups II and IV than for the men in Groups I and III, but
the differences were not statistically significant. No differences were observed
for resting systolic or diastolic blood pressure (p. 131).

CONCLUSION

Cigarette smokers in a group of young adult male industrial workers were not
significantly different from marijuana only smokers and nonsmokers on certain
physiological measures: estimated fat levels, hematocrit, hemoglobin, heart rate
responses during various levels of submaximal work and during maximal volitional
effort, resting heart rate, peak heart rate, and peak oxygen uptake. Cigarette
smokers were different from nonsmokers in two ways: they had higher minute
ventilations, consistent with a decrease in pulmonary diffusion capacity, and they
showed higher levels of perceived exertion, suggesting the possibility that
respiratory factors provide a major stimulus in establishing level of perceived
exertion, since heart rates and oxygen uptakes were identical. In general, the
use of cigarettes and marijuana by young male blue-collar workers does not
seriously impair aerobic power and physical work capacity. Further studies should
focus on long term use of cigarettes and marijuana and perhaps on higher levels of
smoking. Finally, it should be noted that differences in age, height, weight, and
race affected the physiological measures and that statistical control of these
variables tended to reduce differences between the subjects.

AN: 227
AU: Matefy, R.E.
TI: Role-play theory of psychedelic drug flashbacks
SO: Journal of Consulting and Clinical Psychology, 48:551-553, 1980
IN: University of Bridgeport, Bridgeport, Connecticut
RF: 8

SUMMARY TABLE

DRUG: LSD
TYPE: LSD users
NUMBER: initial testing: 87 (34 flashbackers; 29 nonflashbackers; 24
              controls); one year follow-up: 50 (17; 17; 16, respectively)
SEX: male (45); female (42)
AGE: college/university
ETHNICITY: not specified
LOCATION: Bridgeport, Connecticut
METHODOLOGY: comparative survey
INSTRUMENT(S): interview; Experience Inventory; Hypnotic Characteristic
              Inventory; Barber Suggestibility Scale; Betts Vividness of
              Imagery Scale
CONDUCTED: not specified

PURPOSE

The psychedelic drug "flashback" phenomenon was investigated in a research project
with a one year follow-up. Subjects participated in a series of four initial and
four follow-up sessions involving intensive interviews, psychological tests, and
behavioral tasks. It was theorized that a flashback is a reaction that is learned
during the condition of high physiological arousal that accompanies psychedelic
use. In other words, people who experience flashbacks are highly predisposed to
role playing and should demonstrate a greater likelihood for involvement in role
playing activities than those who do not experience flashbacks.

OPERATIONAL DEFINITIONS

Flashbackers: LSD users who experienced flashbacks.

Nonflashbackers: LSD users who did not experience flashbacks.

FINDINGS

1. The flashbackers scored significantly higher than the nonflashbackers on the
total Experience Inventory and on the Role Taking and Peak Experience subscales of
the Experience Inventory (p. 552).

2. The flashbackers scored significantly higher on the role-taking measure
derived from the Hypnotic Characteristic Inventory than the nonflashbackers
(p. 552).

3. Significant differences between flashbackers and nonflashbackers were found in responses to the behavioral tasks of the total Barber Suggestibility Scale, to the Objective subscale (rating how well the subject actually performed on each behavioral task), and to the Subjective subscale (rating how well the subject felt he or she participated on each task) (p. 552).

4. The higher role-playing propensity of the flashbackers, compared with nonflashbackers, persisted after a one-year interval, as measured by the total Experience Inventory and by the Role-Taking, Dissociation, and Peak Experience subscales of the Experience Inventory (p. 552).

5. The flashbackers were prone to imagine more vividly than were the nonflashbackers on the total Vividness of Imagery Scale and on the Auditory and Organic subscales (p. 552).

CONCLUSION

The findings supported aspects of a role-playing theory of flashbacks in which flashbacks are a learned behavior. Flashbackers consistently showed greater proficiency than nonflashbackers in losing themselves during their involvement in various role-playing situations, and they became more deeply engrossed in role playing a hypnotic performance and in imagined activities.

AN: 228
AU: Matefy, R.E.; Hayes, C.; Hirsch, J.
TI: Psychedelic drug flashbacks: Subjective reports and biographical data
SO: Addictive Behavior, 3:161-178, 1978
IN: University of Bridgeport, Bridgeport, Connecticut
RF: 11

SUMMARY TABLE

DRUG: LSD
TYPE: LSD users
NUMBER: initial interviews: 87 (34 flashbackers; 29 nonflashbackers; 24
                 controls); one-year follow-up: 50 (17; 16; 17, respectively)
SEX: male (45); female (42)
AGE: college/university
ETHNICITY: not specified
LOCATION: Bridgeport, Connecticut
METHODOLOGY: longitudinal survey
INSTRUMENT(S):   structured interview
CONDUCTED: not specified

PURPOSE

The aim of this study was to systematically collect subjective information from
psychedelic drug users about flashback experiences, conditions surrounding the
occurrence, drug taking, and other relevant biographical data. The same
information was gathered (where pertinent) from psychedelic drug users not
experiencing flashbacks and from non-drug-using controls. The subjects were also
interviewed in a one year follow-up.

OPERATIONAL DEFINITIONS

Flashbackers: LSD users who experienced flashbacks.

Nonflashbackers: LSD users who did not experience flashbacks.

FINDINGS

1. LSD was overwhelmingly cited as the primary drug causing flashbacks (p. 167).

2. Flashbacks occurred from daily to a few times weekly for 21% of the subjects,
two or three times monthly for 18%, and once a month to once in a very few months
for 43% of the subjects (p. 167).

3. Of those who had experienced flashbacks in the past, 18% reported not
experiencing flashbacks anymore (p. 167).

4. Nearly two-thirds (64%) of the flashbackers reported that the flashbacks had
decreased since first experiencing them, compared to 18% reporting an increase
(p. 167).

5. The delay between drug use and flashbacks varied from within a few days to a week to over two years later (p. 167).

6. Eighty-two percent of the subjects continued to experience flashbacks for a period of one to two years (p. 167).

7. Of the flashbackers interviewed a second time, 18% were still experiencing flashbacks a few times weeky, 18% had them a few times monthly, and 52% had them once a month or less (p. 167).

8. The vast majority (87%) of subjects stated that flashbacks were actually a multidimensional phenomenon, consisting of combinations of characteristics. These characteristics were (in order of prevalence) perceptual illusions; depersonalization; anxiety, tension, or panic; disorientation or confusion; union with the world; bodily sensations; auditory hallucinations; visual hallucinations; unconscious thoughts; feelings of depression; paranoia (p. 168).

9. Most of the subjects (57%) said their flashbacks were exact recurrences of their drug experiences, and 43% said they were similar (p. 169).

10. Fifty-six percent of the subjects experienced their flashback experiences as "fortunate" and 70% perceived them as "non-threatening" (p. 169).

11. Thirty-seven percent considered their past flashbacks pleasant, and 60% viewed their present flashbacks as pleasant (p. 169).

12. The large majority of the subjects (85%) felt their flashbacks were unpredictable (or seldom predictable); 53% claimed their flashbacks were out of control, and 36% reported that they were mostly within their control (p. 169).

13. The dominant factors triggering flashbacks were marijuana or alcohol (22%), pleasurable thoughts and situations (21%), and anxiety-provoking thoughts and situations (20%) (p. 170).

14. The subjects gave four main explanations of their flashbacks: a cue reminded the subject of past "tripping" (58%), psychedelic drugs were released from the brain (50%), flashbacks were a learning or conditioning process (42%), and flashbacks were a release of unconscious thoughts (38%) (p. 170).

15. A comparison of the drug-using flashbackers and drug-using nonflashbackers revealed no significant differences in the drug-taking history of the two groups (p. 171).

16. For both the flashbackers and nonflashbackers, the use of "hard" drugs decreased significantly from the time of the initial interviews to the one year follow-up (p. 171).

17. The major initial reasons for flashbackers and nonflashbackers to take drugs were curiosity, desire to get high, and increased self-awareness (p. 171).

18. The main changes reported by flashbackers and nonflashbackers as a result of drug taking were a deeper appreciation of life's meaning, greater introspection, enhanced understanding of self and others, increased interest in music, art, or nature, personal development noted by significant others, ability to be oneself, and less materialistic or competitive attitude (p. 172).

19. In comparison with nonflashbackers or the controls, the flashbackers described themselves as more frivolous than practical, more spontaneous than controlled, more outspoken than reserved (p. 173).

20. Significantly more flashbackers (64%) said they had consulted a professional for mental health problems than did the nonflashbackers (31%) or the controls (35%) (p. 174).

CONCLUSION

LSD was the primary cause of flashbacks. One cannot predict when flashbacks will be experienced after ingestion. Flashbacks were described by the subjects as almost exact reminiscences of their drug experiences. The following themes of flashbacks were reported: perceptual experiences, depersonalization, feelings of anxiety and tension, disorientation and confusion, union with the world, and bodily sensations. Theories given by the subjects explaining flashbacks involved some sort of conditioning process or a cue associated with a past drug high (getting intoxicated, listening to acid rock music). There were no substantial differences between flashbackers and nonflashbackers in their reasons for taking drugs.

AN: 229
AU: Matefy, R.E.; Hayes, C.; Hirsch, J.
TI: Psychedelic drug flashbacks: Attentional deficits?
SO: Journal of Abnormal Psychology, 88:212-215, 1979
IN: University of Bridgeport, Bridgeport, Connecticut
RF: 18

SUMMARY TABLE

DRUG: LSD
TYPE: LSD users
NUMBER: 87 (34 flashbackers; 29 nonflashbackers; 24 controls)
SEX: male (45); female (42)
AGE: college/university
ETHNICITY: not specified
LOCATION: Bridgeport, Connecticut
METHODOLOGY: experimental research
INSTRUMENT(S):   reaction time test apparatus
CONDUCTED: not specified

PURPOSE

The study tested the validity of claims that psychedelic flashbacks are
manifestations of deficits in attentional processes caused directly or indirectly
by a drug. Psychedelic drug users experiencing flashbacks were compared with
psychedelic drug users not having flashbacks and with a non-drug-using control
group on a reaction time task with various preparatory intervals. The apparatus
consisted of a telegraph key housed in an aluminium case and two small speakers
driven by an oscillator and amplifier. The subjects were instructed to depress
the key as quickly as possible after hearing the stimulus tone. The intervals
between the tones were 25, 15, 10, 7, 5, 3, 2, and 1 seconds. The experiment was
repeated with the same subjects one year later.

OPERATIONAL DEFINITIONS

Flashback group: LSD users who experienced flashbacks.

Nonflashback group: LSD users who did not experience flashbacks.

FINDINGS

1. The reaction times of the flashback group did not differ significantly from
those of the nonflashback group or the control group (p. 213).

2. Both drug-taking groups had faster reaction times than the control group,
particularly for the tasks requiring longer preparatory intervals (p. 213).

3. When the experiment was repeated a year later, the relative differences in the
reaction times for the three groups remained the same: the two drug-using groups
still showed faster reaction times than did the control group (p. 213).

CONCLUSION

The study offers no empirical support for theorists who would explain flashbacks by deficits in attentional processes. The flashbackers' attention was comparable to that of the psychedelic drug users not experiencing flashbacks. Both psychedelic drug-using groups were able to respond quickly and efficiently. The flashbackers, 82% of whom were still flashbacking after one year, did not suffer a fundamental loss of the selective inhibitory process of attention at follow-up. The findings also contradict, indirectly, theorists who assume that flashbacks represent manifestations of psychotic decomposition.

AN: 230
AU: Meier, R.F.; Johnson, W.T.
TI: Deterrence as social control: The legal and extralegal production of
     conformity
SO: American Sociological Review, 42:292-304, 1977
IN: University of California, Irvine
RF: 31

SUMMARY TABLE

DRUG: marijuana
TYPE: general population
NUMBER: 632
SEX: male and female
AGE: 18 and over
ETHNICITY: not specified
LOCATION: Cook County (Chicago), Illinois
METHODOLOGY: statistical analysis
INSTRUMENT(S): interview; questionnaire
CONDUCTED: 1971

PURPOSE

This paper focuses on legal and extra-legal (informal) factors that reinforce
social conformity. The model tested the degree to which compliance or
noncompliance is determined by legal factors (knowledge of the law, legal threat,
perceived certainty and severity of punishment) or by extralegal factors (social
support, social influence, attitudes, and social background characteristics). The
survey data were drawn from self-reports of criminal activity and reasons for its
nonoccurrence. The substantive focus of the study was on a Chicago criminal
statute regarding possession of marijuana. The data used had been gathered in
1971 by Response Analysis Corporation for the National Commission on Marihuana and
Drug Abuse.

FINDINGS

1. The number of friends who used marijuana was the best single predictor of
marijuana use; the influence of friends' use on respondent's use or nonuse was
probably a reinforcing rather than a controlling effect (p. 299).

2. With increasing perceived severity of penalties, use of marijuana increased
(p. 299).

3. Perceived certainty of punishment showed essentially no effect on marijuana
use or nonuse (p. 301).

4. Although legal threat exerted no appreciable direct effect on the use or
nonuse of marijuana, it appeared to indirectly affect use or nonuse through other
variables (p. 301).

5. Social background was strongly correlated with the use or nonuse of marijuana
(p. 301).

6. Age and occupation were strongly correlated with use or nonuse of marijuana (p. 301).

7. The belief that marijuana use is immoral and the perceived physical consequences of using marijuana inhibited marijuana use (p. 301).

CONCLUSION

Marijuana use was a relatively orderly, or at least predictable, phenomenon. Substantial evidence was found to show that social control-compliance was produced by ordinary and extralegal processes and influences. The findings confirmed the importance of age-graded norms, which is consistent with traditional sociological arguments on the topic. However, despite the contemporary emphasis on legal sanctions as a deterrent against crime, the findings of this study showed the primacy of interpersonal influences. Legal factors may only generate some "explanatory power," but most of their influence is indirect.

AN: 231
AU: Naditch, M.P.
TI: Ego functioning and acute adverse reactions to psychoactive drugs
SO: Journal of Personality, 43:305-320, 1975
IN: Department of Psychology, Cornell University, Ithaca, New York
RF: 15

SUMMARY TABLE

DRUG: LSD; mescaline; marijuana
TYPE: psychoactive drug users
NUMBER: 483
SEX: male
AGE: 21.4 years (mean age)
ETHNICITY: white (95%)
LOCATION: not specified
METHODOLOGY: correlational survey
INSTRUMENT(S):   questionnaire
CONDUCTED: 1972

PURPOSE

A number of hypotheses related to the effects of specific ego mechanisms during
marijuana and LSD (or mescaline) experiences were examined. These hypotheses,
with some additional assumptions about plausible ordering of the variables,
suggested the hypothetical model used in this study. The data were collected
using a self-administered questionnaire filled out by 483 male drug users
contacted through a system of chain referrals for this purpose. Approximately 92%
of the subjects had used marijuana, 52% had used LSD, and 55% had used mescaline.
Acute adverse reactions were measured using a 23-item measure of retrospective
experience. Ego mechanisms were measured using items from the MMPI and CPI.

OPERATIONAL DEFINITIONS

Ego mechanisms studied: intellectualization, denial, repression, projection,
regression, regression in the service of the ego, tolerance of ambiguity, and
total coping.

FINDINGS

1. Regression and regression in the service of the ego were each related to
marijuana and LSD use as hypothesized, and there were also small, but
statistically significant negative correlations between intellectualization and
denial and the two kinds of drug use, and between total coping and LSD use
(p. 314).

2. With the exception of repression and projection, each of the ego mechanisms
hypothesized to be related to acute adverse reactions to marijuana correlated
significantly in the hypothesized direction (p. 314).

3. With the exceptions of projection and regression in the service of the ego, each of the ego mechanisms hypothesized to be related to acute adverse reactions to LSD correlated in the hypothesized direction (p. 314).

4. People high in regression were most likely to have acute adverse reactions to marijuana and LSD (p. 314).

5. Subjects using denial as a characteristic defense mechanism were less likely to have had acute adverse reactions to marijuana or LSD (p. 315).

6. Subjects high in use of intellectualization were less likely to have had acute adverse reactions to marijuana or LSD (p. 315).

7. Subjects high in use of regression were more likely to have had acute adverse reactions to marijuana or LSD (p. 315).

8. Subjects with high total coping scores were less likely to have had acute reactions to LSD (p. 315).

9. Both marijuana use and LSD use directly affected acute adverse reactions as hypothesized (p. 315).

10. The ego mechanisms related to drug use accounted for 11% of the variance in both marijuana and LSD use (p. 315).

11. The ego mechanisms taken together, including the effects of use, accounted for 26% of the variance in acute adverse reactions to marijuana, and 29% of the variance in acute adverse reactions to LSD (p. 315).

CONCLUSION

The data from the study were consistent with a causal model in which use of regression was associated with acute adverse reactions to marijuana and LSD. This analysis used a field survey method and consequently had to depend on retrospective data, raising the question whether selective remembering of the drug experience may have affected the results. Earlier studies have suggested that use of retrospective data may not be a problem, and may even have some advantages in the study of adverse reactions. The conceptual scheme used in this study lends itself to the development of a more complex model, which should include the effects of motive, set, and situational influences on the development of acute adverse reactions.

AN: 232
AU: Naditch, M.P.
TI: Ego mechanisms and marihuana usage
SO: In: Lettieri, D.J., ed. Predicting Adolescent Drug Abuse: A Review of
     Issues, Methods and Correlates (National Institute on Drug Abuse, Research
     Issues Series 11). Washington, D.C.: Government Printing Office, 1975. pp.
     207-221.
IN: Department of Psychology, Cornell University, Ithaca, New York
RF: 53

SUMMARY TABLE

DRUG: marijuana
TYPE: psychoactive drug users
NUMBER: 483
SEX: male
AGE: 21.4 years (mean age)
ETHNICITY: white (95%)
LOCATION: not specified
METHODOLOGY: correlational survey
INSTRUMENT(S):   questionnaire
CONDUCTED: 1972

PURPOSE

This study examined the relationship between marijuana use and the ego mechanisms
of coping and defense and, secondarily, the relationship between marijuana use and
a number of variables concerned with discontent and maladaptive behavior. The
data were collected as part of a larger study, the major purpose of which was to
examine acute adverse reactions to marijuana and LSD. Self-administered
questionnaires were distributed to 483 male subjects. The number of times a
subject had used marijuana (or hashish) was correlated with various measures of
coping, defense, discontent, maladjustment, schizophrenia, and paranoia.

FINDINGS

1. The degree of marijuana use was positively correlated with defense regression
and negatively correlated with total coping (p. 211).

2. No relationship was found between marijuana use and repression or
displacement, failing to support the hypothesis that marijuana users would have
problems in impulse control (p. 211).

3. There was a strong correlation between marijuana use and regression in service
of the ego (p. 211).

4. There were no significant correlations between marijuana use and defensive
projection, intellectualization, the coping mechanism of objectivity, or tolerance
of ambiguity (p. 213).

5. Regression in the service of the ego was the most important ego mechanism in
predicting marijuana use and accounted for 7% of the variance in marijuana use
(p. 213).

6. Marijuana use was positively correlated with locus of control and with the pure schizophrenia subscale of the MMPI (p. 213).

7. The pure paranoia subscale of the MMPI was negatively related to marijuana use and made an independent contribution to the variance (p. 213).

8. Marijuana users were differentiated from users of hard drugs in an analysis of four ego mechanisms, which made significant, independent contributions to the variance: regression, regression in the service of the ego, total coping, and denial. Regression in the service of the ego was the only variable to make a significant and independent contribution to the variance in distinguishing nonusers and marijuana users (p. 215).

CONCLUSION

Marijuana users were not found to share the configuration of the ego mechanisms of defense and coping that have been associated with alcoholics and narcotic addicts. The evidence did not support the contention that the degree of marijuana use was itself associated with inadequate coping, characteristic use of defensive regression, or lack of impulse control because of an inability to use regression or displacement effectively. The degree of marijuana use was significantly associated with employment of regression in the service of the ego as a coping mechanism. Marijuana use was not found to be related to measures of discontent and maladaptive behavior. Discriminate function analysis of the differences between marijuana users and users of hard drugs found that the latter group was characterized by regression in service of the ego, ego deficiency, regressive tendencies, and poor coping.

AN: 233
AU: Naditch, M.P.
TI: Relation of motives for drug use and psychopathology in the development of
      acute adverse reactions to psychoactive drugs
SO: Journal of Abnormal Psychology, 84:374-385, 1975
IN: Department of Psychology, Cornell University, Ithaca, New York
RF: 15

SUMMARY TABLE

DRUG: LSD; marijuana; mescaline
ᴛYPE: psychoactive drug users
NUMBER: 483
SEX: male
AGE: 21.4 years (mean age)
ETHNICITY: white (95%)
LOCATION: not specified
METHODOLOGY: correlational survey
INSTRUMENT(S):   questionnaire
CONDUCTED: [1972]

PURPOSE

The study examined the relation among motives for drug use, the degree of drug
use, psychopathology, and acute adverse reactions to marijuana and LSD. The data
were collected using self-administered questionnaires given to 483 male drug
users. Acute adverse reactions were measured with a 23-item measure of
retrospective experience. Acute adverse reactions were correlated with motives
for use (pleasure, self-therapy, social pressure), with psychopathology
(regression, schizophrenia, maladjustment), and with measures of cumulative use of
marijuana and LSD (and/or mescaline).

OPERATIONAL DEFINITIONS

Motive variables: pleasure, self-therapy, social pressure.

Psychopathology variables: regression, schizophrenia, maladjustment.

FINDINGS

1. Each of the three motive variables was positively correlated with acute
adverse reactions to marijuana. The strongest correlation was between
self-therapeutic use and adverse reactions (p. 379).

2. There were significant positive correlations between acute adverse reactions
to marijuana and the degree of marijuana use, schizophrenia, maladjustment, and
regression (p. 379).

3. Use for pleasure or curiosity, when considered independently of use for
self-therapy and social pressure, had no influence on the development of acute
adverse reactions to marijuana. The motive to use drugs for self-therapy and the
motive to use as a response to social pressure continued to make significant

independent contributions to the variance in adverse reactions to marijuana (p. 380).

4. There was no relation between use of LSD motivated by pleasure or curiosity and acute adverse reactions. Use motivated with therapeutic intentions and use as a response to peer pressure each correlated with adverse reactions to LSD and continued to make independent contributions to the variance (p. 381).

5. The three psychopathology motives were each positively correlated with, and made significant independent contributions to, the variance in acute adverse reactions to LSD (p. 381).

6. Increased use of LSD and/or mescaline was related to the development of acute adverse reactions to these drugs in the sample, and this relation was independent both of the motives for use and of the three aspects of psychopathology considered (p. 381).

7. Use motivated for therapeutic reasons accounted for more variance in adverse reactions to marijuana than it did in adverse reactions to LSD (p 381).

8. The most important predictor of adverse reactions to LSD was the extent of current maladjustment: it accounted for approximately 22% of the variance in acute adverse reactions to LSD (p. 381).

9. Each of the three motive variables was strongly correlated with marijuana use; the strongest correlation was between the pleasure and curiosity motives and marijuana use. Drug use for pleasure or curiosity had a significant and strong influence on marijuana use that was independent of therapeutically motivated use, which also made a strong independent contribution to the use rate of marijuana (p. 381).

10. Each of the three psychopathology variables correlated significantly with LSD use rates (p. 382).

11. There was a statistically significant correlation between the motive for the use of drugs for pleasure or curiosity and the pure schizophrenia subscale of the MMPI (p. 383).

12. There was a statistically significant correlation between the motive to use drugs for pleasure or curiosity and a characteristic tendency to use regression as an ego defense (p. 383).

13. The self-therapeutic motive for drug use was positively associated with schizophrenia, maladjustment, and regression (p. 383).

14. The tendency to use regressive modes of problem solving was the most important underlying determinant of the use of drugs as a way to solve problems (p. 383).

CONCLUSION

Use of psychoactive drugs with a therapeutic intent to solve problems was the single most important factor underlying the development of acute adverse reactions to marijuana. The degree of maladjustment was also an important underlying factor in the development of adverse reactions to marijuana. A therapeutic motive for drug use was also important in the development of acute adverse reactions to LSD. The use of drugs for pleasure or curiosity was a more important underlying determinent of marijuana use than of LSD use in this population. Drug use with therapeutic intent was the most important determinant of LSD use. A number of limitations must be considered in generalizing from the results of this study. The sample was not randomly drawn and therefore might not be representative of the general population. The adverse reaction measure was designed to measure acute adverse reactions to marijuana and LSD; hence, the association between independent variables and these measures are not generalizable to other drugs.

AN: 234
AU: Naditch, M.P.; Alker, P.C.; Joffe, P.
TI: Individual differences and setting as determinants of acute adverse reactions
     to psychoactive drugs
SO: Journal of Nervous and Mental Disease, 161:326-335, 1975
IN: Department of Psychology, Cornell University, Ithaca, New York
RF: 19

SUMMARY TABLE

DRUG: LSD; marijuana; mescaline
TYPE: psychoactive drug users
NUMBER: 483
SEX: male
AGE: 21.4 years (mean age)
ETHNICITY: white (95%)
LOCATION: not specified
METHODOLOGY: correlational survey
INSTRUMENT(S): questionnaire
CONDUCTED: 1972

PURPOSE

This study examined the variety of situations that relate to acute adverse reactions to psychoactive drugs and the relationship between these situations and individual differences in drug users. It was hypothesized that supportive settings would be inversely related to the development of acute adverse reactions and that threatening, less supportive settings would be directly related to the development of such reactions. The data were collected by distributing self-administered questionnaires to 483 male drug users. Twenty-three items were used to construct a measure of acute adverse reactions. Acute adverse reactions to LSD and/or mescaline and to marijuana were measured separately. Acute adverse reactions were related to five setting factors: (1) the presence of close friends knowledgeable about drugs, (2) a situation of no support or negative social sanction for drug use, (3) a public setting in which the subject tried to hide his drug taking out of fear of authorities, (4) a setting in which the subject felt pressured to use drugs at a time when he was experiencing interpersonal problems, and (5) a situation in which the person was experiencing interpersonal problems and in which other drug users were experiencing adverse reactions.

FINDINGS

1. There was a strong correlation between pressure to use drugs during a period in which the user was experiencing interpersonal difficulties and acute adverse reactions to LSD (pp. 329-330).

2. There was a significant correlation between acute adverse reactions to LSD and a setting in which a user experiencing interpersonal difficulties found himself in a situation where others were having bad drug experiences (p. 330).

3. There was a significant correlation between acute adverse reactions to LSD and a setting in which the user was in a public place using drugs (p. 330).

4. Neither the extent of social support nor the extent of negative social sanctions was associated with acute adverse reactions to LSD (p. 330).

5. The presence of close friends knowledgeable about drugs, the presence of interpersonal difficulties coupled with pressure to use drugs, and interpersonal difficulties coupled with a situation in which other friends were experiencing adverse reactions made statistically significant contributions to the variance in acute adverse reactions to LSD (p. 330).

6. The largest contributions to the variance in acute adverse reactions to LSD were made by maladjustment, schizophrenic tendencies, and regression (p. 331).

7. For LSD use, there were significant interaction effects between the absence of close friends knowledgeable about drugs and schizophrenic tendencies and maladjustment (p. 331).

8. For LSD use, there was a very substantial interaction effect between the degree of negative sanctions surrounding drug use and schizophrenic tendencies (p. 331).

9. For LSD use, pressure to use drugs during a period of interpersonal difficulties interacted significantly with both regression and maladjustment (p. 331).

10. For LSD use, a setting in which a user experiencing interpersonal difficulties was confronted by others who were having adverse reactions interacted with both schizophrenic tendencies and maladjustment (p. 331).

11. For marijuana use, there was a significant interaction effect between the degree of negative social sanctions for drug use and schizophrenic tendencies (p. 332).

12. There was a small, but significant correlation between pressure to use drugs during a time of interpersonal problems and acute adverse reactions to marijuana (p. 332).

13. For marijuana, there was a significant interaction effect between the use of regression as an ego defense and using drugs at a time of interpersonal problems when others were experiencing adverse drug reactions (p. 332).

CONCLUSION

The findings suggest that the setting in which the drug experience takes place does not by itself have a very significant effect on the development of acute adverse reactions. There were a number of substantial interaction effects between settings surrounding the drug experience and individual differences on the three dimensions of psychopathology considered in this analysis (schizophrenia, maladjustment, and regression). The theoretical importance of these findings should be interpreted with caution. They were not based on specific hypotheses, and a number of them were of small magnitude.

AN: 235
AU: Naditch, M.P.; Fenwick, S.
TI: LSD flashbacks and ego functioning
SO: Journal of Abnormal Psychology, 86:352-359, 1977
IN: Abt Associates, Cambridge, Massachusetts
RF: 27

SUMMARY TABLE

DRUG: LSD
TYPE: LSD users
NUMBER: 235
SEX: male
AGE: 21.2 years (mean age)
ETHNICITY: white (96%)
LOCATION: not specified
METHODOLOGY: correlational survey
INSTRUMENT(S):   questionnaire; interview
CONDUCTED: 1972

PURPOSE

The study examined the relation of flashbacks to a variety of measures of ego
functions and psychopathologies concerned with the ability to exercise volitional
control of experience. It was expected that LSD users who had trouble handling
intrusive cognitive and affective impulses would be more susceptible to
flashbacks. The data for the study were collected through a questionnaire
distributed to 483 male drug users, of whom the 235 who used LSD were chosen as
subjects for the study. Flashbacks were measured by asking subjects whether they
had ever experienced flashbacks or spontaneous recurrences of the LSD experience
nonvolitionally. Subjects were asked to assess their flashback experience and to
respond to various psychological questionnaires. Mean scores of LSD users having
flashbacks were compared with mean scores of LSD users not experiencing
flashbacks.

OPERATIONAL DEFINITIONS

Flashbackers: LSD users who had experienced flashbacks.

Nonflashbackers: LSD users who had not experienced flashbacks.

FINDINGS

1. Twenty-eight percent of the LSD users reported experiencing flashbacks
(p. 354).

2. About 11% of the flashbackers described their flashback experiences as very
frightening, 32% as moderately frightening, 36% as moderately pleasant, and 21% as
very pleasant (p. 354).

3. Approximately 36% of the flashbackers found the experiences to be disruptive of their normal activity, whereas 64% of the flashbackers did not (p. 354-355).

4. Only 16% of the subjects sought clinical help as a result of their flashback experiences (p. 355).

5. Flashbackers were more likely to use repression and much more likely to use regression as ego defenses than were nonflashbackers (p. 355).

6. Flashbackers had lower scores on total coping, had less tolerance of ambiguity, and were less likely to be able to employ intellectualization effectively than were nonflashbackers (p. 353).

7. Subjects who took LSD for self-therapeutic reasons were much more likely to report having experienced flashbacks, and users who tried the drug reluctantly under peer pressure were also somewhat more likely to report experiencing flashbacks (p. 355).

8. Flashbackers had higher levels of drug use and were also much more likely to have experienced a more intense acute adverse reaction than were nonflashbackers (p. 355).

9. Data did not support latent psychopathology explanations of the etiology of LSD flashbacks (p. 356).

10. Inadequate ego capacity and increased rates of LSD use enhanced the probability of flashbacks because they increased the probability of experiencing acute adverse reactions while taking the drug (p. 357).

CONCLUSION

The results suggest that acute adverse reactions occurring during the drug experience and, possibly, the degree of drug use should be considered in theoretical explanations of flashbacks. These findings are limited to a white, middle-class, male normal population and should be replicated in other populations.

AN: 236
AU: Pillard, R.C.; McNair, D.M.; Fisher, S.
TI: Does marijuana enhance experimentally induced anxiety?
SO: Psychopharmacologia, 40:205-210, 1974
IN: Psychopharmacology Laboratory, Division of Psychiatry, Boston University
     School of Medicine, Boston, Massachusetts
RF: 7

SUMMARY TABLE

DRUG: marijuana
TYPE: marijuana users
NUMBER: 48
SEX: male
AGE: 21 years and older
ETHNICITY: not specified
LOCATION: Boston, Massachusetts
METHODOLOGY: experimental research
INSTRUMENT(S):   Situational Anxiety Scale; Profile of Mood States
CONDUCTED: not specified

PURPOSE

In order to find out whether laboratory stressors induce greater or more variable anxiety in marijuana-intoxicated subjects, two experiments were conducted in which subjects were presented with anxiety-inducing situations. All subjects were volunteers who had previously used marijuana. Subjects smoked marijuana or a placebo (THC-free marijuana) until they felt as high as they usually did in social situations. In Experiment 1, a motion picture depicting dental procedures was shown to marijuana and placebo subjects; in Experiment 2, subjects had to give a short videotaped speech.

FINDINGS

1. For both marijuana smokers and placebo subjects, there was a sharp increase in anxiety after viewing a dental film, but it was of the same degree for both groups. There was no evidence of drug effect on anxiety (p. 207).

2. Anxiety response to a public speaking task was the same for both the marijuana smokers and the placebo subjects (noted differences were insignificant) (p. 209).

CONCLUSION

The two experiments showed that marijuana at the dose level studied had no effect either on the average level or on the variability of anxiety in subjects exposed to stressful situations.

AN: 237
AU: Salzman, C.; Kochansky, G.E.; Van der Kolk, B.A.; Shader, R.I.
TI: The effect of marijuana on small group process
SO: American Journal of Drug and Alcohol Abuse, 4:251-255, 1977
IN: Psychopharmacology Research Laboratory, Harvard Medical School, Massachusetts
      Mental Health Center, Boston, Massachusetts
RF: 14

SUMMARY TABLE

DRUG: marijuana
TYPE: marijuana users
NUMBER: 60
SEX: males
AGE: 21-30 years
ETHNICITY: not specified
LOCATION: Boston, Massachusetts
METHODOLOGY: experimental research
INSTRUMENT(S):   Thematic Appercepton Test; videotape observations
CONDUCTED: not specified

PURPOSE

Earlier studies have suggested that the effects of marijuana differ when it is
used in a group setting as compared to when used alone. A small-group, laboratory
study was carried out to investigate the effects of marijuana on affective
communication within three-person groups and on the ability of the groups to work
together toward a common goal.

FINDINGS

1. Placebo groups were unchanged after smoking marijuana in terms of affective
communications and ability to work together. Marijuana groups, on the other hand,
were observed to differ markedly after smoking compared to predrug behavior, with
eight groups appearing more relaxed and friendly and with two groups continuing in
an initial relaxed manner (p. 253).

2. Task-oriented communications decreased in all marijuana groups as members
seemed to begin enjoying themselves more while sharing personal information and
inner experiences (p. 253).

3. Stories produced by marijuana groups after smoking were meager, stereotyped,
or silly and were not more creative or original than stories produced before
smoking or stories produced by placebo groups (p. 253).

4. Placebo groups responded to a frustration stimulus by becoming more hostile,
serious, and task-oriented, while nine of the marijuana groups responded to a the
stimulus by becoming more task-oriented and more determined to work effectively
with evidence of intoxication appearing to decrease (p. 253).

5. In spite of the appearance of more goal-directed behavior, the postfrustration
stories by the marijuana groups were not more creative or elaborate than their
prefrustration stories (p. 253).

CONCLUSION

On the basis of observations of marijuana smokers in a small-group setting, it was concluded that the individuals within the groups were able to temporarily control moderate levels of intoxication. Further, in group functioning they appeared less affected by marijuana and better able to cooperate following a frustration stimulus. However, they did not become more creative in performing an assigned task. Similar findings have previously been reported for individual smokers. It appears that both in individuals and in groups marijuana effects may depend on multiple variables, including the setting, the characteristics of the person and the intoxicant, and the demands placed on the smoker.

AN: 238
AU: Salzman, C.; Van der Kolk, B.A.; Shader, R.I.
TI: Marijuana and hostility in a small-group setting
SO: American Journal of Psychiatry, 133:1029-1033, 1976
IN: Psychopharmacology Research Laboratory, Harvard Medical School, Massachusetts
      Mental Health Center, Boston, Massachusetts
RF: 45

SUMMARY TABLE

DRUG: marijuana
TYPE: marijuana users
NUMBER: 60
SEX: males
AGE: 21-30 years
ETHNICITY: not specified
LOCATION: Boston, Massachusetts
METHODOLOGY: experimental research
INSTRUMENT(S):   Thematic Apperception Test; Buss-Durkee Hostility Inventory;
                 Symptom Checklist; Hostility Interpersonal Rating Scale; Bales'
                 Interaction Process Analysis
CONDUCTED: not specified

PURPOSE

Psychopharmacology studies have suggested that the effects of marijuana on affect
and behavior depend on the social setting and may differ when taken in a group as
compared to taken when alone. In one study, subjects given marijuana individually
became quiet and relaxed, whereas those in a group showed euphoria, elation, and a
lack of sedation. Other investigators have reported decreases in anger, anxiety,
social interaction, and hostile behavior. A controlled study in a laboratory
setting was performed to further investigate these preliminary findings. Sixty
male marijuana users were assigned to three-person groups; the members of each
group smoked marijuana or a placebo according to a double-blind schedule.
Hostility levels were measured before and after smoking one cigarette (marijuana
or placebo) and participating in a group activity.

FINDINGS

1. Change scores on anger-hostility scales were similar for subjects given
marijuana and subjects given placebo in a small-group setting (p. 1030).

2. Following a frustration stimulus, marijuana subjects showed a small,
statistically significant decrease, and placebo subjects a slight increase, in
hostility (p. 1030).

3. Marijuana produced a small, statistically significant increase in sarcastic
communications among members of a small group (p. 1030).

4. Total negative verbal behavior increased significantly following marijuana
smoking by members of small groups (pp. 1030-1031).

5. Following a frustration stimulus given in a small-group setting, negative verbal and sarcastic behaviors decreased significantly for marijuana subjects and increased for placebo subjects (p. 1031).

6. Marijuana-intoxicated subjects in a small-group setting reported a statistically significant decrease in hostile feelings following frustration and placebo subjects reported a slight increase (p. 1031).

CONCLUSION

In a laboratory, small-group study, a moderate marijuana dose and a mild frustration stimulus produced no increase in hostility, but did produce an increase in sarcastic communications. The findings suggest that the marijuana dose served as a disinhibitor, allowing subjects to feel less angry and also less constricted in their verbal interactions. Although in this study marijuana appears to have reduced negative behavior and affect, the literature is not unanimously in agreement with the finding. The possibility remains that other dose levels, different environments, and higher levels of frustration might produce an increase in hostility. The relationship between marijuana and hostility requires further study.

INDEXES

AUTHOR INDEX

BIHARI, B.

054 Entry into methadone maintenance programs: A follow-up study of New York City heroin users detoxified in 1961-1963

BLUM, R.H.

128 Drug education: Further results and recommendations

BONITO, A.J.

004 The veridicality of addicts' self-reports in social research

015 Studying addicts over time: Methodology and preliminary findings

025 Is there a relationship between astrology and addiction? A reexamination

BONNHEIM, M.L.

203 Family interaction and acculturation in Mexican-American inhalant users

BOTTO, R.W.

219 Hypnotic susceptibility during cannabis intoxication

BOURNE, P.

123 A heroin "epidemic" in Asia

BOYLE, J.M.

204 What happened in Harlem? Analysis of a decline in heroin use among a generation unit of urban black youth

207 Patterns of drug involvement: Developmental and secular influences on age at initiation

BROOK, D.W.

129 Perceived paternal relationships, adolescent personality, and female marijuana use

134 Paternal determinants of male adolescent marijuana use

135 Fathers and sons: Their relationship and personality characteristics associated with the son's smoking behavior

BROOK, J.S.

129 Perceived paternal relationships, adolescent personality, and female marijuana use

130 Correlates of adolescent marijuana use as related to age, sex, and ethnicity

131 Peer, family, and personality domains as related to adolescents' drug behavior

132 Family socialization and adolescent personality and their association with adolescent use of marijuana

133 Initiation into adolescent marijuana use

134 Paternal determinants of male adolescent marijuana use

135 Fathers and sons: Their relationship and personality characteristics associated with the son's smoking behavior

136 Maternal and personality determinants of adolescent smoking behavior

137 The role of the father in his son's marijuana use

BROWN, C.H.

209   Sex differences in antecedents of substance use among adolescents

212   Longitudinal community epidemiological studies of drug use: Early aggressiveness, shyness, and learning problems

BRUNSWICK, A.F.

204   What happened in Harlem? Analysis of a decline in heroin use among a generation unit of urban black youth

205   Health and drug behavior: A study of urban black adolescents

206   Black youths and drug-use behavior

207   Patterns of drug involvement: Developmental and secular influences on age at initiation

CAPLOVITZ, D.

005   The working addict

102   Drug use in the construction trade

208   Youngsters Experimenting with Drugs

CARMICHAEL, J.S.

033   Self-concept and substance abuse treatment

055   Focus on the family as a factor in differential treatment outcome

CHAMBERS, C.D.

101   Mexican-American criminals: A comparative study of heroin using and non-using felons

CHITWOOD, D.D.

109   The social problem of drug abuse in ecological perspective

CISIN, I.H.

016   Addict Careers: I. A new typology

017   Addict careers: II. The first ten years

018   Addict careers: III. Trends across time

019   Trends in the age of onset of narcotic addiction

CLAYTON, R.R.

179   Shacking up: Cohabitation in the 1970s

180   Young Men and Drugs in Manhattan: A Causal Analysis

181   Smoking and health, marijuana and use of other illicit drugs: Causal relationships

199   Determinants of early marihuana use

200   Young Men and Drugs--A Nationwide Survey

COATE, D.

059   The impact of drug addiction on criminal earnings

COMITAS, L.

217   Cannabis and work in Jamaica: A refutation of the amotivational syndrome

DAVIDSON, S.T.

182 Changing patterns of drug use among university males

197 The amotivational syndrome and the college student

DAVIS, D.H.

104 Antecedents of narcotic use and addiction: A study of 898 Vietnam veterans

105 Depressive disorders in Vietnam returnees

DE LEON, G.

034 Phoenix House: Psychopathological signs among male and female drug-free residents

035 Therapeutic community dropouts: Psychological changes 2 years after treatment

036 Therapeutic community dropouts: Criminal behavior five years after treatment

037 Phoenix house: Criminal activity of dropouts

038 Male and female drug abusers: Social and psychological status 2 years after treatment in a therapeutic community

039 Phoenix House: Changes in psychopathological signs of resident drug addicts

040 The therapeutic community: Success and improvement rates 5 years after treatment

056 The therapeutic community: Multivariate prediction of retention

076 Are female drug abusers more deviant?

DEWAARD, R.J.

111 Satisfaction with real and simulated jobs in relation to personality variables and drug use

DESMOND, D.P.

006 Street heroin potency and deaths from overdose in San Antonio

012 New light on the maturing out hypothesis in opioid dependence

013 Residence relocation inhibits opioid dependence

041 Religious programs and careers of chronic heroin users

051 Outpatient methadone withdrawal for heroin dependence

060 The effect of probation on behavior of chronic opioid drug users

074 Crime and treatment of heroin users

DODGE, D.L.

183 Survey of students and drugs at the University of Notre Dame: An overview

184 Dimensions of marijuana use in a midwest Catholic university: Subcultural considerations

185 The variation of a midwest Catholic university's drug use pattern from other Catholic university findings: Why?

DOUGLASS, F.M.

103 Three types of extreme drug users identified by a replicated cluster analysis

DUCHAINE, N.S.

010 What is an addict? Empirical patterns and concepts of addiction

062 Daily criminal activities of street drug users: Preliminary findings

DUKES, J.

011 Family ties of heroin addicts

DUPONT, R.L.

075 A preliminary report on crime and addiction within a community-wide population of narcotic addicts

DU TOIT, B.M.

218 Ethnicity and patterning in South African drug use

EDWARDS, R.

211 Drug use among Native American adults

214 Drug use among adolescents of five Southwestern Native American tribes

ELASHOFF, R.M.

032 Therapeutic communities vs methadone maintenance: A prospective controlled study of narcotic addiction treatment: Design and one-year follow-up

ELINSON, J.

138 A Study of Teenage Drug Behavior

EMERY, G.D.

007 Suicidal behavior among heroin addicts: A brief report

028 Correlates of self-reported and clinically assessed depression in male heroin addicts

ENGELSING, T.M.

032 Therapeutic communities vs methadone maintenance: A prospective controlled study of narcotic addiction treatment: Design and one-year follow-up

ENSMINGER, M.E.

209 Sex differences in antecedents of substance use among adolescents

213 Mental health in first grade and teenage drug, alcohol, and cigarette use

ESQUIVEL, M.

051 Outpatient methadone withdrawal for heroin dependence

EVELAND, L.K.

153 Drugs and delinquency: A search for causal connections

FAIRBANKS, L.

107 Qat use in North Yemen and the problem of addiction: A study in medical anthropology

FARBER, P.D.

103 Three types of extreme drug users identified by a replicated cluster analysis

136 Maternal and personality determinants of adolescent smoking behavior

137 The role of the father in his son's marijuana use

GOSHO, C.

083 The relationship between female criminality and drug abuse

GOULD, L.C.

127 The relationship between drug education programs in the greater New Haven schools and changes in drug use and drug-related beliefs and perceptions

139 Sequential patterns of multiple-drug use among high school students

GRAEVEN, D.B.

140 Experimental heroin users: An epidemiologic and psychosocial approach

141 Treated and untreated addicts: Factors associated with participation in treatment and cessation of heroin use

142 Addicts and experimenters: Dynamics of involvement in an adolescent heroin epidemic

143 Personality development and adolescent heroin use

144 Family life and levels of involvement in an adolescent heroin epidemic

GRAEVEN, K.A.

141 Treated and untreated addicts: Factors associated with participation in treatment and cessation of heroin use

HABERMAN, P.

138 A Study of Teenage Drug Behavior

HARBIN, H.

011 Family ties of heroin addicts

HARDING, W.M.

008 Formerly-addicted-now-controlled opiate users

HARRIS, R.

009 Suicide attempts among drug abusers

042 Differential response of heroin and nonheroin abusers to inpatient treatment

043 A comparison of dropouts and disciplinary discharges from a therapeutic community

044 Self-concept and completion of treatment for heroin and nonheroin drug abusers

HAYES, C.

228 Psychedelic drug flashbacks: Subjective reports and biographical data

229 Psychedelic drug flashbacks: Attentional deficits?

HELZER, J.E.

104 Antecedents of narcotic use and addiction: A study of 898 Vietnam veterans

105 Depressive disorders in Vietnam returnees

044 Self-concept and completion of treatment for heroin and nonheroin drug abusers

INCIARDI, J.A.

064 Heroin use and street crime

065 Youth, drugs, and street crime

066 The impact of drug use on street crime

080 Women, heroin, and property crime

081 Black women, heroin and crime: Some empirical notes

101 Mexican-American criminals: A comparative study of heroin using and non-using felons

106 Acute drug reactions among the aged: A research note

JAFFE, J.

036 Therapeutic community dropouts: Criminal behavior five years after treatment

JAINCHILL, N.

038 Male and female drug abusers: Social and psychological status 2 years after treatment in a therapeutic community

040 The therapeutic community: Success and improvement rates 5 years after treatment

076 Are female drug abusers more deviant?

JAMES, J.

082 Prostitution and addiction: An interdisciplinary approach

083 The relationship between female criminality and drug abuse

091 Criminal involvement of female offenders: Psychological characteristics among four groups

222 Sea-Tac and PCP

JOE, G.W.

221 Behavioral correlates and comparisons of current marijuana users, quitters and evasives

223 Behavioral correlates of age at first marijuana use

JOFFE, P.

234 Individual differences and setting as determinants of acute adverse reactions to psychoactive drugs

JOHNSON, B.D.

010 What is an addict? Empirical patterns and concepts of addiction

045 Investigating impact of methadone treatment upon the behavior of New York City street addicts

067 The criminal behavior of street heroin and cocaine users

068 Exploring asymmetries in the hard drug-crime relationship

JOHNSON, W.T.

224 Arrest probabilities for marijuana users as indicators of selective law enforcement

230 Deterrence as social control: The legal and extralegal production of conformity

139 Sequential patterns of multiple-drug use among high school students

172 Sex differences in adolescent drug use: Recent trends

KAY, E.J.

193 A longitudinal study of the personality correlates of marijuana use

KELLAM, S.G.

209 Sex differences in antecedents of substance use among adolescents

212 Longitudinal community epidemiological studies of drug use: Early aggressiveness, shyness, and learning problems

213 Mental health in first grade and teenage drug, alcohol, and cigarette use

KENNEDY, J.G.

107 Qat use in North Yemen and the problem of addiction: A study in medical anthropology

KESSLER, R.C.

160 Antecedents of adolescent initiation to stages of drug use: A development analysis

161 The epidemiology of drug use among New York State high school students: Distribution, trends, and change in rates of use

164 A longitudinal study of onset of drinking among high school students

KHAVARI, K.A.

103 Three types of extreme drug users identified by a replicated cluster analysis

225 Personaltiy correlates of hallucinogen use

KLEBER, H.D.

127 The relationship between drug education programs in the greater New Haven schools and changes in drug use and drug-related beliefs and perceptions

139 Sequential patterns of multiple-drug use among high school students

KLEINMAN, P.H.

046 The magic fix: A critical analysis of methadone maintenance treatment

093 Ethnic differences in factors related to drug use

KLINE, F.G.

165 Aspects of adolescent information acquisition about drugs and alcohol topics

KOCHANSKY, G.E.

237 The effect of marijuana on small group process

KORCHIN, S.J.

177 Project Community: Therapeutic Explorations with Adolescents

132 Family socialization and adolescent personality and their association with adolescent use of marijuana

133 Initiation into adolescent marijuana use

LYONS, A.

193 A longitudinal study of the personality correlates of marijuana use

MABRY, E.

225 Personaltiy correlates of hallucinogen use

McBRIDE, D.C.

069 The relationship between type of drug use and arrest charge in an arrested population

070 Crime and drug-using behavior: An areal analysis

094 A comparison of Spanish and non-Spanish drug users in treatment in Dade County, Florida

106 Acute drug reactions among the aged: A research note

120 Effects of criminal justice and medical definitions of a social problem upon the delivery of treatment: The case of drug abuse

163 Parental and peer influence upon adolescent drug use

McCOY, C.B.

070 Crime and drug-using behavior: An areal analysis

094 A comparison of Spanish and non-Spanish drug users in treatment in Dade County, Florida

109 The social problem of drug abuse in ecological perspective

McGLOTHLIN, W.H.

030 The effect of parole on methadone patient behavior

049 Shutting off methadone: Costs and benefits

050 Long-term follow-up of clients of high- and low-dose methadone programs

071 California civil commitment: A decade later

072 Outcome of the California Civil Addict commitments: 1961-1972

073 Narcotic addiction and crime

McNAIR, D.M.

236 Does marijuana enhance experimentally induced anxiety?

MADANES, C.

011 Family ties of heroin addicts

MADDUX, J.F.

006 Street heroin potency and deaths from overdose in San Antonio

012 New light on the maturing out hypothesis in opioid dependence

013 Residence relocation inhibits opioid dependence

041 Religious programs and careers of chronic heroin users

051 Outpatient methadone withdrawal for heroin dependence

060 The effect of probation on behavior of chronic opioid drug users

MILLER, T.

053 Methadone, wine and welfare

MORRISON, A.J.

165 Aspects of adolescent information acquisition about drugs and alcohol topics

MOSCOSO, M.

170 Drug use among public and private secondary school students in Puerto Rico

MUSTO, D.F.

052 Notes on American medical history: A follow-up study of the New Haven morphine maintenance clinic of 1920

NADITCH, M.P.

231 Ego functioning and acute adverse reactions to psychoactive drugs

232 Ego mechanisms and marihuana usage

233 Relation of motives for drug use and psychopathology in the development of acute adverse reactions to psychoactive drugs

234 Individual differences and setting as determinants of acute adverse reactions to psychoactive drugs

235 LSD flashbacks and ego functioning

NEWMAN, W.

193 A longitudinal study of the personality correlates of marijuana use

NURCO, D.N.

004 The veridicality of addicts' self-reports in social research

014 An analysis of work histories, earnings, and receipts of benefits among a sample of a community-wide population of narcotic addicts

015 Studying addicts over time: Methodology and preliminary findings

016 Addict Careers: I. A new typology

017 Addict careers: II. The first ten years

018 Addict careers: III. Trends across time

019 Trends in the age of onset of narcotic addiction

020 Narcotic abusers and poverty

025 Is there a relationship between astrology and addiction? A reexamination

057 The criminality of heroin addicts when addicted and when off opiates

058 Lifetime criminality of heroin addicts in the United States

075 A preliminary report on crime and addiction within a community-wide population of narcotic addicts

NUTTALL, E.V.

021 Predicting heroin and alcohol usage among young Puerto Ricans

022 Parental correlates of drug use among young Puerto Rican adults

NUTTALL, R.L.

021 Predicting heroin and alcohol usage among young Puerto Ricans

022 Parental correlates of drug use among young Puerto Rican adults

O'DONNELL, J.A.

198 Cigarette smoking as a precursor of illicit drug use

199 Determinants of early marihuana use

200 Young Men and Drugs--A Nationwide Survey

O'MALLEY, P.M.

150 Drugs and the Class of '78: Behaviors, Attitudes, and Recent National Trends

151 Highlights from Student Drug Use in America 1975-1980

152 Marijuana Decriminalization: The Impact on Youth, 1975-1980

153 Drugs and delinquency: A search for causal connections

166 Drug use and military plans of high school seniors

OETTING, E.R.

211 Drug use among Native American adults

214 Drug use among adolescents of five Southwestern Native American tribes

215 Drug use among Native American adolescents

216 Native American Drug Use: Drug Abuse Among Indian Adolescents

ORIVE, R.

167 Personality, attitudinal, and social correlates of drug use

PAGE, J.B.

079 Cuban women, sex role conflicts and the use of prescription drugs

095 The children of exile: Relationships between the acculturation process and drug use among Cuban youth

096 Drug use among Cuban exiles in Miami, Florida: Cultural antecedents and processes

PARKER, R.

063 Addicts, police, and the neighborhood social system

PATON, S.M.

168 Psychological factors and adolescent illicit drug use: Ethnicity and sex differences

169 Depressive mood and adolescent illicit drug use: A longitudinal analysis

PENG, G.

124 Opium and heroin addicts in Laos: I. A comparative study

125 Opium and heroin addicts in Laos: II. A study of matched pairs

PERKINS, M.E.

054 Entry into methadone maintenance programs: A follow-up study of New York City heroin users detoxified in 1961-1963

PERONE, M.

111 Satisfaction with real and simulated jobs in relation to personality variables and drug use

PETERSEN, R.E.

224 Arrest probabilities for marijuana users as indicators of selective law enforcement

PILLARD, R.C.

219 Hypnotic susceptibility during cannabis intoxication

236 Does marijuana enhance experimentally induced anxiety?

POTTIEGER, A.E.

081 Black women, heroin and crime: Some empirical notes

PRATHER, J.E.

084 A valium a day keeps the tension away: Socio-psychological characteristics of minor tranquilizer users

085 Drug usage as an index of stress among women

086 Sex differences in the content and style of medical advertisements

PRATT, T.C.

033 Self-concept and substance abuse treatment

043 A comparison of dropouts and disciplinary discharges from a therapeutic community

048 Cultural factors and attrition in drug abuse treatment

055 Focus on the family as a factor in differential treatment outcome

PREBLE, E.

045 Investigating impact of methadone treatment upon the behavior of New York City street addicts

053 Methadone, wine and welfare

067 The criminal behavior of street heroin and cocaine users

RAMOS, M.R.

052 Notes on American medical history: A follow-up study of the New Haven morphine maintenance clinic of 1920

RATCLIFF, K.S.

097 Risk factors in the continuation of childhood antisocial behavior into adulthood

098 Childhood conduct disorders and later arrest

099 The long-term outcome of truancy

100 Father's alcoholism and children's outcomes

RICHMAN, A.

023 Narcotic addicts, multiple drug abuse and psychological distress

024 Ecological studies of narcotic addiction

054 Entry into methadone maintenance programs: A follow-up study of New York City heroin users detoxified in 1961-1963

SIMON, M.B.

213 Mental health in first grade and teenage drug, alcohol, and cigarette use

SINGER, J.L.

192 Organization of needs in male and female drug and alcohol users

201 Prediction of college drug use from personality and inner experience

202 Reasons for drug and alcohol use by college students

SINGLE, E.W.

161 The epidemiology of drug use among New York State high school students: Distribution, trends, and change in rates of use

162 Adolescent involvement in legal and illegal drug use: A multiple classification analysis

173 The role of buying and selling in illicit drug use

174 Patterns of multiple drug use in high school

SKODOL, A.

039 Phoenix House: Changes in psychopathological signs of resident drug addicts

SLATIN, G.T.

200 Young Men and Drugs--A Nationwide Survey

SMITH, G.M.

175 Teenage drug use: A search for causes and consequenses

176 Psychological predictors of early use, late use, and nonuse of marijuana among teenage students

SOMERS, R.H.

196 Drug use, academic performance, and career indecision: Longitudinal data in search of a model

197 The amotivational syndrome and the college student

SOSKIN, W.F.

177 Project Community: Therapeutic Explorations with Adolescents

SPECKART, G.

030 The effect of parole on methadone patient behavior

SPOTTS, J.V.

027 The Life Styles of Nine American Opiate Users (Executive Summary)

116 The Life Styles of Nine American Amphetamine Users (Executive Summary)

117 Cocaine Users: A Representative Case Approach

118 Life Styles of Nine American Barbiturate/Sedative-Hypnotic Drug Users (Executive Summary)

119 Life Styles of Nine American Non-Users of Drugs (Executive Summary)

STEER, R.A.

007 Suicidal behavior among heroin addicts: A brief report

026 The structure of depression in heroin addicts

028 Correlates of self-reported and clinically assessed depression in male heroin addicts

029 Types of psychopathology displayed by heroin addicts

STEIN, K.B.

177 Project Community: Therapeutic Explorations with Adolescents

STELMACK, S.M.

008 Formerly-addicted-now-controlled opiate users

SUDIT, M.

158 The epidemiology of adolescent drug use in France and Israel

TEAGUE, J.

107 Qat use in North Yemen and the problem of addiction: A study in medical anthropology

THOMPSON, W.D.

127 The relationship between drug education programs in the greater New Haven schools and changes in drug use and drug-related beliefs and perceptions

139 Sequential patterns of multiple-drug use among high school students

TOWNES, B.D.

091 Criminal involvement of female offenders: Psychological characteristics among four groups

TREIMAN, D.

162 Adolescent involvement in legal and illegal drug use: A multiple classification analysis

TREVION, A.

006 Street heroin potency and deaths from overdose in San Antonio

TRIMBOLI, F.

194 A psychiatric emergency room study of inhalant use

TUROFF, B.S.

001 Deaths of persons using methadone in New York City--1971

VAN DER KOLK, B.A.

237 The effect of marijuana on small group process

238 Marijuana and hostility in a small-group setting

VAN STONE, W.W.

032 Therapeutic communities vs methadone maintenance: A prospective controlled study of narcotic addiction treatment: Design and one-year follow-up

VOSS, H.L.

179 Shacking up: Cohabitation in the 1970s

180 Young Men and Drugs in Manhattan: A Causal Analysis

181 Smoking and health, marijuana and use of other illicit drugs: Causal relationships

200 Young Men and Drugs--A Nationwide Survey

WEBB, N.L.

033 Self-concept and substance abuse treatment

048 Cultural factors and attrition in drug abuse treatment

055 Focus on the family as a factor in differential treatment outcome

WELLS, K.S.

106 Acute drug reactions among the aged: A research note

120 Effects of criminal justice and medical definitions of a social problem upon the delivery of treatment: The case of drug abuse

WELLS, L.E.

224 Arrest probabilities for marijuana users as indicators of selective law enforcement

WEPPNER, R.S.

094 A comparison of Spanish and non-Spanish drug users in treatment in Dade County, Florida

120 Effects of criminal justice and medical definitions of a social problem upon the delivery of treatment: The case of drug abuse

WEST, P.A.

100 Father's alcoholism and children's outcomes

WESTERMEYER, J.

121 Narcotic addiction in two Asian cultures: A comparison and analysis

122 Influence of opium availability on addiction rates in Laos

123 A heroin "epidemic" in Asia

124 Opium and heroin addicts in Laos: I. A comparative study

125 Opium and heroin addicts in Laos: II. A study of matched pairs

WEXLER, H.K.

036 Therapeutic community dropouts: Criminal behavior five years after treatment

040 The therapeutic community: Success and improvement rates 5 years after treatment

056 The therapeutic community: Multivariate prediction of retention

WHITE, O.Z.

101 Mexican-American criminals: A comparative study of heroin using and non-using felons

WHITEMAN, M.

130 Correlates of adolescent marijuana use as related to age, sex, and ethnicity

131 Peer, family, and personality domains as related to adolescents' drug behavior

132 Family socialization and adolescent personality and their association with adolescent use of marijuana

133 Initiation into adolescent marijuana use

134 Paternal determinants of male adolescent marijuana use

135 Fathers and sons: Their relationship and personality characteristics associated with the son's smoking behavior

136 Maternal and personality determinants of adolescent smoking behavior

137 The role of the father in his son's marijuana use

WILSON, B.D.

072 Outcome of the California Civil Addict commitments: 1961-1972

073 Narcotic addiction and crime

WINGARD, J.A.

146 Adolescent drug use and intentions to use drugs in the future: A concurrent analysis

147 Beginning adolescent drug use and peer and adult interaction patterns

148 Longitudinal analysis of the role of peer support, adult models, and peer subcultures in beginning adolescent substance use: An application of setwise canonical correlation methods

149 Intentions to use drugs among adolescents: A longitudinal analysis

178 The relationship of personality structure to patterns of adolescent substance use

WISH, E.

114 Vietnam veterans three years after Vietnam: How our study changed our view on heroin

115 Polydrug and alcohol use by veterans and nonveterans

WOHL, R.W.

083 The relationship between female criminality and drug abuse

ZANES, A.

138 A Study of Teenage Drug Behavior

ZARCONE, V.P.

032 Therapeutic communities vs methadone maintenance: A prospective controlled study of narcotic addiction treatment: Design and one-year follow-up

ZINBERG, N.E.

008 Formerly-addicted-now-controlled opiate users

TOPIC INDEX

Topic Index

Addiction Mechanisms and Effects

ABSTINENCE

012 New light on the maturing out
hypothesis in opioid dependence
(1, 3, 5, 6, 7)

013 Residence relocation inhibits
opioid dependence
(2, 3, 4, 6, 7, 8, 10, 11, 12)

015 Studying addicts over time:
Methodology and preliminary findings
(5, 7, 9)

016 Addict Careers: I. A new
typology
(6)

017 Addict careers: II. The first
ten years
(6, 7, 8, 10, 11, 13)

031 What we need to know
(1)

041 Religious programs and careers of
chronic heroin users
(1, 2, 3, 5)

049 Shutting off methadone: Costs and
benefits
(11)

050 Long-term follow-up of clients of
high- and low-dose methadone programs
(12)

051 Outpatient methadone withdrawal
for heroin dependence
(1, 5, 6)

052 Notes on American medical history:
A follow-up study of the New Haven
morphine maintenance clinic of 1920
(12)

057 The criminality of heroin addicts
when addicted and when off opiates
(3)

060 The effect of probation on
behavior of chronic opioid drug users
(2, 3, 4)

071 California civil commitment: A
decade later
(8)

073 Narcotic addiction and crime
(6)

089 Sex roles among deviants: The
woman addict
(8)

107 Qat use in North Yemen and the
problem of addiction: A study in
medical anthropology
(7)

112 Drug treatment after return in
Vietnam veterans
(3)

114 Vietnam veterans three years after
Vietnam: How our study changed our
view on heroin
(10)

141 Treated and untreated addicts:
Factors associated with participation
in treatment and cessation of heroin
use
(15, 17, 18, 19, 20, 21, 22, 24, 25,
26)

142 Addicts and experimenters:
Dynamics of involvement in an
adolescent heroin epidemic
(6)

151 Highlights from Student Drug Use
in America 1975-1980
(4)

182 Changing patterns of drug use
among university males
(12, 14)

206 Black youths and drug-use behavior
(8)

ABUSE LIABILITY

085   Drug usage as an index of stress among women
(6)

DEATH (DRUG RELATED)

001   Deaths of persons using methadone in New York City--1971
(1, 2, 3, 5, 6, 7)

006   Street heroin potency and deaths from overdose in San Antonio
(2, 3)

052   Notes on American medical history: A follow-up study of the New Haven morphine maintenance clinic of 1920
(12)

EUPHORIA

087   Becoming addicted: The woman addict
(9, 12, 14)

107   Qat use in North Yemen and the problem of addiction: A study in medical anthropology
(19)

117   Cocaine Users: A Representative Case Approach
(7)

OVERDOSE/ACUTE INTOXICATION

090   Women addicts' experience of the heroin world: Risk, chaos, and inundation
(2)

106   Acute drug reactions among the aged: A research note
(5)

118   Life Styles of Nine American Barbiturate/Sedative-Hypnotic Drug Users (Executive Summary)
(14)

PHYSICAL DEPENDENCE

010   What is an addict? Empirical patterns and concepts of addiction
(6)

087   Becoming addicted: The woman addict
(4, 8, 9, 10, 11, 12, 14)

089   Sex roles among deviants: The woman addict
(4)

114   Vietnam veterans three years after Vietnam: How our study changed our view on heroin
(3, 8)

115   Polydrug and alcohol use by veterans and nonveterans
(10, 11, 12, 20)

117   Cocaine Users: A Representative Case Approach
(10)

121   Narcotic addiction in two Asian cultures: A comparison and analysis
(2)

124   Opium and heroin addicts in Laos: I. A comparative study
(7)

125   Opium and heroin addicts in Laos: II. A study of matched pairs
(3)

142   Addicts and experimenters: Dynamics of involvement in an adolescent heroin epidemic
(7)

165   Aspects of adolescent information acquisition about drugs and alcohol topics
(12)

183   Survey of students and drugs at the University of Notre Dame: An overview
(20)

031 What we need to know
(1)

032 Therapeutic communities vs
methadone maintenance: A prospective
controlled study of narcotic addiction
treatment: Design and one-year
follow-up
(7)

036 Therapeutic community dropouts:
Criminal behavior five years after
treatment
(4)

037 Phoenix house: Criminal activity
of dropouts
(1, 2, 3, 4, 5)

041 Religious programs and careers of
chronic heroin users
(4)

046 The magic fix: A critical
analysis of methadone maintenance
treatment
(6)

049 Shutting off methadone: Costs and
benefits
(1, 4, 12)

050 Long-term follow-up of clients of
high- and low-dose methadone programs
(3, 9)

051 Outpatient methadone withdrawal
for heroin dependence
(3)

060 The effect of probation on
behavior of chronic opioid drug users
(5)

064 Heroin use and street crime
(6, 7)

065 Youth, drugs, and street crime
(15, 16, 17)

066 The impact of drug use on street
crime
(6, 7, 11, 14)

081 Black women, heroin and crime:
Some empirical notes
(5, 7)

091 Criminal involvement of female
offenders: Psychological
characteristics among four groups
(3, 5)

101 Mexican-American criminals: A
comparative study of heroin using and
non-using felons
(7, 8, 10)

141 Treated and untreated addicts:
Factors associated with participation
in treatment and cessation of heroin
use
(16, 23, 25)

200 Young Men and Drugs--A Nationwide
Survey
(9)

204 What happened in Harlem? Analysis
of a decline in heroin use among a
generation unit of urban black youth
(3)

224 Arrest probabilities for marijuana
users as indicators of selective law
enforcement
(1, 2, 3, 4, 5, 6, 7, 8, 9, 10, 11)

IMPACT OF LAWS AND LAW ENFORCEMENT
  STRATEGIES

012 New light on the maturing out
hypothesis in opioid dependence
(4)

049 Shutting off methadone: Costs and
benefits
(10)

063 Addicts, police, and the
neighborhood social system
(10)

092 Puerto Rican Addicts and
Non-addicts: A Comparison
(4)

224 Arrest probabilities for marijuana users as indicators of selective law enforcement
(1, 2, 3, 4, 5, 6, 7, 8, 9, 10, 11)

INCARCERATION

017 Addict careers: II. The first ten years
(8, 9, 10, 12)

032 Therapeutic communities vs methadone maintenance: A prospective controlled study of narcotic addiction treatment: Design and one-year follow-up
(7)

050 Long-term follow-up of clients of high- and low-dose methadone programs
(2, 3, 12)

066 The impact of drug use on street crime
(6)

069 The relationship between type of drug use and arrest charge in an arrested population
(1, 2, 3, 4, 5)

071 California civil commitment: A decade later
(1, 3, 8)

080 Women, heroin, and property crime
(3)

089 Sex roles among deviants: The woman addict
(8)

141 Treated and untreated addicts: Factors associated with participation in treatment and cessation of heroin use
(5)

171 A report on the dropout study
(11)

200 Young Men and Drugs--A Nationwide Survey
(9)

LEGAL STATUS OF DRUGS

150 Drugs and the Class of '78: Behaviors, Attitudes, and Recent National Trends
(17, 18, 19)

151 Highlights from Student Drug Use in America 1975-1980
(24)

152 Marijuana Decriminalization: The Impact on Youth, 1975-1980
(1, 2, 3, 4, 5, 6, 7, 8, 9, 10)

183 Survey of students and drugs at the University of Notre Dame: An overview
(21, 22)

184 Dimensions of marijuana use in a midwest Catholic university: Subcultural considerations
(10, 11)

230 Deterrence as social control: The legal and extralegal production of conformity
(2, 3, 4)

PAROLE/PROBATION

012 New light on the maturing out hypothesis in opioid dependence
(7)

036 Therapeutic community dropouts: Criminal behavior five years after treatment
(4)

060 The effect of probation on behavior of chronic opioid drug users
(1, 2, 3)

073 Narcotic addiction and crime
(10)

140 Experimental heroin users: An epidemiologic and psychosocial approach
(17)

080 Women, heroin, and property crime
(3, 4, 5, 6, 7, 8)

081 Black women, heroin and crime:
Some empirical notes
(4, 5, 6, 7, 8, 9)

083 The relationship between female
criminality and drug abuse
(1, 2, 4, 5, 6, 7, 8, 9, 10, 11, 12,
13, 14, 15, 16)

089 Sex roles among deviants: The
woman addict
(7, 9)

090 Women addicts' experience of the
heroin world: Risk, chaos, and
inundation
(2, 6, 8, 10, 11)

091 Criminal involvement of female
offenders: Psychological
characteristics among four groups
(7)

094 A comparison of Spanish and
non-Spanish drug users in treatment in
Dade County, Florida
(9)

098 Childhood conduct disorders and
later arrest
(1, 2, 3, 4, 5, 6)

101 Mexican-American criminals: A
comparative study of heroin using and
non-using felons
(5, 6, 7, 8, 10, 11, 12, 13, 14)

108 The drug problems of industry
(18)

114 Vietnam veterans three years after
Vietnam: How our study changed our
view on heroin
(13)

153 Drugs and delinquency: A search
for causal connections
(1, 2, 3, 4, 5, 6, 7)

164 A longitudinal study of onset of
drinking among high school students
(6)

167 Personality, attitudinal, and
social correlates of drug use
(6)

198 Cigarette smoking as a precursor
of illicit drug use
(4)

199 Determinants of early marihuana
use
(8)

200 Young Men and Drugs--A Nationwide
Survey
(9)

SURVEILLANCE AND INTELLIGENCE

062 Daily criminal activities of
street drug users: Preliminary
findings
(2, 3, 4, 5, 6, 7)

063 Addicts, police, and the
neighborhood social system
(9)

Cultural Factors

SUBCULTURAL FACTORS

010 What is an addict? Empirical
patterns and concepts of addiction
(4)

079 Cuban women, sex role conflicts
and the use of prescription drugs
(5)

082 Prostitution and addiction: An
interdisciplinary approach
(7)

092 Puerto Rican Addicts and
Non-addicts: A Comparison
(16)

095 The children of exile:
Relationships between the acculturation
process and drug use among Cuban youth
(4)

114 Vietnam veterans three years after Vietnam: How our study changed our view on heroin
(2, 5, 6, 7, 11)

115 Polydrug and alcohol use by veterans and nonveterans
(1, 2, 6, 8, 9, 15, 16, 18, 19, 20)

117 Cocaine Users: A Representative Case Approach
(4)

118 Life Styles of Nine American Barbiturate/Sedative-Hypnotic Drug Users (Executive Summary)
(15, 16)

119 Life Styles of Nine American Non-Users of Drugs (Executive Summary)
(9)

120 Effects of criminal justice and medical definitions of a social problem upon the delivery of treatment: The case of drug abuse
(1, 2, 3, 4)

123 A heroin "epidemic" in Asia
(5, 8)

128 Drug education: Further results and recommendations
(1, 2, 4, 5, 8)

131 Peer, family, and personality domains as related to adolescents' drug behavior
(1)

133 Initiation into adolescent marijuana use
(2)

138 A Study of Teenage Drug Behavior
(3, 4, 5, 6, 7, 9, 12, 13, 14, 22)

140 Experimental heroin users: An epidemiologic and psychosocial approach
(1, 4, 8, 9, 10, 11, 12, 13, 14, 15)

141 Treated and untreated addicts: Factors associated with participation in treatment and cessation of heroin use
(12, 13, 15, 21, 22, 23)

142 Addicts and experimenters: Dynamics of involvement in an adolescent heroin epidemic
(4, 5, 7)

143 Personality development and adolescent heroin use
(1)

146 Adolescent drug use and intentions to use drugs in the future: A concurrent analysis
(1, 2, 3)

150 Drugs and the Class of '78: Behaviors, Attitudes, and Recent National Trends
(2, 3, 4, 5, 6, 7, 8, 9, 10)

151 Highlights from Student Drug Use in America 1975-1980
(2, 5, 6, 7, 8, 9, 10, 13, 16, 17)

152 Marijuana Decriminalization: The Impact on Youth, 1975-1980
(1, 2, 3, 4, 5, 6)

158 The epidemiology of adolescent drug use in France and Israel
(7, 8, 9, 10)

160 Antecedents of adolescent initiation to stages of drug use: A development analysis
(12)

161 The epidemiology of drug use among New York State high school students: Distribution, trends, and change in rates of use
(11, 19, 20)

180 Young Men and Drugs in Manhattan: A Causal Analysis
(12, 17)

181 Smoking and health, marijuana and use of other illicit drugs: Causal relationships
(3)

182 Changing patterns of drug use among university males
(6, 7, 9, 15, 17, 18)

POLYDRUG USE

010 What is an addict? Empirical patterns and concepts of addiction
(2)

023 Narcotic addicts, multiple drug abuse and psychological distress
(1, 2, 3, 4, 5, 6, 7, 8, 9)

045 Investigating impact of methadone treatment upon the behavior of New York City street addicts
(14)

053 Methadone, wine and welfare
(2, 4)

054 Entry into methadone maintenance programs: A follow-up study of New York City heroin users detoxified in 1961-1963
(10)

064 Heroin use and street crime
(2, 3, 4)

065 Youth, drugs, and street crime
(10, 12, 13)

066 The impact of drug use on street crime
(3, 4, 13)

080 Women, heroin, and property crime
(1, 2)

081 Black women, heroin and crime: Some empirical notes
(1, 2, 3)

084 A valium a day keeps the tension away: Socio-psychological characteristics of minor tranquilizer users
(2, 5)

085 Drug usage as an index of stress among women
(2, 7)

094 A comparison of Spanish and non-Spanish drug users in treatment in Dade County, Florida
(10, 12)

095 The children of exile: Relationships between the acculturation process and drug use among Cuban youth
(1, 2)

103 Three types of extreme drug users identified by a replicated cluster analysis
(1, 2)

114 Vietnam veterans three years after Vietnam: How our study changed our view on heroin
(5, 7)

117 Cocaine Users: A Representative Case Approach
(2)

118 Life Styles of Nine American Barbiturate/Sedative-Hypnotic Drug Users (Executive Summary)
(13)

119 Life Styles of Nine American Non-Users of Drugs (Executive Summary)
(8)

138 A Study of Teenage Drug Behavior
(19, 22)

139 Sequential patterns of multiple-drug use among high school students
(3, 4, 5, 6, 7, 8, 9, 10, 11)

140 Experimental heroin users: An epidemiologic and psychosocial approach
(7, 8, 9, 12)

141 Treated and untreated addicts: Factors associated with participation in treatment and cessation of heroin use
(14, 21, 22)

142 Addicts and experimenters: Dynamics of involvement in an adolescent heroin epidemic
(8, 9, 10, 11, 12)

143 Personality development and adolescent heroin use
(1, 5)

145 Is coca paste currently a drug of abuse among high school students? (1, 2)

150 Drugs and the Class of '78: Behaviors, Attitudes, and Recent National Trends (1, 2, 4, 6, 7, 8)

151 Highlights from Student Drug Use in America 1975-1980 (1, 2, 3, 5, 6, 8, 9, 10, 11, 12, 13, 14, 15, 16, 17)

152 Marijuana Decriminalization: The Impact on Youth, 1975-1980 (1, 2, 3, 4, 5, 6)

156 Reaching the hard-to-reach: Illicit drug use among high school absentees (1, 3, 4, 5, 6)

158 The epidemiology of adolescent drug use in France and Israel (1, 2, 3, 4, 5, 6, 15)

159 Sequences and stages in patterns of adolescent drug use (1, 2, 3, 4, 5)

161 The epidemiology of drug use among New York State high school students: Distribution, trends, and change in rates of use (1, 2, 3, 4, 5, 6, 7, 8, 9, 10, 12, 13, 14, 15, 16, 17, 18)

162 Adolescent involvement in legal and illegal drug use: A multiple classification analysis (10)

167 Personality, attitudinal, and social correlates of drug use (1)

170 Drug use among public and private secondary school students in Puerto Rico (1, 2, 3, 4, 5, 6, 7, 8, 9, 10, 11)

171 A report on the dropout study (1, 2, 3, 4, 5, 6, 7)

172 Sex differences in adolescent drug use: Recent trends (1, 2, 3, 4, 5, 6, 7, 8, 9, 10, 11, 12, 13, 14, 15, 16, 17, 18, 19, 20, 21, 22, 23, 24)

174 Patterns of multiple drug use in high school (1, 2, 11, 12)

175 Teenage drug use: A search for causes and consequenses (1)

177 Project Community: Therapeutic Explorations with Adolescents (1, 2, 3, 4)

178 The relationship of personality structure to patterns of adolescent substance use (1, 2)

180 Young Men and Drugs in Manhattan: A Causal Analysis (1, 2, 3, 4, 5, 6, 7, 8, 9, 10, 11)

182 Changing patterns of drug use among university males (3, 4, 5, 6, 8, 10, 11, 12, 13, 14, 16, 18)

184 Dimensions of marijuana use in a midwest Catholic university: Subcultural considerations (1, 2, 3)

185 The variation of a midwest Catholic university's drug use pattern from other Catholic university findings: Why? (1, 2, 3, 4, 5)

186 Getting high in high school: The meaning of adolescent drug usage (11)

190 Judging the shape of things to come: Lessons learned from comparisons of student drug users in 1968 and 1970 (4, 5, 6, 7)

197 The amotivational syndrome and the college student (2, 5, 6)

199 Determinants of early marihuana use
(3)

200 Young Men and Drugs--A Nationwide Survey
(1, 3, 5, 6, 7, 11)

204 What happened in Harlem? Analysis of a decline in heroin use among a generation unit of urban black youth
(1, 2, 3, 4, 5, 6)

206 Black youths and drug-use behavior
(1, 2, 3, 11, 12)

207 Patterns of drug involvement: Developmental and secular influences on age at initiation
(1, 2, 3, 4, 5, 8, 10)

208 Youngsters Experimenting with Drugs
(1, 2, 3)

209 Sex differences in antecedents of substance use among adolescents
(1)

210 Inhalant abuse among the Pueblo tribes of New Mexico
(1, 2, 14)

211 Drug use among Native American adults
(1, 3, 4, 5, 6, 10)

212 Longitudinal community epidemiological studies of drug use: Early aggressiveness, shyness, and learning problems
(1)

213 Mental health in first grade and teenage drug, alcohol, and cigarette use
(1)

214 Drug use among adolescents of five Southwestern Native American tribes
(1, 2)

215 Drug use among Native American adolescents
(1, 2, 3, 4, 5, 6, 7, 10)

216 Native American Drug Use: Drug Abuse Among Indian Adolescents
(5, 6, 7)

218 Ethnicity and patterning in South African drug use
(1, 2, 8, 9, 10, 11, 12, 13, 14)

220 Phencyclidine use in high school: Tests of models
(1)

222 Sea-Tac and PCP
(1, 2, 4)

230 Deterrence as social control: The legal and extralegal production of conformity
(2, 3, 4, 5, 6)

233 Relation of motives for drug use and psychopathology in the development of acute adverse reactions to psychoactive drugs
(2, 5, 6, 9, 10)

STAGES OF DRUG USE (STEPPINGSTONE HYPOTHESIS)

064 Heroin use and street crime
(2, 3)

065 Youth, drugs, and street crime
(9, 11)

066 The impact of drug use on street crime
(1, 2)

080 Women, heroin, and property crime
(2)

081 Black women, heroin and crime: Some empirical notes
(1)

139 Sequential patterns of multiple-drug use among high school students
(6, 7, 8, 9, 10, 11)

146 Adolescent drug use and intentions to use drugs in the future: A concurrent analysis
(2, 3)

Prevention Programs

DRUG INFORMATION PROGRAM

MULTIDIMENSIONAL PREVENTION

STUDENT PREVENTION PROGRAM, COLLEGE/UNIVERSITY

STUDENT PREVENTION PROGRAM, K-12

Psychobehavioral Factors

AGGRESSION AND VIOLENCE

027 The Life Styles of Nine American
Opiate Users (Executive Summary)
(9)

117 Cocaine Users: A Representative
Case Approach
(15, 18)

153 Drugs and delinquency: A search
for causal connections
(6)

194 A psychiatric emergency room study
of inhalant use
(6, 7)

213 Mental health in first grade and
teenage drug, alcohol, and cigarette
use
(10)

ALTERED STATE OF CONSCIOUSNESS

202 Reasons for drug and alcohol use
by college students
(6)

219 Hypnotic susceptibility during
cannabis intoxication
(1)

ATTENTION AND AROUSAL

107 Qat use in North Yemen and the
problem of addiction: A study in
medical anthropology
(19)

117 Cocaine Users: A Representative
Case Approach
(6, 7)

212 Longitudinal community
epidemiological studies of drug use:
Early aggressiveness, shyness, and
learning problems
(9)

229 Psychedelic drug flashbacks:
Attentional deficits?
(1, 2, 3)

ATTITUDE/PERCEPTION TOWARD DRUG
  USE/USERS

022 Parental correlates of drug use
among young Puerto Rican adults
(3, 4, 10, 14)

047 Attrition of older alcoholics from
treatment
(9, 10)

063 Addicts, police, and the
neighborhood social system
(1, 2, 3, 4, 5, 6, 7, 8, 9, 10)

078 Employment status, role
dissatisfaction and the housewife
syndrome
(2, 5)

087 Becoming addicted: The woman
addict
(2, 14)

088 Difficulties in taking care of
business: Women addicts as mothers
(3)

090 Women addicts' experience of the
heroin world: Risk, chaos, and
inundation
(9)

092 Puerto Rican Addicts and
Non-addicts: A Comparison
(5)

095 The children of exile:
Relationships between the acculturation
process and drug use among Cuban youth
(3)

107 Qat use in North Yemen and the
problem of addiction: A study in
medical anthropology
(20)

108 The drug problems of industry
(4)

221   Behavioral correlates and comparisons of current marijuana users, quitters and evasives
(8)

230   Deterrence as social control: The legal and extralegal production of conformity
(7)

234   Individual differences and setting as determinants of acute adverse reactions to psychoactive drugs
(4, 8, 11)

COGNITION AND INFORMATION PROCESSING

082   Prostitution and addiction: An interdisciplinary approach
(8)

091   Criminal involvement of female offenders: Psychological characteristics among four groups
(1, 3, 4, 6, 7)

116   The Life Styles of Nine American Amphetamine Users (Executive Summary)
(1)

117   Cocaine Users: A Representative Case Approach
(6, 7)

194   A psychiatric emergency room study of inhalant use
(3, 10)

206   Black youths and drug-use behavior
(23)

213   Mental health in first grade and teenage drug, alcohol, and cigarette use
(5)

COMMUNICATION SKILLS

191   Personality characteristics of students who became drug users: An MMPI study of an avant-garde
(1)

DEATH (NONDRUG RELATED)

001   Deaths of persons using methadone in New York City--1971
(4, 8)

052   Notes on American medical history: A follow-up study of the New Haven morphine maintenance clinic of 1920
(10, 11)

205   Health and drug behavior: A study of urban black adolescents
(12)

DRUG KNOWLEDGE/AWARENESS

022   Parental correlates of drug use among young Puerto Rican adults
(2, 5, 6, 8, 13, 15, 16)

084   A valium a day keeps the tension away: Socio-psychological characteristics of minor tranquilizer users
(12)

108   The drug problems of industry
(5, 13)

110   What everybody in Cuzco knows about coca
(1, 2, 3, 4, 5, 6, 7)

118   Life Styles of Nine American Barbiturate/Sedative-Hypnotic Drug Users (Executive Summary)
(16)

127   The relationship between drug education programs in the greater New Haven schools and changes in drug use and drug-related beliefs and perceptions
(5, 6)

128   Drug education: Further results and recommendations
(9)

140   Experimental heroin users: An epidemiologic and psychosocial approach
(16)

176 Psychological predictors of early use, late use, and nonuse of marijuana among teenage students
(3)

201 Prediction of college drug use from personality and inner experience
(1, 2, 3)

209 Sex differences in antecedents of substance use among adolescents
(2, 3)

212 Longitudinal community epidemiological studies of drug use: Early aggressiveness, shyness, and learning problems
(3, 4, 5, 6, 7, 8, 9, 10, 11)

213 Mental health in first grade and teenage drug, alcohol, and cigarette use
(2, 3, 4, 5, 6, 9, 11, 13)

225 Personaltiy correlates of hallucinogen use
(7, 8)

230 Deterrence as social control: The legal and extralegal production of conformity
(1)

INTERPERSONAL SKILLS

082 Prostitution and addiction: An interdisciplinary approach
(9)

177 Project Community: Therapeutic Explorations with Adolescents
(5)

191 Personality characteristics of students who became drug users: An MMPI study of an avant-garde
(1, 3, 4)

LEARNING

116 The Life Styles of Nine American Amphetamine Users (Executive Summary)
(1)

209 Sex differences in antecedents of substance use among adolescents
(3)

212 Longitudinal community epidemiological studies of drug use: Early aggressiveness, shyness, and learning problems
(3, 9, 11)

213 Mental health in first grade and teenage drug, alcohol, and cigarette use
(2, 4)

MEMORY

194 A psychiatric emergency room study of inhalant use
(9)

MOOD AND EMOTION

027 The Life Styles of Nine American Opiate Users (Executive Summary)
(7)

047 Attrition of older alcoholics from treatment
(8)

086 Sex differences in the content and style of medical advertisements
(4)

107 Qat use in North Yemen and the problem of addiction: A study in medical anthropology
(19)

194 A psychiatric emergency room study of inhalant use
(11, 12)

205 Health and drug behavior: A study of urban black adolescents
(5)

206 Black youths and drug-use behavior
(23)

ONSET OF SUBSTANCE USE/ADDICTION

008 Formerly-addicted-now-controlled
opiate users
(1)

015 Studying addicts over time:
Methodology and preliminary findings
(3)

016 Addict Careers: I. A new
typology
(1, 3, 4)

018 Addict careers: III. Trends
across time
(1, 4)

019 Trends in the age of onset of
narcotic addiction
(1, 2, 3, 4, 5, 8)

057 The criminality of heroin addicts
when addicted and when off opiates
(11)

064 Heroin use and street crime
(1, 3)

065 Youth, drugs, and street crime
(1, 9, 11, 18)

066 The impact of drug use on street
crime
(1, 2, 13)

073 Narcotic addiction and crime
(1)

080 Women, heroin, and property crime
(2)

081 Black women, heroin and crime:
Some empirical notes
(1)

082 Prostitution and addiction: An
interdisciplinary approach
(1, 2, 3, 4, 6, 7, 10)

083 The relationship between female
criminality and drug abuse
(6)

087 Becoming addicted: The woman
addict
(1, 2, 3, 5, 6, 8)

089 Sex roles among deviants: The
woman addict
(1)

097 Risk factors in the continuation
of childhood antisocial behavior into
adulthood
(1, 2, 3)

112 Drug treatment after return in
Vietnam veterans
(2)

113 The interaction of setting and
predisposition in explaining novel
behavior: Drug initiations before, in,
and after Vietnam
(2, 3, 4, 5, 6, 7, 8, 9, 10, 11, 12)

117 Cocaine Users: A Representative
Case Approach
(1, 2, 3)

121 Narcotic addiction in two Asian
cultures: A comparison and analysis
(2)

123 A heroin "epidemic" in Asia
(7)

124 Opium and heroin addicts in Laos:
I. A comparative study
(6)

125 Opium and heroin addicts in Laos:
II. A study of matched pairs
(3)

126 Attitude and behavior: A
specification of the contingent
consistency hypothesis
(2, 3)

133 Initiation into adolescent
marijuana use
(1, 2, 3, 4, 5, 6, 7, 8, 9, 10)

140 Experimental heroin users: An
epidemiologic and psychosocial approach
(2, 3, 4, 14, 15)

194 A psychiatric emergency room study of inhalant use
(8)

203 Family interaction and acculturation in Mexican-American inhalant users
(2)

205 Health and drug behavior: A study of urban black adolescents
(5)

236 Does marijuana enhance experimentally induced anxiety?
(1, 2)

DELUSIONS

117 Cocaine Users: A Representative Case Approach
(18)

DEPRESSION

009 Suicide attempts among drug abusers
(5)

026 The structure of depression in heroin addicts
(1, 2, 3, 4, 5)

028 Correlates of self-reported and clinically assessed depression in male heroin addicts
(1, 2, 3)

034 Phoenix House: Psychopathological signs among male and female drug-free residents
(10)

042 Differential response of heroin and nonheroin abusers to inpatient treatment
(2)

047 Attrition of older alcoholics from treatment
(6, 7)

105 Depressive disorders in Vietnam returnees
(1, 2, 3, 4)

117 Cocaine Users: A Representative Case Approach
(8)

160 Antecedents of adolescent initiation to stages of drug use: A development analysis
(13)

162 Adolescent involvement in legal and illegal drug use: A multiple classification analysis
(8)

168 Psychological factors and adolescent illicit drug use: Ethnicity and sex differences
(1, 2, 3, 4, 5, 6, 7)

169 Depressive mood and adolescent illicit drug use: A longitudinal analysis
(1, 2, 3, 4, 5, 6, 7, 8, 9)

205 Health and drug behavior: A study of urban black adolescents
(3)

FLASHBACKS

227 Role-play theory of psychedelic drug flashbacks
(1, 2, 3, 4, 5)

228 Psychedelic drug flashbacks: Subjective reports and biographical data
(1, 2, 3, 4, 5, 6, 7, 8, 9, 10, 11, 12, 13, 14, 15)

235 LSD flashbacks and ego functioning
(1, 2, 3, 4, 5, 6, 7, 8, 9, 10)

GENERAL PSYCHOLOGICAL HEALTH STATUS

023 Narcotic addicts, multiple drug abuse and psychological distress
(7, 9)

118 Life Styles of Nine American
Barbiturate/Sedative-Hypnotic Drug
Users (Executive Summary)
(4, 6)

191 Personality characteristics of
students who became drug users: An
MMPI study of an avant-garde
(2)

194 A psychiatric emergency room study
of inhalant use
(4)

196 Drug use, academic performance,
and career indecision: Longitudinal
data in search of a model
(8)

225 Personaltiy correlates of
hallucinogen use
(5)

233 Relation of motives for drug use
and psychopathology in the development
of acute adverse reactions to
psychoactive drugs
(2, 5, 6, 8, 10, 12, 13, 14)

234 Individual differences and setting
as determinants of acute adverse
reactions to psychoactive drugs
(1, 6, 7, 8, 9, 10, 11)

235 LSD flashbacks and ego functioning
(9)

RELATIONSHIP PROBLEMS

205 Health and drug behavior: A study
of urban black adolescents
(4)

SCHIZOPHRENIA

232 Ego mechanisms and marihuana usage
(6)

233 Relation of motives for drug use
and psychopathology in the development
of acute adverse reactions to
psychoactive drugs
(2, 5, 6, 10, 11, 13)

234 Individual differences and setting
as determinants of acute adverse
reactions to psychoactive drugs
(8, 10, 11)

SENSORY HALLUCINATIONS

117 Cocaine Users: A Representative
Case Approach
(9, 15)

Social Factors

ACADEMIC PERFORMANCE/FACTORS

016 Addict Careers: I. A new
typology
(4)

018 Addict careers: III. Trends
across time
(2)

021 Predicting heroin and alcohol
usage among young Puerto Ricans
(1, 4, 5, 13)

031 What we need to know
(4)

032 Therapeutic communities vs
methadone maintenance: A prospective
controlled study of narcotic addiction
treatment: Design and one-year
follow-up
(8, 9, 10, 11, 13)

044 Self-concept and completion of
treatment for heroin and nonheroin drug
abusers
(5)

054 Entry into methadone maintenance
programs: A follow-up study of New
York City heroin users detoxified in
1961-1963
(3)

056 The therapeutic community:
Multivariate prediction of retention
(6)

AGE

131 Peer, family, and personality domains as related to adolescents' drug behavior
(2)

138 A Study of Teenage Drug Behavior
(1, 2, 3, 4, 5, 6, 7, 8, 9, 20, 23)

139 Sequential patterns of multiple-drug use among high school students
(1)

141 Treated and untreated addicts: Factors associated with participation in treatment and cessation of heroin use
(3)

150 Drugs and the Class of '78: Behaviors, Attitudes, and Recent National Trends
(11)

158 The epidemiology of adolescent drug use in France and Israel
(11)

161 The epidemiology of drug use among New York State high school students: Distribution, trends, and change in rates of use
(6, 14)

162 Adolescent involvement in legal and illegal drug use: A multiple classification analysis
(1)

172 Sex differences in adolescent drug use: Recent trends
(1, 20)

180 Young Men and Drugs in Manhattan: A Causal Analysis
(4, 10)

184 Dimensions of marijuana use in a midwest Catholic university: Subcultural considerations
(4)

194 A psychiatric emergency room study of inhalant use
(13)

199 Determinants of early marihuana use
(2, 4, 5, 7, 8)

200 Young Men and Drugs--A Nationwide Survey
(4, 5)

204 What happened in Harlem? Analysis of a decline in heroin use among a generation unit of urban black youth
(5)

206 Black youths and drug-use behavior
(16)

207 Patterns of drug involvement: Developmental and secular influences on age at initiation
(8, 9, 10)

208 Youngsters Experimenting with Drugs
(2, 3, 10)

210 Inhalant abuse among the Pueblo tribes of New Mexico
(5, 13)

214 Drug use among adolescents of five Southwestern Native American tribes
(2)

215 Drug use among Native American adolescents
(2, 3, 4, 9)

216 Native American Drug Use: Drug Abuse Among Indian Adolescents
(9)

218 Ethnicity and patterning in South African drug use
(1, 2, 3, 4, 5, 6, 7)

221 Behavioral correlates and comparisons of current marijuana users, quitters and evasives
(1, 2, 4)

222 Sea-Tac and PCP
(8)

224 Arrest probabilities for marijuana users as indicators of selective law enforcement
(5, 9)

230 Deterrence as social control: The legal and extralegal production of conformity
(6)

COMMUNICATION AND SOCIAL NETWORK

089 Sex roles among deviants: The woman addict
(2)

090 Women addicts' experience of the heroin world: Risk, chaos, and inundation
(4)

096 Drug use among Cuban exiles in Miami, Florida: Cultural antecedents and processes
(3)

116 The Life Styles of Nine American Amphetamine Users (Executive Summary)
(7, 8)

117 Cocaine Users: A Representative Case Approach
(14)

147 Beginning adolescent drug use and peer and adult interaction patterns
(1, 2, 3, 4, 5, 6, 7)

154 Inter- and intragenerational influences on adolescent marijuana use
(6)

155 Interpersonal influences on adolescent illegal drug use
(6)

170 Drug use among public and private secondary school students in Puerto Rico
(12)

203 Family interaction and acculturation in Mexican-American inhalant users
(4, 11)

205 Health and drug behavior: A study of urban black adolescents
(9)

208 Youngsters Experimenting with Drugs
(16)

213 Mental health in first grade and teenage drug, alcohol, and cigarette use
(8, 9, 10, 12, 13)

217 Cannabis and work in Jamaica: A refutation of the amotivational syndrome
(7)

237 The effect of marijuana on small group process
(1, 2, 3, 4, 5)

238 Marijuana and hostility in a small-group setting
(3, 4, 5)

DEMOGRAPHY/ENVIRONMENT

021 Predicting heroin and alcohol usage among young Puerto Ricans
(8)

042 Differential response of heroin and nonheroin abusers to inpatient treatment
(1)

052 Notes on American medical history: A follow-up study of the New Haven morphine maintenance clinic of 1920
(5)

054 Entry into methadone maintenance programs: A follow-up study of New York City heroin users detoxified in 1961-1963
(3)

077 Psychotropic drug use by women: Health, attitudinal, personality and demographic correlates
(4)

097 Risk factors in the continuation of childhood antisocial behavior into adulthood
(1)

109 The social problem of drug abuse in ecological perspective
(1, 2, 3, 4, 5, 6, 7, 8, 9, 10, 11)

170 Drug use among public and private secondary school students in Puerto Rico
(15, 16)

186 Getting high in high school: The meaning of adolescent drug usage
(1)

210 Inhalant abuse among the Pueblo tribes of New Mexico
(6)

216 Native American Drug Use: Drug Abuse Among Indian Adolescents
(4)

230 Deterrence as social control: The legal and extralegal production of conformity
(5)

ECONOMIC FACTORS

005 The working addict
(4)

014 An analysis of work histories, earnings, and receipts of benefits among a sample of a community-wide population of narcotic addicts
(1, 2, 3, 4, 5)

017 Addict careers: II. The first ten years
(5, 11)

018 Addict careers: III. Trends across time
(11)

020 Narcotic abusers and poverty
(1, 2, 3)

021 Predicting heroin and alcohol usage among young Puerto Ricans
(7, 16)

024 Ecological studies of narcotic addiction
(5)

027 The Life Styles of Nine American Opiate Users (Executive Summary)
(3)

052 Notes on American medical history: A follow-up study of the New Haven morphine maintenance clinic of 1920
(6, 8)

053 Methadone, wine and welfare
(1, 5)

059 The impact of drug addiction on criminal earnings
(2, 3, 4, 5, 6, 7, 8)

061 Getting over: Economic alternatives to predatory crime among street drug users
(1, 2, 3, 4, 5, 6, 7, 8, 9, 10, 11)

062 Daily criminal activities of street drug users: Preliminary findings
(2, 3, 4, 5, 6, 7)

064 Heroin use and street crime
(8)

065 Youth, drugs, and street crime
(19)

066 The impact of drug use on street crime
(8)

068 Exploring asymmetries in the hard drug-crime relationship
(1, 2, 3, 5, 6, 7, 8, 9)

082 Prostitution and addiction: An interdisciplinary approach
(10)

083 The relationship between female criminality and drug abuse
(11, 15, 16)

050 Long-term follow-up of clients of high- and low-dose methadone programs
(11)

051 Outpatient methadone withdrawal for heroin dependence
(2)

052 Notes on American medical history: A follow-up study of the New Haven morphine maintenance clinic of 1920
(7)

054 Entry into methadone maintenance programs: A follow-up study of New York City heroin users detoxified in 1961-1963
(6)

059 The impact of drug addiction on criminal earnings
(1, 5, 6, 7)

060 The effect of probation on behavior of chronic opioid drug users
(5)

061 Getting over: Economic alternatives to predatory crime among street drug users
(7)

062 Daily criminal activities of street drug users: Preliminary findings
(3)

071 California civil commitment: A decade later
(5)

073 Narcotic addiction and crime
(8, 9)

078 Employment status, role dissatisfaction and the housewife syndrome
(2, 3)

079 Cuban women, sex role conflicts and the use of prescription drugs
(2)

084 A valium a day keeps the tension away: Socio-psychological characteristics of minor tranquilizer users
(7, 8, 9)

085 Drug usage as an index of stress among women
(11)

092 Puerto Rican Addicts and Non-addicts: A Comparison
(12)

094 A comparison of Spanish and non-Spanish drug users in treatment in Dade County, Florida
(7, 8)

101 Mexican-American criminals: A comparative study of heroin using and non-using felons
(5)

102 Drug use in the construction trade
(1, 2, 3, 4, 5, 6, 7, 8, 9, 10, 11, 12, 13, 14, 15, 16, 17, 18, 19, 20, 21, 22, 23)

103 Three types of extreme drug users identified by a replicated cluster analysis
(5)

104 Antecedents of narcotic use and addiction: A study of 898 Vietnam veterans
(4)

108 The drug problems of industry
(1, 2, 3, 4, 5, 6, 7, 8, 9, 10, 11, 12, 13, 14, 15, 16, 17, 18, 19, 20, 21, 22, 23, 24, 25, 26, 27, 28)

109 The social problem of drug abuse in ecological perspective
(8)

111 Satisfaction with real and simulated jobs in relation to personality variables and drug use
(2, 3)

ETHNIC FACTORS

MARITAL STATUS

085 Drug usage as an index of stress among women
(12, 13)

087 Becoming addicted: The woman addict
(5)

089 Sex roles among deviants: The woman addict
(1)

093 Ethnic differences in factors related to drug use
(6)

101 Mexican-American criminals: A comparative study of heroin using and non-using felons
(4)

109 The social problem of drug abuse in ecological perspective
(6)

121 Narcotic addiction in two Asian cultures: A comparison and analysis
(1)

123 A heroin "epidemic" in Asia
(7)

124 Opium and heroin addicts in Laos: I. A comparative study
(4)

125 Opium and heroin addicts in Laos: II. A study of matched pairs
(1)

141 Treated and untreated addicts: Factors associated with participation in treatment and cessation of heroin use
(4, 16)

179 Shacking up: Cohabitation in the 1970s
(1, 2, 3, 4)

180 Young Men and Drugs in Manhattan: A Causal Analysis
(8)

200 Young Men and Drugs--A Nationwide Survey
(11)

206 Black youths and drug-use behavior
(19)

221 Behavioral correlates and comparisons of current marijuana users, quitters and evasives
(1, 4)

MILITARY SERVICE

166 Drug use and military plans of high school seniors
(1, 2, 3, 4, 5, 6, 7, 8)

PARENTAL, FAMILY, SIBLING
    INFLUENCE/RELATIONSHIPS

011 Family ties of heroin addicts
(1, 2, 3, 4, 5, 6)

017 Addict careers: II. The first ten years
(6)

021 Predicting heroin and alcohol usage among young Puerto Ricans
(2, 6, 9, 12)

022 Parental correlates of drug use among young Puerto Rican adults
(1, 2, 3, 4, 5, 6, 7, 8, 9, 10, 11, 12, 13, 14, 15, 16)

024 Ecological studies of narcotic addiction
(5)

027 The Life Styles of Nine American Opiate Users (Executive Summary)
(4)

048 Cultural factors and attrition in drug abuse treatment
(2, 3)

055 Focus on the family as a factor in differential treatment outcome
(1, 2, 3, 4, 5)

056 The therapeutic community:
Multivariate prediction of retention
(5)

061 Getting over: Economic
alternatives to predatory crime among
street drug users
(9)

079 Cuban women, sex role conflicts
and the use of prescription drugs
(4)

085 Drug usage as an index of stress
among women
(14)

088 Difficulties in taking care of
business: Women addicts as mothers
(4, 5, 6, 7, 8, 9)

090 Women addicts' experience of the
heroin world: Risk, chaos, and
inundation
(6, 12)

092 Puerto Rican Addicts and
Non-addicts: A Comparison
(2, 3, 12, 13, 14, 15)

094 A comparison of Spanish and
non-Spanish drug users in treatment in
Dade County, Florida
(6)

096 Drug use among Cuban exiles in
Miami, Florida: Cultural antecedents
and processes
(1)

100 Father's alcoholism and children's
outcomes
(1, 2, 3, 4, 5)

104 Antecedents of narcotic use and
addiction: A study of 898 Vietnam
veterans
(2)

116 The Life Styles of Nine American
Amphetamine Users (Executive Summary)
(10, 11)

118 Life Styles of Nine American
Barbiturate/Sedative-Hypnotic Drug
Users (Executive Summary)
(1)

119 Life Styles of Nine American
Non-Users of Drugs (Executive Summary)
(1, 9)

121 Narcotic addiction in two Asian
cultures: A comparison and analysis
(1)

123 A heroin "epidemic" in Asia
(4)

125 Opium and heroin addicts in Laos:
II. A study of matched pairs
(1)

126 Attitude and behavior: A
specification of the contingent
consistency hypothesis
(6)

129 Perceived paternal relationships,
adolescent personality, and female
marijuana use
(1, 3, 4)

130 Correlates of adolescent marijuana
use as related to age, sex, and
ethnicity
(5, 6, 7)

131 Peer, family, and personality
domains as related to adolescents' drug
behavior
(4, 5, 6)

132 Family socialization and
adolescent personality and their
association with adolescent use of
marijuana
(1, 2, 3, 4)

133 Initiation into adolescent
marijuana use
(4, 5, 6, 8, 9, 10)

134 Paternal determinants of male
adolescent marijuana use
(1, 2, 4, 5, 6, 7)

RELIGIOUS FACTORS

012 New light on the maturing out hypothesis in opioid dependence
(7)

054 Entry into methadone maintenance programs: A follow-up study of New York City heroin users detoxified in 1961-1963
(5)

060 The effect of probation on behavior of chronic opioid drug users
(4)

138 A Study of Teenage Drug Behavior
(16)

158 The epidemiology of adolescent drug use in France and Israel
(14)

162 Adolescent involvement in legal and illegal drug use: A multiple classification analysis
(6)

164 A longitudinal study of onset of drinking among high school students
(11)

170 Drug use among public and private secondary school students in Puerto Rico
(14)

186 Getting high in high school: The meaning of adolescent drug usage
(1)

205 Health and drug behavior: A study of urban black adolescents
(10)

210 Inhalant abuse among the Pueblo tribes of New Mexico
(3)

215 Drug use among Native American adolescents
(21)

216 Native American Drug Use: Drug Abuse Among Indian Adolescents
(1)

SEX

021 Predicting heroin and alcohol usage among young Puerto Ricans
(10)

023 Narcotic addicts, multiple drug abuse and psychological distress
(3, 8)

024 Ecological studies of narcotic addiction
(1, 2)

029 Types of psychopathology displayed by heroin addicts
(2)

034 Phoenix House: Psychopathological signs among male and female drug-free residents
(2, 5, 9, 10, 11, 12)

038 Male and female drug abusers: Social and psychological status 2 years after treatment in a therapeutic community
(1, 2, 3, 4, 5, 7, 8, 9, 10, 11, 12, 13, 14, 15)

052 Notes on American medical history: A follow-up study of the New Haven morphine maintenance clinic of 1920
(2, 4)

054 Entry into methadone maintenance programs: A follow-up study of New York City heroin users detoxified in 1961-1963
(2)

064 Heroin use and street crime
(3, 4, 5)

066 The impact of drug use on street crime
(2, 3, 7, 12)

122 Influence of opium availability on addiction rates in Laos
(7, 8)

126 Attitude and behavior: A specification of the contingent consistency hypothesis
(2, 3)

206 Black youths and drug-use behavior
(20)

210 Inhalant abuse among the Pueblo tribes of New Mexico
(6)

234 Individual differences and setting as determinants of acute adverse reactions to psychoactive drugs
(1, 2, 3, 4, 5, 10, 12, 13)

237 The effect of marijuana on small group process
(1, 2, 3, 4, 5)

238 Marijuana and hostility in a small-group setting
(1, 2, 3, 4, 5, 6)

SOCIAL STATUS AND ROLE

016 Addict Careers: I. A new typology
(2)

017 Addict careers: II. The first ten years
(12)

018 Addict careers: III. Trends across time
(2)

079 Cuban women, sex role conflicts and the use of prescription drugs
(2)

084 A valium a day keeps the tension away: Socio-psychological characteristics of minor tranquilizer users
(8)

085 Drug usage as an index of stress among women
(8, 14)

090 Women addicts' experience of the heroin world: Risk, chaos, and inundation
(7)

094 A comparison of Spanish and non-Spanish drug users in treatment in Dade County, Florida
(6)

104 Antecedents of narcotic use and addiction: A study of 898 Vietnam veterans
(1)

109 The social problem of drug abuse in ecological perspective
(5, 11)

158 The epidemiology of adolescent drug use in France and Israel
(13)

167 Personality, attitudinal, and social correlates of drug use
(4)

194 A psychiatric emergency room study of inhalant use
(16)

222 Sea-Tac and PCP
(8)

TYPE OF SCHOOL (PUBLIC, PRIVATE, RELIGIOUS, ETC.)

170 Drug use among public and private secondary school students in Puerto Rico
(7, 8, 9, 10, 11, 12, 15)

172 Sex differences in adolescent drug use: Recent trends
(21, 22, 23, 24)

210 Inhalant abuse among the Pueblo tribes of New Mexico
(6)

014 An analysis of work histories, earnings, and receipts of benefits among a sample of a community-wide population of narcotic addicts
(6)

033 Self-concept and substance abuse treatment
(1, 2, 3, 4, 5, 6, 7)

045 Investigating impact of methadone treatment upon the behavior of New York City street addicts
(1, 2, 3, 4, 5, 6, 7, 8, 9, 10, 12, 13, 14)

049 Shutting off methadone: Costs and benefits
(5)

112 Drug treatment after return in Vietnam veterans
(4, 6, 7, 8)

123 A heroin "epidemic" in Asia
(9, 10)

124 Opium and heroin addicts in Laos: I. A comparative study
(9)

125 Opium and heroin addicts in Laos: II. A study of matched pairs
(4)

141 Treated and untreated addicts: Factors associated with participation in treatment and cessation of heroin use
(1, 2, 3, 4, 5, 6, 7, 8, 9, 10, 11, 12, 13, 14, 15, 17, 19, 20, 22, 23, 24, 26)

200 Young Men and Drugs--A Nationwide Survey
(10)

206 Black youths and drug-use behavior
(24, 25, 26, 27, 28, 29)

DETOXIFICATION

032 Therapeutic communities vs methadone maintenance: A prospective controlled study of narcotic addiction treatment: Design and one-year follow-up
(13)

050 Long-term follow-up of clients of high- and low-dose methadone programs
(5)

054 Entry into methadone maintenance programs: A follow-up study of New York City heroin users detoxified in 1961-1963
(7)

114 Vietnam veterans three years after Vietnam: How our study changed our view on heroin
(9)

121 Narcotic addiction in two Asian cultures: A comparison and analysis
(3)

124 Opium and heroin addicts in Laos: I. A comparative study
(12)

125 Opium and heroin addicts in Laos: II. A study of matched pairs
(6)

FOLLOW-UP/EVALUATION

013 Residence relocation inhibits opioid dependence
(1, 2, 3, 4, 5, 6, 7, 8, 9, 10, 11, 12)

030 The effect of parole on methadone patient behavior
(1, 2, 3, 4, 5, 6, 7, 8, 9, 10, 11, 12, 13)

031 What we need to know
(1, 2, 3, 4)

032 Therapeutic communities vs methadone maintenance: A prospective controlled study of narcotic addiction treatment
(1, 2, 3, 4, 5, 6, 7, 8, 9, 10, 11, 12)

049 Shutting off methadone: Costs and benefits
(1, 2, 3, 4, 5, 6, 7, 8, 9, 10, 11, 12)

050 Long-term follow-up of clients of high- and low-dose methadone programs
(1, 2, 3, 4, 5, 6, 7, 8, 9, 10, 11, 12)

051 Outpatient methadone withdrawal for heroin dependence
(1, 2, 3, 4, 5, 6)

054 Entry into methadone maintenance programs: A follow-up study of New York City heroin users detoxified in 1961-1963
(1, 2, 3, 4, 5, 6, 7, 8, 9, 10, 11)

071 California civil commitment: A decade later
(4, 6, 7)

073 Narcotic addiction and crime
(11)

074 Crime and treatment of heroin users
(1, 2, 3)

112 Drug treatment after return in Vietnam veterans
(10)

206 Black youths and drug-use behavior
(27)

PROGRAM DROPOUTS

033 Self-concept and substance abuse treatment
(1, 2, 3, 4, 5, 6, 7)

034 Phoenix House: Psychopathological signs among male and female drug-free residents
(5)

035 Therapeutic community dropouts: Psychological changes 2 years after treatment
(1, 2, 3)

037 Phoenix house: Criminal activity of dropouts
(1, 2, 3, 4)

038 Male and female drug abusers: Social and psychological status 2 years after treatment in a therapeutic community
(1, 2, 3, 4, 5, 6, 7, 8, 9, 10, 11, 12, 13, 14, 15)

040 The therapeutic community: Success and improvement rates 5 years after treatment
(2, 3, 4, 6, 7, 8, 9, 10, 11, 12, 13)

043 A comparison of dropouts and disciplinary discharges from a therapeutic community
(1, 2, 3, 4)

044 Self-concept and completion of treatment for heroin and nonheroin drug abusers
(1, 2, 3, 4, 5)

046 The magic fix: A critical analysis of methadone maintenance treatment
(1)

047 Attrition of older alcoholics from treatment
(1, 2, 3, 4, 5, 7, 8, 9, 10, 11)

048 Cultural factors and attrition in drug abuse treatment
(1, 3, 4, 5, 6, 7, 8)

050 Long-term follow-up of clients of high- and low-dose methadone programs
(1)

056 The therapeutic community: Multivariate prediction of retention
(1, 2, 3, 4, 5, 6, 7, 8)

PSYCHOTHERAPY

206 Black youths and drug-use behavior
(27)

READDICTION

013 Residence relocation inhibits opioid dependence
(12)

028 Correlates of self-reported and clinically assessed depression in male heroin addicts
(3)

041 Religious programs and careers of chronic heroin users
(2)

046 The magic fix: A critical analysis of methadone maintenance treatment
(2, 3)

049 Shutting off methadone: Costs and benefits
(2, 6, 10, 12)

050 Long-term follow-up of clients of high- and low-dose methadone programs
(7, 8)

112 Drug treatment after return in Vietnam veterans
(3, 11)

114 Vietnam veterans three years after Vietnam: How our study changed our view on heroin
(9, 11)

125 Opium and heroin addicts in Laos: II. A study of matched pairs
(7)

RELIGIOUS PROGRAM

015 Studying addicts over time: Methodology and preliminary findings
(5, 10)

041 Religious programs and careers of chronic heroin users
(1, 2, 3, 4, 5, 6)

THERAPEUTIC COMMUNITY

032 Therapeutic communities vs methadone maintenance: A prospective controlled study of narcotic addiction treatment: Design and one-year follow-up
(1, 2, 3, 4, 5, 6, 7, 8, 9, 10, 11, 12)

034 Phoenix House: Psychopathological signs among male and female drug-free residents
(1, 2, 3, 4, 5, 6, 7, 8, 9, 10, 11, 12)

035 Therapeutic community dropouts: Psychological changes 2 years after treatment
(1, 2, 3)

036 Therapeutic community dropouts: Criminal behavior five years after treatment
(1, 2, 3, 4, 5, 6, 7)

037 Phoenix house: Criminal activity of dropouts
(1, 2, 3, 4, 5)

038 Male and female drug abusers: Social and psychological status 2 years after treatment in a therapeutic community
(1, 2, 3, 4, 5, 6, 7, 8, 9, 10, 11, 12, 13, 14, 15)

039 Phoenix House: Changes in psychopathological signs of resident drug addicts
(1, 2, 3, 4)

040 The therapeutic community: Success and improvement rates 5 years after treatment
(1, 2, 3, 4, 5, 6, 7, 8, 9, 10, 11, 12, 13, 14, 15, 16)

056 The therapeutic community: Multivariate prediction of retention
(1, 2, 3, 4, 5, 6, 7, 8)

076 Are female drug abusers more deviant?
(5)

VOCATIONAL REHABILITATION PROGRAM

048 Cultural factors and attrition in
drug abuse treatment
(2)

YOUTH PROGRAM

177 Project Community: Therapeutic
Explorations with Adolescents
(1, 2, 3, 4, 5, 6, 7, 8)

DRUG INDEX

Alcohol

012 New light on the maturing out hypothesis in opioid dependence
(7)

013 Residence relocation inhibits opioid dependence
(10)

021 Predicting heroin and alcohol usage among young Puerto Ricans
(10, 11, 12, 13, 14, 15, 16)

022 Parental correlates of drug use among young Puerto Rican adults
(12, 13, 14, 15, 16)

023 Narcotic addicts, multiple drug abuse and psychological distress
(4)

033 Self-concept and substance abuse treatment
(1, 4, 5, 6, 7)

035 Therapeutic community dropouts: Psychological changes 2 years after treatment
(1, 2, 3)

040 The therapeutic community: Success and improvement rates 5 years after treatment
(16)

045 Investigating impact of methadone treatment upon the behavior of New York City street addicts
(13)

047 Attrition of older alcoholics from treatment
(1, 2, 3, 4, 5, 6, 7, 8, 9, 10, 11)

049 Shutting off methadone: Costs and benefits
(3, 8)

050 Long-term follow-up of clients of high- and low-dose methadone programs
(6, 11)

055 Focus on the family as a factor in differential treatment outcome
(1, 2, 3, 4, 5)

064 Heroin use and street crime
(1)

065 Youth, drugs, and street crime
(1)

098 Childhood conduct disorders and later arrest
(6)

100 Father's alcoholism and children's outcomes
(1, 2, 3, 4, 5)

101 Mexican-American criminals: A comparative study of heroin using and non-using felons
(9)

102 Drug use in the construction trade
(16, 17, 18, 19, 20, 21)

105 Depressive disorders in Vietnam returnees
(1)

108 The drug problems of industry
(12, 13, 14, 15, 16, 17, 18, 19, 20, 21, 22, 23, 24, 25)

115 Polydrug and alcohol use by veterans and nonveterans
(19)

127 The relationship between drug education programs in the greater New Haven schools and changes in drug use and drug-related beliefs and perceptions
(12)

138 A Study of Teenage Drug Behavior
(1)

144 Family life and levels of involvement in an adolescent heroin epidemic
(11)

148 Longitudinal analysis of the role of peer support, adult models, and peer subcultures in beginning adolescent substance use: An application of setwise canonical correlation methods
(3, 4)

149 Intentions to use drugs among adolescents: A longitudinal analysis
(4)

150 Drugs and the Class of '78: Behaviors, Attitudes, and Recent National Trends
(5, 8, 13)

151 Highlights from Student Drug Use in America 1975-1980
(5, 16, 21, 28)

154 Inter- and intragenerational influences on adolescent marijuana use
(4, 5)

155 Interpersonal influences on adolescent illegal drug use
(4, 5)

158 The epidemiology of adolescent drug use in France and Israel
(7, 9, 10)

160 Antecedents of adolescent initiation to stages of drug use: A development analysis
(1, 2, 3, 4, 5, 10)

161 The epidemiology of drug use among New York State high school students: Distribution, trends, and change in rates of use
(3, 4, 7, 14, 16, 21)

162 Adolescent involvement in legal and illegal drug use: A multiple classification analysis
(10, 11)

164 A longitudinal study of onset of drinking among high school students
(14)

165 Aspects of adolescent information acquisition about drugs and alcohol topics
(1, 2, 3, 4, 5, 6, 7, 8, 9, 10, 11, 12, 13, 14)

166 Drug use and military plans of high school seniors
(3)

167 Personality, attitudinal, and social correlates of drug use
(1)

170 Drug use among public and private secondary school students in Puerto Rico
(6)

171 A report on the dropout study
(5, 14)

172 Sex differences in adolescent drug use: Recent trends
(11, 18)

174 Patterns of multiple drug use in high school
(4, 9)

179 Shacking up: Cohabitation in the 1970s
(1)

186 Getting high in high school: The meaning of adolescent drug usage
(10)

191 Personality characteristics of students who became drug users: An MMPI study of an avant-garde
(6)

192 Organization of needs in male and female drug and alcohol users
(1, 2, 3, 4)

196 Drug use, academic performance, and career indecision: Longitudinal data in search of a model
(8)

198 Cigarette smoking as a precursor of illicit drug use
(1, 2, 3, 8, 10)

126 Attitude and behavior: A specification of the contingent consistency hypothesis
(1, 2, 3, 4, 5, 6)

127 The relationship between drug education programs in the greater New Haven schools and changes in drug use and drug-related beliefs and perceptions
(7, 12)

129 Perceived paternal relationships, adolescent personality, and female marijuana use
(1, 2, 3, 4)

130 Correlates of adolescent marijuana use as related to age, sex, and ethnicity
(1, 2, 3, 4, 5, 6, 7, 8)

131 Peer, family, and personality domains as related to adolescents' drug behavior
(1, 2, 3, 4, 5, 6)

132 Family socialization and adolescent personality and their association with adolescent use of marijuana
(1, 2, 3, 4)

133 Initiation into adolescent marijuana use
(1, 2, 3, 4, 5, 6, 7, 8, 9, 10)

134 Paternal determinants of male adolescent marijuana use
(1, 2, 3, 4, 5, 6, 7)

137 The role of the father in his son's marijuana use
(1, 2, 3, 4)

138 A Study of Teenage Drug Behavior
(3, 16, 22, 23)

148 Longitudinal analysis of the role of peer support, adult models, and peer subcultures in beginning adolescent substance use: An application of setwise canonical correlation methods
(3, 4)

149 Intentions to use drugs among adolescents: A longitudinal analysis
(4)

150 Drugs and the Class of '78: Behaviors, Attitudes, and Recent National Trends
(19)

151 Highlights from Student Drug Use in America 1975-1980
(2, 6, 7, 18, 22, 24, 25)

152 Marijuana Decriminalization: The Impact on Youth, 1975-1980
(1, 2, 3, 4, 5, 6, 7, 8, 9, 10)

153 Drugs and delinquency: A search for causal connections
(6)

154 Inter- and intragenerational influences on adolescent marijuana use
(1, 2, 3, 4, 5, 6, 7, 8, 9, 10)

155 Interpersonal influences on adolescent illegal drug use
(1, 5, 7, 8, 9, 12)

157 On variations in adolescent subcultures
(1, 4, 5, 6, 7)

158 The epidemiology of adolescent drug use in France and Israel
(4, 9, 10)

159 Sequences and stages in patterns of adolescent drug use
(8)

160 Antecedents of adolescent initiation to stages of drug use: A development analysis
(6, 7, 8, 12)

161 The epidemiology of drug use among New York State high school students: Distribution, trends, and change in rates of use
(14, 16, 21)

162 Adolescent involvement in legal and illegal drug use: A multiple classification analysis
(1, 2, 3, 4, 5, 6, 7, 8, 9, 10)

166 Drug use and military plans of high school seniors
(2, 7)

167 Personality, attitudinal, and social correlates of drug use
(1, 2, 5)

169 Depressive mood and adolescent illicit drug use: A longitudinal analysis
(2, 3, 4, 5, 6, 8, 9)

170 Drug use among public and private secondary school students in Puerto Rico
(2, 4)

171 A report on the dropout study
(2, 3, 6)

173 The role of buying and selling in illicit drug use
(1, 2, 3, 4, 5, 6)

174 Patterns of multiple drug use in high school
(3, 8, 9)

176 Psychological predictors of early use, late use, and nonuse of marijuana among teenage students
(1, 2, 3)

177 Project Community: Therapeutic Explorations with Adolescents
(1, 4, 5, 6)

180 Young Men and Drugs in Manhattan: A Causal Analysis
(2, 13, 14, 15, 16)

181 Smoking and health, marijuana and use of other illicit drugs: Causal relationships
(1, 2, 3, 4, 5, 6)

182 Changing patterns of drug use among university males
(7, 9, 10, 13, 17, 18)

183 Survey of students and drugs at the University of Notre Dame: An overview
(1, 2, 3, 4, 11, 13, 14, 15, 16, 17, 18, 19, 20, 21, 22, 23)

184 Dimensions of marijuana use in a midwest Catholic university: Subcultural considerations
(1, 2, 3, 4, 5, 6, 7, 8, 9, 10, 11, 12, 13, 14, 15)

185 The variation of a midwest Catholic university's drug use pattern from other Catholic university findings: Why?
(1, 2, 4, 5, 6)

186 Getting high in high school: The meaning of adolescent drug usage
(1, 2, 3, 4, 5, 6, 8, 10, 11)

187 Motivations for psychoactive drug use among students
(1, 2, 3)

190 Judging the shape of things to come: Lessons learned from comparisons of student drug users in 1968 and 1970
(1, 2, 3, 4, 5, 6, 8, 9)

191 Personality characteristics of students who became drug users: An MMPI study of an avant-garde
(1, 2, 3, 4, 5, 6, 7)

193 A longitudinal study of the personality correlates of marijuana use
(1, 2, 3, 4, 5, 6, 7)

196 Drug use, academic performance, and career indecision: Longitudinal data in search of a model
(7)

197 The amotivational syndrome and the college student
(3, 4, 5, 7, 8)

198 Cigarette smoking as a precursor of illicit drug use
(1, 2, 3, 4, 5, 6, 7, 8, 9, 10)

199 Determinants of early marihuana use
(1, 2, 4, 5, 6, 7, 8, 9, 10, 11, 12, 13)

201 Prediction of college drug use from personality and inner experience
(1, 2, 3)

Depressants

BARBITURATES

METHAQUALONE

SEDATIVES-HYPNOTICS

Hallucinogens

HALLUCINOGENS (GENERAL)

174 Patterns of multiple drug use in high school
(11)

188 Students' evaluations of their psychoactive drug use
(6)

191 Personality characteristics of students who became drug users: An MMPI study of an avant-garde
(1, 2, 3, 4, 5, 6, 7)

211 Drug use among Native American adults
(9)

225 Personaltiy correlates of hallucinogen use
(1, 2, 3, 4, 5, 6, 7, 8)

LSD

138 A Study of Teenage Drug Behavior
(6)

151 Highlights from Student Drug Use in America 1975-1980
(15)

186 Getting high in high school: The meaning of adolescent drug usage
(3)

187 Motivations for psychoactive drug use among students
(1)

190 Judging the shape of things to come: Lessons learned from comparisons of student drug users in 1968 and 1970
(7, 8, 10)

214 Drug use among adolescents of five Southwestern Native American tribes
(5)

218 Ethnicity and patterning in South African drug use
(3, 8)

225 Personaltiy correlates of hallucinogen use
(1, 2, 3, 4, 5, 6, 7, 8)

227 Role-play theory of psychedelic drug flashbacks
(1, 2, 3, 4, 5)

228 Psychedelic drug flashbacks: Subjective reports and biographical data
(1, 2, 3, 4, 5, 6, 7, 8, 9, 10, 11, 12, 13, 14, 15, 16, 17, 18, 19, 20)

229 Psychedelic drug flashbacks: Attentional deficits?
(1, 2, 3)

231 Ego functioning and acute adverse reactions to psychoactive drugs
(1, 3, 4, 5, 6, 7, 8, 9, 10, 11)

233 Relation of motives for drug use and psychopathology in the development of acute adverse reactions to psychoactive drugs
(4, 5, 6, 7, 8, 10, 11, 12, 13, 14)

234 Individual differences and setting as determinants of acute adverse reactions to psychoactive drugs
(1, 2, 3, 4, 5, 6, 7, 8, 9, 10)

235 LSD flashbacks and ego functioning
(1, 2, 3, 4, 5, 6, 7, 8, 9, 10)

MESCALINE

187 Motivations for psychoactive drug use among students
(1)

231 Ego functioning and acute adverse reactions to psychoactive drugs
(1, 3, 4, 5, 6, 7, 8, 9, 10, 11)

234 Individual differences and setting as determinants of acute adverse reactions to psychoactive drugs
(1, 2, 3, 4, 5, 6, 7, 8, 9, 10)

PCP (PHENCYCLIDINE)

151 Highlights from Student Drug Use in America 1975-1980
(15)

220 Phencyclidine use in high school: Tests of models
(1, 2, 3, 4, 5, 6, 7)

222 Sea-Tac and PCP
(1, 2, 3, 4, 5, 6, 7, 8)

PEYOTE

214 Drug use among adolescents of five Southwestern Native American tribes
(5)

Inhalants

095 The children of exile: Relationships between the acculturation process and drug use among Cuban youth
(5)

138 A Study of Teenage Drug Behavior
(7)

151 Highlights from Student Drug Use in America 1975-1980
(9)

194 A psychiatric emergency room study of inhalant use
(1, 2, 3, 4, 5, 6, 7, 8, 9, 10, 11, 12, 13, 14, 15, 16)

203 Family interaction and acculturation in Mexican-American inhalant users
(1, 2, 3, 4, 5, 6, 7, 8, 9, 10, 11)

210 Inhalant abuse among the Pueblo tribes of New Mexico
(1, 2, 3, 4, 5, 6, 7, 8, 9, 10, 11, 12, 13, 14)

211 Drug use among Native American adults
(5)

214 Drug use among adolescents of five Southwestern Native American tribes
(7)

215 Drug use among Native American adolescents
(4, 8, 10, 18, 23)

216 Native American Drug Use: Drug Abuse Among Indian Adolescents
(3, 5, 6, 9, 10, 13, 14, 16)

218 Ethnicity and patterning in South African drug use
(5, 7, 10, 15, 16)

Multidrug

001 Deaths of persons using methadone in New York City--1971
(1, 6)

009 Suicide attempts among drug abusers
(1, 2, 3, 4, 5)

019 Trends in the age of onset of narcotic addiction
(1, 2, 3, 4, 5, 7, 8)

023 Narcotic addicts, multiple drug abuse and psychological distress
(1, 2, 3, 5, 6, 7, 8, 9)

033 Self-concept and substance abuse treatment
(1, 2, 3, 5, 6, 7)

035 Therapeutic community dropouts: Psychological changes 2 years after treatment
(1, 2, 3)

038 Male and female drug abusers: Social and psychological status 2 years after treatment in a therapeutic community
(1, 2, 3, 4, 5, 6, 7, 8, 9, 10, 11, 12, 13, 14, 15)

040 The therapeutic community: Success and improvement rates 5 years after treatment
(1, 2, 3, 4, 5, 6, 7, 8, 9, 10, 11, 12, 13, 14, 15)

042 Differential response of heroin and nonheroin abusers to inpatient treatment
(1, 2)

043 A comparison of dropouts and disciplinary discharges from a therapeutic community
(1, 2, 3, 4)

044 Self-concept and completion of treatment for heroin and nonheroin drug abusers
(1, 2, 3, 4, 5)

045 Investigating impact of methadone treatment upon the behavior of New York City street addicts
(14)

048 Cultural factors and attrition in drug abuse treatment
(1, 2, 3, 4, 5, 6, 7, 8)

053 Methadone, wine and welfare
(1, 2, 4, 5, 6, 7)

054 Entry into methadone maintenance programs: A follow-up study of New York City heroin users detoxified in 1961-1963
(10)

055 Focus on the family as a factor in differential treatment outcome
(1, 2, 3, 4, 5)

059 The impact of drug addiction on criminal earnings
(1, 3, 4, 5, 6, 7, 8)

062 Daily criminal activities of street drug users: Preliminary findings
(2)

064 Heroin use and street crime
(2, 3, 4)

065 Youth, drugs, and street crime
(2, 3, 4, 5, 6, 7, 8, 9, 10, 11, 12, 13, 14, 15, 17, 18, 19)

066 The impact of drug use on street crime
(1, 2, 3, 4, 13, 14, 15, 16)

069 The relationship between type of drug use and arrest charge in an arrested population
(1, 2, 3, 5)

070 Crime and drug-using behavior: An areal analysis
(1)

076 Are female drug abusers more deviant?
(1, 2, 3, 4, 5)

081 Black women, heroin and crime: Some empirical notes
(1, 2, 3)

093 Ethnic differences in factors related to drug use
(1, 2, 3, 4, 5, 6, 7, 8, 9)

094 A comparison of Spanish and non-Spanish drug users in treatment in Dade County, Florida
(1, 2, 3, 4, 5, 6, 7, 8, 9, 10, 11, 12)

095 The children of exile: Relationships between the acculturation process and drug use among Cuban youth
(1, 2, 3)

096 Drug use among Cuban exiles in Miami, Florida: Cultural antecedents and processes
(1, 2, 3, 4, 5)

097 Risk factors in the continuation of childhood antisocial behavior into adulthood
(1, 2, 3)

098 Childhood conduct disorders and later arrest
(1, 2, 3, 4, 5)

099 The long-term outcome of truancy
(1, 2, 3, 4, 5, 6, 7)

102 Drug use in the construction trade
(1, 2, 6, 7, 8, 13, 14, 15, 22, 23)

103 Three types of extreme drug users identified by a replicated cluster analysis
(1, 2, 3, 4, 5)

106 Acute drug reactions among the aged: A research note
(1, 2, 3, 4, 5, 6)

108   The drug problems of industry
(3, 5, 6, 7, 8, 9, 10, 11, 18, 19, 20,
21, 22, 24, 25, 26, 27, 28)

109   The social problem of drug abuse
in ecological perspective
(1, 2, 3, 4, 5, 6, 7, 8, 9, 10, 11)

111   Satisfaction with real and
simulated jobs in relation to
personality variables and drug use
(1, 2, 3)

112   Drug treatment after return in
Vietnam veterans
(8, 9, 10, 11)

113   The interaction of setting and
predisposition in explaining novel
behavior: Drug initiations before, in,
and after Vietnam
(1, 2, 3, 4, 6, 8, 9, 10, 11, 12)

114   Vietnam veterans three years after
Vietnam: How our study changed our
view on heroin
(1, 2, 5, 7, 15, 16)

115   Polydrug and alcohol use by
veterans and nonveterans
(1, 2, 3, 4, 5, 6, 7, 8, 9, 10, 11, 14,
16, 17, 18, 19, 20)

117   Cocaine Users: A Representative
Case Approach
(2)

119   Life Styles of Nine American
Non-Users of Drugs (Executive Summary)
(1, 2, 3, 4, 5, 6, 7, 8, 9)

120   Effects of criminal justice and
medical definitions of a social problem
upon the delivery of treatment: The
case of drug abuse
(5, 6)

127   The relationship between drug
education programs in the greater New
Haven schools and changes in drug use
and drug-related beliefs and
perceptions
(1, 2, 3, 4, 5, 6, 8, 9, 10, 11, 13,
14, 15)

128   Drug education: Further results
and recommendations
(1, 2, 3, 4, 5, 6, 7, 8, 9)

131   Peer, family, and personality
domains as related to adolescents' drug
behavior
(1, 2, 3, 4, 5, 6)

138   A Study of Teenage Drug Behavior
(10, 11, 12, 13, 14, 17, 18, 19, 20,
21, 23, 24)

139   Sequential patterns of
multiple-drug use among high school
students
(1, 2, 3, 4, 5, 6, 7, 8, 9, 10, 11)

144   Family life and levels of
involvement in an adolescent heroin
epidemic
(7, 9, 10)

146   Adolescent drug use and intentions
to use drugs in the future: A
concurrent analysis
(1, 2, 3)

147   Beginning adolescent drug use and
peer and adult interaction patterns
(1, 2, 4, 5, 6, 7)

148   Longitudinal analysis of the role
of peer support, adult models, and peer
subcultures in beginning adolescent
substance use: An application of
setwise canonical correlation methods
(1, 2, 3, 4)

149   Intentions to use drugs among
adolescents: A longitudinal analysis
(1, 2, 3)

150   Drugs and the Class of '78:
Behaviors, Attitudes, and Recent
National Trends
(1, 2, 3, 4, 6, 7, 9, 10, 11, 12, 14,
15, 16, 17, 18, 20, 21, 22, 23, 24)

151   Highlights from Student Drug Use
in America 1975-1980
(1, 3, 4, 26)

153 Drugs and delinquency: A search for causal connections
(1, 2, 3, 4, 5, 6, 7)

155 Interpersonal influences on adolescent illegal drug use
(2, 3, 4, 5, 6, 7, 10, 11, 13)

156 Reaching the hard-to-reach: Illicit drug use among high school absentees
(1, 2, 3, 4, 5, 6)

157 On variations in adolescent subcultures
(1, 2, 3)

158 The epidemiology of adolescent drug use in France and Israel
(1, 2, 3, 5, 6, 9, 11, 12, 13, 14, 15)

159 Sequences and stages in patterns of adolescent drug use
(1, 2, 3, 4, 5, 6, 7, 8, 9, 10, 11, 12)

160 Antecedents of adolescent initiation to stages of drug use: A development analysis
(9, 10, 11, 12, 13)

161 The epidemiology of drug use among New York State high school students: Distribution, trends, and change in rates of use
(1, 2, 3, 5, 6, 7, 8, 9, 10, 11, 12, 13, 15, 17, 18, 19, 20)

162 Adolescent involvement in legal and illegal drug use: A multiple classification analysis
(7, 8, 9)

163 Parental and peer influence upon adolescent drug use
(1, 2, 3)

165 Aspects of adolescent information acquisition about drugs and alcohol topics
(1, 2, 3, 4, 5, 6, 7, 8, 11, 12, 14)

166 Drug use and military plans of high school seniors
(1, 4, 8)

167 Personality, attitudinal, and social correlates of drug use
(3, 4, 6, 7, 8, 9, 10, 11, 12)

168 Psychological factors and adolescent illicit drug use: Ethnicity and sex differences
(1, 2, 3, 4, 5, 6, 7)

169 Depressive mood and adolescent illicit drug use: A longitudinal analysis
(1, 3, 6, 7, 8, 9)

170 Drug use among public and private secondary school students in Puerto Rico
(1, 3, 5, 7, 8, 9, 10, 11, 12, 13, 14, 15, 16)

171 A report on the dropout study
(1, 4, 8, 9, 10, 13, 16)

172 Sex differences in adolescent drug use: Recent trends
(1, 2, 3, 4, 5, 6, 7, 8, 9, 10, 13, 14, 15, 16, 17, 20, 21, 22, 23, 24)

173 The role of buying and selling in illicit drug use
(1, 2, 3, 4, 5, 6)

174 Patterns of multiple drug use in high school
(1, 2, 3, 4, 5, 6, 7, 8, 10, 12)

175 Teenage drug use: A search for causes and consequenses
(1, 2)

177 Project Community: Therapeutic Explorations with Adolescents
(1, 2, 3, 7, 8)

178 The relationship of personality structure to patterns of adolescent substance use
(1, 2, 3, 4, 5)

179 Shacking up: Cohabitation in the 1970s
(2, 3, 4)

180   Young Men and Drugs in Manhattan:
A Causal Analysis
(1, 4, 5, 6, 7, 8, 9, 14, 17, 18, 20)

182   Changing patterns of drug use
among university males
(1, 2, 3, 4, 5, 6, 8, 10, 11, 12, 13,
14, 15, 16, 17, 18)

183   Survey of students and drugs at
the University of Notre Dame: An
overview
(5, 6, 7, 8, 9, 10, 12)

185   The variation of a midwest
Catholic university's drug use pattern
from other Catholic university
findings: Why?
(3)

186   Getting high in high school: The
meaning of adolescent drug usage
(4, 7, 8, 9)

187   Motivations for psychoactive drug
use among students
(4)

188   Students' evaluations of their
psychoactive drug use
(1, 2, 3, 4, 5)

189   Whither the epidemic?
Psychoactive drug-use career patterns
of college students
(1, 2, 3, 4, 5, 6, 7, 8)

192   Organization of needs in male and
female drug and alcohol users
(1, 2, 3, 4)

195   Psychoactive drugs: A course
evaluation
(1, 3, 4)

196   Drug use, academic performance,
and career indecision: Longitudinal
data in search of a model
(1, 2, 3, 4, 5, 6, 8)

197   The amotivational syndrome and the
college student
(1, 2, 3, 4, 6, 7, 8, 9, 10, 11, 12,
13)

198   Cigarette smoking as a precursor
of illicit drug use
(3, 4, 6, 7, 9)

199   Determinants of early marihuana
use
(3, 4, 9, 10)

200   Young Men and Drugs--A Nationwide
Survey
(1, 2, 4, 5, 6, 7, 8, 9, 11)

201   Prediction of college drug use
from personality and inner experience
(1, 2, 3)

202   Reasons for drug and alcohol use
by college students
(7, 8)

205   Health and drug behavior: A study
of urban black adolescents
(1, 2, 3, 4, 5, 6, 7, 8, 9, 10, 11, 12)

206   Black youths and drug-use behavior
(2, 3, 4, 5, 6, 7, 8, 9, 11, 14, 15,
16, 20, 21, 22, 23)

207   Patterns of drug involvement:
Developmental and secular influences on
age at initiation
(1, 2, 3, 4, 5, 6, 7, 8, 9, 10)

208   Youngsters Experimenting with
Drugs
(1, 2, 4, 5, 6, 7, 8, 10, 11, 12, 13,
14, 15, 16, 17, 18, 19)

211   Drug use among Native American
adults
(6, 7, 8, 10)

212   Longitudinal community
epidemiological studies of drug use:
Early aggressiveness, shyness, and
learning problems
(2, 3, 4, 10, 11)

213   Mental health in first grade and
teenage drug, alcohol, and cigarette
use
(1, 2, 4, 5, 6, 7, 8, 9, 10, 11, 12,
13)

214 Drug use among adolescents of five Southwestern Native American tribes
(1, 5, 6)

215 Drug use among Native American adolescents
(1, 5, 6, 7, 8, 9, 10, 11, 12, 13, 14, 15, 16, 17, 18, 19, 20, 21, 22, 23)

216 Native American Drug Use: Drug Abuse Among Indian Adolescents
(1, 2, 3, 4, 10, 15)

218 Ethnicity and patterning in South African drug use
(1, 2)

Narcotics

CODEINE

018 Addict careers: III. Trends across time
(5)

019 Trends in the age of onset of narcotic addiction
(6)

HEROIN

001 Deaths of persons using methadone in New York City--1971
(7)

002 Some research notes on the sexual life of the addict
(1, 2, 3, 4, 5)

003 Junkie work, "hustles" and social status among heroin addicts
(1, 2, 3, 4, 5, 6, 7, 8, 9, 10, 11, 12, 13, 14, 15)

005 The working addict
(1, 2, 3, 4, 5, 6, 7, 8, 9, 10, 11, 12)

006 Street heroin potency and deaths from overdose in San Antonio
(1, 2, 3)

007 Suicidal behavior among heroin addicts: A brief report
(1, 2)

008 Formerly-addicted-now-controlled opiate users
(1, 2, 3, 4, 5, 6, 7)

010 What is an addict? Empirical patterns and concepts of addiction
(1, 2, 3, 4, 5, 6)

011 Family ties of heroin addicts
(1, 2, 3, 4, 5, 6)

013 Residence relocation inhibits opioid dependence
(1, 2, 3, 4, 5, 6, 7, 8, 9, 10, 11, 12)

017 Addict careers: II. The first ten years
(3)

019 Trends in the age of onset of narcotic addiction
(6)

021 Predicting heroin and alcohol usage among young Puerto Ricans
(1, 2, 3, 4, 5, 6, 7, 8, 9)

022 Parental correlates of drug use among young Puerto Rican adults
(1, 2, 3, 4, 5, 6, 7, 8, 9, 10, 11, 12, 13, 14, 15, 16)

023 Narcotic addicts, multiple drug abuse and psychological distress
(1, 2, 3, 4, 5, 6, 7, 8, 9)

024 Ecological studies of narcotic addiction
(1, 2, 3, 4, 5)

026 The structure of depression in heroin addicts
(1, 2, 3, 4, 5)

028 Correlates of self-reported and clinically assessed depression in male heroin addicts
(1, 2, 3)

124 Opium and heroin addicts in Laos:
I. A comparative study
(1, 2, 3, 4, 5, 6, 7, 8, 9, 10, 11, 12)

125 Opium and heroin addicts in Laos:
II. A study of matched pairs
(1, 2, 3, 4, 5, 6, 7)

138 A Study of Teenage Drug Behavior
(9)

140 Experimental heroin users: An
epidemiologic and psychosocial approach
(1, 2, 3, 4, 5, 6, 7, 8, 9, 10, 11, 12,
13, 14, 15, 16, 17, 18, 19, 20)

141 Treated and untreated addicts:
Factors associated with participation
in treatment and cessation of heroin
use
(1, 2, 3, 4, 5, 6, 7, 8, 9, 10, 11, 12,
13, 14, 15, 16, 17, 18, 19, 20, 21, 22,
23, 24, 25, 26)

142 Addicts and experimenters:
Dynamics of involvement in an
adolescent heroin epidemic
(1, 2, 3, 4, 5, 6, 7, 8, 9, 10, 11, 12,
13, 14, 15, 16, 17, 18, 19)

143 Personality development and
adolescent heroin use
(1, 2, 3, 4, 5, 6, 7, 8, 9, 10, 11, 12,
13, 14, 15, 16)

144 Family life and levels of
involvement in an adolescent heroin
epidemic
(1, 2, 3, 4, 5, 6, 7, 8, 9, 10, 11)

151 Highlights from Student Drug Use
in America 1975-1980
(13)

153 Drugs and delinquency: A search
for causal connections
(5)

171 A report on the dropout study
(2, 7, 11, 12, 15)

174 Patterns of multiple drug use in
high school
(11)

180 Young Men and Drugs in Manhattan:
A Causal Analysis
(2, 3, 10, 11, 12, 15, 16, 19)

181 Smoking and health, marijuana and
use of other illicit drugs: Causal
relationships
(1, 2, 3, 4, 5, 6)

186 Getting high in high school: The
meaning of adolescent drug usage
(3)

198 Cigarette smoking as a precursor
of illicit drug use
(4)

199 Determinants of early marihuana
use
(1, 5, 6)

200 Young Men and Drugs--A Nationwide
Survey
(10)

204 What happened in Harlem? Analysis
of a decline in heroin use among a
generation unit of urban black youth
(1, 2, 3, 4, 5, 6, 7, 8, 9, 10, 11, 12)

206 Black youths and drug-use behavior
(10, 13, 16, 17, 18, 19, 24, 25, 26,
27, 28, 29)

215 Drug use among Native American
adolescents
(7)

METHADONE

001 Deaths of persons using methadone
in New York City--1971
(1, 2, 3, 4, 5, 6, 7, 8)

010 What is an addict? Empirical
patterns and concepts of addiction
(5)

012 New light on the maturing out
hypothesis in opioid dependence
(2)

030 The effect of parole on methadone patient behavior
(1, 2, 3, 4, 5, 6, 7, 8, 9, 10, 11, 12, 13)

045 Investigating impact of methadone treatment upon the behavior of New York City street addicts
(1, 2, 3, 4, 5, 6, 7, 8, 9, 10, 11, 12, 13, 14)

046 The magic fix: A critical analysis of methadone maintenance treatment
(1, 2, 3, 4, 5, 6, 7)

049 Shutting off methadone: Costs and benefits
(1, 2, 3, 4, 5, 6, 7, 8, 9, 10, 11, 12)

050 Long-term follow-up of clients of high- and low-dose methadone programs
(1, 2, 3, 4, 5, 6, 7, 8, 9, 10, 11, 12)

051 Outpatient methadone withdrawal for heroin dependence
(1, 2, 3, 4, 5, 6)

053 Methadone, wine and welfare
(1, 2, 3, 4, 5, 6, 7, 8)

121 Narcotic addiction in two Asian cultures: A comparison and analysis
(3)

124 Opium and heroin addicts in Laos: I. A comparative study
(12)

125 Opium and heroin addicts in Laos: II. A study of matched pairs
(6)

MORPHINE

052 Notes on American medical history: A follow-up study of the New Haven morphine maintenance clinic of 1920
(1, 2, 3, 4, 5, 6, 7, 8, 9, 10, 11, 12)

123 A heroin "epidemic" in Asia
(5)

NARCOTICS (GENERAL)

004 The veridicality of addicts' self-reports in social research
(1, 2, 3, 4, 5, 6, 7)

014 An analysis of work histories, earnings, and receipts of benefits among a sample of a community-wide population of narcotic addicts
(1, 2, 3, 4, 5, 6)

015 Studying addicts over time: Methodology and preliminary findings
(1, 2, 3, 4, 5, 6, 7, 8, 9, 10)

016 Addict Careers: I. A new typology
(1, 2, 3, 4, 5, 6, 7, 8, 9, 10)

017 Addict careers: II. The first ten years
(1, 2, 3, 4, 5, 6, 7, 8, 9, 10, 11, 12, 13)

018 Addict careers: III. Trends across time
(1, 2, 3, 4, 5, 6, 7, 8, 9, 10, 11)

020 Narcotic abusers and poverty
(1, 2, 3)

024 Ecological studies of narcotic addiction
(1, 2, 3, 4, 5)

025 Is there a relationship between astrology and addiction? A reexamination
(1)

027 The Life Styles of Nine American Opiate Users (Executive Summary)
(1, 2, 3, 4, 5, 6, 7, 8, 9, 10, 11)

066 The impact of drug use on street crime
(1, 2, 3, 4, 5, 6, 7, 8, 9, 10, 11, 12, 13, 14, 15, 16, 17, 18)

069 The relationship between type of drug use and arrest charge in an arrested population
(1, 2, 3, 4, 5)

121 Narcotic addiction in two Asian cultures: A comparison and analysis
(1, 2, 3)

122 Influence of opium availability on addiction rates in Laos
(1, 2, 3, 4, 5, 6, 7, 8)

123 A heroin "epidemic" in Asia
(5, 8)

124 Opium and heroin addicts in Laos: I. A comparative study
(1, 2, 3, 4, 5, 6, 7, 8, 9, 10, 11, 12)

125 Opium and heroin addicts in Laos: II. A study of matched pairs
(1, 2, 3, 4, 5, 6, 7)

218 Ethnicity and patterning in South African drug use
(6, 11)

Prescription Drugs

077 Psychotropic drug use by women: Health, attitudinal, personality and demographic correlates
(1, 2, 3, 4, 5, 6, 7, 8)

078 Employment status, role dissatisfaction and the housewife syndrome
(1, 2, 3, 5)

079 Cuban women, sex role conflicts and the use of prescription drugs
(1, 2, 3, 4, 5, 6)

085 Drug usage as an index of stress among women
(1, 2, 3, 4, 5, 6, 7, 8, 9, 10, 11, 12, 13, 14)

086 Sex differences in the content and style of medical advertisements
(1, 2, 3, 4, 5, 6)

108 The drug problems of industry
(1, 2)

120 Effects of criminal justice and medical definitions of a social problem upon the delivery of treatment: The case of drug abuse
(4)

154 Inter- and intragenerational influences on adolescent marijuana use
(1, 2, 3)

155 Interpersonal influences on adolescent illegal drug use
(1, 3, 8)

160 Antecedents of adolescent initiation to stages of drug use: A development analysis
(10)

Stimulants

AMPHETAMINES

027 The Life Styles of Nine American Opiate Users (Executive Summary)
(1, 3, 4, 7, 8, 10)

102 Drug use in the construction trade
(3, 4)

105 Depressive disorders in Vietnam returnees
(2, 3)

113 The interaction of setting and predisposition in explaining novel behavior: Drug initiations before, in, and after Vietnam
(5)

114 Vietnam veterans three years after Vietnam: How our study changed our view on heroin
(4, 6)

116 The Life Styles of Nine American Amphetamine Users (Executive Summary)
(1, 2, 3, 4, 5, 6, 7, 8, 9, 10, 11)

117 Cocaine Users: A Representative Case Approach
(18)

206   Black youths and drug-use behavior
(16)

222   Sea-Tac and PCP
(2)

COCA LEAVES

110   What everybody in Cuzco knows
about coca
(1, 2, 3, 4, 5, 6, 7)

KHAT

107   Qat use in North Yemen and the
problem of addiction: A study in
medical anthropology
(1, 2, 3, 4, 5, 6, 7, 8, 9, 10, 11, 12,
13, 14, 15, 16, 17, 18, 19, 20)

Tobacco (Cigarettes)

021   Predicting heroin and alcohol
usage among young Puerto Ricans
(14)

022   Parental correlates of drug use
among young Puerto Rican adults
(12)

135   Fathers and sons: Their
relationship and personality
characteristics associated with the
son's smoking behavior
(1, 2, 3, 4, 5, 6, 7)

136   Maternal and personality
determinants of adolescent smoking
behavior
(1, 2, 3, 4, 5, 6)

138   A Study of Teenage Drug Behavior
(2)

147   Beginning adolescent drug use and
peer and adult interaction patterns
(3)

150   Drugs and the Class of '78:
Behaviors, Attitudes, and Recent
National Trends
(5, 8, 10)

151   Highlights from Student Drug Use
in America 1975-1980
(5, 17, 19, 21, 23, 27)

154   Inter- and intragenerational
influences on adolescent marijuana use
(5)

155   Interpersonal influences on
adolescent illegal drug use
(4)

158   The epidemiology of adolescent
drug use in France and Israel
(8, 10)

159   Sequences and stages in patterns
of adolescent drug use
(11)

160   Antecedents of adolescent
initiation to stages of drug use: A
development analysis
(5)

161   The epidemiology of drug use among
New York State high school students:
Distribution, trends, and change in
rates of use
(3, 14)

162   Adolescent involvement in legal
and illegal drug use: A multiple
classification analysis
(10)

164   A longitudinal study of onset of
drinking among high school students
(14)

166   Drug use and military plans of
high school seniors
(5, 6)

171   A report on the dropout study
(5)

172   Sex differences in adolescent drug
use: Recent trends
(12, 19)

174   Patterns of multiple drug use in
high school
(4, 6)

179 Shacking up: Cohabitation in the 1970s
(1)

198 Cigarette smoking as a precursor of illicit drug use
(1, 5, 7, 8, 9, 10)

200 Young Men and Drugs--A Nationwide Survey
(3)

205 Health and drug behavior: A study of urban black adolescents
(6)

206 Black youths and drug-use behavior
(1)

209 Sex differences in antecedents of substance use among adolescents
(1, 2, 3, 4, 5, 6, 7)

212 Longitudinal community epidemiological studies of drug use: Early aggressiveness, shyness, and learning problems
(1, 5, 6, 7)

216 Native American Drug Use: Drug Abuse Among Indian Adolescents
(16)

226 Physiological responses to exercise in chronic cigarette and marijuana users
(1, 2, 3)

Tranquilizers

CHLORDIAZEPOXIDE (LIBRIUM)

078 Employment status, role dissatisfaction and the housewife syndrome
(4)

138 A Study of Teenage Drug Behavior
(15)

DIAZEPAM (VALIUM)

078 Employment status, role dissatisfaction and the housewife syndrome
(4)

TRANQUILIZERS (GENERAL)

070 Crime and drug-using behavior: An areal analysis
(4)

084 A valium a day keeps the tension away: Socio-psychological characteristics of minor tranquilizer users
(1, 2, 3, 4, 5, 6, 7, 8, 9, 10, 11, 12)

120 Effects of criminal justice and medical definitions of a social problem upon the delivery of treatment: The case of drug abuse
(1)

151 Highlights from Student Drug Use in America 1975-1980
(12)

195 Psychoactive drugs: A course evaluation
(2)

SAMPLE TYPE INDEX

ADDICTS

002 Some research notes on the sexual
life of the addict
(1, 2, 3, 4, 5)

003 Junkie work, "hustles" and social
status among heroin addicts
(1, 2, 3, 4, 5, 6, 7, 8, 9, 10, 11, 12,
13, 14, 15)

004 The veridicality of addicts'
self-reports in social research
(1, 2, 3, 4, 5, 6, 7)

005 The working addict
(1, 2, 3, 4, 5, 6, 7, 8, 9, 10, 11, 12)

007 Suicidal behavior among heroin
addicts: A brief report
(1, 2)

011 Family ties of heroin addicts
(1, 2, 3, 4, 5, 6)

012 New light on the maturing out
hypothesis in opioid dependence
(1, 2, 3, 4, 5, 6, 7)

013 Residence relocation inhibits
opioid dependence
(1, 2, 3, 4, 5, 6, 7, 8, 9, 10, 11, 12)

014 An analysis of work histories,
earnings, and receipts of benefits
among a sample of a community-wide
population of narcotic addicts
(1, 2, 3, 4, 5, 6)

015 Studying addicts over time:
Methodology and preliminary findings
(1, 2, 3, 4, 5, 6, 7, 8, 9, 10)

016 Addict Careers: I. A new
typology
(1, 2, 3, 4, 5, 6, 7, 8, 9, 10)

017 Addict careers: II. The first
ten years
(1, 2, 3, 4, 5, 6, 7, 8, 9, 10, 11, 12,
13)

018 Addict careers: III. Trends
across time
(1, 2, 3, 4, 5, 6, 7, 8, 9, 10, 11)

019 Trends in the age of onset of
narcotic addiction
(1, 2, 3, 4, 5, 6, 7, 8)

024 Ecological studies of narcotic
addiction
(1, 2, 3, 4, 5)

025 Is there a relationship between
astrology and addiction? A
reexamination
(1)

026 The structure of depression in
heroin addicts
(1, 2, 3, 4, 5)

027 The Life Styles of Nine American
Opiate Users (Executive Summary)
(1, 2, 3, 4, 5, 6, 7, 8, 9, 10, 11)

028 Correlates of self-reported and
clinically assessed depression in male
heroin addicts
(1, 2, 3)

029 Types of psychopathology displayed
by heroin addicts
(1, 2)

032 Therapeutic communities vs
methadone maintenance: A prospective
controlled study of narcotic addiction
treatment: Design and one-year
follow-up
(1, 2, 3, 4, 5, 6, 7, 8, 9, 10, 11, 12,
13)

051 Outpatient methadone withdrawal
for heroin dependence
(1, 2, 3, 4, 5, 6)

052 Notes on American medical history:
A follow-up study of the New Haven
morphine maintenance clinic of 1920
(1, 2, 3, 4, 5, 6, 7, 8, 9, 10, 11, 12)

054 Entry into methadone maintenance
programs: A follow-up study of New
York City heroin users detoxified in
1961-1963
(1, 2, 3, 4, 5, 6, 7, 8, 9, 10, 11)

055 Focus on the family as a factor in differential treatment outcome
(1, 2, 3, 4, 5)

057 The criminality of heroin addicts when addicted and when off opiates
(1, 2, 3, 4, 5, 6, 7, 8, 9, 10, 11, 12, 13, 14, 15)

058 Lifetime criminality of heroin addicts in the United States
(1, 2, 3, 4, 5, 6, 7, 8, 9, 10)

062 Daily criminal activities of street drug users: Preliminary findings
(1, 2, 3, 4, 5, 6, 7)

071 California civil commitment: A decade later
(1, 2, 3, 4, 5, 6, 7, 8)

072 Outcome of the California Civil Addict commitments: 1961-1972
(1, 2, 3, 4, 5, 6, 7, 8, 9, 10, 11, 12, 13, 14, 15, 16)

073 Narcotic addiction and crime
(1, 2, 3, 4, 5, 6, 7, 8, 9, 10, 11)

075 A preliminary report on crime and addiction within a community-wide population of narcotic addicts
(1, 2, 3, 4, 5, 6, 7, 8)

082 Prostitution and addiction: An interdisciplinary approach
(1, 2, 3, 4, 5, 6, 7, 8, 9, 10)

083 The relationship between female criminality and drug abuse
(1, 2, 3, 4, 5, 6, 7, 8, 9, 10, 11, 12, 13, 14, 15, 16)

087 Becoming addicted: The woman addict
(1, 2, 3, 4, 5, 6, 7, 8, 9, 10, 11, 12, 13, 14)

088 Difficulties in taking care of business: Women addicts as mothers
(1, 2, 3, 4, 5, 6, 7, 8, 9)

089 Sex roles among deviants: The woman addict
(1, 2, 3, 4, 5, 6, 7, 8, 9, 10)

090 Women addicts' experience of the heroin world: Risk, chaos, and inundation
(1, 2, 3, 4, 5, 6, 7, 8, 9, 10, 11, 12)

091 Criminal involvement of female offenders: Psychological characteristics among four groups
(1, 2, 3, 4, 5, 6, 7)

092 Puerto Rican Addicts and Non-addicts: A Comparison
(1, 2, 3, 4, 5, 6, 7, 8, 9, 10, 11, 12, 13, 14, 15, 16, 17, 18, 19, 20, 21)

114 Vietnam veterans three years after Vietnam: How our study changed our view on heroin
(9, 11, 13, 14, 16)

121 Narcotic addiction in two Asian cultures: A comparison and analysis
(1, 2, 3)

122 Influence of opium availability on addiction rates in Laos
(1, 2, 3, 4, 5, 6, 7, 8)

123 A heroin "epidemic" in Asia
(1, 2, 3, 4, 5, 6, 7, 8, 9, 10)

124 Opium and heroin addicts in Laos: I. A comparative study
(1, 2, 3, 4, 5, 6, 7, 8, 9, 10, 11, 12)

125 Opium and heroin addicts in Laos: II. A study of matched pairs
(1, 2, 3, 4, 5, 6, 7)

140 Experimental heroin users: An epidemiologic and psychosocial approach
(2, 3, 5, 6)

141 Treated and untreated addicts: Factors associated with participation in treatment and cessation of heroin use
(1, 2, 3, 4, 5, 6, 7, 8, 9, 10, 11, 12, 13, 14, 15, 16, 18, 21, 23, 24, 25)

142 Addicts and experimenters: Dynamics of involvement in an adolescent heroin epidemic
(1, 2, 4, 6, 7, 8, 9, 10, 11, 12, 13, 15, 16, 17, 18, 19)

ALCOHOLICS

047 Attrition of older alcoholics from treatment
(1, 2, 3, 4, 5, 6, 7, 8, 9, 10, 11)

055 Focus on the family as a factor in differential treatment outcome
(1, 2, 3, 4, 5)

100 Father's alcoholism and children's outcomes
(1, 2, 3, 4, 5)

COCAINE USERS

067 The criminal behavior of street heroin and cocaine users
(1, 2, 3, 4, 5, 6, 7, 8, 9)

068 Exploring asymmetries in the hard drug-crime relationship
(1, 2, 3, 4, 5, 6, 7, 8, 9)

117 Cocaine Users: A Representative Case Approach
(1, 2, 3, 4, 5, 6, 7, 8, 9, 10, 11, 12, 13, 14, 15, 16, 17, 18, 19)

COLLEGE STUDENTS

065 Youth, drugs, and street crime
(1, 2, 3, 4, 5, 6, 7)

134 Paternal determinants of male adolescent marijuana use
(1, 2, 3, 4, 5, 6, 7)

135 Fathers and sons: Their relationship and personality characteristics associated with the son's smoking behavior
(1, 2, 3, 4, 5, 6, 7)

182 Changing patterns of drug use among university males
(1, 2, 3, 4, 5, 6, 7, 8, 9, 10, 11, 12, 13, 14, 15, 16, 17, 18)

183 Survey of students and drugs at the University of Notre Dame: An overview
(1, 2, 3, 4, 5, 6, 7, 8, 9, 10, 11, 12, 13, 14, 15, 16, 17, 18, 19, 20, 21, 22, 23)

184 Dimensions of marijuana use in a midwest Catholic university: Subcultural considerations
(1, 2, 3, 4, 5, 6, 7, 8, 9, 10, 11, 12, 13, 14, 15)

185 The variation of a midwest Catholic university's drug use pattern from other Catholic university findings: Why?
(1, 2, 3, 4, 5, 6)

186 Getting high in high school: The meaning of adolescent drug usage
(1, 2, 3, 4, 5, 6, 7, 8, 9, 10, 11)

187 Motivations for psychoactive drug use among students
(1, 2, 3, 4)

189 Whither the epidemic? Psychoactive drug-use career patterns of college students
(1, 2, 3, 4, 5, 6, 7, 8)

190 Judging the shape of things to come: Lessons learned from comparisons of student drug users in 1968 and 1970
(1, 2, 3, 4, 5, 6, 7, 8, 9, 10)

192 Organization of needs in male and female drug and alcohol users
(1, 2, 3, 4)

193 A longitudinal study of the personality correlates of marijuana use
(1, 2, 3, 4, 5, 6, 7)

195 Psychoactive drugs: A course evaluation
(1, 2, 3, 4)

038 Male and female drug abusers:
Social and psychological status 2 years
after treatment in a therapeutic
community
(1, 2, 3, 4, 5, 6, 7, 8, 9, 10, 11, 12,
13, 14, 15)

039 Phoenix House: Changes in
psychopathological signs of resident
drug addicts
(1, 2, 3, 4)

040 The therapeutic community:
Success and improvement rates 5 years
after treatment
(1, 2, 3, 4, 5, 6, 7, 8, 9, 10, 11, 12,
13, 14, 15, 16)

042 Differential response of heroin
and nonheroin abusers to inpatient
treatment
(1, 2)

043 A comparison of dropouts and
disciplinary discharges from a
therapeutic community
(1, 2, 3, 4)

044 Self-concept and completion of
treatment for heroin and nonheroin drug
abusers
(1, 2, 3, 4, 5)

047 Attrition of older alcoholics from
treatment
(1, 2, 3, 4, 5, 6, 7, 8, 9, 10, 11)

048 Cultural factors and attrition in
drug abuse treatment
(1, 2, 3, 4, 5, 6, 7, 8)

056 The therapeutic community:
Multivariate prediction of retention
(1, 2, 3, 4, 5, 6, 7, 8)

076 Are female drug abusers more
deviant?
(1, 2, 3, 4, 5)

DRUG TREATMENT OUTPATIENTS

028 Correlates of self-reported and
clinically assessed depression in male
heroin addicts
(1, 2, 3)

030 The effect of parole on methadone
patient behavior
(1, 2, 3, 4, 5, 6, 7, 8, 9, 10, 11, 12,
13)

045 Investigating impact of methadone
treatment upon the behavior of New York
City street addicts
(1, 2, 3, 4, 5, 6, 7, 8, 9, 10, 11, 12,
13, 14)

046 The magic fix: A critical
analysis of methadone maintenance
treatment
(1, 2, 3, 4, 5, 6, 7)

049 Shutting off methadone: Costs and
benefits
(1, 2, 3, 4, 5, 6, 7, 8, 9, 10, 11, 12)

050 Long-term follow-up of clients of
high- and low-dose methadone programs
(1, 2, 3, 4, 5, 6, 7, 8, 9, 10, 11, 12)

051 Outpatient methadone withdrawal
for heroin dependence
(1, 2, 3, 4, 5, 6)

052 Notes on American medical history:
A follow-up study of the New Haven
morphine maintenance clinic of 1920
(1, 2, 3, 4, 5, 6, 7, 8, 9, 10, 11, 12)

074 Crime and treatment of heroin
users
(1, 2, 3)

DRUG TREATMENT PATIENTS

041 Religious programs and careers of
chronic heroin users
(1, 2, 3, 4, 5, 6)

059 The impact of drug addiction on
criminal earnings
(1, 2, 3, 4, 5, 6, 7, 8)

094 A comparison of Spanish and
non-Spanish drug users in treatment in
Dade County, Florida
(1, 2, 3, 4, 5, 6, 7, 8, 9, 10, 11, 12)

095 The children of exile:
Relationships between the acculturation
process and drug use among Cuban youth
(1, 2, 3, 4, 5, 6, 7)

109 The social problem of drug abuse
in ecological perspective
(1, 2, 3, 4, 5, 6, 7, 8, 9, 10, 11)

141 Treated and untreated addicts:
Factors associated with participation
in treatment and cessation of heroin
use
(1, 2, 3, 4, 5, 6, 7, 8, 9, 10, 11, 12,
13, 14, 15, 17, 19, 20, 22, 23, 24, 26)

ELEMENTARY SCHOOL STUDENTS

128 Drug education: Further results
and recommendations
(1, 2, 3, 4, 5, 6, 7, 8, 9)

216 Native American Drug Use: Drug
Abuse Among Indian Adolescents
(10, 11, 12, 13, 14, 15, 16)

EMPLOYEES

005 The working addict
(1, 2, 3, 4, 5, 6, 7, 8, 9, 10, 11, 12)

102 Drug use in the construction trade
(1, 2, 3, 4, 5, 6, 7, 8, 9, 10, 11, 12,
13, 14, 15, 16, 17, 18, 19, 20, 21, 22,
23)

108 The drug problems of industry
(1, 2, 3, 4, 5, 6, 7, 8, 9, 10, 11, 12,
13, 14, 15, 16, 17, 18, 19, 20, 21, 22,
23, 24, 25, 26, 27, 28)

111 Satisfaction with real and
simulated jobs in relation to
personality variables and drug use
(1, 2, 3)

226 Physiological responses to
exercise in chronic cigarette and
marijuana users
(1, 2, 3)

EX-USERS/EX-ADDICTS

108 The drug problems of industry
(26, 27, 28)

114 Vietnam veterans three years after
Vietnam: How our study changed our
view on heroin
(10)

119 Life Styles of Nine American
Non-Users of Drugs (Executive Summary)
(1, 2, 3, 4, 5, 6, 7, 8, 9)

141 Treated and untreated addicts:
Factors associated with participation
in treatment and cessation of heroin
use
(16, 17, 18, 19, 20, 21, 22, 25, 26)

GENERAL POPULATION

021 Predicting heroin and alcohol
usage among young Puerto Ricans
(1, 2, 3, 4, 5, 6, 7, 8, 9, 10, 11, 12,
13, 14, 15, 16)

022 Parental correlates of drug use
among young Puerto Rican adults
(1, 2, 3, 4, 5, 6, 7, 8, 9, 10, 11, 12,
13, 14, 15, 16)

063 Addicts, police, and the
neighborhood social system
(1, 2, 3, 4, 5, 6, 7, 8, 9, 10)

077 Psychotropic drug use by women:
Health, attitudinal, personality and
demographic correlates
(1, 2, 3, 4, 5, 6, 7, 8)

078 Employment status, role
dissatisfaction and the housewife
syndrome
(1, 2, 3, 4, 5)

084 A valium a day keeps the tension
away: Socio-psychological
characteristics of minor tranquilizer
users
(1, 2, 3, 4, 5, 6, 7, 8, 9, 10, 11, 12)

HALLUCINOGEN USERS

227 Role-play theory of psychedelic drug flashbacks
(1, 2, 3, 4, 5)

228 Psychedelic drug flashbacks: Subjective reports and biographical data
(1, 2, 3, 4, 5, 6, 7, 8, 9, 10, 11, 12, 13, 14, 15, 16, 17, 18, 19, 20)

229 Psychedelic drug flashbacks: Attentional deficits?
(1, 2, 3)

231 Ego functioning and acute adverse reactions to psychoactive drugs
(1, 3, 4, 5, 6, 7, 9, 10, 11)

232 Ego mechanisms and marihuana usage
(1, 2, 3, 4, 5, 6, 7, 8)

233 Relation of motives for drug use and psychopathology in the development of acute adverse reactions to psychoactive drugs
(1, 2, 3, 4, 5, 6, 7, 8, 9, 10, 11, 12, 13, 14)

234 Individual differences and setting as determinants of acute adverse reactions to psychoactive drugs
(1, 2, 3, 4, 5, 6, 7, 8, 9, 10)

235 LSD flashbacks and ego functioning
(1, 2, 3, 4, 5, 6, 7, 8, 9, 10)

HIGH SCHOOL STUDENTS

126 Attitude and behavior: A specification of the contingent consistency hypothesis
(1, 2, 3, 4, 5, 6)

127 The relationship between drug education programs in the greater New Haven schools and changes in drug use and drug-related beliefs and perceptions
(1, 2, 3, 4, 5, 6, 7, 8, 9, 10, 11, 12, 13, 14, 15)

129 Perceived paternal relationships, adolescent personality, and female marijuana use
(1, 2, 3, 4)

130 Correlates of adolescent marijuana use as related to age, sex, and ethnicity
(1, 2, 3, 4, 5, 6, 7, 8)

131 Peer, family, and personality domains as related to adolescents' drug behavior
(1, 2, 3, 4, 5, 6)

132 Family socialization and adolescent personality and their association with adolescent use of marijuana
(1, 2, 3, 4)

133 Initiation into adolescent marijuana use
(1, 2, 3, 4, 5, 6, 7, 8, 9, 10)

137 The role of the father in his son's marijuana use
(1, 2, 3, 4)

138 A Study of Teenage Drug Behavior
(1, 2, 3, 4, 5, 6, 7, 8, 9, 10, 11, 12, 13, 14, 15, 16, 17, 23, 24)

139 Sequential patterns of multiple-drug use among high school students
(1, 2, 3, 4, 5, 6, 7, 8, 9, 10, 11)

145 Is coca paste currently a drug of abuse among high school students?
(1, 2, 3, 4)

151 Highlights from Student Drug Use in America 1975-1980
(1, 2, 3, 4, 5, 6, 7, 8, 9, 10, 11, 12, 13, 14, 15, 16, 17, 18, 19, 20, 21, 22, 23, 24, 25, 26, 27, 28)

152 Marijuana Decriminalization: The Impact on Youth, 1975-1980
(1, 2, 3, 4, 5, 6, 7, 8, 9, 10)

153 Drugs and delinquency: A search for causal connections
(1, 2, 3, 4, 5, 6, 7)

154 Inter- and intragenerational influences on adolescent marijuana use
(1, 2, 3, 4, 5, 6, 7, 8, 9, 10)

155 Interpersonal influences on adolescent illegal drug use
(1, 2, 3, 4, 5, 6, 7, 8, 9, 10, 11, 12, 13)

156 Reaching the hard-to-reach: Illicit drug use among high school absentees
(1, 2, 3, 4, 5, 6)

157 On variations in adolescent subcultures
(1, 2, 3, 4, 5, 6, 7)

159 Sequences and stages in patterns of adolescent drug use
(1, 2, 3, 4, 5, 6, 7, 8, 9, 10, 11, 12)

160 Antecedents of adolescent initiation to stages of drug use: A development analysis
(1, 2, 3, 4, 5, 6, 7, 8, 9, 10, 11, 12, 13)

161 The epidemiology of drug use among New York State high school students: Distribution, trends, and change in rates of use
(1, 2, 3, 4, 5, 6, 7, 8, 9, 10, 11, 12, 13, 14, 15, 16, 17, 18, 19, 20, 21)

162 Adolescent involvement in legal and illegal drug use: A multiple classification analysis
(1, 2, 3, 4, 5, 6, 7, 8, 9, 10, 11)

163 Parental and peer influence upon adolescent drug use
(1, 2, 3)

164 A longitudinal study of onset of drinking among high school students
(1, 2, 3, 4, 5, 6, 7, 8, 9, 10, 11, 12, 13, 14)

165 Aspects of adolescent information acquisition about drugs and alcohol topics
(1, 2, 3, 4, 5, 6, 7, 8, 9, 10, 11, 12, 13, 14)

166 Drug use and military plans of high school seniors
(1, 2, 3, 4, 5, 6, 7, 8)

168 Psychological factors and adolescent illicit drug use: Ethnicity and sex differences
(1, 2, 3, 4, 5, 6, 7)

169 Depressive mood and adolescent illicit drug use: A longitudinal analysis
(1, 2, 3, 4, 5, 6, 7, 8, 9)

170 Drug use among public and private secondary school students in Puerto Rico
(1, 2, 3, 4, 5, 6, 7, 8, 9, 10, 11, 12, 13, 14, 15, 16)

172 Sex differences in adolescent drug use: Recent trends
(1, 2, 3, 4, 5, 6, 7, 8, 9, 10, 11, 12, 13, 14, 15, 16, 17, 18, 19, 20, 21, 22, 23, 24)

173 The role of buying and selling in illicit drug use
(1, 2, 3, 4, 5, 6)

174 Patterns of multiple drug use in high school
(1, 2, 3, 4, 5, 6, 7, 8, 9, 10, 11, 12)

175 Teenage drug use: A search for causes and consequenses
(1, 2)

176 Psychological predictors of early use, late use, and nonuse of marijuana among teenage students
(1, 2, 3)

177 Project Community: Therapeutic Explorations with Adolescents
(1, 2, 3, 4, 5, 6, 7, 8)

209 Sex differences in antecedents of substance use among adolescents
(1, 2, 3, 4, 5, 6, 7)

210 Inhalant abuse among the Pueblo tribes of New Mexico
(1, 2, 3, 4, 5, 6, 7, 8, 9, 10, 11, 12, 13, 14)

212 Longitudinal community epidemiological studies of drug use: Early aggressiveness, shyness, and learning problems
(1, 2, 3, 4, 5, 6, 7, 8, 9, 10, 11)

213 Mental health in first grade and teenage drug, alcohol, and cigarette use
(1, 2, 3, 4, 5, 6, 7, 8, 9, 10, 11, 12, 13)

214 Drug use among adolescents of five Southwestern Native American tribes
(1, 2, 3, 4, 5, 6, 7)

215 Drug use among Native American adolescents
(1, 2, 3, 4, 5, 6, 7, 8, 9, 10, 11, 12, 13, 14, 15, 16, 17, 18, 19, 20, 21, 22, 23)

216 Native American Drug Use: Drug Abuse Among Indian Adolescents
(1, 2, 3, 4, 5, 6, 7, 8, 9)

220 Phencyclidine use in high school: Tests of models
(1, 2, 3, 4, 5, 6, 7)

INHALANT USERS

194 A psychiatric emergency room study of inhalant use
(1, 2, 3, 4, 5, 6, 7, 8, 9, 10, 11, 12, 13, 14, 15, 16)

203 Family interaction and acculturation in Mexican-American inhalant users
(1, 2, 3, 4, 5, 6, 7, 8, 9, 10, 11)

JUNIOR HIGH SCHOOL STUDENTS

127 The relationship between drug education programs in the greater New Haven schools and changes in drug use and drug-related beliefs and perceptions
(1, 2, 3, 4, 5, 6, 7, 8, 9, 10, 11, 12, 13, 14, 15)

130 Correlates of adolescent marijuana use as related to age, sex, and ethnicity
(1, 2, 3, 4, 5, 6, 7, 8)

131 Peer, family, and personality domains as related to adolescents' drug behavior
(1, 2, 3, 4, 5, 6)

138 A Study of Teenage Drug Behavior
(1, 2, 3, 4, 5, 6, 7, 8, 9, 10, 11, 12, 13, 14, 15, 16, 18, 19, 20, 21)

146 Adolescent drug use and intentions to use drugs in the future: A concurrent analysis
(1, 2, 3)

147 Beginning adolescent drug use and peer and adult interaction patterns
(1, 2, 3, 4, 5, 6, 7)

148 Longitudinal analysis of the role of peer support, adult models, and peer subcultures in beginning adolescent substance use: An application of setwise canonical correlation methods
(1, 2, 3, 4)

149 Intentions to use drugs among adolescents: A longitudinal analysis
(1, 2, 3, 4)

165 Aspects of adolescent information acquisition about drugs and alcohol topics
(1, 2, 3, 4, 5, 6, 7, 8, 9, 10, 11, 12, 13, 14)

167 Personality, attitudinal, and social correlates of drug use
(1, 2, 3, 4, 5, 6, 7, 8, 9, 10, 11, 12)

172 Sex differences in adolescent drug use: Recent trends
(1, 2, 3, 4, 5, 6, 7, 8, 9, 10, 11, 12, 13, 14, 15, 16, 17, 18, 19, 20, 21, 22, 23, 24)

175 Teenage drug use: A search for causes and consequenses
(1, 2)

MEDICAL PATIENTS

106 Acute drug reactions among the aged: A research note
(1, 2, 3, 4, 5, 6)

120 Effects of criminal justice and medical definitions of a social problem upon the delivery of treatment: The case of drug abuse
(1, 2, 3, 4, 5, 6)

MILITARY PERSONNEL/VETERANS

009 Suicide attempts among drug abusers
(1, 2, 3, 4, 5)

033 Self-concept and substance abuse treatment
(1, 2, 3, 4, 5, 6, 7)

042 Differential response of heroin and nonheroin abusers to inpatient treatment
(1, 2)

043 A comparison of dropouts and disciplinary discharges from a therapeutic community
(1, 2, 3, 4)

044 Self-concept and completion of treatment for heroin and nonheroin drug abusers
(1, 2, 3, 4, 5)

048 Cultural factors and attrition in drug abuse treatment
(1, 2, 3, 4, 5, 6, 7, 8)

104 Antecedents of narcotic use and addiction: A study of 898 Vietnam veterans
(1, 2, 3, 4, 5, 6, 7)

105 Depressive disorders in Vietnam returnees
(1, 2, 3, 4)

112 Drug treatment after return in Vietnam veterans
(1, 2, 3, 4, 5, 6, 7, 8, 9, 10, 11)

113 The interaction of setting and predisposition in explaining novel behavior: Drug initiations before, in, and after Vietnam
(1, 2, 3, 4, 5, 6, 7, 8, 9, 10, 11, 12)

114 Vietnam veterans three years after Vietnam: How our study changed our view on heroin
(1, 2, 3, 4, 5, 6, 7, 8, 9, 10, 11, 12, 13, 14, 15, 16)

115 Polydrug and alcohol use by veterans and nonveterans
(1, 2, 3, 4, 5, 6, 7, 8, 9, 10, 11, 12, 13, 14, 15, 16, 17, 18, 19, 20)

200 Young Men and Drugs--A Nationwide Survey
(7)

223 Behavioral correlates of age at first marijuana use
(1, 2, 3)

NARCOTIC USERS

001 Deaths of persons using methadone in New York City--1971
(1, 2, 3, 4, 5, 6, 7, 8)

006 Street heroin potency and deaths from overdose in San Antonio
(1, 2, 3)

008 Formerly-addicted-now-controlled opiate users
(1, 2, 3, 4, 5, 6, 7)

010 What is an addict? Empirical patterns and concepts of addiction
(1, 2, 3, 4, 5, 6)

020 Narcotic abusers and poverty
(1, 2, 3)

027 The Life Styles of Nine American Opiate Users (Executive Summary)
(1, 2, 3, 4, 5, 6, 7, 8, 9, 10, 11)

041 Religious programs and careers of chronic heroin users
(1, 2, 3, 4, 5, 6)

045 Investigating impact of methadone treatment upon the behavior of New York City street addicts
(1, 2, 3, 4, 5, 6, 7, 8, 9, 10, 11, 12, 13, 14)

053 Methadone, wine and welfare
(1, 2, 3, 4, 5, 6, 7, 8)

059 The impact of drug addiction on criminal earnings
(1, 2, 3, 4, 5, 6, 7, 8)

060 The effect of probation on behavior of chronic opioid drug users
(1, 2, 3, 4, 5)

061 Getting over: Economic alternatives to predatory crime among street drug users
(1, 2, 3, 4, 5, 6, 7, 8, 9, 10, 11)

064 Heroin use and street crime
(1, 2, 3, 4, 5, 6, 7, 8, 9, 10, 11, 12, 13, 14, 15)

065 Youth, drugs, and street crime
(8, 9, 10, 12, 14, 15, 16, 18, 19)

066 The impact of drug use on street crime
(1, 2, 3, 4, 5, 6, 7, 8, 9, 10, 11, 12, 13, 14, 15, 16, 17, 18)

067 The criminal behavior of street heroin and cocaine users
(1, 2, 3, 4, 5, 6, 7, 8, 9)

068 Exploring asymmetries in the hard drug-crime relationship
(1, 2, 3, 4, 5, 6, 7, 8, 9)

070 Crime and drug-using behavior: An areal analysis
(1, 2, 3, 5)

074 Crime and treatment of heroin users
(1, 2, 3)

080 Women, heroin, and property crime
(1, 2, 3, 4, 5, 6, 7, 8)

081 Black women, heroin and crime: Some empirical notes
(1, 2, 3, 4, 5, 6, 7, 8, 9)

101 Mexican-American criminals: A comparative study of heroin using and non-using felons
(1, 2, 3, 4, 5, 6, 7, 8, 9, 10, 11, 12, 13, 14)

114 Vietnam veterans three years after Vietnam: How our study changed our view on heroin
(12)

140 Experimental heroin users: An epidemiologic and psychosocial approach
(1, 3, 4, 7, 8, 9, 10, 11, 12, 13, 14, 15, 16, 17, 18, 19, 20)

143 Personality development and adolescent heroin use
(1, 2, 3, 4, 5, 6, 7, 8, 9, 10, 11, 12, 13, 14, 15, 16)

144 Family life and levels of involvement in an adolescent heroin epidemic
(1, 2, 3, 4, 5, 6, 7, 8, 9, 10, 11)

204 What happened in Harlem? Analysis of a decline in heroin use among a generation unit of urban black youth
(1, 2, 3, 4, 5, 6, 7, 8, 9, 10, 11, 12)

205 Health and drug behavior: A study of urban black adolescents
(1, 2, 3, 4, 5, 6, 7, 8, 9, 10, 11, 12)

POLYDRUG USERS

065 Youth, drugs, and street crime
(8, 11, 13, 14, 15, 17, 18, 19)

066 The impact of drug use on street crime
(13, 14, 15, 16)

095 The children of exile: Relationships between the acculturation process and drug use among Cuban youth
(1, 2, 3, 4, 5, 6, 7)

096 Drug use among Cuban exiles in Miami, Florida: Cultural antecedents and processes
(1, 2, 3, 4, 5)

103 Three types of extreme drug users identified by a replicated cluster analysis
(1, 2, 3, 4, 5)

194 A psychiatric emergency room study of inhalant use
(1, 2, 3, 4, 5, 6, 7, 8, 9, 10, 11, 12, 13, 14, 15, 16)

222 Sea-Tac and PCP
(1, 2, 3, 4, 5, 6, 7, 8)

PRISONERS

002 Some research notes on the sexual life of the addict
(1, 2, 3, 4, 5)

003 Junkie work, "hustles" and social status among heroin addicts
(1, 2, 3, 4, 5, 6, 7, 8, 9, 10, 11, 12, 13, 14, 15)

069 The relationship between type of drug use and arrest charge in an arrested population
(1, 2, 3, 4, 5)

089 Sex roles among deviants: The woman addict
(1, 2, 3, 4, 5, 6, 7, 8, 9, 10)

PROBATIONERS

060 The effect of probation on behavior of chronic opioid drug users
(1, 2, 3, 4, 5)

138 A Study of Teenage Drug Behavior
(22)

PROSTITUTES

082 Prostitution and addiction: An interdisciplinary approach
(1, 2, 3, 4, 5, 6, 7, 8, 9, 10)

083 The relationship between female criminality and drug abuse
(1, 2, 3, 4, 5, 6, 7, 8, 9, 10, 11, 12, 13, 14, 15, 16)

091 Criminal involvement of female offenders: Psychological characteristics among four groups
(1, 2, 3, 4, 5, 6, 7)

PSYCHOTHERAPEUTIC DRUG USERS

079 Cuban women, sex role conflicts and the use of prescription drugs
(1, 2, 3, 4, 5, 6)

RECREATIONAL USERS/EXPERIMENTERS

070 Crime and drug-using behavior: An areal analysis
(4)

140 Experimental heroin users: An epidemiologic and psychosocial approach
(1, 2, 4, 5, 6, 7, 8, 9, 10, 11, 12, 13, 14, 15, 16, 17, 18, 19, 20)

142 Addicts and experimenters: Dynamics of involvement in an adolescent heroin epidemic
(2, 3, 5, 8, 9, 10, 11, 14, 15, 16, 18, 19)

SCHOOL DROPOUTS

171 A report on the dropout study
(1, 2, 3, 4, 5, 6, 7, 8, 9, 10, 11, 12, 13, 14, 15, 16)

STIMULANT USERS

107 Qat use in North Yemen and the problem of addiction: A study in medical anthropology
(1, 2, 3, 4, 5, 6, 7, 8, 9, 10, 11, 12, 13, 14, 15, 16, 17, 18, 19, 20)

116 The Life Styles of Nine American Amphetamine Users (Executive Summary)
(1, 2, 3, 4, 5, 6, 7, 8, 9, 10, 11)

120 Effects of criminal justice and
medical definitions of a social problem
upon the delivery of treatment: The
case of drug abuse
(1, 2, 3, 4, 5, 6)

SEX INDEX

171 A report on the dropout study
(1, 3, 8)

212 Longitudinal community
epidemiological studies of drug use:
Early aggressiveness, shyness, and
learning problems
(4)

213 Mental health in first grade and
teenage drug, alcohol, and cigarette
use
(3, 13)

MALE

004 The veridicality of addicts'
self-reports in social research
(1, 2, 3, 4, 5, 6, 7)

009 Suicide attempts among drug
abusers
(1, 2, 3, 4, 5)

010 What is an addict? Empirical
patterns and concepts of addiction
(1, 2, 3, 4, 5, 6)

011 Family ties of heroin addicts
(1, 2, 3, 4, 5, 6)

012 New light on the maturing out
hypothesis in opioid dependence
(1, 2, 3, 4, 5, 6, 7)

013 Residence relocation inhibits
opioid dependence
(1, 2, 3, 4, 5, 6, 7, 8, 9, 10, 11, 12)

014 An analysis of work histories,
earnings, and receipts of benefits
among a sample of a community-wide
population of narcotic addicts
(1, 2, 3, 4, 5, 6)

015 Studying addicts over time:
Methodology and preliminary findings
(1, 2, 3, 4, 5, 6, 7, 8, 9, 10)

016 Addict Careers: I. A new
typology
(1, 2, 3, 4, 5, 6, 7, 8, 9, 10)

017 Addict careers: II. The first
ten years
(1, 2, 3, 4, 5, 6, 7, 8, 9, 10, 11, 12,
13)

018 Addict careers: III. Trends
across time
(1, 2, 3, 4, 5, 6, 7, 8, 9, 10, 11)

019 Trends in the age of onset of
narcotic addiction
(1, 2, 3, 4, 5, 6, 7, 8)

022 Parental correlates of drug use
among young Puerto Rican adults
(1, 2, 3, 4, 5, 6, 7, 12, 13, 14, 15)

025 Is there a relationship between
astrology and addiction? A
reexamination
(1)

026 The structure of depression in
heroin addicts
(1, 2, 3, 4, 5)

027 The Life Styles of Nine American
Opiate Users (Executive Summary)
(1, 2, 3, 4, 5, 6, 7, 8, 9, 10, 11)

028 Correlates of self-reported and
clinically assessed depression in male
heroin addicts
(1, 2, 3)

030 The effect of parole on methadone
patient behavior
(1, 2, 3, 4, 5, 6, 7, 8, 9, 10, 11, 12,
13)

032 Therapeutic communities vs
methadone maintenance: A prospective
controlled study of narcotic addiction
treatment: Design and one-year
follow-up
(1, 2, 3, 4, 5, 6, 7, 8, 9, 10, 11, 12,
13)

033 Self-concept and substance abuse
treatment
(1, 2, 3, 4, 5, 6, 7)

034 Phoenix House: Psychopathological
signs among male and female drug-free
residents
(11)

181 Smoking and health, marijuana and use of other illicit drugs: Causal relationships
(1, 2, 3, 4, 5, 6)

182 Changing patterns of drug use among university males
(1, 2, 3, 4, 5, 6, 7, 8, 9, 10, 11, 12, 13, 14, 15, 16, 17, 18)

183 Survey of students and drugs at the University of Notre Dame: An overview
(1, 2, 3, 4, 5, 6, 7, 8, 9, 10, 11, 12, 13, 14, 15, 16, 17, 18, 19, 20, 21, 22, 23)

184 Dimensions of marijuana use in a midwest Catholic university: Subcultural considerations
(1, 2, 3, 4, 5, 6, 7, 8, 9, 10, 11, 12, 13, 14, 15)

185 The variation of a midwest Catholic university's drug use pattern from other Catholic university findings: Why?
(1, 2, 3, 4, 5, 6)

193 A longitudinal study of the personality correlates of marijuana use
(1, 2, 3, 4, 5, 6, 7)

196 Drug use, academic performance, and career indecision: Longitudinal data in search of a model
(1, 2, 3, 4, 5, 6, 7, 8)

197 The amotivational syndrome and the college student
(1, 2, 3, 4, 5, 6, 7, 8, 9, 10, 11, 12, 13)

198 Cigarette smoking as a precursor of illicit drug use
(1, 2, 3, 4, 5, 6, 7, 8, 9, 10)

199 Determinants of early marihuana use
(1, 2, 3, 4, 5, 6, 7, 8, 9, 10, 11, 12, 13)

200 Young Men and Drugs--A Nationwide Survey
(1, 2, 3, 4, 5, 6, 7, 8, 9, 10, 11)

203 Family interaction and acculturation in Mexican-American inhalant users
(1, 2, 3, 4, 5, 6, 7, 8, 9, 10, 11)

208 Youngsters Experimenting with Drugs
(1, 2, 3, 4, 5, 6, 7, 8, 9, 10, 11, 12, 13, 14, 15, 16, 17, 18, 19)

212 Longitudinal community epidemiological studies of drug use: Early aggressiveness, shyness, and learning problems
(5)

213 Mental health in first grade and teenage drug, alcohol, and cigarette use
(2, 9, 10, 11, 12)

217 Cannabis and work in Jamaica: A refutation of the amotivational syndrome
(1, 2, 3, 4, 5, 6, 7, 8, 9)

219 Hypnotic susceptibility during cannabis intoxication
(1)

223 Behavioral correlates of age at first marijuana use
(1, 2, 3)

226 Physiological responses to exercise in chronic cigarette and marijuana users
(1, 2, 3)

231 Ego functioning and acute adverse reactions to psychoactive drugs
(1, 2, 3, 4, 5, 6, 7, 8, 9, 10, 11)

232 Ego mechanisms and marihuana usage
(1, 2, 3, 4, 5, 6, 7, 8)

233 Relation of motives for drug use and psychopathology in the development of acute adverse reactions to psychoactive drugs
(1, 2, 3, 4, 5, 6, 7, 8, 9, 10, 11, 12, 13, 14)

234 Individual differences and setting
as determinants of acute adverse
reactions to psychoactive drugs
(1, 2, 3, 4, 5, 6, 7, 8, 9, 10, 11, 12,
13)

235 LSD flashbacks and ego functioning
(1, 2, 3, 4, 5, 6, 7, 8, 9, 10)

236 Does marijuana enhance
experimentally induced anxiety?
(1, 2)

237 The effect of marijuana on small
group process
(1, 2, 3, 4, 5)

238 Marijuana and hostility in a
small-group setting
(1, 2, 3, 4, 5, 6)

MALE AND FEMALE

001 Deaths of persons using methadone
in New York City--1971
(1, 2, 3, 4, 5, 6, 7, 8)

002 Some research notes on the sexual
life of the addict
(1, 2, 3, 4, 5)

003 Junkie work, "hustles" and social
status among heroin addicts
(1, 2, 3, 4, 5, 6, 7, 8, 9, 10, 11, 12,
13, 14, 15)

005 The working addict
(1, 2, 3, 4, 5, 6, 7, 8, 9, 10, 11, 12)

007 Suicidal behavior among heroin
addicts: A brief report
(1, 2)

008 Formerly-addicted-now-controlled
opiate users
(1, 2, 3, 4, 5, 6, 7)

020 Narcotic abusers and poverty
(1, 2, 3)

021 Predicting heroin and alcohol
usage among young Puerto Ricans
(1, 2, 3, 4, 5, 6, 7, 8, 9, 10, 11, 12,
13, 14, 15, 16)

023 Narcotic addicts, multiple drug
abuse and psychological distress
(1, 2, 3, 4, 5, 6, 7, 8, 9)

024 Ecological studies of narcotic
addiction
(1, 2, 3, 4, 5)

029 Types of psychopathology displayed
by heroin addicts
(1, 2)

034 Phoenix House: Psychopathological
signs among male and female drug-free
residents
(1, 2, 3, 4, 5, 6, 7, 8, 9, 10)

035 Therapeutic community dropouts:
Psychological changes 2 years after
treatment
(1, 2, 3)

037 Phoenix house: Criminal activity
of dropouts
(1, 2, 3, 4, 5)

038 Male and female drug abusers:
Social and psychological status 2 years
after treatment in a therapeutic
community
(1, 2, 3, 4, 5, 6, 7, 8, 9, 10, 11, 12,
13, 14, 15)

039 Phoenix House: Changes in
psychopathological signs of resident
drug addicts
(1, 2, 3, 4)

040 The therapeutic community:
Success and improvement rates 5 years
after treatment
(1, 2, 3, 4, 5, 6, 7, 8, 9, 10, 11, 12,
13, 14, 15, 16)

045 Investigating impact of methadone
treatment upon the behavior of New York
City street addicts
(1, 2, 3, 4, 5, 6, 7, 8, 9, 10, 11, 12,
13, 14)

046 The magic fix: A critical
analysis of methadone maintenance
treatment
(1, 2, 3, 4, 5, 6, 7)

049 Shutting off methadone: Costs and benefits
(1, 2, 3, 4, 5, 6, 7, 8, 9, 10, 11, 12)

051 Outpatient methadone withdrawal for heroin dependence
(1, 2, 3)

052 Notes on American medical history: A follow-up study of the New Haven morphine maintenance clinic of 1920
(1, 2, 3, 4, 5, 6, 7, 8, 9, 10, 11, 12)

053 Methadone, wine and welfare
(1, 2, 3, 4, 5, 6, 7, 8)

054 Entry into methadone maintenance programs: A follow-up study of New York City heroin users detoxified in 1961-1963
(1, 2, 3, 4, 5, 6, 7, 8, 9, 10, 11)

056 The therapeutic community: Multivariate prediction of retention
(1, 2, 3, 4, 5, 6, 7, 8)

059 The impact of drug addiction on criminal earnings
(1, 2, 3, 4, 5, 6, 7, 8)

061 Getting over: Economic alternatives to predatory crime among street drug users
(1, 2, 3, 4, 5, 6, 7, 8, 9, 10, 11)

062 Daily criminal activities of street drug users: Preliminary findings
(1, 2, 3, 4, 5, 6, 7)

063 Addicts, police, and the neighborhood social system
(1, 2, 3, 4, 5, 6, 7, 8, 9, 10)

064 Heroin use and street crime
(1, 2, 3, 4, 5, 6, 7, 8, 15)

065 Youth, drugs, and street crime
(1, 2, 3, 4, 5, 6, 7, 8, 9, 10, 11, 12, 13, 14, 15, 16, 17, 18, 19)

066 The impact of drug use on street crime
(1, 2, 3, 4, 5, 6, 7, 8, 9, 10, 11, 12, 13, 14, 15, 16, 17, 18)

067 The criminal behavior of street heroin and cocaine users
(1, 2, 3, 4, 5, 6, 7, 8, 9)

068 Exploring asymmetries in the hard drug-crime relationship
(1, 2, 3, 4, 5, 6, 7, 8, 9)

070 Crime and drug-using behavior: An areal analysis
(1, 2, 3, 4, 5)

072 Outcome of the California Civil Addict commitments: 1961-1972
(1, 2, 3, 4, 5, 6, 7, 8, 9, 10, 11, 12, 13, 14, 15, 16)

076 Are female drug abusers more deviant?
(1, 2, 3, 4, 5)

089 Sex roles among deviants: The woman addict
(1, 4, 5, 6, 7)

093 Ethnic differences in factors related to drug use
(1, 2, 3, 4, 5, 6, 7, 8, 9)

094 A comparison of Spanish and non-Spanish drug users in treatment in Dade County, Florida
(1, 2, 3, 4, 5, 6, 7, 8, 9, 10, 11, 12)

100 Father's alcoholism and children's outcomes
(1, 2, 3, 4, 5)

101 Mexican-American criminals: A comparative study of heroin using and non-using felons
(1, 3, 4, 5, 6, 7, 8, 9, 10, 11, 12, 13, 14)

103 Three types of extreme drug users identified by a replicated cluster analysis
(1, 2, 3, 4, 5)

106 Acute drug reactions among the aged: A research note
(1, 2, 3, 4, 5, 6)

167 Personality, attitudinal, and social correlates of drug use
(1, 2, 3, 4, 5, 6, 7, 8, 9, 10, 11, 12)

168 Psychological factors and adolescent illicit drug use: Ethnicity and sex differences
(1, 2, 3, 4, 5)

169 Depressive mood and adolescent illicit drug use: A longitudinal analysis
(1, 2, 3, 4, 5, 6, 7, 8, 9)

170 Drug use among public and private secondary school students in Puerto Rico
(1, 2, 3, 4, 5, 6, 8, 9, 11, 13, 14, 15, 16)

171 A report on the dropout study
(5, 6, 10, 13, 14, 16)

172 Sex differences in adolescent drug use: Recent trends
(1, 2, 3, 4, 5, 6, 7, 8, 9, 10, 11, 12, 13, 14, 15, 16, 17, 18, 19, 20, 21, 22, 23, 24)

173 The role of buying and selling in illicit drug use
(1, 2, 3, 4, 5, 6)

174 Patterns of multiple drug use in high school
(1, 2, 3, 4, 5, 6, 7, 8, 9, 10, 11, 12)

175 Teenage drug use: A search for causes and consequenses
(1, 2)

176 Psychological predictors of early use, late use, and nonuse of marijuana among teenage students
(1, 2, 3)

177 Project Community: Therapeutic Explorations with Adolescents
(1, 2, 3, 4, 5, 6, 7, 8)

178 The relationship of personality structure to patterns of adolescent substance use
(1, 2, 3, 4, 5)

186 Getting high in high school: The meaning of adolescent drug usage
(1, 2, 3, 4, 5, 6, 7, 8, 9, 10, 11)

187 Motivations for psychoactive drug use among students
(1, 2, 3, 4)

188 Students' evaluations of their psychoactive drug use
(1, 2, 3, 4, 5, 6)

189 Whither the epidemic? Psychoactive drug-use career patterns of college students
(1, 2, 3, 4, 5, 6, 7, 8)

190 Judging the shape of things to come: Lessons learned from comparisons of student drug users in 1968 and 1970
(1, 2, 3, 4, 5, 6, 7, 8, 9, 10)

191 Personality characteristics of students who became drug users: An MMPI study of an avant-garde
(1, 2, 3, 4, 5, 6, 7)

192 Organization of needs in male and female drug and alcohol users
(1, 2, 3, 4)

194 A psychiatric emergency room study of inhalant use
(1, 2, 3, 4, 5, 6, 7, 8, 9, 10, 11, 12, 13, 14, 15, 16)

195 Psychoactive drugs: A course evaluation
(1, 2, 3, 4)

201 Prediction of college drug use from personality and inner experience
(1, 2, 3)

202 Reasons for drug and alcohol use by college students
(1, 2, 3, 4, 5, 6, 7, 8)

204 What happened in Harlem? Analysis of a decline in heroin use among a generation unit of urban black youth
(1, 2, 3, 4, 5, 6, 7, 8, 9, 10, 11, 12)

069 The relationship between type of
drug use and arrest charge in an
arrested population
(1, 2, 3, 4, 5)

074 Crime and treatment of heroin
users
(1, 2, 3)

086 Sex differences in the content and
style of medical advertisements
(1, 2, 3, 4, 5, 6)

108 The drug problems of industry
(1, 2, 3, 4, 5, 6, 7, 8, 9, 10, 11, 12,
13, 14, 15, 16, 17, 18, 19, 20, 21, 22,
23, 24, 25, 26, 27, 28)

AGE INDEX

147 Beginning adolescent drug use and
peer and adult interaction patterns
(1, 2, 3, 4, 5, 6, 7)

148 Longitudinal analysis of the role
of peer support, adult models, and peer
subcultures in beginning adolescent
substance use: An application of
setwise canonical correlation methods
(1, 2, 3, 4)

149 Intentions to use drugs among
adolescents: A longitudinal analysis
(1, 2, 3, 4)

150 Drugs and the Class of '78:
Behaviors, Attitudes, and Recent
National Trends
(1, 2, 3, 4, 5, 6, 7, 8, 9, 10, 11, 12,
13, 14, 15, 16, 17, 18, 19, 20, 21, 22,
23, 24)

151 Highlights from Student Drug Use
in America 1975-1980
(1, 2, 3, 4, 5, 6, 7, 8, 9, 10, 11, 12,
13, 14, 15, 16, 17, 18, 19, 20, 21, 22,
23, 24, 25, 26, 27, 28)

152 Marijuana Decriminalization: The
Impact on Youth, 1975-1980
(1, 2, 3, 4, 5, 6, 7, 8, 9, 10)

153 Drugs and delinquency: A search
for causal connections
(1, 2, 3, 4, 5, 6, 7)

154 Inter- and intragenerational
influences on adolescent marijuana use
(1, 2, 3, 4, 5, 6, 7, 8, 9, 10)

155 Interpersonal influences on
adolescent illegal drug use
(1, 2, 3, 4, 5, 6, 7, 8, 9, 10, 11, 12,
13)

156 Reaching the hard-to-reach:
Illicit drug use among high school
absentees
(1, 2, 3, 4, 5, 6)

157 On variations in adolescent
subcultures
(1, 2, 3, 4, 5, 6, 7)

158 The epidemiology of adolescent
drug use in France and Israel
(1, 2, 3, 4, 5, 6, 7, 8, 9, 10, 11, 12,
13, 14, 15)

159 Sequences and stages in patterns
of adolescent drug use
(1, 2, 3, 4, 5, 6, 7, 8, 9, 10, 11, 12)

160 Antecedents of adolescent
initiation to stages of drug use: A
development analysis
(1, 2, 3, 4, 5, 6, 7, 8, 9, 10, 11, 12,
13)

161 The epidemiology of drug use among
New York State high school students:
Distribution, trends, and change in
rates of use
(1, 2, 3, 4, 5, 6, 7, 8, 9, 10, 11, 12,
13, 14, 15, 16, 17, 18, 19, 20, 21)

162 Adolescent involvement in legal
and illegal drug use: A multiple
classification analysis
(1, 2, 3, 4, 5, 6, 7, 8, 9, 10, 11)

163 Parental and peer influence upon
adolescent drug use
(1, 2, 3)

164 A longitudinal study of onset of
drinking among high school students
(1, 2, 3, 4, 5, 6, 7, 8, 9, 10, 11, 12,
13, 14)

165 Aspects of adolescent information
acquisition about drugs and alcohol
topics
(1, 2, 3, 4, 5, 6, 7, 8, 9, 10, 11, 12,
13, 14)

166 Drug use and military plans of
high school seniors
(1, 2, 3, 4, 5, 6, 7, 8)

167 Personality, attitudinal, and
social correlates of drug use
(1, 2, 3, 4, 5, 6, 7, 8, 9, 10, 11, 12)

168 Psychological factors and
adolescent illicit drug use: Ethnicity
and sex differences
(1, 2, 3, 4, 5, 6, 7)

153 Drugs and delinquency: A search
for causal connections
(1, 2, 3, 4, 5, 6, 7)

167 Personality, attitudinal, and
social correlates of drug use
(1, 2, 3, 4, 5, 6, 7, 8, 9, 10, 11, 12)

179 Shacking up: Cohabitation in the
1970s
(1, 2, 3, 4)

180 Young Men and Drugs in Manhattan:
A Causal Analysis
(1, 2, 3, 4, 5, 6, 7, 8, 9, 10, 11, 12,
13, 14, 15, 16, 17, 18, 19, 20)

181 Smoking and health, marijuana and
use of other illicit drugs: Causal
relationships
(1, 2, 3, 4, 5, 6)

194 A psychiatric emergency room study
of inhalant use
(1, 2, 3, 4, 5, 6, 7, 8, 9, 10, 11, 12,
13, 14, 15, 16)

198 Cigarette smoking as a precursor
of illicit drug use
(1, 2, 3, 4, 5, 6, 7, 8, 9, 10)

199 Determinants of early marihuana
use
(1, 2, 3, 4, 5, 6, 7, 8, 9, 10, 11, 12,
13)

200 Young Men and Drugs--A Nationwide
Survey
(1, 2, 3, 4, 5, 6, 7, 8, 9, 10, 11)

204 What happened in Harlem? Analysis
of a decline in heroin use among a
generation unit of urban black youth
(1, 2, 3, 4, 5, 6, 7, 8, 9, 10, 11, 12)

206 Black youths and drug-use behavior
(1, 2, 3, 4, 5, 6, 7, 8, 9, 10, 11, 12,
13, 14, 15, 16, 17, 18, 19, 20, 21, 22,
23, 24, 25, 26, 27, 28, 29)

207 Patterns of drug involvement:
Developmental and secular influences on
age at initiation
(1, 2, 3, 4, 5, 6, 7, 8, 9, 10)

218 Ethnicity and patterning in South
African drug use
(3, 4, 5, 6, 7, 8, 9, 10, 11, 12, 13,
14, 16, 17)

219 Hypnotic susceptibility during
cannabis intoxication
(1)

225 Personaltiy correlates of
hallucinogen use
(1, 2, 3, 4, 5, 6, 7, 8)

233 Relation of motives for drug use
and psychopathology in the development
of acute adverse reactions to
psychoactive drugs
(1, 2, 3, 4, 5, 6, 7, 8, 9, 10, 11, 12,
13, 14)

237 The effect of marijuana on small
group process
(1, 2, 3, 4, 5)

238 Marijuana and hostility in a
small-group setting
(1, 2, 3, 4, 5, 6)

ADULT I (23-40)

002 Some research notes on the sexual
life of the addict
(1, 2, 3, 4, 5)

003 Junkie work, "hustles" and social
status among heroin addicts
(1, 2, 3, 4, 5, 6, 7, 8, 9, 10, 11, 12,
13, 14, 15)

005 The working addict
(1, 2, 3, 4, 5, 6, 7, 8, 9, 10, 11, 12)

007 Suicidal behavior among heroin
addicts: A brief report
(1, 2)

008 Formerly-addicted-now-controlled
opiate users
(1, 2, 3, 4, 5, 6, 7)

009 Suicide attempts among drug
abusers
(1, 2, 3, 4, 5)

125 Opium and heroin addicts in Laos:
II. A study of matched pairs
(1, 2, 3, 4, 5, 6, 7)

179 Shacking up: Cohabitation in the
1970s
(1, 2, 3, 4)

180 Young Men and Drugs in Manhattan:
A Causal Analysis
(1, 2, 3, 4, 5, 6, 7, 8, 9, 10, 11, 12,
13, 14, 15, 16, 17, 18, 19, 20)

181 Smoking and health, marijuana and
use of other illicit drugs: Causal
relationships
(1, 2, 3, 4, 5, 6)

198 Cigarette smoking as a precursor
of illicit drug use
(1, 2, 3, 4, 5, 6, 7, 8, 9, 10)

199 Determinants of early marihuana
use
(1, 2, 3, 4, 5, 6, 7, 8, 9, 10, 11, 12,
13)

200 Young Men and Drugs--A Nationwide
Survey
(1, 2, 3, 4, 5, 6, 7, 8, 9, 10, 11)

218 Ethnicity and patterning in South
African drug use
(3, 4, 5, 6, 7, 8, 9, 10, 11, 12, 13,
14, 16, 17, 18, 19)

219 Hypnotic susceptibility during
cannabis intoxication
(1)

225 Personaltiy correlates of
hallucinogen use
(1, 2, 3, 4, 5, 6, 7, 8)

226 Physiological responses to
exercise in chronic cigarette and
marijuana users
(1, 2, 3)

230 Deterrence as social control: The
legal and extralegal production of
conformity
(1, 2, 3, 4, 5, 6, 7)

236 Does marijuana enhance
experimentally induced anxiety?
(1, 2)

237 The effect of marijuana on small
group process
(1, 2, 3, 4, 5)

238 Marijuana and hostility in a
small-group setting
(1, 2, 3, 4, 5, 6)

ADULT II (41-65)

025 Is there a relationship between
astrology and addiction? A
reexamination
(1)

027 The Life Styles of Nine American
Opiate Users (Executive Summary)
(1, 2, 3, 4, 5, 6, 7, 8, 9, 10, 11)

033 Self-concept and substance abuse
treatment
(1, 2, 3, 4, 5, 6, 7)

060 The effect of probation on
behavior of chronic opioid drug users
(1, 2, 3, 4, 5)

118 Life Styles of Nine American
Barbiturate/Sedative-Hypnotic Drug
Users (Executive Summary)
(1, 2, 3, 4, 5, 6, 7, 8, 9, 10, 11, 12,
13, 14, 15, 16, 17)

121 Narcotic addiction in two Asian
cultures: A comparison and analysis
(1, 2, 3)

124 Opium and heroin addicts in Laos:
I. A comparative study
(1, 2, 3, 4, 5, 6, 7, 8, 9, 10, 11, 12)

152 Marijuana Decriminalization: The
Impact on Youth, 1975-1980
(1, 2, 3, 4, 5, 6, 7, 8, 9, 10)

230 Deterrence as social control: The
legal and extralegal production of
conformity
(1, 2, 3, 4, 5, 6, 7)

MULTIPLE AGE GROUPS

020 Narcotic abusers and poverty
(1, 2, 3)

037 Phoenix house: Criminal activity
of dropouts
(1, 2, 3, 4, 5)

047 Attrition of older alcoholics from
treatment
(1, 2, 3, 4, 5, 6, 7, 8, 9, 10, 11)

052 Notes on American medical history:
A follow-up study of the New Haven
morphine maintenance clinic of 1920
(1, 2, 3, 4, 5, 6, 7, 8, 9, 10, 11, 12)

063 Addicts, police, and the
neighborhood social system
(1, 2, 3, 4, 5, 6, 7, 8, 9, 10)

070 Crime and drug-using behavior: An
areal analysis
(1, 2, 3, 4, 5)

077 Psychotropic drug use by women:
Health, attitudinal, personality and
demographic correlates
(1, 2, 3, 4, 5, 6, 7, 8)

078 Employment status, role
dissatisfaction and the housewife
syndrome
(1, 2, 3, 4, 5)

083 The relationship between female
criminality and drug abuse
(1, 2, 3, 4, 5, 6, 7, 8, 9, 10, 11, 12,
13, 14, 15, 16)

084 A valium a day keeps the tension
away: Socio-psychological
characteristics of minor tranquilizer
users
(1, 2, 3, 4, 5, 6, 7, 8, 9, 10, 11, 12)

085 Drug usage as an index of stress
among women
(1, 2, 3, 4, 5, 6, 7, 8, 9, 10, 11, 12,
13, 14)

091 Criminal involvement of female
offenders: Psychological
characteristics among four groups
(1, 2, 3, 4, 5, 6, 7)

093 Ethnic differences in factors
related to drug use
(1, 2, 3, 4, 5, 6, 7, 8, 9)

096 Drug use among Cuban exiles in
Miami, Florida: Cultural antecedents
and processes
(1, 2, 3, 4, 5)

101 Mexican-American criminals: A
comparative study of heroin using and
non-using felons
(1, 2, 3, 4, 5, 6, 7, 8, 9, 10, 11, 12,
13, 14)

103 Three types of extreme drug users
identified by a replicated cluster
analysis
(1, 2, 3, 4, 5)

105 Depressive disorders in Vietnam
returnees
(1, 2, 3, 4)

106 Acute drug reactions among the
aged: A research note
(1, 2, 3, 4, 5, 6)

109 The social problem of drug abuse
in ecological perspective
(1, 2, 3, 4, 5, 6, 7, 8, 9, 10, 11)

117 Cocaine Users: A Representative
Case Approach
(1, 2, 3, 4, 5, 6, 7, 8, 9, 10, 11, 12,
13, 14, 15, 16, 17, 18, 19)

120 Effects of criminal justice and
medical definitions of a social problem
upon the delivery of treatment: The
case of drug abuse
(1, 2, 3, 4, 5, 6)

123 A heroin "epidemic" in Asia
(1, 2, 3, 4, 5, 6, 7, 8, 9, 10)

221 Behavioral correlates and
comparisons of current marijuana users,
quitters and evasives
(1, 2, 3, 4, 5, 6, 7, 8)

222 Sea-Tac and PCP
(1, 2, 3, 4, 5, 6, 7, 8)

224 Arrest probabilities for marijuana users as indicators of selective law enforcement
(1, 2, 3, 4, 5, 6, 7, 8, 9, 10, 11)

AGE GROUP COMPARISON

024 Ecological studies of narcotic addiction
(1, 2, 3, 4, 5)

218 Ethnicity and patterning in South African drug use
(1, 2)

AGE UNSPECIFIED

001 Deaths of persons using methadone in New York City--1971
(1, 2, 3, 4, 5, 6, 7, 8)

004 The veridicality of addicts' self-reports in social research
(1, 2, 3, 4, 5, 6, 7)

006 Street heroin potency and deaths from overdose in San Antonio
(1, 2, 3)

010 What is an addict? Empirical patterns and concepts of addiction
(1, 2, 3, 4, 5, 6)

014 An analysis of work histories, earnings, and receipts of benefits among a sample of a community-wide population of narcotic addicts
(1, 2, 3, 4, 5, 6)

015 Studying addicts over time: Methodology and preliminary findings
(1, 2, 3, 4, 5, 6, 7, 8, 9, 10)

016 Addict Careers: I. A new typology
(1, 2, 3, 4, 5, 6, 7, 8, 9, 10)

017 Addict careers: II. The first ten years
(1, 2, 3, 4, 5, 6, 7, 8, 9, 10, 11, 12, 13)

018 Addict careers: III. Trends across time
(1, 2, 3, 4, 5, 6, 7, 8, 9, 10, 11)

019 Trends in the age of onset of narcotic addiction
(1, 2, 3, 4, 5, 6, 7, 8)

023 Narcotic addicts, multiple drug abuse and psychological distress
(1, 2, 3, 4, 5, 6, 7, 8, 9)

031 What we need to know
(1, 2, 3, 4)

035 Therapeutic community dropouts: Psychological changes 2 years after treatment
(1, 2, 3)

045 Investigating impact of methadone treatment upon the behavior of New York City street addicts
(1, 2, 3, 4, 5, 6, 7, 8, 9, 10, 11, 12, 13, 14)

046 The magic fix: A critical analysis of methadone maintenance treatment
(1, 2, 3, 4, 5, 6, 7)

050 Long-term follow-up of clients of high- and low-dose methadone programs
(1, 2, 3, 4, 5, 6, 7, 8, 9, 10, 11, 12)

054 Entry into methadone maintenance programs: A follow-up study of New York City heroin users detoxified in 1961-1963
(1, 2, 3, 4, 5, 6, 7, 8, 9, 10, 11)

056 The therapeutic community: Multivariate prediction of retention
(1, 2, 3, 4, 5, 6, 7, 8)

059 The impact of drug addiction on criminal earnings
(1, 2, 3, 4, 5, 6, 7, 8)

069 The relationship between type of drug use and arrest charge in an arrested population
(1, 2, 3, 4, 5)

074 Crime and treatment of heroin
users
(1, 2, 3)

075 A preliminary report on crime and
addiction within a community-wide
population of narcotic addicts
(1, 2, 3, 4, 5, 6, 7, 8)

076 Are female drug abusers more
deviant?
(1, 2, 3, 4, 5)

079 Cuban women, sex role conflicts
and the use of prescription drugs
(1, 2, 3, 4, 5, 6)

082 Prostitution and addiction: An
interdisciplinary approach
(1, 2, 3, 4, 5, 6, 7, 8, 9, 10)

086 Sex differences in the content and
style of medical advertisements
(1, 2, 3, 4, 5, 6)

087 Becoming addicted: The woman
addict
(1, 2, 3, 4, 5, 6, 7, 8, 9, 10, 11, 12,
13, 14)

088 Difficulties in taking care of
business: Women addicts as mothers
(1, 2, 3, 4, 5, 6, 7, 8, 9)

090 Women addicts' experience of the
heroin world: Risk, chaos, and
inundation
(1, 2, 3, 4, 5, 6, 7, 8, 9, 10, 11, 12)

094 A comparison of Spanish and
non-Spanish drug users in treatment in
Dade County, Florida
(1, 2, 3, 4, 5, 6, 7, 8, 9, 10, 11, 12)

102 Drug use in the construction trade
(1, 2, 3, 4, 5, 6, 7, 8, 9, 10, 11, 12,
13, 14, 15, 16, 17, 18, 19, 20, 21, 22,
23)

104 Antecedents of narcotic use and
addiction: A study of 898 Vietnam
veterans
(1, 2, 3, 4, 5, 6, 7)

107 Qat use in North Yemen and the
problem of addiction: A study in
medical anthropology
(1, 2, 3, 4, 5, 6, 7, 8, 9, 10, 11, 12,
13, 14, 15, 16, 17, 18, 19, 20)

108 The drug problems of industry
(1, 2, 3, 4, 5, 6, 7, 8, 9, 10, 11, 12,
13, 14, 15, 16, 17, 18, 19, 20, 21, 22,
23, 24, 25, 26, 27, 28)

110 What everybody in Cuzco knows
about coca
(1, 2, 3, 4, 5, 6, 7)

112 Drug treatment after return in
Vietnam veterans
(1, 2, 3, 4, 5, 6, 7, 8, 9, 10, 11)

122 Influence of opium availability on
addiction rates in Laos
(1, 2, 3, 4, 5, 6, 7, 8)

217 Cannabis and work in Jamaica: A
refutation of the amotivational
syndrome
(1, 2, 3, 4, 5, 6, 7, 8, 9)

223 Behavioral correlates of age at
first marijuana use
(1, 2, 3)

ETHNICITY INDEX

ASIAN-AMERICAN/ORIENTAL

121 Narcotic addiction in two Asian cultures: A comparison and analysis
(1, 2, 3)

122 Influence of opium availability on addiction rates in Laos
(1, 2, 3, 4, 5, 6, 7, 8)

123 A heroin "epidemic" in Asia
(1, 2, 3, 4, 5, 9)

124 Opium and heroin addicts in Laos: I. A comparative study
(1, 2, 3, 4, 5, 6, 7, 8, 9, 10, 11, 12)

125 Opium and heroin addicts in Laos: II. A study of matched pairs
(1, 2, 3, 4, 5, 6, 7)

161 The epidemiology of drug use among New York State high school students: Distribution, trends, and change in rates of use
(10)

182 Changing patterns of drug use among university males
(1, 2, 3, 4, 5, 6, 7, 8, 9, 10, 11, 12, 13, 14, 15, 16, 17, 18)

196 Drug use, academic performance, and career indecision: Longitudinal data in search of a model
(1, 2, 3, 4, 5, 6, 7, 8)

197 The amotivational syndrome and the college student
(1, 2, 3, 4, 5, 6, 7, 8, 9, 10, 11, 12, 13)

BLACK

001 Deaths of persons using methadone in New York City--1971
(1, 2, 3, 4, 5, 6, 7, 8)

003 Junkie work, "hustles" and social status among heroin addicts
(1, 2, 3, 4, 5, 6, 7, 8, 9, 10, 11, 12, 13, 14, 15)

004 The veridicality of addicts' self-reports in social research
(1, 2, 3, 4, 5, 6, 7)

005 The working addict
(1, 2, 3, 4, 5, 6, 7, 8, 9, 10, 11, 12)

007 Suicidal behavior among heroin addicts: A brief report
(1, 2)

008 Formerly-addicted-now-controlled opiate users
(1, 2, 3, 4, 5, 6, 7)

009 Suicide attempts among drug abusers
(1, 2, 3, 4, 5)

011 Family ties of heroin addicts
(1, 2, 3, 4, 5, 6)

012 New light on the maturing out hypothesis in opioid dependence
(1, 2, 3, 4, 5, 6, 7)

014 An analysis of work histories, earnings, and receipts of benefits among a sample of a community-wide population of narcotic addicts
(1, 2, 3, 4, 5, 6)

015 Studying addicts over time: Methodology and preliminary findings
(1, 2, 3, 4, 5, 6, 7, 8, 9, 10)

016 Addict Careers: I. A new typology
(1, 2, 3, 4, 5, 6, 7, 8, 9, 10)

017 Addict careers: II. The first ten years
(1, 2, 3, 4, 5, 6, 7, 8, 9, 10, 11, 12, 13)

018 Addict careers: III. Trends across time
(1, 2, 3, 4, 5, 6, 7, 8, 9, 10, 11)

019 Trends in the age of onset of narcotic addiction
(1, 2, 3, 4, 5, 6, 7, 8)

023 Narcotic addicts, multiple drug abuse and psychological distress
(1, 2, 3, 4, 5, 6, 7, 8, 9)

024 Ecological studies of narcotic addiction
(1, 2, 3, 4, 5)

025 Is there a relationship between astrology and addiction? A reexamination
(1)

026 The structure of depression in heroin addicts
(1, 2, 3, 4, 5)

027 The Life Styles of Nine American Opiate Users (Executive Summary)
(1, 2, 3, 4, 5, 6, 7, 8, 9, 10, 11)

028 Correlates of self-reported and clinically assessed depression in male heroin addicts
(1, 2, 3)

029 Types of psychopathology displayed by heroin addicts
(1, 2)

030 The effect of parole on methadone patient behavior
(1, 2, 3, 4, 5, 6, 7, 8, 9, 10, 11, 12, 13)

033 Self-concept and substance abuse treatment
(1, 2, 3, 4, 5, 6, 7)

034 Phoenix House: Psychopathological signs among male and female drug-free residents
(1, 2, 3, 4, 5, 6, 7, 8, 9, 10, 11, 12)

035 Therapeutic community dropouts: Psychological changes 2 years after treatment
(1, 2, 3)

036 Therapeutic community dropouts: Criminal behavior five years after treatment
(1, 2, 3, 4, 5, 6, 7)

037 Phoenix house: Criminal activity of dropouts
(1, 2, 3, 4, 5)

038 Male and female drug abusers: Social and psychological status 2 years after treatment in a therapeutic community
(1, 2, 3, 4, 5, 6, 7, 8, 9, 10, 11, 12, 13, 14, 15)

039 Phoenix House: Changes in psychopathological signs of resident drug addicts
(1, 2, 3, 4)

040 The therapeutic community: Success and improvement rates 5 years after treatment
(1, 2, 3, 4, 5, 6, 7, 8, 9, 10, 11, 12, 13, 14, 15, 16)

042 Differential response of heroin and nonheroin abusers to inpatient treatment
(1, 2)

043 A comparison of dropouts and disciplinary discharges from a therapeutic community
(1, 2, 3, 4)

044 Self-concept and completion of treatment for heroin and nonheroin drug abusers
(1, 2, 3, 4, 5)

047 Attrition of older alcoholics from treatment
(1, 2, 3, 4, 5, 6, 7, 8, 9, 10, 11)

048 Cultural factors and attrition in drug abuse treatment
(1, 2, 3, 4, 5, 6, 7, 8)

049 Shutting off methadone: Costs and benefits
(1, 2, 3, 4, 5, 6, 7, 8, 9, 10, 11, 12)

050 Long-term follow-up of clients of high- and low-dose methadone programs
(1, 2, 3, 4, 5, 6, 7, 8, 9, 10, 11, 12)

051 Outpatient methadone withdrawal
for heroin dependence
(1, 2, 3, 4, 5, 6)

052 Notes on American medical history:
A follow-up study of the New Haven
morphine maintenance clinic of 1920
(1, 2, 3, 4, 5, 6, 7, 8, 9, 10, 11, 12)

054 Entry into methadone maintenance
programs: A follow-up study of New
York City heroin users detoxified in
1961-1963
(1, 2, 3, 4, 5, 6, 7, 8, 9, 10, 11)

055 Focus on the family as a factor in
differential treatment outcome
(1, 2, 3, 4, 5)

056 The therapeutic community:
Multivariate prediction of retention
(1, 2, 3, 4, 5, 6, 7, 8)

057 The criminality of heroin addicts
when addicted and when off opiates
(1, 2, 3, 4, 5, 6, 7, 8, 9, 10, 11, 12,
13, 14, 15)

058 Lifetime criminality of heroin
addicts in the United States
(1, 2, 3, 4, 5, 6, 7, 8, 9, 10)

060 The effect of probation on
behavior of chronic opioid drug users
(1, 2, 3, 4, 5)

061 Getting over: Economic
alternatives to predatory crime among
street drug users
(1, 2, 3, 4, 5, 6, 7, 8, 9, 10, 11)

062 Daily criminal activities of
street drug users: Preliminary
findings
(1, 2, 3, 4, 5, 6, 7)

064 Heroin use and street crime
(1, 2, 3, 4, 5, 6, 7, 8, 9, 10, 11, 12,
13, 14, 15)

066 The impact of drug use on street
crime
(1, 2, 3, 4, 5, 6, 7, 8, 9, 10, 11, 12,
13, 14, 15, 16, 17, 18)

067 The criminal behavior of street
heroin and cocaine users
(1, 2, 3, 4, 5, 6, 7, 8, 9)

068 Exploring asymmetries in the hard
drug-crime relationship
(1, 2, 3, 4, 5, 6, 7, 8, 9)

071 California civil commitment: A
decade later
(1, 2, 3, 4, 5, 6, 7, 8)

072 Outcome of the California Civil
Addict commitments: 1961-1972
(1, 2, 3, 4, 5, 6, 7, 8, 9, 10, 11, 12,
13, 14, 15, 16)

073 Narcotic addiction and crime
(1, 2, 3, 4, 5, 6, 7, 8, 9, 10, 11)

075 A preliminary report on crime and
addiction within a community-wide
population of narcotic addicts
(1, 2, 3, 4, 5, 6, 7, 8)

076 Are female drug abusers more
deviant?
(1, 2, 3, 4, 5)

080 Women, heroin, and property crime
(1, 2, 3, 4, 5, 6, 7, 8)

081 Black women, heroin and crime:
Some empirical notes
(1, 2, 3, 4, 5, 6, 7, 8, 9)

082 Prostitution and addiction: An
interdisciplinary approach
(1, 2, 3, 4, 5, 6, 7, 8, 9, 10)

083 The relationship between female
criminality and drug abuse
(1, 2, 3, 4, 5, 6, 7, 8, 9, 10, 11, 12,
13, 14, 15, 16)

087 Becoming addicted: The woman
addict
(1, 2, 3, 4, 5, 6, 7, 8, 9, 10, 11, 12,
13, 14)

088 Difficulties in taking care of
business: Women addicts as mothers
(1, 2, 3, 4, 5, 6, 7, 8, 9)

089 Sex roles among deviants: The woman addict
(1, 2, 3, 4, 5, 6, 7, 8, 9, 10)

090 Women addicts' experience of the heroin world: Risk, chaos, and inundation
(1, 2, 3, 4, 5, 6, 7, 8, 9, 10, 11, 12)

091 Criminal involvement of female offenders: Psychological characteristics among four groups
(1, 2, 3, 4, 5, 6, 7)

093 Ethnic differences in factors related to drug use
(1, 2, 3, 4, 5, 6, 7, 8, 9)

094 A comparison of Spanish and non-Spanish drug users in treatment in Dade County, Florida
(1, 2, 3, 4, 5, 6, 7, 8, 9, 10, 11, 12)

097 Risk factors in the continuation of childhood antisocial behavior into adulthood
(1, 2, 3)

098 Childhood conduct disorders and later arrest
(1, 2, 3, 4, 5, 6)

099 The long-term outcome of truancy
(1, 2, 3, 4, 5, 6, 7)

100 Father's alcoholism and children's outcomes
(1, 2, 3, 4, 5)

102 Drug use in the construction trade
(1, 2, 3, 4, 5, 6, 7, 8, 9, 10, 11, 12, 13, 14, 15, 16, 17, 18, 19, 20, 21, 22, 23)

103 Three types of extreme drug users identified by a replicated cluster analysis
(1, 2, 3, 4, 5)

105 Depressive disorders in Vietnam returnees
(1, 2, 3, 4)

106 Acute drug reactions among the aged: A research note
(1, 2, 3, 4, 5, 6)

109 The social problem of drug abuse in ecological perspective
(1, 2, 3, 4, 5, 6, 7, 8, 9, 10, 11)

116 The Life Styles of Nine American Amphetamine Users (Executive Summary)
(1, 2, 3, 4, 5, 6, 7, 8, 9, 10, 11)

117 Cocaine Users: A Representative Case Approach
(1, 2, 3, 4, 5, 6, 7, 8, 9, 10, 11, 12, 13, 14, 15, 16, 17, 18, 19)

118 Life Styles of Nine American Barbiturate/Sedative-Hypnotic Drug Users (Executive Summary)
(1, 2, 3, 4, 5, 6, 7, 8, 9, 10, 11, 12, 13, 14, 15, 16, 17)

119 Life Styles of Nine American Non-Users of Drugs (Executive Summary)
(1, 2, 3, 4, 5, 6, 7, 8, 9)

120 Effects of criminal justice and medical definitions of a social problem upon the delivery of treatment: The case of drug abuse
(1, 2, 3, 4, 5, 6)

126 Attitude and behavior: A specification of the contingent consistency hypothesis
(1, 2, 3, 4, 5, 6)

127 The relationship between drug education programs in the greater New Haven schools and changes in drug use and drug-related beliefs and perceptions
(1, 2, 3, 4, 5, 6, 7, 8, 9, 10, 11, 12, 13, 14, 15)

130 Correlates of adolescent marijuana use as related to age, sex, and ethnicity
(1, 2, 3, 4, 5, 6, 7, 8)

131 Peer, family, and personality domains as related to adolescents' drug behavior
(1, 2, 3, 4, 5, 6)

199 Determinants of early marihuana use
(1, 2, 3, 4, 5, 6, 7, 8, 9, 10, 11, 12, 13)

200 Young Men and Drugs--A Nationwide Survey
(1, 2, 3, 4, 5, 6, 7, 8, 9, 10, 11)

204 What happened in Harlem? Analysis of a decline in heroin use among a generation unit of urban black youth
(1, 2, 3, 4, 5, 6, 7, 8, 9, 10, 11, 12)

205 Health and drug behavior: A study of urban black adolescents
(1, 2, 3, 4, 5, 6, 7, 8, 9, 10, 11, 12)

206 Black youths and drug-use behavior
(1, 2, 3, 4, 5, 6, 7, 8, 9, 10, 11, 12, 13, 14, 15, 16, 17, 18, 19, 20, 21, 22, 23, 24, 25, 26, 27, 28, 29)

207 Patterns of drug involvement: Developmental and secular influences on age at initiation
(1, 2, 3, 4, 5, 6, 7, 8, 9, 10)

208 Youngsters Experimenting with Drugs
(1, 2, 3, 4, 5, 6, 7, 8, 9, 10, 11, 12, 13, 14, 15, 16, 17, 18, 19)

209 Sex differences in antecedents of substance use among adolescents
(1, 2, 3, 4, 5, 6, 7)

212 Longitudinal community epidemiological studies of drug use: Early aggressiveness, shyness, and learning problems
(1, 2, 3, 4, 5, 6, 7, 8, 9, 10, 11)

213 Mental health in first grade and teenage drug, alcohol, and cigarette use
(1, 2, 3, 4, 5, 6, 7, 8, 9, 10, 11, 12, 13)

217 Cannabis and work in Jamaica: A refutation of the amotivational syndrome
(1, 2, 3, 4, 5, 6, 7, 8, 9)

221 Behavioral correlates and comparisons of current marijuana users, quitters and evasives
(1, 2, 3, 4, 5, 6, 7, 8)

222 Sea-Tac and PCP
(1, 2, 3, 4, 5, 6, 7, 8)

223 Behavioral correlates of age at first marijuana use
(1, 2, 3)

224 Arrest probabilities for marijuana users as indicators of selective law enforcement
(1, 2, 3, 4, 5, 6, 7, 8, 9, 10, 11)

CHICANO/MEXICAN-AMERICAN

003 Junkie work, "hustles" and social status among heroin addicts
(1, 2, 3, 4, 5, 6, 7, 8, 9, 10, 11, 12, 13, 14, 15)

013 Residence relocation inhibits opioid dependence
(1, 2, 3, 4, 5, 6, 7, 8, 9, 10, 11, 12)

030 The effect of parole on methadone patient behavior
(1, 2, 3, 4, 5, 6, 7, 8, 9, 10, 11, 12, 13)

041 Religious programs and careers of chronic heroin users
(1, 2, 3, 4, 5, 6)

049 Shutting off methadone: Costs and benefits
(1, 2, 3, 4, 5, 6, 7, 8, 9, 10, 11, 12)

050 Long-term follow-up of clients of high- and low-dose methadone programs
(1, 2, 3, 4, 5, 6, 7, 8, 9, 10, 11, 12)

051 Outpatient methadone withdrawal for heroin dependence
(1, 2, 3, 4, 5, 6)

060 The effect of probation on behavior of chronic opioid drug users
(1, 2, 3, 4, 5)

071 California civil commitment: A decade later
(1, 2, 3, 4, 5, 6, 7, 8)

072 Outcome of the California Civil Addict commitments: 1961-1972
(1, 2, 3, 4, 5, 6, 7, 8, 9, 10, 11, 12, 13, 14, 15, 16)

073 Narcotic addiction and crime
(1, 2, 3, 4, 5, 6, 7, 8, 9, 10, 11)

087 Becoming addicted: The woman addict
(1, 2, 3, 4, 5, 6, 7, 8, 9, 10, 11, 12, 13, 14)

088 Difficulties in taking care of business: Women addicts as mothers
(1, 2, 3, 4, 5, 6, 7, 8, 9)

089 Sex roles among deviants: The woman addict
(1, 2, 3, 4, 5, 6, 7, 8, 9, 10)

090 Women addicts' experience of the heroin world: Risk, chaos, and inundation
(1, 2, 3, 4, 5, 6, 7, 8, 9, 10, 11, 12)

101 Mexican-American criminals: A comparative study of heroin using and non-using felons
(1, 2, 3, 4, 5, 6, 7, 8, 9, 10, 11, 12, 13, 14)

142 Addicts and experimenters: Dynamics of involvement in an adolescent heroin epidemic
(1, 2, 3, 4, 5, 6, 7, 8, 9, 10, 11, 12, 13, 14, 15, 16, 17, 18, 19)

143 Personality development and adolescent heroin use
(1, 2, 3, 4, 5, 6, 7, 8, 9, 10, 11, 12, 13, 14, 15, 16)

144 Family life and levels of involvement in an adolescent heroin epidemic
(1, 2, 3, 4, 5, 6, 7, 8, 9, 10, 11)

167 Personality, attitudinal, and social correlates of drug use
(1, 2, 3, 4, 5, 6, 7, 8, 9, 10, 11, 12)

194 A psychiatric emergency room study of inhalant use
(1, 2, 3, 4, 5, 6, 7, 8, 9, 10, 11, 12, 13, 14, 15, 16)

203 Family interaction and acculturation in Mexican-American inhalant users
(1, 2, 3, 4, 5, 6, 7, 8, 9, 10, 11)

CUBAN

079 Cuban women, sex role conflicts and the use of prescription drugs
(1, 2, 3, 4, 5, 6)

095 The children of exile: Relationships between the acculturation process and drug use among Cuban youth
(1, 2, 3, 4, 5, 6, 7)

096 Drug use among Cuban exiles in Miami, Florida: Cultural antecedents and processes
(1, 2, 3, 4, 5)

ETHNICITY UNSPECIFIED

006 Street heroin potency and deaths from overdose in San Antonio
(1, 2, 3)

010 What is an addict? Empirical patterns and concepts of addiction
(1, 2, 3, 4, 5, 6)

031 What we need to know
(1, 2, 3, 4)

046 The magic fix: A critical analysis of methadone maintenance treatment
(1, 2, 3, 4, 5, 6, 7)

059 The impact of drug addiction on criminal earnings
(1, 2, 3, 4, 5, 6, 7, 8)

069 The relationship between type of drug use and arrest charge in an arrested population
(1, 2, 3, 4, 5)

070 Crime and drug-using behavior: An areal analysis
(1, 2, 3, 4, 5)

074 Crime and treatment of heroin users
(1, 2, 3)

078 Employment status, role dissatisfaction and the housewife syndrome
(1, 2, 3, 4, 5)

086 Sex differences in the content and style of medical advertisements
(1, 2, 3, 4, 5, 6)

108 The drug problems of industry
(1, 2, 3, 4, 5, 6, 7, 8, 9, 10, 11, 12, 13, 14, 15, 16, 17, 18, 19, 20, 21, 22, 23, 24, 25, 26, 27, 28)

111 Satisfaction with real and simulated jobs in relation to personality variables and drug use
(1, 2, 3)

150 Drugs and the Class of '78: Behaviors, Attitudes, and Recent National Trends
(1, 2, 3, 4, 5, 6, 7, 8, 9, 10, 11, 12, 13, 14, 15, 16, 17, 18, 19, 20, 21, 22, 23, 24)

151 Highlights from Student Drug Use in America 1975-1980
(1, 2, 3, 4, 5, 6, 7, 8, 9, 10, 11, 12, 13, 14, 15, 16, 17, 18, 19, 20, 21, 22, 23, 24, 25, 26, 27, 28)

152 Marijuana Decriminalization: The Impact on Youth, 1975-1980
(1, 2, 3, 4, 5, 6, 7, 8, 9, 10)

154 Inter- and intragenerational influences on adolescent marijuana use
(1, 2, 3, 4, 5, 6, 7, 8, 9, 10)

165 Aspects of adolescent information acquisition about drugs and alcohol topics
(1, 2, 3, 4, 5, 6, 7, 8, 9, 10, 11, 12, 13, 14)

166 Drug use and military plans of high school seniors
(1, 2, 3, 4, 5, 6, 7, 8)

183 Survey of students and drugs at the University of Notre Dame: An overview
(1, 2, 3, 4, 5, 6, 7, 8, 9, 10, 11, 12, 13, 14, 15, 16, 17, 18, 19, 20, 21, 22, 23)

184 Dimensions of marijuana use in a midwest Catholic university: Subcultural considerations
(1, 2, 3, 4, 5, 6, 7, 8, 9, 10, 11, 12, 13, 14, 15)

185 The variation of a midwest Catholic university's drug use pattern from other Catholic university findings: Why?
(1, 2, 3, 4, 5, 6)

186 Getting high in high school: The meaning of adolescent drug usage
(1, 2, 3, 4, 5, 6, 7, 8, 9, 10, 11)

187 Motivations for psychoactive drug use among students
(1, 2, 3, 4)

190 Judging the shape of things to come: Lessons learned from comparisons of student drug users in 1968 and 1970
(1, 2, 3, 4, 5, 6, 7, 8, 9, 10)

191 Personality characteristics of students who became drug users: An MMPI study of an avant-garde
(1, 2, 3, 4, 5, 6, 7)

192 Organization of needs in male and female drug and alcohol users
(1, 2, 3, 4)

193 A longitudinal study of the personality correlates of marijuana use
(1, 2, 3, 4, 5, 6, 7)

195 Psychoactive drugs: A course evaluation
(1, 2, 3, 4)

201 Prediction of college drug use
from personality and inner experience
(1, 2, 3)

202 Reasons for drug and alcohol use
by college students
(1, 2, 3, 4, 5, 6, 7, 8)

219 Hypnotic susceptibility during
cannabis intoxication
(1)

225 Personaltiy correlates of
hallucinogen use
(1, 2, 3, 4, 5, 6, 7, 8)

226 Physiological responses to
exercise in chronic cigarette and
marijuana users
(1, 2, 3)

227 Role-play theory of psychedelic
drug flashbacks
(1, 2, 3, 4, 5)

228 Psychedelic drug flashbacks:
Subjective reports and biographical
data
(1, 2, 3, 4, 5, 6, 7, 8, 9, 10, 11, 12,
13, 14, 15, 16, 17, 18, 19, 20)

229 Psychedelic drug flashbacks:
Attentional deficits?
(1, 2, 3)

230 Deterrence as social control: The
legal and extralegal production of
conformity
(1, 2, 3, 4, 5, 6, 7)

236 Does marijuana enhance
experimentally induced anxiety?
(1, 2)

237 The effect of marijuana on small
group process
(1, 2, 3, 4, 5)

238 Marijuana and hostility in a
small-group setting
(1, 2, 3, 4, 5, 6)

MULTIETHNIC

002 Some research notes on the sexual
life of the addict
(1, 2, 3, 4, 5)

032 Therapeutic communities vs
methadone maintenance: A prospective
controlled study of narcotic addiction
treatment: Design and one-year
follow-up
(1, 2, 3, 4, 5, 6, 7, 8, 9, 10, 11, 12,
13)

063 Addicts, police, and the
neighborhood social system
(1, 2, 3, 4, 5, 6, 7, 8, 9, 10)

065 Youth, drugs, and street crime
(8, 9, 10, 11, 12, 13, 14, 15, 16, 17,
18, 19)

104 Antecedents of narcotic use and
addiction: A study of 898 Vietnam
veterans
(1, 2, 3, 4, 5, 6, 7)

112 Drug treatment after return in
Vietnam veterans
(1, 2, 3, 4, 5, 6, 7, 8, 9, 10, 11)

113 The interaction of setting and
predisposition in explaining novel
behavior: Drug initiations before, in,
and after Vietnam
(1, 2, 3, 4, 5, 6, 7, 8, 9, 10, 11, 12)

114 Vietnam veterans three years after
Vietnam: How our study changed our
view on heroin
(1, 2, 3, 4, 5, 6, 7, 8, 9, 10, 11, 12,
13, 14, 15, 16)

115 Polydrug and alcohol use by
veterans and nonveterans
(1, 2, 3, 4, 5, 6, 7, 8, 9, 10, 11, 12,
13, 14, 15, 16, 17, 18, 19, 20)

122 Influence of opium availability on
addiction rates in Laos
(1, 2, 3, 4, 5, 6, 7, 8)

138 A Study of Teenage Drug Behavior
(1, 2, 3, 4, 5, 6, 7, 8, 9, 10, 11, 12,
13, 14, 15, 16, 17, 18, 19, 20, 21, 22)

145 Is coca paste currently a drug of abuse among high school students?
(1, 2, 3, 4)

146 Adolescent drug use and intentions to use drugs in the future: A concurrent analysis
(1, 2, 3)

147 Beginning adolescent drug use and peer and adult interaction patterns
(1, 2, 3, 4, 5, 6, 7)

148 Longitudinal analysis of the role of peer support, adult models, and peer subcultures in beginning adolescent substance use: An application of setwise canonical correlation methods
(1, 2, 3, 4)

149 Intentions to use drugs among adolescents: A longitudinal analysis
(1, 2, 3, 4)

161 The epidemiology of drug use among New York State high school students: Distribution, trends, and change in rates of use
(1, 2, 3, 4, 5, 6, 7, 8, 11, 12, 13, 14, 15, 16, 17, 18, 19, 20, 21)

178 The relationship of personality structure to patterns of adolescent substance use
(1, 2, 3, 4, 5)

189 Whither the epidemic? Psychoactive drug-use career patterns of college students
(1, 2, 3, 4, 5, 6, 7, 8)

218 Ethnicity and patterning in South African drug use
(1, 2, 3, 4, 5, 6, 7, 8, 9, 10, 11, 12, 13, 14, 15, 16, 17, 18, 19)

220 Phencyclidine use in high school: Tests of models
(1, 2, 3, 4, 5, 6, 7)

NORTH AMERICAN INDIAN

161 The epidemiology of drug use among New York State high school students: Distribution, trends, and change in rates of use
(9)

210 Inhalant abuse among the Pueblo tribes of New Mexico
(1, 2, 3, 4, 5, 6, 7, 8, 9, 10, 11, 12, 13, 14)

211 Drug use among Native American adults
(1, 2, 3, 4, 5, 6, 7, 8, 9, 10)

214 Drug use among adolescents of five Southwestern Native American tribes
(1, 2, 3, 4, 5, 6, 7)

215 Drug use among Native American adolescents
(1, 2, 3, 4, 5, 6, 7, 8, 9, 10, 11, 12, 13, 14, 15, 16, 17, 18, 19, 20, 21, 22, 23)

216 Native American Drug Use: Drug Abuse Among Indian Adolescents
(1, 2, 3, 4, 5, 6, 7, 8, 9, 10, 11, 12, 13, 14, 15, 16)

PUERTO RICAN

001 Deaths of persons using methadone in New York City--1971
(1, 2, 3, 4, 5, 6, 7, 8)

005 The working addict
(1, 2, 3, 4, 5, 6, 7, 8, 9, 10, 11, 12)

021 Predicting heroin and alcohol usage among young Puerto Ricans
(1, 2, 3, 4, 5, 6, 7, 8, 9, 10, 11, 12, 13, 14, 15, 16)

022 Parental correlates of drug use among young Puerto Rican adults
(1, 2, 3, 4, 5, 6, 7, 8, 9, 10, 11, 12, 13, 14, 15, 16)

039 Phoenix House: Changes in psychopathological signs of resident drug addicts
(1, 2, 3, 4)

092 Puerto Rican Addicts and
Non-addicts: A Comparison
(1, 2, 3, 4, 5, 6, 7, 8, 9, 10, 11, 12,
13, 14, 15, 16, 17, 18, 19, 20, 21)

126 Attitude and behavior: A
specification of the contingent
consistency hypothesis
(1, 2, 3, 4, 5, 6)

138 A Study of Teenage Drug Behavior
(24)

139 Sequential patterns of
multiple-drug use among high school
students
(1, 2, 3, 4, 5, 6, 7, 8, 9, 10, 11)

168 Psychological factors and
adolescent illicit drug use: Ethnicity
and sex differences
(1, 2, 3, 4, 6, 7)

170 Drug use among public and private
secondary school students in Puerto
Rico
(1, 2, 3, 4, 5, 6, 7, 8, 9, 10, 11, 12,
13, 14, 15, 16)

171 A report on the dropout study
(1, 2, 3, 4, 5, 6, 7, 8, 9, 10, 11, 12,
13, 14, 15, 16)

173 The role of buying and selling in
illicit drug use
(1, 2, 3, 4, 5, 6)

SPANISH/SPANISH-SPEAKING

012 New light on the maturing out
hypothesis in opioid dependence
(1, 2, 3, 4, 5, 6, 7)

023 Narcotic addicts, multiple drug
abuse and psychological distress
(1, 2, 3, 4, 5, 6, 7, 8, 9)

034 Phoenix House: Psychopathological
signs among male and female drug-free
residents
(1, 2, 3, 4, 5, 6, 7, 8, 9, 10, 11, 12)

035 Therapeutic community dropouts:
Psychological changes 2 years after
treatment
(1, 2, 3)

036 Therapeutic community dropouts:
Criminal behavior five years after
treatment
(1, 2, 3, 4, 5, 6, 7)

037 Phoenix house: Criminal activity
of dropouts
(1, 2, 3, 4, 5)

038 Male and female drug abusers:
Social and psychological status 2 years
after treatment in a therapeutic
community
(1, 2, 3, 4, 5, 6, 7, 8, 9, 10, 11, 12,
13, 14, 15)

040 The therapeutic community:
Success and improvement rates 5 years
after treatment
(1, 2, 3, 4, 5, 6, 7, 8, 9, 10, 11, 12,
13, 14, 15, 16)

054 Entry into methadone maintenance
programs: A follow-up study of New
York City heroin users detoxified in
1961-1963
(1, 2, 3, 4, 5, 6, 7, 8, 9, 10, 11)

056 The therapeutic community:
Multivariate prediction of retention
(1, 2, 3, 4, 5, 6, 7, 8)

061 Getting over: Economic
alternatives to predatory crime among
street drug users
(1, 2, 3, 4, 5, 6, 7, 8, 9, 10, 11)

062 Daily criminal activities of
street drug users: Preliminary
findings
(1, 2, 3, 4, 5, 6, 7)

064 Heroin use and street crime
(1, 2, 3, 4, 5, 6, 7, 8, 9, 10, 11, 12,
13, 14, 15)

066 The impact of drug use on street
crime
(1, 2, 3, 4, 5, 6, 7, 8, 9, 10, 11, 12,
13, 14, 15, 16, 17, 18)

067 The criminal behavior of street
heroin and cocaine users
(1, 2, 3, 4, 5, 6, 7, 8, 9)

068 Exploring asymmetries in the hard
drug-crime relationship
(1, 2, 3, 4, 5, 6, 7, 8, 9)

076 Are female drug abusers more
deviant?
(1, 2, 3, 4, 5)

080 Women, heroin, and property crime
(1, 2, 3, 4, 5, 6, 7, 8)

094 A comparison of Spanish and
non-Spanish drug users in treatment in
Dade County, Florida
(1, 2, 3, 4, 5, 6, 7, 8, 9, 10, 11, 12)

105 Depressive disorders in Vietnam
returnees
(1, 2, 3, 4)

106 Acute drug reactions among the
aged: A research note
(1, 2, 3, 4, 5, 6)

109 The social problem of drug abuse
in ecological perspective
(1, 2, 3, 4, 5, 6, 7, 8, 9, 10, 11)

110 What everybody in Cuzco knows
about coca
(1, 2, 3, 4, 5, 6, 7)

120 Effects of criminal justice and
medical definitions of a social problem
upon the delivery of treatment: The
case of drug abuse
(1, 2, 3, 4, 5, 6)

163 Parental and peer influence upon
adolescent drug use
(1, 2, 3)

198 Cigarette smoking as a precursor
of illicit drug use
(1, 2, 3, 4, 5, 6, 7, 8, 9, 10)

200 Young Men and Drugs--A Nationwide
Survey
(1, 2, 3, 4, 5, 6, 7, 8, 9, 10, 11)

208 Youngsters Experimenting with
Drugs
(1, 2, 3, 4, 5, 6, 7, 8, 9, 10, 11, 12,
13, 14, 15, 16, 17, 18, 19)

WHITE

001 Deaths of persons using methadone
in New York City--1971
(1, 2, 3, 4, 5, 6, 7, 8)

003 Junkie work, "hustles" and social
status among heroin addicts
(1, 2, 3, 4, 5, 6, 7, 8, 9, 10, 11, 12,
13, 14, 15)

004 The veridicality of addicts'
self-reports in social research
(1, 2, 3, 4, 5, 6, 7)

005 The working addict
(1, 2, 3, 4, 5, 6, 7, 8, 9, 10, 11, 12)

007 Suicidal behavior among heroin
addicts: A brief report
(1, 2)

008 Formerly-addicted-now-controlled
opiate users
(1, 2, 3, 4, 5, 6, 7)

009 Suicide attempts among drug
abusers
(1, 2, 3, 4, 5)

012 New light on the maturing out
hypothesis in opioid dependence
(1, 2, 3, 4, 5, 6, 7)

014 An analysis of work histories,
earnings, and receipts of benefits
among a sample of a community-wide
population of narcotic addicts
(1, 2, 3, 4, 5, 6)

015 Studying addicts over time:
Methodology and preliminary findings
(1, 2, 3, 4, 5, 6, 7, 8, 9, 10)

016 Addict Careers: I. A new
typology
(1, 2, 3, 4, 5, 6, 7, 8, 9, 10)

045 Investigating impact of methadone treatment upon the behavior of New York City street addicts
(1, 2, 3, 4, 5, 6, 7, 8, 9, 10, 11, 12, 13, 14)

047 Attrition of older alcoholics from treatment
(1, 2, 3, 4, 5, 6, 7, 8, 9, 10, 11)

048 Cultural factors and attrition in drug abuse treatment
(1, 2, 3, 4, 5, 6, 7, 8)

049 Shutting off methadone: Costs and benefits
(1, 2, 3, 4, 5, 6, 7, 8, 9, 10, 11, 12)

050 Long-term follow-up of clients of high- and low-dose methadone programs
(1, 2, 3, 4, 5, 6, 7, 8, 9, 10, 11, 12)

051 Outpatient methadone withdrawal for heroin dependence
(1, 2, 3, 4, 5, 6)

052 Notes on American medical history: A follow-up study of the New Haven morphine maintenance clinic of 1920
(1, 2, 3, 4, 5, 6, 7, 8, 9, 10, 11, 12)

053 Methadone, wine and welfare
(1, 2, 3, 4, 5, 6, 7, 8)

054 Entry into methadone maintenance programs: A follow-up study of New York City heroin users detoxified in 1961-1963
(1, 2, 3, 4, 5, 6, 7, 8, 9, 10, 11)

055 Focus on the family as a factor in differential treatment outcome
(1, 2, 3, 4, 5)

056 The therapeutic community: Multivariate prediction of retention
(1, 2, 3, 4, 5, 6, 7, 8)

057 The criminality of heroin addicts when addicted and when off opiates
(1, 2, 3, 4, 5, 6, 7, 8, 9, 10, 11, 12, 13, 14, 15)

058 Lifetime criminality of heroin addicts in the United States
(1, 2, 3, 4, 5, 6, 7, 8, 9, 10)

061 Getting over: Economic alternatives to predatory crime among street drug users
(1, 2, 3, 4, 5, 6, 7, 8, 9, 10, 11)

062 Daily criminal activities of street drug users: Preliminary findings
(1, 2, 3, 4, 5, 6, 7)

064 Heroin use and street crime
(1, 2, 3, 4, 5, 6, 7, 8, 9, 10, 11, 12, 13, 14, 15)

065 Youth, drugs, and street crime
(1, 2, 3, 4, 5, 6, 7)

066 The impact of drug use on street crime
(1, 2, 3, 4, 5, 6, 7, 8, 9, 10, 11, 12, 13, 14, 15, 16, 17, 18)

067 The criminal behavior of street heroin and cocaine users
(1, 2, 3, 4, 5, 6, 7, 8, 9)

068 Exploring asymmetries in the hard drug-crime relationship
(1, 2, 3, 4, 5, 6, 7, 8, 9)

071 California civil commitment: A decade later
(1, 2, 3, 4, 5, 6, 7, 8)

072 Outcome of the California Civil Addict commitments: 1961-1972
(1, 2, 3, 4, 5, 6, 7, 8, 9, 10, 11, 12, 13, 14, 15, 16)

073 Narcotic addiction and crime
(1, 2, 3, 4, 5, 6, 7, 8, 9, 10, 11)

075 A preliminary report on crime and addiction within a community-wide population of narcotic addicts
(1, 3, 4, 5, 6, 7, 8)

076 Are female drug abusers more deviant?
(1, 2, 3, 4, 5)

077 Psychotropic drug use by women:
Health, attitudinal, personality and
demographic correlates
(1, 2, 3, 4, 5, 6, 7, 8)

078 Employment status, role
dissatisfaction and the housewife
syndrome
(1, 2, 3, 4, 5)

080 Women, heroin, and property crime
(1, 2, 3, 4, 5, 6, 7, 8)

082 Prostitution and addiction: An
interdisciplinary approach
(1, 2, 3, 4, 5, 6, 7, 8, 9, 10)

083 The relationship between female
criminality and drug abuse
(1, 2, 3, 4, 5, 6, 7, 8, 9, 10, 11, 12,
13, 14, 15, 16)

084 A valium a day keeps the tension
away: Socio-psychological
characteristics of minor tranquilizer
users
(1, 2, 3, 4, 5, 6, 7, 8, 9, 10, 11, 12)

085 Drug usage as an index of stress
among women
(1, 2, 3, 4, 5, 6, 7, 8, 9, 10, 11, 12,
13, 14)

087 Becoming addicted: The woman
addict
(1, 2, 3, 4, 5, 6, 7, 8, 9, 10, 11, 12,
13, 14)

088 Difficulties in taking care of
business: Women addicts as mothers
(1, 2, 3, 4, 5, 6, 7, 8, 9)

089 Sex roles among deviants: The
woman addict
(1, 2, 3, 4, 5, 6, 7, 8, 9, 10)

090 Women addicts' experience of the
heroin world: Risk, chaos, and
inundation
(1, 2, 3, 4, 5, 6, 7, 8, 9, 10, 11, 12)

091 Criminal involvement of female
offenders: Psychological
characteristics among four groups
(1, 2, 3, 4, 5, 6, 7)

093 Ethnic differences in factors
related to drug use
(1, 2, 3, 4, 5, 6, 7, 8, 9)

094 A comparison of Spanish and
non-Spanish drug users in treatment in
Dade County, Florida
(1, 2, 3, 4, 5, 6, 7, 8, 9, 10, 11, 12)

102 Drug use in the construction trade
(1, 2, 3, 4, 5, 6, 7, 8, 9, 10, 11, 12,
13, 14, 15, 16, 17, 18, 19, 20, 21, 22,
23)

103 Three types of extreme drug users
identified by a replicated cluster
analysis
(1, 2, 3, 4, 5)

105 Depressive disorders in Vietnam
returnees
(1, 2, 3, 4)

106 Acute drug reactions among the
aged: A research note
(1, 2, 3, 4, 5, 6)

109 The social problem of drug abuse
in ecological perspective
(1, 2, 3, 4, 5, 6, 7, 8, 9, 10, 11)

116 The Life Styles of Nine American
Amphetamine Users (Executive Summary)
(1, 2, 3, 4, 5, 6, 7, 8, 9, 10, 11)

117 Cocaine Users: A Representative
Case Approach
(1, 2, 3, 4, 5, 6, 7, 8, 9, 10, 11, 12,
13, 14, 15, 16, 17, 18, 19)

118 Life Styles of Nine American
Barbiturate/Sedative-Hypnotic Drug
Users (Executive Summary)
(1, 2, 3, 4, 5, 6, 7, 8, 9, 10, 11, 12,
13, 14, 15, 16, 17)

119 Life Styles of Nine American
Non-Users of Drugs (Executive Summary)
(1, 2, 3, 4, 5, 6, 7, 8, 9)

120 Effects of criminal justice and
medical definitions of a social problem
upon the delivery of treatment: The
case of drug abuse
(1, 2, 3, 4, 5, 6)

123 A heroin "epidemic" in Asia
(1, 2, 6, 7, 8, 10)

126 Attitude and behavior: A
specification of the contingent
consistency hypothesis
(1, 2, 3, 4, 5, 6)

127 The relationship between drug
education programs in the greater New
Haven schools and changes in drug use
and drug-related beliefs and
perceptions
(1, 2, 3, 4, 5, 6, 7, 8, 9, 10, 11, 12,
13, 14, 15)

128 Drug education: Further results
and recommendations
(1, 2, 3, 4, 5, 6, 7, 8, 9)

129 Perceived paternal relationships,
adolescent personality, and female
marijuana use
(1, 2, 3, 4)

130 Correlates of adolescent marijuana
use as related to age, sex, and
ethnicity
(1, 2, 3, 4, 5, 6, 7, 8)

131 Peer, family, and personality
domains as related to adolescents' drug
behavior
(1, 2, 3, 4, 5, 6)

132 Family socialization and
adolescent personality and their
association with adolescent use of
marijuana
(1, 2, 3, 4)

133 Initiation into adolescent
marijuana use
(1, 2, 3, 4, 5, 6, 7, 8, 9, 10)

134 Paternal determinants of male
adolescent marijuana use
(1, 2, 3, 4, 5, 6, 7)

135 Fathers and sons: Their
relationship and personality
characteristics associated with the
son's smoking behavior
(1, 2, 3, 4, 5, 6, 7)

136 Maternal and personality
determinants of adolescent smoking
behavior
(1, 2, 3, 4, 5, 6)

137 The role of the father in his
son's marijuana use
(1, 2, 3, 4)

138 A Study of Teenage Drug Behavior
(23)

139 Sequential patterns of
multiple-drug use among high school
students
(1, 2, 3, 4, 5, 6, 7, 8, 9, 10, 11)

140 Experimental heroin users: An
epidemiologic and psychosocial approach
(1, 2, 3, 4, 5, 6, 7, 8, 9, 10, 11, 12,
13, 14, 15, 16, 17, 18, 19, 20)

141 Treated and untreated addicts:
Factors associated with participation
in treatment and cessation of heroin
use
(1, 2, 3, 4, 5, 6, 7, 8, 9, 10, 11, 12,
13, 14, 15, 16, 17, 18, 19, 20, 21, 22,
23, 24, 25, 26)

142 Addicts and experimenters:
Dynamics of involvement in an
adolescent heroin epidemic
(1, 2, 3, 4, 5, 6, 7, 8, 9, 10, 11, 12,
13, 14, 15, 16, 17, 18, 19)

143 Personality development and
adolescent heroin use
(1, 2, 3, 4, 5, 6, 7, 8, 9, 10, 11, 12,
13, 14, 15, 16)

144 Family life and levels of
involvement in an adolescent heroin
epidemic
(1, 2, 3, 4, 5, 6, 7, 8, 9, 10, 11)

153 Drugs and delinquency: A search
for causal connections
(1, 2, 3, 4, 5, 6, 7)

155 Interpersonal influences on
adolescent illegal drug use
(1, 2, 3, 4, 5, 6, 7, 8, 9, 10, 11, 12,
13)

194 A psychiatric emergency room study
of inhalant use
(1, 2, 3, 4, 5, 6, 7, 8, 9, 10, 11, 12,
13, 14, 15, 16)

196 Drug use, academic performance,
and career indecision: Longitudinal
data in search of a model
(1, 2, 3, 4, 5, 6, 7, 8)

197 The amotivational syndrome and the
college student
(1, 2, 3, 4, 5, 6, 7, 8, 9, 10, 11, 12,
13)

198 Cigarette smoking as a precursor
of illicit drug use
(1, 2, 3, 4, 5, 6, 7, 8, 9, 10)

199 Determinants of early marihuana
use
(1, 2, 3, 4, 5, 6, 7, 8, 9, 10, 11, 12,
13)

200 Young Men and Drugs--A Nationwide
Survey
(1, 2, 3, 4, 5, 6, 7, 8, 9, 10, 11)

208 Youngsters Experimenting with
Drugs
(1, 2, 3, 4, 5, 6, 7, 8, 9, 10, 11, 12,
13, 14, 15, 16, 17, 18, 19)

221 Behavioral correlates and
comparisons of current marijuana users,
quitters and evasives
(1, 2, 3, 4, 5, 6, 7, 8)

222 Sea-Tac and PCP
(1, 2, 3, 4, 5, 6, 7, 8)

223 Behavioral correlates of age at
first marijuana use
(1, 2, 3)

231 Ego functioning and acute adverse
reactions to psychoactive drugs
(1, 2, 3, 4, 5, 6, 7, 8, 9, 10, 11)

232 Ego mechanisms and marihuana usage
(1, 2, 3, 4, 5, 6, 7, 8)

233 Relation of motives for drug use
and psychopathology in the development
of acute adverse reactions to
psychoactive drugs
(1, 2, 3, 4, 5, 6, 7, 8, 9, 10, 11, 12,
13, 14)

234 Individual differences and setting
as determinants of acute adverse
reactions to psychoactive drugs
(1, 2, 3, 4, 5, 6, 7, 8, 9, 10, 11, 12,
13)

235 LSD flashbacks and ego functioning
(1, 2, 3, 4, 5, 6, 7, 8, 9, 10)

LOCATION INDEX

METHODOLOGY INDEX

CROSS-SECTIONAL SURVEY

ECONOMETRIC ANALYSIS

ETHNOGRAPHY/PARTICIPANT OBSERVATION

096 Drug use among Cuban exiles in Miami, Florida: Cultural antecedents and processes

107 Qat use in North Yemen and the problem of addiction: A study in medical anthropology

217 Cannabis and work in Jamaica: A refutation of the amotivational syndrome

222 Sea-Tac and PCP

EXPERIMENTAL RESEARCH

165 Aspects of adolescent information acquisition about drugs and alcohol topics

177 Project Community: Therapeutic Explorations with Adolescents

195 Psychoactive drugs: A course evaluation

219 Hypnotic susceptibility during cannabis intoxication

226 Physiological responses to exercise in chronic cigarette and marijuana users

229 Psychedelic drug flashbacks: Attentional deficits?

236 Does marijuana enhance experimentally induced anxiety?

237 The effect of marijuana on small group process

238 Marijuana and hostility in a small-group setting

EXPLORATORY/DESCRIPTIVE SURVEY

001 Deaths of persons using methadone in New York City--1971

002 Some research notes on the sexual life of the addict

003 Junkie work, "hustles" and social status among heroin addicts

005 The working addict

007 Suicidal behavior among heroin addicts: A brief report

010 What is an addict? Empirical patterns and concepts of addiction

014 An analysis of work histories, earnings, and receipts of benefits among a sample of a community-wide population of narcotic addicts

020 Narcotic abusers and poverty

023 Narcotic addicts, multiple drug abuse and psychological distress

052 Notes on American medical history: A follow-up study of the New Haven morphine maintenance clinic of 1920

054 Entry into methadone maintenance programs: A follow-up study of New York City heroin users detoxified in 1961-1963

061 Getting over: Economic alternatives to predatory crime among street drug users

062 Daily criminal activities of street drug users: Preliminary findings

063 Addicts, police, and the neighborhood social system

064 Heroin use and street crime

065 Youth, drugs, and street crime

066 The impact of drug use on street crime

067 The criminal behavior of street heroin and cocaine users

068 Exploring asymmetries in the hard drug-crime relationship

INSTRUMENT INDEX

038 Male and female drug abusers: Social and psychological status 2 years after treatment in a therapeutic community

040 The therapeutic community: Success and improvement rates 5 years after treatment

042 Differential response of heroin and nonheroin abusers to inpatient treatment

043 A comparison of dropouts and disciplinary discharges from a therapeutic community

044 Self-concept and completion of treatment for heroin and nonheroin drug abusers

045 Investigating impact of methadone treatment upon the behavior of New York City street addicts

048 Cultural factors and attrition in drug abuse treatment

049 Shutting off methadone: Costs and benefits

050 Long-term follow-up of clients of high- and low-dose methadone programs

055 Focus on the family as a factor in differential treatment outcome

057 The criminality of heroin addicts when addicted and when off opiates

065 Youth, drugs, and street crime

066 The impact of drug use on street crime

093 Ethnic differences in factors related to drug use

097 Risk factors in the continuation of childhood antisocial behavior into adulthood

099 The long-term outcome of truancy

100 Father's alcoholism and children's outcomes

116 The Life Styles of Nine American Amphetamine Users (Executive Summary)

117 Cocaine Users: A Representative Case Approach

118 Life Styles of Nine American Barbiturate/Sedative-Hypnotic Drug Users (Executive Summary)

119 Life Styles of Nine American Non-Users of Drugs (Executive Summary)

129 Perceived paternal relationships, adolescent personality, and female marijuana use

130 Correlates of adolescent marijuana use as related to age, sex, and ethnicity

131 Peer, family, and personality domains as related to adolescents' drug behavior

132 Family socialization and adolescent personality and their association with adolescent use of marijuana

133 Initiation into adolescent marijuana use

136 Maternal and personality determinants of adolescent smoking behavior

137 The role of the father in his son's marijuana use

140 Experimental heroin users: An epidemiologic and psychosocial approach

143 Personality development and adolescent heroin use

144 Family life and levels of involvement in an adolescent heroin epidemic

INTERVIEW (UNSPECIFIED)